*The Formation of Ch'an Ideology*
*in China and Korea*

*Princeton Library of Asian Translations*

# THE FORMATION
# OF CH'AN IDEOLOGY
# IN CHINA AND KOREA

## The *Vajrasamādhi-Sūtra*,
## a Buddhist Apocryphon

ROBERT E. BUSWELL, JR.

*Princeton University Press*
*Princeton, New Jersey*

Randall Library UNC-W

Copyright ©1989 by Princeton University Press
Published by Princeton University Press, 41 William Street,
Princeton, New Jersey 08540
In the United Kingdom: Princeton University Press, Oxford

Library of Congress Cataloging-in-Publication Data
Buswell, Robert E.
The formation of Ch'an ideology in China and Korea : the Vajrasamādhi-Sūtra, a
Buddhist Apocryphon / by Robert E. Buswell, Jr.
p.    cm. — (Princeton library of Asian translations)
Bibliography: p.
Includes index.
ISBN 0-691-07336-8
1. Chin kang san mei ching—Criticism, interpretation, etc.    2. Zen Buddhism—
China—Doctrines—History.    3. Zen Buddhism—Korea—Doctrines—History.
I. Chin kang san mei ching. English.    II. Title.    III. Series.
BQ2240.V357B87    1989
294.3′927—dc19                                                          88-37437
                                                                           CIP

This book has been composed in Linotron Bembo

Clothbound editions of Princeton University Press books
are printed on acid-free paper, and binding materials are
chosen for strength and durability. Paperbacks, although satisfactory
for personal collections, are not usually suitable for library rebinding

Printed in the United States of America by Princeton University Press,
Princeton, New Jersey

To K. T.

# CONTENTS

# ILLUSTRATIONS

The Recovery of the *Vajrasamādhi*:
Plates from the *Kegon engi emaki*
*Following p. 45*

See Chapter 2

# TABLES

# PREFACE

This book began as an examination of syncretic tendencies in Korean Buddhist thought and was intended to allow me to combine work in two areas of Buddhist studies that particularly interested me: Korean Buddhist and especially Sŏn (Zen) philosophy, and indigenous Chinese Buddhist scriptures. In my earlier book, *The Korean Approach to Zen: The Collected Works of Chinul*, I had surveyed the attempts during the Koryŏ dynasty to unify the Sŏn and doctrinal schools of medieval Korean Buddhism but had been able but to broach the possible antecedents of this tendency in earlier Korean thought. Looking for its origins, I decided to turn to the works of Wŏnhyo, where many of the distinctive features that characterize later Korean Buddhism may be traced. Among Wŏnhyo's treatises, his *Exposition of the Book of Adamantine Absorption* seemed to provide the most thorough and mature outline of his syncretic vision. As that commentary was also based on what was thought to be an indigenous Chinese scripture, I thought that a study of his *Exposition* might also provide some valuable indications as to the role such "apocryphal" sūtras played in the development of uniquely East Asian forms of Buddhism.

But as I read the scripture on which that commentary was based—the *Book of Adamantine Absorption*, or the *Vajrasamādhi-sūtra* as it is commonly known in Western scholarship—I began to feel increasingly uncomfortable with earlier work on the sūtra itself. It ultimately became clear to me that the significance of Wŏnhyo's commentary in the development of Korean Buddhist thought would be forthcoming only by undertaking first a thorough treatment of the *Vajrasamādhi* itself. In particular, the pronounced Sŏn elements in the text, to which Wŏnhyo was completely oblivious, immediately attracted my attention and suggested that there was more to the scripture than Wŏnhyo himself had known. The principal focus of my research therefore changed: rather than examining the role of Wŏnhyo's commentary in forging a syncretic outlook toward Buddhist doctrine, I instead would attempt a wholesale reevaluation of the *Vajrasamādhi* itself, including its dating, provenance, authorship, and philosophy. That reevaluation led in turn to an extensive exploration of the formation of Ch'an ideology in both China and Korea—hence the title of the book. This contextualization will suggest that it is no longer tenable to treat East Asian Buddhism in terms of its separate national traditions. I propose we must look instead for a broader "East Asian" tradition of Buddhism, which is something more than its Chinese, Korean, Japanese, or Vietnamese constituents.

This new vision of the *Vajrasamādhi* and its importance in East Asian Buddhism is presented in part 1. Chapter 1 discusses the background of the *Vajrasamādhi* and critiques traditional views about its origins. In chapter 2, I turn to the biographies of Wŏnhyo to ferret out information on the dating and provenance of the sūtra. Chapter 3 discusses the *Vajrasamādhi*'s attempts to draw out the practical implications of the fundamental sinitic doctrine of the inherence of enlightenment in all beings. The last chapter explores the evolution of sinitic Ch'an ideology in China and Korea, as a means of determining the possible authorship of the scripture.

In part 2, I present a complete, annotated translation of the *Vajrasamādhi*, the first in a Western language. My translation is heavily indebted to Wŏnhyo's interpretations of the often-problematic literary Chinese of the *Vajrasamādhi*. His comments and glosses are either translated or paraphrased in the annotation or included in brackets in the main body of the translation. Though Wŏnhyo's interpretations are occasionally forced, they tell us much about how a Silla Buddhist who was a contemporary of the *Vajrasamādhi*'s author understood the text. While a complete translation of Wŏnhyo's commentary to the sūtra may also have been desirable, its length made it impractical for this book. Still, much that is of philosophical or philological interest in Wŏnhyo's commentary is brought out. What I have consistently omitted is the complex hermeneutical schema Wŏnhyo creates to explicate the text. While East Asian commentarial style demands the use of such an interpretive superstructure, it holds considerably less interest for the contemporary reader.

I also refer occasionally in the annotation to Chu-chen's Ch'ing dynasty commentary on the sūtra, which is an insightful and often provocative exegesis; I would have drawn from it much more extensively were it not for the late date of its composition. Yüan-ch'eng's seventeenth-century commentary is considerably less useful, and I have mentioned it only rarely.

As far as translation style is concerned, I have tried to maintain close fidelity to the Chinese text, without being rigidly literal in the process—no easy task, as any translator can attest. There are a few places where the Chinese of the text itself is either corrupt or stylistically impaired, and my translation is occasionally tentative. The more problematic of these passages are noted in the annotation.

From the way in which the study evolved, it should be clear that I do not intend to propose in this book a general methodology by which to evaluate the authenticity of sinitic Buddhist sūtras. However, the approach I follow in resolving the problems surrounding the origins of the *Vajrasamādhi* exemplifies techniques that may be of help in ferreting out other possible "apocryphal" scriptures. This approach will also illustrate the crossfertilization that I believe must occur between Buddhist studies and other of the humanistic disciplines of Sinology and Koreanology. We are at the stage in the development of Buddhist studies where the text-critical methodologies of the traditionally trained Buddhologist alone are no longer adequate to treat the questions the scholar of the indigenous Buddhist traditions of East Asia must ask.

In addition to its other aims, I hope too that this study will contribute to opening Korean Buddhism to further scholarly inquiry, especially its manifold points of symbiosis with the Chinese tradition. Despite the plethora of materials available in Sino-Korean, which are readily accessible to all Sinologists or Buddhologists who read literary Chinese, Korean Buddhism remains shamefully neglected in both Western and Japanese scholarship. It will give particular satisfaction to me if this book helps in its own small way to mitigate that neglect.

I would like to take this opportunity to thank all of my academic advisers at the University of California, Berkeley, for their guidance, support, and fellowship during the course of my undergraduate and graduate studies there. In particular I am grateful to Lewis Lancaster, Michel Strickmann, and Michael Rogers, my three readers on the dissertation to which this book owes its own origins. I will be satisfied if my work but partially emulates the superb model of scholarship that they have each provided. Several people have also read portions of the manuscript and offered valuable comments and suggestions, including Bernard Faure, Han Kidu, Ko Ikchin, Daniel Overmyer, and Henrik Sorensen. I am especially indebted to the Press's two readers, John McRae and Peter Gregory, as well as to John Jorgensen, each of whom went through the manuscript with great care and offered judicious input on a number of key points. Karen Brock helped me to procure plates of the Japanese scroll that illustrates these pages. Kōzanji, which owns the scroll, kindly gave permission to reprint sections of the scroll, with plates provided from Kyoto National Museum. There are few instances in which Buddhist scholars can find relevant illustrative material for their research.

Considering my advocacy of an East Asian tradition of Buddhism, I was pleased to find illustrated in a Japanese scroll this Chinese legend about the origins of a Korean scripture. Several graduate students at UCLA have served as my research assistants over the last two years and have helped much in getting this book to press; especially deserving of mention are Chi-wah Chan, Ding-hwa Hsieh, Sarah Lubman, Adam Schorr, and Daniel Alt-schuler, who prepared the index. Finally, I would like to thank my colleagues in the Department of East Asian Languages and Cultures at UCLA, who offered me a nonteaching quarter so that I could finish the research and writing of the book. I of course take full responsibility for any errors of fact or interpretation that may remain.

Research on this book was sponsored by the Joint Committee on Korean Studies of the American Council of Learned Societies and the Social Science Research Council, with funds provided by the National Endowment for the Humanities and the Ford Foundation. Funds for research assistantships were provided by the Committee on Research of the UCLA Academic Senate. The assistance of both these agencies is gratefully acknowledged.

Finally, I would like to thank my wife, Kyoko Tokuno, who does triple duty as my closest friend and colleague. The dedication of this book to her is but a small token of my debt of gratitude for her inspiration, learning, and support.

# ABBREVIATIONS AND CONVENTIONS

| | |
|---|---|
| Ch. | Chinese |
| *ch.* | *chüan* |
| *IBK* | *Indogaku bukkyōgaku kenkyū* |
| *k.* | *kwŏn* |
| Ko Ikchin | "Wŏnhyo ŭi sasang ŭi silch'ŏn wŏlli" |
| Kor. | Korean |
| *KSGR* | *Kŭmgang sammaegyŏng-ron* |
| Liebenthal | "Notes on the 'Vajrasamādhi' " |
| Mizuno | "Bodaidaruma no *Ninyūshigyōsetsu* to *Kongōzammaikyō*" |
| McRae | *The Northern School and the Formation of Early Ch'an Buddhism* |
| *PGHP* | *Pulgyo hakpo* |
| *SGYS* | *Samguk yusa* |
| *SKSC* | *Sung Kao-seng chuan* |
| *T* | *Taishō shinshū daizōkyō* |
| *VS* | *Vajrasamādhi-sūtra* |
| *ZZ* | *Dai-Nihon zokuzōkyō* |

Citations from the *Taishō* canon are listed in the following fashion: title (with Sanskrit title, if relevant, in parentheses) and fascicle number; *T*[*aishō*]; *Taishō* serial number; *Taishō* volume number; page, register (a, b, or c), line number(s). E.g., *Ta-fang-kuang fo hua-yen ching* (*Avataṃsaka-sūtra*) 23, *T* 278.9.542c27–543a1.

Citations from the *Zokuzōkyō* are listed as follows: Title and fascicle number; *ZZ*; series; case; volume; page, column (a, b, c, or d), line number(s). E.g., *Shih-men Hung Chüeh-fan lin-chien lu* 1, *ZZ* 2b, 21, 4, 303d13.

Transliterations of Asian languages follow the systems commonly used in the scholarly community: Wade-Giles for Chinese, revised Hepburn for Japanese, McCune-Reischauer for Korean. I have adopted many of the modifications and enhancements of the McCune-Reischauer romanization proposed in Robert Austerlitz et al., "Report of the Workshop Conference on Korean Romanization." I have also adapted their recommendation concerning the treatment of quasi-free Sino-Korean suffixes and category designates (e.g., I write *Kŭmgang sammaegyŏng-ron*, not *Kŭmgang sammae kyŏng non*).

All Buddhist terminology that appears in *Webster's Third New International Dictionary* I regard as English and leave unitalicized: this includes such technical terms as dhāraṇī, dhyāna, skandha, and tathāgatagarbha. For a convenient listing of a hundred such words, see Roger Jackson, "Terms of Sanskrit and Pali Origin Acceptable as English Words." I have, however, expanded the list to include compounds formed from accepted words, for example, vajrasamādhi and tathāgatadhyāna. I also romanize ālayavijñāna and amalavijñāna, because of their frequent appearance in this book.

Since I consider the *Vajrasamādhi-sūtra* to be a Korean composition, I transliterate the indigenous technical terminology of East Asian Buddhism according to the Korean pronunciation of the literary Chinese, followed by the Chinese, where relevant: for example, *pon'gak/pen-chüeh*, *haengnip/hsing-ju*. Standard, pan-Buddhistic terms (e.g., *kleśa*, *saṃyojana*) are cited only in Sanskrit.

In rendering Buddhist technical terms, where the Chinese is a translation, I translate; where it is a transcription, I transcribe. Thus, whenever a term is italicized (e.g., *kṣāntipāramitā*), the Chinese has been a transcription. The only exception is technical terminology that has now entered the English language (e.g., skandha); such terms typically are translated in the Chinese.

Since my own reading of the *Vajrasamādhi* relies heavily on Wŏnhyo's commentary, in translating the sūtra I have followed the recension of the *Vajrasamādhi* embedded there, unless otherwise noted. I also often follow Wŏnhyo's interpretations because I believe he and his coterie were the prime target audience of the sūtra's author. For ease in consulting the Chinese text of the sūtra, however, page and column references bracketed in the body of the translation are keyed to the *Taishō* edition of the *Vajrasamādhi* (*T* 273). In the annotation, I refer to my translation of the *Vajrasamādhi* appearing in part 2 by chapter and note number (e.g., *VS*, chap. 5, at n. 74).

# Part One

## *Study*

# CHAPTER ONE

# THE *VAJRASAMĀDHI-SŪTRA* AS AN APOCRYPHAL SCRIPTURE

This book is the story of a Buddhist scripture, the *Vajrasamādhi-sūtra*, or *Book of Adamantine Absorption*.[1] Until the middle of this century, this scripture was thought to be a translation into Chinese of an Indian Buddhist text, made some three centuries after Buddhism's introduction into China. Modern scholars have raised questions about this assumption, some proposing that the text may actually have been written in China—that is, be "apocryphal." The story I seek to tell here, though, will take us in rather a different direction, not just to China but also to Korea. And its plot will not be limited to issues of scriptural authenticity but will also involve the origins of one of the foremost branches of East Asian Buddhism: the school of Ch'an or, as it is usually known in the West, Zen.

---

[1] *Chin-kang san-mei ching*; Korean *Kŭmgang sammae-kyŏng*; Jpn. *Kongōzammaikyō*; T 273.9.365c–374b; hereafter abbreviated in the notes as *VS* and cited only by page, register, and line. Several undated Tun-huang fragments of *VS* are also extant: Stein nos. 2368, 2445, 2610, 2794 (the only complete MS.), 3615; and Peking nos. Huang 93 and Yü 81. The Tibetan recension (Tib. *Rdo-rjehi tiṅ-ṅe-ḥdsin-gyi chos-kyi yi-ge*), which is translated from Chinese, is no. 803 in the Peking collection, no. 135 in the *Tōhoku* catalogue, and also available in two Tun-huang MSS. (Pelliot nos. 623 and 116). The Tibetan translation was probably made sometime between the late eighth and early ninth centuries, since *VS* is listed in the Lden-kar scriptural catalogue, which Yoshimura Shūki dates to ca. 824 ("The Denkar-Ma, An Oldest Catalogue of the Tibetan Buddhist Canons," pp. 113–14). For a survey of *VS* manuscripts, see Okabe Kazuo, "Zensō no chūsho ni gigi kyōten," pp. 360–61.

Lionel Giles (*A Descriptive Catalogue of the Chinese Manuscripts from Tunhuang in the British Museum*, p. 176, entry no. 5726) has suggested that Stein no. 2368, which includes a fragment of *VS* on the verso side, is written in a "somewhat later hand" than the recto copy of *Ssu-fen chieh-pen su*, which he considers to be a "fairly good MS. of 6th cent." In fact, these fragments were copied at least some one hundred years after the recto text, given that they contain a passage taken from Hsüan-tsang's 649 translation of the *Heart Sūtra* (*Po-jo po-lo-mi hsin ching*, T 251.8.848c = *VS*, chap. 6, at n. 95). Techniques for dating the Tun-huang manuscripts have been developed by Fujieda Akira; for a summary of his methodology, see his "The Tun-huang Manuscripts," pp. 121–23.

## Problems and Prospects of Studying the *Vajrasamādhi-Sūtra*

### *The Symbiotic Relationship between Chinese and Korean Buddhism*

Given the dominance the Chinese exerted over the political and cultural life of East Asia throughout most of history, it is easy to forget that Koreans are a distinct race with a unique language, culture, and society, as different from the Chinese and Japanese as the French are from Germans or Italians. The close relationships between China and the Korean peninsula since the inception of the common era brought Korea inextricably within the web of sinitic civilization. The coalescence of the tribal leagues of prehistoric Korea into the three kingdoms of Koguryŏ, Paekche, and Silla occurred simultaneous with the gradual infiltration of Chinese culture from the mainland. This infiltration was speeded through the missionary activities of the Buddhists, who brought not only their religious teachings and rituals but also Chinese secular culture to new regions of Asia. To a considerable extent it was Buddhism, with its large body of written scriptures, that fostered among the Koreans literacy in written Chinese, the lingua franca of educated discourse in East Asia. Knowledge of Chinese logographs was indispensable in order to have access to the written scriptures of Mahāyāna Buddhism. But full literacy in the commentarial and exegetical materials of Chinese Buddhism demanded familiarity as well with the full range of Chinese secular writing, including Confucian philosophy and ritual, belles lettres, calendrics, and divination. It was perhaps inevitable, then, that the diffusion of Buddhism occurred in tandem with expanding fluency in the Chinese writing system.[2] Buddhism thus played a crucial role in the evolution of Sino-Korean civilization. Eventually much of Korea's indigenous culture was eclipsed (though never fully subsumed) by the incoming sinitic civilization and this alien religion of Buddhism. The challenge Buddhism presented to the domestic worldview, and its co-option of autochthonous myth to justify its naturalization in Korea, will be one of the backdrops against which is played out this story of the *Vajrasamādhi*.

Despite their apparent geographical isolation from the major scholastic and practice centers of Buddhism in China, Korean adherents of the religion maintained close contacts with their brethren on the mainland. Korea's

---

[2] For an insightful discussion of the Buddhist role in transmitting sinitic culture in general to the rest of East Asia, see Inoue Hideo, "Chōsen ni okeru bukkyō juyō to shinkan'nen," pp. 45–52. I have made an annotated translation of this article in "The Reception of Buddhism in Korea and Its Impact on Indigenous Culture."

proximity to North China via the overland route through Manchuria assured the establishment of diplomatic and cultural ties between the peninsula and the mainland. But during its Three Kingdoms (first century A.D.–668) and Unified Silla (669–936) periods, Korea was the veritable Phoenicia of East Asia, and its nautical prowess and well-developed sea lanes made the peninsula's seaports the hubs of regional commerce. It was thus relatively easy for Korean monks to accompany trading parties to China, where they could learn from, and train together with, Chinese adepts. Ennin (793–864), a Japanese pilgrim in China during the middle of the ninth century, reported on the large Korean contingent among the foreign monks in the Chinese capital of Ch'ang-an. All along China's eastern littoral were permanent communities of Koreans, which were granted extraterritorial privileges and had their own autonomous political administration. Temples were established in those communities, which served as centers for the many Korean monks and traders operating in China.[3]

Although most Korean pilgrims eventually returned to their homeland, several remained behind in China and became prominent leaders of T'ang dynasty Buddhist schools. The Koguryŏ monk Sŭngnang (Ch. Seng-lang; fl. ca. 490), for instance, was an important vaunt courier in the San-lun school, the Chinese counterpart of the Madhyamaka branch of Indian philosophical exegesis. Wŏnch'ŭk (Ch. Yüan-tse; 613–696) in the Fa-hsiang (Yogācāra) school was one of the two main disciples of the preeminent Chinese pilgrim-translator Hsüan-tsang (d. 664). Still today, Wŏnch'ŭk remains well known to Tibetans through his renowned commentary to the *Saṃdhinirmocana-sūtra*, which was extremely influential in the evolution of Tibetan Buddhism. Later, during the Sung dynasty, Ch'egwan (Ch. Ti-kuan; d. 971) revived a moribund Chinese T'ien-t'ai school and wrote the definitive treatise on its doctrinal taxonomy, the *T'ien-t'ai ssu-chiao i* (An outline of the fourfold teachings).[4]

This ready interchange between Korea and China allowed indigenous Korean contributions to Buddhist thought to become known to the Chinese as well. Writings produced in either of the two regions were often transmitted to the other with relative dispatch, so that scholars in both traditions were kept well apprised of advances made by their colleagues. Thus doc-

[3] See Edwin O. Reischauer, *Ennin's Travels in T'ang China*, especially chap. 8, "The Koreans in China." For a survey of Buddhist monastic life in such a Korean colony, see Henrik Sorensen, "Ennin's Account of a Korean Buddhist Monastery, 839–840 A.D.," pp. 141–55.

[4] I emphasize the need to take into account these Korean contributions to Chinese Buddhism in my article "Buddhism in Korea," pp. 421–26.

trinal treatises and scriptural commentaries written in Silla Korea by such monks as Ŭisang (625–702) and Wŏnhyo (617–686) were much admired in China, and their insights heavily influenced, for example, the thought of Fa-tsang (643–712), the systematizer of the Chinese Hua-yen school. And so it was with Fa-tsang's works in Korea. Wŏnhyo, in particular, will be a central figure in this investigation of the origins of the *Vajrasamādhi*. The legends told about the events leading up to his authorship of *Kŭmgang sammaegyŏng-ron* (hereafter *KSGR*),[5] the earliest commentary to the *Vajrasamādhi*, will prove vital in ascertaining the scripture's provenance, dating, and doctrinal approach.

## *New Approaches to the Origins of Ch'an*

Such contacts between Chinese and Korean Buddhism are especially pronounced in the case of Ch'an—known in Korea as Sŏn. Two of the earliest "schools" of Ch'an—if one can call "schools" the small coteries of students gathered around isolated teachers during this period of incipiency[6]—were

---

[5] *Kŭmgang sammaegyŏng-ron*, *T* 1730.34.961a–1008a (hereafter abbreviated as *KSGR* and cited only by page, register, and line). Korean vernacular translations appear in Rhi Ki-yong [Yi Kiyŏng], trans., *Han'guk ŭi Pulgyo sasang*, pp. 138–240; Rhi Ki-yong, trans., *Kŭmgang sammaegyŏng-ron*; Sŏng Nakhun, trans., *Wŏnhyo, Wŏnch'ŭk, Ŭisang, Hyech'o, Ch'egwan, Ŭich'ŏn*, pp. 133–281; and most recently Kim Talchin, trans., *Kŭmgang sammaegyŏng-ron*. See also the studies mentioned *infra* by Ko Ikchin and Han Kidu. In addition to Wŏnhyo's work, another Korean commentary to *VS* is mentioned by Ŭich'ŏn (1055–1101) in his bibliographical catalogue, *Sinp'yŏn chejong kyojang ch'ongnok* 1, *T* 2184.55.1171b11. This text, the *Kŭmgang sammaegyŏng-chu*, is attributed to Tullyun (alt., Toryun, Sŭngdun; d.u.), a Silla monk about whom little is known. Eighteen works are attributed to him, of which only one is extant; see listings in Tongguk taehakkyo Pulgyo munhwa yŏn'guso, ed., *Han'guk Pulgyo ch'ansul munhŏn ch'ongnok*, pp. 67–69. Tullyun's commentary is quoted in the section on amalavijñāna in *Fan-i ming-i chi* 6, *T* 2131.54.1158b–c, suggesting that the text remained in circulation at least through 1143. Chu-chen mentions this citation of Tullyun's commentary and says that he was in the Fa-yen lineage of Ch'an, which is impossible; *Chin-kang san-mei ching t'ung-tsung chi* 1, *ZZ* 1, 55, 3, 228a3; hereafter cited only by page and register. Four nonextant, anonymous commentaries to *VS*, apparently by Japanese authors, are listed in the 1094 Japanese catalogue, *Tōiki dentō mokuroku*; see *T* 2183.55.1152a27 (*Kongōzammaikyō ronso*); 1152a28 (*Kongōzammaikyōgi*); 1152a29 (*Kongōzammaikyō shiki*); 1152b1 (*Kongōzammaikyō shiji*). These are listed in my article "Did Wŏnhyo Write Two Versions of His *Kŭmgang sammaegyŏng-ron* [Exposition of the *Book of Adamantine Absorption*]?: An Issue in Korean Buddhist Textual History."

[6] See Stanley Weinstein's admonition about using "school" to translate the Chinese *tsung* in his article "Chinese Buddhism," pp. 482–87; McRae ("The Ox-Head School of Chinese Ch'an Buddhism: From Early Ch'an to the Golden Age," p. 199) also warns that these early factions of Ch'an were not schools "in any organizational or institutional sense. . . . [Instead, they] represented a religious ideal with which one might empathize, a loose sense of fellowship rather than a precisely defined clique."

the Ching-chung and Pao-t'ang, centered in what was then the wild Szech-wan frontier of southwestern China. Both factions claimed as their patriarch a Ch'an master of Korean extraction named Musang (Ch. Wu-hsiang; 680/4–762), who is better known as Reverend Kim (Kim *hwasang*), using his native Korean surname.[7] While this tale of the *Vajrasamādhi* will deal only tangentially with Musang, one of its major subplots will concern the inti-mate connections between Korea and China during the early evolution of the Ch'an tradition. Indeed, the Ch'an components that can be isolated in the *Vajrasamādhi* will provide compelling clues as to its authorship and the motives underlying its composition.

Ch'an has traditionally prided itself on being a transmission of Buddhism that was separate from the doctrinal teachings of the religion. Ch'an claimed that its dissemination occurred through direct spiritual experience, not the indirect medium of the spoken or written word. To justify this distinctive view of itself, Ch'an created an elaborate pseudohistory tracing its spiritual lineage back to the Buddha himself. This history was populated with leg-endary patriarchs in India and China who transmitted the Buddha's enlight-enment down through the ages, followed by successive generations of emi-nent masters throughout East Asia who formalized Ch'an teaching styles into a variety of different schools or "houses" (*chia*). All these men were then knit together in systematic, lineal fashion by intricate primary and collateral lineages. While the historical origins of Ch'an are still a matter of consider-able scholarly debate, Ch'an's diachronic portrayal of its own history is now all but totally debunked. The lives of the patriarchs are shrouded in obscu-rity, and the connections between the successive generations of its teachers are often tenuous at best, if not patently contrived. As retrospective views of how the mature Ch'an schools perceived their own evolution, these ac-counts are invaluable; but as reliable historical sources for ascertaining the earliest filiations of the nascent Ch'an tradition, they are most unsatisfactory.

---

[7] For Musang, see Jan Yün-hua, "Tung-hai ta-shih Wu-hsiang chuan yen-chiu," pp. 47–60; Yamaguchi Zuihō, "Chibetto bukkyō to Shiragi Kin oshō," pp. 1–36; Broughton, "Early Ch'an Schools in Tibet," pp. 1–68 passim, who points out that there were no lineal connections between the Ching-chung school of Musang and the Pao-t'ang school of his presumed succes-sor, Wu-chu (714–74); and Yanagida, "Li-tai fa-pao chi," p. 18. For further sources on his life and thought, see Buswell, *The Korean Approach to Zen: The Collected Works of Chinul*, p. 77 n. 51. Obata Hironobu, "Chibetto no Zenshū to *Rekidai hōbōki*," pp. 139–76, has noted that it is probably because of its associations with the Pao-t'ang school of early Ch'an that *VS* came to be translated into Tibetan. See the summary of the article in Ueyama Daishun, "The Study of Tibetan Ch'an Manuscripts Recovered from Tun-huang: A Review of the Field and Its Pros-pects," pp. 332–33.

The present approach to determining the origins of Ch'an must take a different, more synchronic, tack.[8]

An innovative approach to describing early Ch'an teachings has been made by John McRae in his recent book on the Northern school (Pei tsung). Rather than treating Ch'an in terms of its traditional lineages—what he terms a "string of pearls" approach—McRae seeks instead to examine early Ch'an teachings as elaborations of two metaphors: a more static image of the luminous sun adventitiously covered by passing clouds, and a more active metaphor of a mirror reflecting everything universally. These metaphors are then interpreted as the conceptual matrices within which much of early Ch'an doctrine is expressed.[9] If accepted, McRae's account makes obsolete many of the older rubrics with which early Ch'an doctrine has been analyzed—particularly the sudden/gradual dichotomy that has dominated most Ch'an scholarship to date. Such a focus on metaphor would also seem to be particularly promising for analyzing the literature of the mature Ch'an tradition—especially the massive anecdotal collections, with their rich, if sometimes stultifying, imagery.

The *Vajrasamādhi* provides a different perspective on developing such a thematic approach. Rather than forcing us to interpret the imagery of explicitly Ch'an texts, this sūtra allows us instead to look at the doctrinal context within which Ch'an elements are placed in apocryphal sūtras oriented toward Ch'an, such as the text under consideration here. The *Vajrasamādhi* contains extensive references to many of the major trends occurring in contemporary Buddhist exegesis. But the ways in which such trends were made to relate to Ch'an ideas provide an invaluable guide for evaluating the doctrinal affinities and intellectual confluences of the Ch'an movement. The *Vajrasamādhi* will show first and foremost that the teachings of Ch'an must be viewed as part and parcel of the mainstream of sinitic Buddhist doc-

---

[8] A compelling indictment of this "string of pearls" approach to the study of Ch'an is found in John R. McRae, *The Northern School and the Formation of Early Ch'an Buddhism*, esp. pp. 7–8. See also his comments on p. 120 concerning the need for a synchronic approach to studying the teachings of early Ch'an.

[9] The sun-and-cloud metaphor McRae (esp. pp. 146–47, 246–50) equates with the East Mountain meditative approach of "guarding the mind," as well as with the "access of principle" found in the *Erh-ju ssu-hsing lun* of Bodhidharma. He sees the mirror metaphor conducing to a more dynamic gnoseology, in which the interactions occurring in ordinary life are themselves enlightenment. This second metaphor is adumbrated in the Bodhidharma text's access of practice and provides the principal focus of Northern school soteriology. The use of imagery in buddhological research has also been explored with considerable success by Steven Collins in his recent book on the meaning of "non-self" (*anattā*) doctrine in the Pali Buddhist tradition; see his *Selfless Persons: Imagery and Thought in Theravāda Buddhism*.

trine—whatever the school's persistent protestations to the contrary. The relationship the author draws between Ch'an praxis and the seminal doctrinal concepts of the wider sinitic tradition will show that, while Ch'an may "not," as it claims, "rely on words and letters," it nevertheless has drawn creatively, and with little real reticence, on the scriptural teachings of the larger Buddhist tradition.

The *Vajrasamādhi* dates from the incipiency of Ch'an, when its earliest clearly historical factions were forming and the school's adepts were showing their first concerns with their own "sectarian" identity. In the period between the last half of the seventh century and the early years of the eighth, a class of monks appeared who began to view themselves as having a distinctive pedigree, unique within Chinese Buddhism. These monks presumed themselves heirs to a lineage that could be traced back to an Indian patriarch, Bodhidharma (P'u-t'i ta-mo; d. ca. 530?),[10] whom they claimed had introduced a new type of Buddhism to China. It is these monks whom I shall identify as belonging to the "Ch'an school," to distinguish them from other Chinese adepts who also practiced *ch'an*, or meditation.[11] The *Vajrasamādhi* includes references to teachings that derive from two distinct factions of these early Ch'an adepts: the "two accesses" soteriology attributed to this putative first Chinese patriarch of Ch'an, Bodhidharma; and the "guarding the one"/"guarding the mind" meditative theory of the traditional fourth and fifth patriarchs, Tao-hsin (580–651) and Hung-jen (601–674). However, these teachings appear not in an explicitly Ch'an text, but instead in the guise of a sūtra, a sermon attributed to the Buddha himself, which provides the basis for the doctrinal teachings of Buddhism. This sūtra draws heavily from Tathāgatagarbha (lit., "womb" or "embryo" of buddhahood) thought, a strand of Buddhist philosophy based on the universal immanence of enlightenment. The doctrines presented in the *Vajrasamādhi* that contextualize these Ch'an teachings may not in themselves offer precise information about the historical evolution of Ch'an. Nevertheless, they do give important indications concerning the philosophical sensitivities and religious interests of the early Ch'an adepts who probably wrote the sūtra. Despite Ch'an's own vision of its independence from the rest of the Bud-

---

[10] This dating is suggested by McRae, p. 18. Bodhidharma's dates are given variously as ?–495; ?–436; 346–495; and ?–528 in Zengaku Daijiten Hensansho, ed., *Zengaku daijiten*, s.v. "Bodaidaruma."

[11] Here I follow Griffith Foulk's critique of previous scholarly attempts to define the Ch'an school and his convincing argument for a more "stipulative" definition; see his recent dissertation "The 'Ch'an School' and Its Place in the Buddhist Monastic Tradition," pp. 164–244.

dhist tradition, this book will show that it in fact evolves out of an attempt
to elaborate the praxis aspects of Tathāgatagarbha thought.

The *Vajrasamādhi* plays an important role too in expanding the scope of
*ch'an* ("meditation") to take in the highest reaches of Mahāyāna Buddhist
spiritual experience: the nonproduction of all dharmas (*anutpattikadharmakṣānti*). In so doing, *ch'an* was freed from the purely contemplative role it
played in earlier Indian and Chinese Buddhism so that, as Ch'an, it could
become a complete religious and ideological system.[12] Inspired by the Tathāgatagarbha ideal and motivated by the aspiration to make enlightenment
accessible to all, Ch'an was thus part of the trend that was strong during the
fifth through eighth centuries to "sinicize" Buddhism—that is, to assimilate
the imported Indian tradition with indigenous religious needs, cultural ex-
pectations, and social mores. Ch'an's conjunctions with its native counter-
parts in Chinese Buddhism are much more compelling than its alleged dis-
junctions. These commonalities Ch'an strove to gainsay with elaborate
legends of ancient masters and complex lineages proving the independence
of its transmission. This is not to deny that Ch'an was a distinctive school
of Chinese Buddhism by the Sung dynasty, but its uniqueness derives not so
much from its religious doctrines as its unusual rhetorical styles, pedagogical techniques, and meditative practices.[13] The *Vajrasamādhi* will reveal that
the philosophical underpinnings of these distinctive Ch'an features are remarkably similar to those of other, more explicitly "doctrinal" schools of
the indigenous sinitic traditions of Buddhism.

As a text with an implicit Ch'an agenda, but without an explicit Ch'an
pedigree, the *Vajrasamādhi* is in a unique position to corroborate teachings
that later Ch'an doxographic works attribute to earlier patriarchs. This sūtra
will emerge as one of the oldest works affiliated with Ch'an, apparently an-
tedated only by a treatise attributed to Bodhidharma, the *Erh-ju ssu-hsing lun*
(Treatise on the two accesses and four practices), the basic outlines of which
are included in the *Vajrasamādhi*. And the *Vajrasamādhi* itself predates all of
the sectarian doxographic anthologies of the Northern school, such as *Leng-
ch'ieh shih-tzu chi* (Records of the masters and disciples of the *Laṅkā[vatāra]*),
which heretofore were the only sources of information on the early East
Mountain school (Tung-shan fa-men) of Tao-hsin and Hung-jen. The *Vajra-*

---

[12] See discussion in part 1, chapter 4, " 'Guarding the One' and Early Ch'an Meditation."
This point is made also by Foulk, "The 'Ch'an School,' " pp. 117–18.

[13] For discussion on this point, see my article "The 'Short-Cut' Approach of *K'an-hua* Meditation: The Evolution of a Practical Subitism in Chinese Ch'an Buddhism," esp. pp. 321–27.
As I mention there, I believe the Sung period was the "Golden Age" of Ch'an.

*samādhi* in fact provides the only independent corroboration of these later accounts of the East Mountain teachings. The structure of the section in the *Vajrasamādhi* that includes these early Ch'an components also reveals its author's bias in favor of the East Mountain faction and lends credence to the claim I will make here that this sūtra was written by a Ch'an author, specifically a Korean associated with that school. But in its synthesis of these teachings, the *Vajrasamādhi* is implicitly connecting the East Mountain faction to Bodhidharma, suggesting in the process the lineality of the Ch'an transmission. This lineality will be crucial in the evolution of an independent self-identity for the Ch'an school.

The *Vajrasamādhi* is even more important for our knowledge of early Sŏn in Korea. The so-called Nine Mountain Gates of Sŏn (Kusan Sŏnmun) are presumed to have evolved during the last century of the Unified Silla dynasty, and all but two of those schools derive from Chinese Ch'an teachers associated with the Hung-chou school of the middle Ch'an period.[14] The oldest of these nine, the Hŭiyang-san school, traces its origins to an indigenous Sŏn lineage that began with Tao-hsin in China, as combined with a Chinese Northern school transmission. But the few extant sources that discuss the foundation of the Nine Mountains schools all date from the ninth century, fully two centuries after the *Vajrasamādhi*. If my scenario of the Korean Sŏn authorship of this sūtra is accepted, it will be the first evidence of the type of Sŏn that was practiced on the peninsula at the school's inception. And that proto-Sŏn will derive not from the "Southern school" of the Sixth Patriarch, Hui-neng (638–713), as most Korean exponents have heretofore claimed, but from the East Mountain school.

Despite Ch'an's later preeminence in the mature East Asian traditions of Buddhism, it did not always find a receptive audience for its new message. This it often had to earn through pitched debates with its rivals, if not blatant propaganda. The process of disseminating a religious ideology into new regions, and thence establishing an independent sectarian identity for itself, will be one of the major themes of this book. A religion such as Mahāyāna Buddhism, with its expansive worldview, elaborate doctrinal systems, complex spiritual practices, and methodical ritual life, might easily arouse the curiosity of potential converts. But sustaining that interest was a far more

---

[14] Only the last of the schools to form, the Sumi-san school, claims a different lineage—through Ch'ing-yüan Hsing-ssu (d. 740), in what would become the Ts'ao-t'ung line. For the Nine Mountains schools, see part 1, chap. 4, "Early Korean Sŏn and and the Legend of Pŏmnang." For my tripartite periodization of Ch'an into early, middle, and classical periods, see my article, "The 'Short-Cut' Approach of *K'an-Hua* Meditation," pp. 327–28.

difficult undertaking—difficult, but vital, if the religion was to flourish in the targeted region.

Silla was the last of the three kingdoms of ancient Korea to form and, in turn, the last to adopt sinitic culture, including Buddhism. Its isolated geographical position in the far southeast of the Korean peninsula kept Silla from becoming part of the formal tributary system that governed relations between the Chinese empire and its peripheral regions until the middle of the sixth century. Silla thus did not receive any direct transmission of Buddhism from the Chinese court until 549, almost two centuries after Koguryŏ and Paekche. But Buddhism seems to have been filtering into Silla from Koguryŏ at the local level by the middle of the fifth century, in tandem with important political changes occurring in the kingdom. At that time, Silla was evolving from a tribal confederation into a hereditary monarchy. This process culminated in the creation of a sinicized state during the reign of King Pŏphŭng (r. 514–539), which put in place a centralized bureaucracy modeled after Chinese political institutions.

But a unifying ideology was crucial to the successful completion of this process of state formation and, especially, to justify the concentration of power in the monarchy. Some texts of Mahāyāna Buddhism, such as the *Jen-wang ching* (Book of benevolent kings), which will figure in the story of the recovery of the *Vajrasamādhi*, and the *Chin-kuang-ming ching* (Sūtra of golden light), provided ideological justification for allegiance to the king, helping to loosen persistent tribal and clan ties. Such political exigencies may have contributed to Pŏphŭng's decision to force the aristocracy to recognize Buddhism as the official state religion. Though the nobility resisted the move, they were eventually won over, according to legend, by the martyrdom of one of their fellow vassals, the grand secretary Ich'adon (d.u.), in 529. Subsequent kings lent vigorous support to the adopted religion, constructing monasteries, sponsoring Buddhist ceremonies, and even becoming monks themselves. Pŏphŭng's successor, Chinhŭng (r. 540–575), brought the aristocracy into this politico-religious nexus by forming the *hwarang* (lit., "flower boys"), a military and religious organization of noble youths trained according to Buddhist principles, charging it with responsibility for the moral and military protection of the nation. As the drive for peninsular unification intensified, Silla support for Buddhism became ever stronger. It is no surprise, then, that in the years leading up to the 669 unification of the Korean peninsula under the Silla banner, there was a massive flowering of Buddhist scholastic studies in Korea, which produced advancements in

Buddhist philosophy rivaling anything then found on the Chinese mainland.[15]

The doctrinal teachings that came to be supported in Silla were those that helped to justify at an ideological level a centralized bureaucracy reporting to an autocratic monarch. It was the Hwaŏm school in particular that reaped the benefits of such political interests. Its doctrine of "consummate interfusion" (*wŏnyung/yüan-jung*)—in which, as the Korean Hwaŏm founder Ŭisang (625–702) says, "in one is all and in the many is one; one is all and the many are one"—was ideally suited to such a system of statecraft.[16] In return for its ideological sanction of the Silla monarchy, Hwaŏm received munificent official support and established a nexus of state-sponsored monasteries throughout the realm. The first of these Hwaŏm monasteries, Pusŏk-sa, was built in 676, at the very time, I propose, the *Vajrasamādhi* was written.

Now fully committed to Buddhism, the Silla state and the Buddhist religion became intricately intertwined, the state supplying munificent material donations and extensive political support to the religion, the religion interceding with the powerful deities and bodhisattvas of Buddhism on behalf of the state and its welfare. The political investment of the court in the status quo—especially the Hwaŏm school—would make it extremely difficult for rival interpretations of Buddhism even to be heard, let alone disseminated. Imagine, then, the problems that would have faced Sŏn missionaries expounding a new and reputedly superior form of Buddhism, which claimed not to be beholden to the scriptures that the other Buddhist schools of the peninsula followed. Sŏn's impudence was a gauntlet that challenged not only the authority of the entrenched scholastic schools, but the spiritual foundations of the nation. How could these first Sŏn adepts hope to convince Koreans, especially those holding positions of ecclesiastical and polit-

[15] Perhaps the best treatment of the close connections between Buddhism and the state in ancient Korea appears in Ko Ikchin, "Han'guk kodae ŭi Pulgyo sasang," pp. 11–106. For accessible treatments of the role of Buddhism in state formation in Three Kingdoms Korea, see An Kye-Hyŏn, "Silla Buddhism and the Spirit of the Protection of the Fatherland," pp. 27–29; Hee Sung Keel, "Buddhism and Political Power in Korean History," esp. pp. 12–16; Tamura Enchō, "Japan and the Eastward Permeation of Buddhism," pp. 10–12. For the *hwarang* system see Richard Rutt, "The Flower Boys of Silla (Hwarang)," pp. 1–66. The legend of Ich'adon appears in the biography of Pŏpkong in *Haedong kosŭng-chŏn* (*T* 2065.50.1018c–1019a); see Peter H. Lee, trans., *Lives of Eminent Korean Monks: The Haedong Kosŭng chŏn*, pp. 58–63. For an attempt at a general theory of the evolution of Buddhism and other missionary religions, which draws on Korean examples, see James Huntly Grayson, *Early Buddhism and Christianity in Korea: A Study in the Emplantation of Religion*.

[16] See *Hwaŏm ilsŭng pŏpkye-to* (*T* 1887A.45.711a). For the importance of Hwaŏm Buddhism in Silla national ideology, see Ki-Baek Lee, *A New History of Korea*, p. 81.

ical power, that their form of Buddhism was truer to the Buddha's intent than were the sūtras themselves and their learned expositions in the doctrinal schools? In the story of the *Vajrasamādhi*, I will pay close attention to the artifices—such as scriptural composition—that the first Sŏn missionaries might have employed to spread their new, and in some ways radical, message.

*Apocryphal Texts and the Sinicization of Buddhism*

I have referred already several times to the indigenous sūtras of East Asian Buddhism as "apocryphal" texts, what the Chinese cataloguers generally call *i-ching* ("books of doubtful authenticity") or *wei-ching* ("spurious books"). In using such terms as "apocrypha" to refer to indigenous scriptures like the *Vajrasamādhi*, in no way do I mean to convey any such pejorative connotation. Etymologically, "apocrypha" refers to works that are "secret" or "hidden away," either too profound or perhaps too dangerous for public circulation. Three principal usages of the term are noted in Occidental religious literature: laudatory, minatory, and pejorative.[17] But the criteria employed in the Judeo-Christian tradition to distinguish between apocryphal and canonical are so inconsistent as to be virtually useless for the present purposes—especially so when one considers that Buddhism had no corpora of texts, like the biblical Apocrypha, that were distinct from the revealed teachings of the religion. These criteria hardly provide a worthy model for discussion of Buddhist texts in East Asia, where the principal standard of canonicity was, as will be seen, whether a sūtra was of "foreign," that is, Indian or Central Asian, origin.

One must also remain on guard lest the use of such a term as "apocrypha" to refer exclusively to native scriptures imply a value judgment about the relative value of Indian versus sinitic materials that is inappropriate, if not utterly misleading, in the context of East Asian Buddhism. If scriptures are deemed "apocryphal" merely because they were written by native authors, then the vast majority of Indian—and especially Indian Mahāyāna—sūtras should be similarly labeled, since their redactions certainly postdate the Buddha's own lifetime. Admittedly, apocryphal texts did often try to "hide" their origins in order to better their chances of acceptance. But the use of such false attributions was not merely intended as subterfuge. There was in

---

[17] For these three distinct connotations of the term "apocrypha," see R. H. Charles, *The Apocrypha and Pseudepigrapha of the Old Testament in English*, vol. 1, p. viii.

fact a long tradition, deriving ultimately from India, of writing texts and attributing them to previous saints, out of respect for one's predecessors. Provided that the term is used with due diligence, one may appropriate "apocrypha" to refer to indigenous Buddhist scriptures, composed outside the Indian cultural sphere, which follow the narrative structure of Indian or Central Asian sūtras.[18]

The composition of apocryphal texts was part of the sinicization process by which the imported Indian and Central Asian traditions of Buddhism were adapted to indigenous East Asian culture. This process of assimilation took place in several phases. The first was for the Chinese to seek to understand the incoming tradition in terms of their own native intellectual and religious traditions.[19] In the second, as more texts were made available in translation, and as the Chinese apprehension of Buddhism became increasingly sophisticated, exegetical schools began to develop that sought to interpret Buddhist texts on their own terms, free of much of the obscuring veil of indigenous philosophy. Careful study of these commentarial exegeses and doctrinal elaborations of originally Indian materials tell much about the Chinese understanding of Indian Buddhism and help to clarify problematic areas in Indian thought. In fact, one reason scholars of Buddhism first took an interest in Chinese sources was to gain access both to Indian texts that are no longer available in Sanskrit or Middle Indic and to indigenous commentaries that would help in interpreting those texts. But by limiting attention to exegeses of originally Indian materials, scholars ran the risk of treating the East Asian traditions of Buddhism as mere appendages of India.

A third phase, which more recently has received the lion's share of scholarly attention, was the creative response to Indian Buddhism, as seen especially in the evolution of uniquely sinitic schools of Buddhism, such as T'ien-t'ai, Hua-yen, and Ch'an.[20] Such schools sought to respond to issues raised in Indian Buddhist texts by interpreting and remolding them in light

---

[18] I have discussed in more detail the problem of using "apocrypha" and alternate terms to refer to indigenous sūtras in my "Prolegomenon to the Study of Buddhist Apocryphal Literature," in Buswell, ed., *Chinese Buddhist Apocrypha*.

[19] This phase of sinicization is brilliantly handled in Erik Zürcher's *The Buddhist Conquest of China*.

[20] The rise of such indigenous schools has been discussed in Stanley Weinstein's "Imperial Patronage in the Formation of T'ang Buddhism," pp. 265–306; and more recently in Robert Gimello's "Chih-yen (602–668) and the Foundations of Hua-yen Buddhism." Both of these studies are based on the pioneering work of Yūki Reimon. Valuable comments on the issue of sinicization appear in Robert Gimello, "Random Reflections on the 'Sinicization' of Buddhism," pp. 52–89.

of indigenous intellectual traditions and cultural mores. But there was still another way in which such assimilation could take place: not through forming a new learned school, but by composing a new sūtra—an "apocryphal" scripture. One of the most startling discoveries of East Asian Buddhist scholarship has been that many of the seminal texts of the sinitic tradition were not translated sūtras at all, but such indigenous compositions. Apocryphal texts often satisfied East Asian religious presumptions and needs in ways that translated Indian scriptures, which targeted Indian or Central Asian audiences, simply could not. Like the indigenous learned schools of Buddhism, indigenous sūtras also sought to fashion East Asian forms of Buddhism, without precise analogues within the Indian tradition. In such scriptures, motifs and concepts drawn from translated texts were combined with beliefs and practices deriving from the native culture. These components were then arranged in a familiar sūtra narrative structure: the scripture is spoken by the Buddha at an Indian site, to an audience of Indians (or at least persons with pseudo-Indian names). In the *Vajrasamādhi*, these two strands of new scriptures and new learned movements converge.

But apocryphal texts were not mere passive reflections of developments taking place within the indigenous schools of sinitic Buddhism; they often actively catalyzed or sustained those developments. Scriptural testimony was one of the principal standards of authority accepted in Buddhism, and doctrinal innovations could be justified if supported by citations from the sūtras. It was in scriptures that we now know to be apocryphal that such support was often found, thus accounting for their copious citation in the writings of East Asian scholiasts.[21] As these texts were studied and quoted by eminent Buddhist exegetes, doubts about their provenance began to fade, until they were entered into the canon alongside translated scriptures. Thus many apocryphal sūtras eventually became part of the mainstream of the Buddhist traditions of East Asia. This is precisely what happened to the *Vajrasamādhi*. Whatever aspersions may initially have been cast on its

---

[21] Even the most casual perusal of Chinese exegetical writings will reveal copious quotations from such apocryphal scriptures as *Jen-wang ching*, *P'u-sa ying-lo pen-yeh ching*, *T'i-wei Po-li ching*, and the *Vajrasamādhi*, as will be seen in the course of this study. Mizuno Kōgen, in his study of the apocryphal *Fa-chü ching* (*Dharmapada*), has suggested that "The San-lun, the T'ien-t'ai, the Fa-hsiang, the Hua-yen and other schools attached great importance to the sacred books and depended solely on genuine books. They took no notice of the pseudo-scriptures [viz., apocrypha]. The pseudo-scriptures made no appeal whatsoever to them" ("On the Pseudo-Fa-ku-king," p. 395). This is most certainly wrong. As two of many examples to the contrary, see the extensive citations to apocryphal scriptures in Tao-cho's *An-lo chi*, given in Satō Ken, "Anrakushū to gikyō," pp. 79–134; for Chih-i's use of apocryphal scriptures, see Makita Tairyō, "Tendai daishi no gikyō kan," pp. 201–15.

origins, the text eventually silenced its critics by being cited frequently in the writings of the scholarly elite in East Asian Buddhism.

The discovery of such apocryphal texts threatens to force an extensive rethinking of many traditionally held views about the history of East Asian Buddhism. East Asians assumed that their Buddhist canons contained faithful translations of Sanskrit or Middle Indic *texta recepta*, which were then accurately commented upon by native exegetes. Attempts were usually made to anchor such scriptures in time and place by adding a colophon describing where and when it was translated, and by whom. Such colophons assured that the original text had been brought from the "Outer Regions" (Wai-yü; viz., India or Central Asia)—foreign origin being the principal criterion of textual authenticity for the East Asians.[22] But the discovery that many of the seminal scriptures of East Asian Buddhism are in fact indigenous compositions calls much of that textual history into question. Some sūtras in the sinitic Buddhist canons—the tripiṭaka (*san-tsang*; lit., "three repositories")—were unequivocally authentic translations and were quite rightly accepted into the canon by the bibliographical catalloguers, the arbiters of canonicity. Others were just as unequivocally spurious and banned from the canon, ultimately dropping from circulation. It is only in the last hundred years that several of these long-lost apocrypha were recovered from the Tun-huang cave site and made available for scholarly study. But a number of other scriptures contained moot points, or had checkered pasts, which at one time or another had brought their authenticity into question. These scriptures—which include such influential texts as *Ta-sheng ch'i-hsin lun* (Treatise on the awakening of faith according to the Mahāyāna), *Yüan-chüeh ching* (Book of consummate enlightenment), *Shou-leng-yen ching* (*Śūraṃgama-sūtra*), and the *Vajrasamādhi*—had to battle for acceptance. Eventually, however, their victory won, they were deemed bona fide—even if there were occasional pockets of dissent among the native commentators—and reprinted continually in the East Asia tripiṭakas. When such significant texts are recognized as being indigenous compositions, many of our most basic presumptions about the forces that influenced the evolution of sinitic Buddhist systems of thought are challenged. What we find is that the inspiration for many indigenous developments came not from India, but China.

It is especially the Ch'an school that relied heavily on the testimony of

---

[22] Note the comments of the cataloguer Seng-yu: "[Apocryphal sūtras are scriptures that,] on the one hand, I have not heard that someone has gone afar to the Outer Regions [to obtain], or, on the other hand, I have not seen that they have been either received from, or translated by, Western visitors [i.e., foreign missionaries]." *Chu san-tsang chi-chi* 5, *T* 2145.55.39a2.

apocryphal texts to authenticate its novel perspectives on the teachings of Buddhism. This should not be unexpected. Ch'an is commonly (if not sometimes stereotypically) regarded as the most quintessentially sinitic of all the indigenous schools of East Asian Buddhism, incorporating into its doctrine, praxis, and rhetoric many elements deriving from the native tradition (often incorrectly labeled "Taoist"). Given that apocryphal texts too display a similar adaptation to East Asian religious and social milieux, it is no surprise that later Ch'an exegetes, such as Tsung-mi (780–841) and Yen-shou (904–975), would have made frequent use of apocryphal scriptures to justify their positions. That they may not have realized that some of these apocryphal texts, such as the *Vajrasamādhi*, were originally written by Ch'an adherents precisely to provide such justification only attests to the skill with which those authors did their work. Furthermore, the Ch'an school's use of such texts occurred despite its claim that it "does not rely on words and letters." When texts fulfilled a necessary purpose, even the most sacrosanct of shibboleths were conveniently ignored.

One of the major reasons for composing sūtras would have been to convey one's message in a guise familiar to the Buddhist believer, especially the ecclesiastical elite. For an apocryphal text to earn a niche in the tradition, it was vital to win over the scholarly arbiters of Buddhism, by orienting its message in a way that would be appealing to these opinion makers. One of the prominent features of sinitic Buddhism, which apocryphal texts often exhibit, has been a syncretic approach to doctrine. East Asians were the inheritors of a highly developed Buddhist tradition, which was already split into a number of competing schools, some Indian, some Chinese in provenance. Buddhism was also not received en masse in East Asia but was introduced by successive waves of missionaries and translators who arrived initially from Central Asian kingdoms and Serindian oases, and eventually from the Buddhist homeland of India itself. All of these people claimed to be Buddhist, but to the East Asians their teachings must often have seemed diametrically opposed. Reconciling these variant strands of Buddhism occupied much of the attention of scholiasts in both China and Korea. Most indigenous schools of Chinese Buddhism had their own hermeneutical taxonomies (*p'an-chiao*; Kor. *pan'gyo*) by which they sought to bring order to this pandemonium of doctrines. Reconciling the disparate teachings of Buddhism was the principal focus of many of the works of Wŏnhyo, the preeminent Silla scholiast, especially his *Simmun hwajaeng-ron* (Ten approaches to the reconciliation of doctrinal controversy), *Kisillon-so* and *pyŏlgi* (his commentary and autocommentary to the *Awakening of Faith*), and *Kŭmgang sam-*

*maegyŏng-ron*, his exegesis of the *Vajrasamādhi*. The syncretic concerns in Wŏnhyo's thought strongly influenced the subsequent development of Korean Buddhism, and syncretism would become the watchword of the tradition from his time forward. The *Vajrasamādhi* too resonates closely with this Korean penchant for doctrinal harmony. Indeed, its emphasis on a comprehensive approach to Buddhist doctrine may account for much of its success in attracting the attention of Silla scholiasts.

*The* Vajrasamādhi *as a Sinitic Apocryphon*

Although the *Vajrasamādhi* ultimately is recognized by the tradition as a canonical scripture, its authenticity did not go unchallenged. The text was alleged to have been translated anonymously during the Northern Liang dynasty (A.D. 397–439), but suspicions remained about its origins until well into the twelfth century, and perhaps were never fully allayed given the continued scholarly interest in the topic. Ch'an polemicists like Chüeh-fan Hui-hung (1071–1128), the compiler of *Shih-men Hung Chüeh-fan lin-chien lu* (Forest records of Chüeh-fan Hui-hung), conveniently circumvented such concerns by declaring that "because [the *Vajrasamādhi*] has timelessness (*wu-shih*) and absence of nature (*wu-hsing*) as its principal themes, the prefatory sections of the sūtra do not indicate the time and place [of its preaching] and the histories, furthermore, do not record any information as to the era of its translation."[23] Iryŏn (1206–1289), the author of one of the biographies of Wŏnhyo that will figure in dating the *Vajrasamādhi*, remarked with regard to another Buddhist apocryphon, *Chan-ch'a shan-o yeh-pao ching* (Book on divining the karmic retribution of salutary and unsalutary actions), which similarly lacks information as to translator, provenance, or dating: "To doubt [the authenticity of] the text [because of such concerns] is like carrying away the hemp but leaving the gold."[24]

But modern scholars of Buddhist apocrypha cannot so easily demur from such fundamental issues. Indeed, given the preliminary stage of research on Buddhist apocrypha, authenticity questions have dominated scholarly attention. Resolving such seemingly narrow textual concerns, however, often demands attention to the wider philosophical, ecclesiastical, and even political milieux that helped shape apocryphal materials. If the study of Buddhist apocrypha is to realize its full potential, a breadth of approach is required

[23] *Shih-men Hung Chüeh-fan lin-chien lu*, *ZZ* 2b, 21, 4, 303a.
[24] *Samguk yusa* (hereafter *SGYS*), *T* 2039.49.1008a4–5.

that goes beyond the different disciplines *sensu strictu* of East Asian humanities. The individual buddhologist, sinologist, folklorist, or historian of religion would be able to glean only so much about the origins of suspect scriptures. The classically trained buddhologist, for example, might be able to determine the textual filiations and doctrinal affinities of apocryphal texts like the *Vajrasamādhi*, but probably very little about the indigenous milieux that contextualize those scriptures. The sinologist, on the other hand, might be sensitive to the social and political contexts of apocrypha but would often have little interest in their doctrinal components. As this study will show, however, it is only when the methodologies of each of these disciplines are brought to bear on the study of the *Vajrasamādhi* that the real identity and significance of the scripture in East Asian Buddhism will be forthcoming. Hence, I hope that the approach I take here will contribute at least partially to breaking through some of the barriers that compartmentalize the various fields of East Asian studies and reveal some of the benefits that might be forthcoming from their crossfertilization.

My work on the *Vajrasamādhi* suggests as well that the study of apocryphal scriptures—if not of Buddhism as a whole—can be impeded by the very structure of the discipline of Buddhist studies. Buddhologists typically specialize in Indian, Chinese, Japanese, or Tibetan Buddhism, even though there are other divisions of the field that would be ideologically more felicitous, and historically more meaningful. Such specialization is especially pernicious when it obscures the manifold points of symbiosis across international borders that may themselves have contributed to the development of the national varieties of Buddhism. Just as the continental approach toward sinology pioneered by Peter Boodberg has come to be recognized as essential in the study of China, so too in Buddhist studies we must look at Buddhism as the organic whole it has always been, rather than in the splendid isolation of our artificial academic categorizations.[25]

Previous research on the *Vajrasamādhi* epitomizes the types of problems that can occur when research is conducted along national lines. Because of the dominant role played by China in the evolution of East Asian Buddhism, virtually by default the search for the origins of texts written in

---

[25] Alvin P. Cohen, ed., *Selected Works of Peter A. Boodberg*, pp. xii–xiii. See my remarks about the need for a "pan-East Asiatic" perspective on sinitic Buddhism in my article "Chinul's Systematization of Chinese Meditative Techniques in Korean Sŏn Buddhism," pp. 199–200. Cf. Gari Ledyard's comments about the need for a broader "East Asian history," which would be "something greater than the sum of the history of its constituent parts" in his "Yin and Yang in the China-Manchuria-Korea Triangle," p. 350.

Chinese has been limited to China alone, to the neglect of other areas of East Asia where Buddhism also flourished and where literary Chinese was also the principal vehicle of learned communication. Obviously, through sheer size alone the monolith of China would tend to dominate the creative work of East Asian Buddhism. But this need not imply that innovations did not take place elsewhere in Asia, which may have had a profound effect in neighboring lands as well. In fact, it is becoming increasingly apparent that we ignore at our peril the place of the "peripheral regions"—Tibet, Vietnam, Japan, and especially my main subject here, Korea—in any comprehensive description of "Chinese" Buddhism. I have already alluded to the contributions made by both domestic and expatriate Koreans in the development of Chinese Buddhism. But Korea was subject to many of the same forces and motivations that prompted the production of apocryphal texts in China. Korea also had access to virtually all the same sources that served as exemplars for composing Chinese native compositions. Clearly, there is no reason why the Koreans—or, indeed, any of the other peoples of East Asia—could not have written their own Buddhist scriptures, also in literary Chinese, which would have been able to exert as pervasive an influence as scriptures produced in China proper. And given the organic nature of the traditions, there is no reason why such a "peripheral" creation could not have found its way to China and been accepted by the Chinese as readily as one of its own indigenous compositions. This I will seek to show was the case with the *Vajrasamādhi*.

In evaluating a sūtra like the *Vajrasamādhi* that is suspected of being indigenous, there is a variety of information that must be weighed. Wording that is evocative of the argot and style of identifiable Chinese translations can indicate that a text already available in Chinese was the model for its composition. The doctrines showcased in the texts, the terminology it uses, even the type of Sanskrit transliterations it adopts will often parallel other explicitly apocryphal compositions. The intrusion of such typically Chinese notions as *yin/yang* cosmology may sometimes be enough to warrant suspicions about the origins of a scripture.[26] Specific examples of all such signs can be found in the *Vajrasamādhi*, leaving little doubt of the text's non-Indian provenance. Thanks especially to the efforts of two pioneering scholars in

---

[26] Considerable care must be used, of course, in distinguishing such "indigenous elements." See the monitions about interpreting filial piety (*hsiao*) as an exclusively East Asian moral concept in Gregory Schopen, "Filial Piety and the Monk in the Practice of Indian Buddhism: A Question of 'Sinicization' Viewed from the Other Side," pp. 110–26.

the study of apocryphal scriptures, Mizuno Kōgen and Walter Liebenthal, some of the mystery surrounding the textual sources of the *Vajrasamādhi* has begun to fade.[27] We now have several well-documented examples of direct borrowing by the author of the *Vajrasamādhi* from Chinese translations of other scriptures and treatises. Chapter 6 of the text includes, for example, a passage taken verbatim from Hsüan-tsang's definitive 649 translation of the *Heart Sūtra*, which provides the terminus a quo of the composition of the *Vajrasamādhi*.[28] Certain transliterations of Sanskrit adopted by the writer from earlier translators—such as *amala* ("immaculate")—contribute to our understanding of the indigenous literature with which the author was famil-iar.[29] The terminology used in the sūtra includes names of specific Chinese rivers, which would immediately cast doubts on the Indian authorship of the text.[30] These factors will receive further coverage later, and specific tex-tual appropriations will be highlighted in the annotation to my translation of the *Vajrasamādhi*.

But while we may know that the *Vajrasamādhi* is not a translation of an Indian or Serindian text, earlier scholars have all worked under the tacit as-sumption that the text was composed in China just because it was written in Chinese.[31] Thus, glaring evidence of the scripture's Korean origins has been ignored; and even when the suggestion was broached that the *Vajrasamādhi* might have been written in Korea, that opinion was based more on ad hoc stereotypes about the syncretic tendencies of Korean Buddhism than on a careful weighing of the relevant evidence.[32] Korean scholars working on the

[27] Mizuno Kōgen, "Bodaidaruma no *Ninyūshigyō setsu* to *Kongōzammaikyō*," pp. 33–57; Walter Liebenthal, "Notes on the 'Vajrasamādhi,' " pp. 347–86. A recent summary of the text, which closely follows Mizuno's account, appears in Okabe Kazuo, "Zenso no chūsho to gigi kyōten," pp. 360–62. The contributions these scholars have made to our understanding of *VS* will be treated in the course of my discussion of the text.

[28] *Mo-ho po-jo po-lo-mi-to hsin ching* (*Mahāprajñāpāramitāhṛdaya-sūtra*), T 251.8.848c14–15; see discussion in Mizuno, p. 46.

[29] See discussion in Mizuno, p. 45; Liebenthal, pp. 370–74; and see the annotation to my translation.

[30] Mizuno, p. 42; Liebenthal, p. 361.

[31] Mizuno (p. 40) assumed that *VS* must have been written in the Shan-tung or Liao-tung regions of northeastern China because of the role of the Dragon King in revealing the scripture; Liebenthal (pp. 377–86) looked to North China instead. Their arguments will be countered elsewhere in this book. It should be noted that Mizuno's dating of the composition of *VS* at between 650 and 665 (p. 40) or 660 and 680 ("Gisaku no *Hokkukyō* ni tsuite," p. 32) is com-pletely arbitrary, based neither on any account concerning the text appearing in Wŏnhyo's bi-ographies nor on catalogue references.

[32] See especially Kimura Senshō, "*Kongōzammaikyō* no shingi mondai," pp. 115–16. Al-though Kimura broaches the possibility of a Korean origin for the text, he provides no evidence for his hypothesis, and his reasoning is decidedly circular. After summarizing the earlier re-

sūtra have also been excessively provincial: while contributing valuable studies on the importance of Wŏnhyo's commentary to the *Vajrasamādhi* in the
development of Korean Buddhist thought, they have carefully skirted coverage of the scripture itself or the issue of its authenticity.[33]

Based on my own research on this text, I feel that many of the problems
surrounding the *Vajrasamādhi* can be resolved, first, through close consideration of the documentation concerning the text available in Buddhist bibliographical catalogues and evidence from its textual lineages. This examination must be followed by careful comparison with information gleaned
from the hagiographies of the Buddhist figure most closely linked with the
sūtra, the Korean scholiast Wŏnhyo, who wrote the first commentary to the
text sometime during the latter part of the seventh century. Wŏnhyo's associations with the *Vajrasamādhi* are far from adventitious and clearly figure
more importantly in forming a workable hypothesis about the sūtra's
origins than modern scholars have heretofore dared to suspect. Finally, the
unique doctrines of the text must be examined with reference to the ecclesiastical and political conditions prevalent in the Korean kingdom of Silla,
where I judge the text to have been composed; this comparison will narrow
considerably the possible candidates for authorship. Catalogue evidence,
textual filiations, hagiographical accounts, doctrinal innovations, and the
prospective cultural and religious milieux taken in isolation will not be sufficient to make any credible judgment about the dating, provenance, and
authorship of the text. Taken together, however, such factors serve as crucial
pieces of a complex puzzle, which will indicate that the *Vajrasamādhi* was
written in Korea, sometime around A.D. 685, by an early adept of the nascent Sŏn tradition on the peninsula, a man I shall call Pŏmnang.

---

search of Mizuno, Liebenthal, and Yanagida Seizan, Kimura simply notes that the syncretic
focus of *VS* tallies well with the ecumenical religious climate commonly considered to characterize Unified Silla Buddhism (668–935), and he suggests that the Silla origins of the text should
be explored. While I intend to show that aspects of this suggestion are correct, on the basis of
his approach to the question of origin, the corollary—that *VS* was popular in Silla precisely
*because* it was so close to the sympathies of Silla Buddhists—would be equally valid.

[33] An outstanding study of Wŏnhyo's commentary to *VS* has been made by Ko Ikchin,
"Wŏnhyo ŭi sasang ŭi silch'ŏn wŏlli," pp. 225–55; Ko, however, ignores the problems of the
sūtra's authenticity and focuses only on the place of the commentary in Wŏnhyo's thought.
Han Kidu (*Silla sidae ŭi Sŏn sasang*, pp. 23–34) has discussed insightfully many of the major
issues raised in both text and commentary and views the commentary as an integral part of the
Silla Sŏn tradition. Han suggests (p. 23) that without the impetus provided by *KSGR* to the
study of Sŏn, the pilgrimage of Koreans to the Chinese mainland to receive instruction directly
from Ch'an masters might never have taken place. Han's treatment adumbrates the close connections between *VS* and Korean Buddhism that I will explore in this study.

Despite the apparent aplomb with which I tell this story of the *Vajrasa-mādhi*, I more than anyone am aware of how tentative some of my conclu-sions must be. On the dating and provenance of the text, I am quite confi-dent; on the final question of authorship I am rather less sure. I have at times been tempted to offer the reader a choice of possible endings to this tale. I have refrained, however, and give what I perceive to be the most plausible scenario, based on my evaluation of the available evidence. The authorship case I make is, I believe, strong, but mostly circumstantial; smoking guns rarely survive a millennium, especially in the face of a determined coverup or widespread indifference. Finally, I portray the putative author of the text as more a shell for the type of person who would have been able to compose the *Vajrasamādhi*, rather than a real historical figure. But for texts separated from us by such vast temporal, geographical, and linguistic gulfs, it is a matter of some satisfaction that we will be able to come as far as we do. That the evidence does not allow us to resolve each and every outstanding ques-tion about the text seems hardly reason to despair and withhold the story indefinitely. We must glean as much from the evidence as it may support, and hope that others will see more in the material presented here, or find other supporting evidence that will reveal new things.

Let me first proceed to a survey of the contents of the *Vajrasamādhi* and the traditional view of its message.

## The Eclecticism of the *Vajrasamādhi*

The *Kŭmgang sammae-kyŏng*—which is usually known in Western scholar-ship as the *Vajrasamādhi-sūtra*, after the Sanskrit reconstruction of its title— is one of the many scriptures classified in China as *samādhi-sūtra*s (*san-mei ching*). Such texts were recognized since the late fifth century as a distinct genre of sūtra literature. They may have been important in the early evolu-tion of Ch'an, as seen, for example, with the *Hui-yin san-mei ching* (Book of [the tathāgatas'] seal of wisdom samādhi), which is thought to have been influential in Bodhidharma's teachings.[34] The plethora of citations from the *Vajrasamādhi* appearing in East Asian exegetical, didactic, and doxographic works shows that the text pervaded the sinitic Buddhist tradition, rivalling

---

[34] See Seng-yu's reference to the "*samādhi-sūtra* class" (*san-mei-ching lei*) in *Chu-san-tsang chi-chi* 9, *T* 2145.55.62b8–9. For a survey of this genre of sūtra, see Ōminami Ryūshō, "Sanmai kyōten no yakushutsu to juyō." For Bodhidharma's use of *Hui-yin san-mei ching* (*T* 632.15.460c–468a), see McRae, pp. 20–21.

the influence exerted by many translated Indian scriptures. This is especially so when the importance of the *Vajrasamādhi* to Ch'an is taken into account, a topic I shall return to often in the course of this book.

As the traditional commentators to the *Vajrasamādhi* have sought to explain, the vision implicit in the sūtra is that of a grand synthesis of Mahāyāna doctrine, something akin to what is found in the *Laṅkāvatāra-sūtra*, one of the more popular models for Chinese apocryphal scriptures. This eclecticism is suggested in the preface to Wŏnhyo's commentary to the *Vajrasamādhi*: "There are none of the Mahāyāna's dharma-characteristics that are not encompassed [by this scripture], nor none of [the Mahāyāna's] theme that has unlimited meaning that is not included in it. This is why it is said that its [three different] titles are not frivolously given."[35] The two alternate titles given to the text in its Epilogue are clear indications of this synthetic concern: *Compendium of Mahāyāna Sūtra* (*Sŏp taesŭng-kyŏng*; *Mahāyānasaṃgraha-sūtra*) and *Source of Immeasurable Doctrine Sūtra* (*Muryangŭijong-kyŏng*; *Anantanirdeśasiddhānta*).[36] Chu-chen (d.u.), the Ch'ing dynasty commentator to the *Vajrasamādhi*, also points out how elements from each of the "three repositories" of the Buddhist canon appear in the sūtra:

> Now this *Vajrasamādhi-sūtra* originally belonged to the scriptural repository (*sūtrapiṭaka*). However, the reference in the scripture to the three moral codes includes the repository of discipline (*vinayapiṭaka*). Its dialogues, from beginning to end, all thoroughly analyze profound principles and it thus includes as well the entire repository of exegetical writing (*śāstrapiṭaka*). Hence, all the tripiṭaka is included therein.[37]

From a variety of standpoints, then, and according to different commentators of varying times and places, a syncretic approach to Buddhist thought has been considered the *Vajrasamādhi*'s predominant concern.

This synthesis was not, however, an end in itself. The sūtra's first commentator, Wŏnhyo, for example, suggests a higher purpose: to supply the foundation for a workable soteriology by providing a comprehensive system of meditative praxis. Following Wŏnhyo's hermeneutic of the text, chapter 1, "Prologue," surveys the basic qualities of the adamantine absorption (vajrasamādhi) after which the text is named. There, the vajrasamādhi is said

---

[35] *KSGR* 1, p. 961b7–8.

[36] The significance of these titles is discussed in Takamine Ryōshū, *Kegon to Zen to no tsūro*, pp. 150–51.

[37] Chu-chen, *T'ung-tsung chi* 1, p. 225a16–17.

to be a unique variety of absorption accessed by the Buddha himself, in which all doubts are resolved and all things incorporated into the one, all-encompassing buddha-vehicle. Chapters 2 through 7 are a progressive exposition of the actual process of contemplation practice (*kwanhaeng*) undertaken by the adept during the Semblance Age of the dharma (Hsiang-fa; Pratirūpaka), when Buddhism was in its initial stages of degeneration. Chapter 2, "The Signless Dharma," explains the technique of signless contemplation, which frees the meditator from the tendency to assume that both person and dharmas are ultimately real. Chapter 3, "The Practice of Nonproduction," describes a type of practice in which one trains to become completely unattached even to the fruits of meditation, thus allowing the mind to achieve perfect calm. Chapter 4, "The Inspiration of Original Enlightenment," explains how the practitioner may thence continue on to benefit all sentient beings through relying on the powers inherent in the innate enlightenment of his mind. Chapter 5, "Approaching the Edge of Reality," describes the transition from illusory perception to true reality. Chapter 6, "The Voidness of the True Nature," explains that all spiritual practices derive from the innate voidness of the true nature. This contemplative process culminates in chapter 7, "The Tathāgatagarbha," which reveals that all the approaches to practice discussed previously culminate in access to the tathā-gatagarbha, the womb or embryo of buddhahood—the realization of the original enlightenment that is inherent in all beings. The final chapter, "Dhāraṇī," removes any lingering doubts on the part of the audience as to the message of the sūtra and transmits the scripture to posterity.[38]

This soteriological orientation of the *Vajrasamādhi* is brought out also by Chu-chen. His exegesis interprets each chapter in terms of a specific stage, or *bhūmi*, on the bodhisattva path (mārga). The "Prologue" is the section in which faith is aroused concerning the one buddha-vehicle; this faith then serves as the proleptic cause for the eventual fruition of buddhahood. "Signless Dharma" is the chapter dealing with prajñā (wisdom) and refers specifically to the sixth *bhūmi* of the bodhisattva path, "Disposed toward Enlightenment" (*hsien-ch'ien ti*; *abhimukhībhūmi*). "Practice of Nonproduction" discusses the acquiescence to the nonproduction of dharmas (*anutpattika-dharmakṣānti*) that takes place on the seventh *bhūmi*, "Far-reaching" (*yüan-hsing ti*; *dūraṃgamābhūmi*). "Inspiration of Original Enlightenment" outlines

---

[38] *KSGR* 1, pp. 963c3–964a16; Wŏnhyo gives an alternative exegesis at 963c21ff. This section is discussed also in Han Kidu, *Silla sidae ŭi Sŏn sasang*, pp. 24–26, and Ko Ikchin, pp. 231–36.

the process by which the ordinary sensory consciousnesses are transformed into the four types of wisdom; it corresponds to the eighth *bhūmi*, the "Unshakable" (*pu-tung ti*; *acalābhūmi*). "Approaching the Edge of Reality" explains the achievement of analytical knowledge (*pratisaṃvid*) that occurs on the ninth *bhūmi* of "Effective Intelligence" (*shan-hui ti*; *sādhumatībhūmi*). "Voidness of the True Nature" describes the consummation of progress through the *bhūmi*s; it corresponds to the tenth and final stage of "Dharma Cloud" (*fa-yün ti*; *dharmameghābhūmi*). "Tathāgatagarbha" describes the knowledge that is gained at the level of "equal enlightenment" (*teng-chüeh*), the initial stage of buddhahood itself, in which one achieves the understanding that is "equal" in all the buddhas. "Dhāraṇī" represents the perfection of enlightenment that takes place at the level of "sublime enlightenment" (*miao-chüeh*), in which the adept is able to act out the myriad of salutary qualities gained through complete, perfect enlightenment (*anuttarasamyaksaṃbodhi*). Finally, Chu-chen separates a concluding "Epilogue" from the rest of the final chapter, which discusses the need for proselytism and the transmission of the sūtra.[39] However, in a manner reminiscent of the *Avataṃsaka-sūtra*, which was so important to both Hua-yen and Ch'an, Chu-chen advocates that both the beginning and end of the *Vajrasamādhi* actually include all the other chapters: "The 'Signless Dharma' chapter completely incorporates the teachings of the latter six chapters, while the final 'Dhāraṇī' chapter in fact amalgamates the teachings of the preceding six chapters."[40] Chu-chen thus saw the sūtra as directed principally at an audience of advanced bodhisattvas on the final stages of the *mārga*: "This [*Vajra*]*samādhi* is not something that can be known by bodhisattvas [still training] in the provisional teachings who are on the levels of the [ten] abidings (*chu*) and [ten] practices (*hsing*) and working toward the *bhūmi*s. Rather, it is only bodhisattvas following the absolute teachings of the one [buddha] vehicle, who have already ascended to the last five *bhūmi*s and the two stages of equal and sublime enlightenments, who can realize and access it."[41]

Accepting such systematic outlines of the *Vajrasamādhi* requires a consid-

[39] Chu-chen, *T'ung-tsung chi* 1, p. 228c–d. See discussion of this *mārga* schema in Takamine Ryōshū, *Kegon to Zen to no tsūro*, p. 155.

[40] Chu-chen, *T'ung-tsung chi* 1, p. 228b10–12. The Hua-yen parallel is the claim in the "Brahmacaryā Chapter" (Fan-hsing p'in) that the inception and consummation of religious cultivation are identical: "The initial arousing of the *bodhicitta* is the attainment of *anuttarasam-yaksaṃbodhi*." *Ta-fang-kuang fo hua-yen ching* 8, T 278.9.449c14; *Ta-fang-kuang fo hua-yen ching* 17, T 279.10.89a1–2.

[41] Chu-chen, *T'ung-tsung chi* 1, p. 228b7–9.

erable leap of faith, though their premise is not utterly far-fetched. There is some continuity of interest in the *Vajrasamādhi*, especially in the emphasis seen through most of the sūtra on such seminal Mahāyāna concepts as "non-production" (*anutpādatva*) and "signlessness" (*alakṣaṇatva*). And it is true that the major orientation of the scripture is soteriological, given its stress on the concepts of samādhi, tathāgatagarbha, and enlightenment. Rather than the systematic "synthesis" that its commentators perceived, however, an eclectic "amalgam" may be a somewhat more accurate portrayal. The *Vajrasamādhi* provides a cross-section of the philosophical interests of contemporary East Asian Buddhist exegetes. But its examination of these debates is hardly rigorous, and the sūtra is most certainly not the methodical exposition of scholastic doctrine that its commentators perceive. There is, finally, relatively little sustained argumentation through the scripture, a fact adumbrated by the change of interlocutor from chapter to chapter.[42]

But our author need not be taken unduly to task for the haphazard quality of his text. In his defense, such a tendency to anthologize is not unique to sinitic apocrypha, but is actually quite common in Mahāyāna scriptures, if not in the sūtra genre as a whole.[43] D. T. Suzuki's characterization of *Laṅkāvatāra-sūtra*, a distant relative of our text, is apposite in reading the *Vajrasamādhi*: "The whole *Laṅkāvatāra* is just a collection of notes unsystematically strung together, and, frankly speaking, it is a useless task to attempt to divide them into sections, or chapters (*parivarta*), under some specific titles. Some commentators have tried to create a system in the *Laṅkāvatāra* by making each paragraph somewhat connected in meaning with the preceding as well as the succeeding one, but one can at once detect that there is something quite constrained or far-fetched about the attempt."[44] In his neglect of organization, then, the author was in the best of company and can hardly be faulted.

My own reading of the *Vajrasamādhi* suggests that its author had an additional, and perhaps overriding, agenda supplementing the synthesis the commentators saw: to embed a new interpretation of Buddhism—Ch'an—within a doctrinal framework familiar to the scholiasts of his age, ensuring that it would be noticed and, with any luck, preserved. This agenda is particularly noticable in chapter 5, "Approaching the Edge of Reality," which

---

[42] A similar change of interlocutors is found also in the apocryphal *Yüan-chüeh ching*, T 842.17.913aff.

[43] A possibility raised by Luis Gómez, "The Structure and Meaning of a Pali *Sutta*."

[44] Suzuki, *Studies*, p. 17; and note also his *Essays in Zen Buddhism*, series 1, p. 75.

includes the most prominent Ch'an elements. The text that brackets the discussion of the "two accesses" and of "guarding the one" there is quite difficult to construe and seems to be merely a vehicle for introducing these concepts from Ch'an. The forest of purposes of apocryphal texts can often be obscured by the trees (sometimes it seems more like the brambles) of their doctrinal allusions. As I seek to show was the case with the *Vajrasamādhi*, the teachings adopted in the scripture may in one sense be seen as a subterfuge for a strong polemical motive supporting Ch'an positions.

## The Model for the *Vajrasamādhi*'s Narrative Structure

While the overriding message and general style of the *Vajrasamādhi* may be akin to those found in the *Laṅkāvatāra*, the narrative structure of the sūtra is modeled after another influential Indian sūtra: the *Saddharmapuṇḍarīka-sūtra* (*Miao-fa lien-hua ching*), the renowned *Lotus Sūtra*. The first chapters in both texts were considered to be prologues to the actual texts of the *Lotus* and *Vajrasamādhi* sūtras themselves, which follow subsequently. During the time described in those prologues, the Buddha delivers a completely different sūtra—in the *Vajrasamādhi*'s case, an "expanded scripture" (*vaipulyasūtra*)—the titles of which are rubrics for the topics they treat. Once that initial scripture is finished, the Buddha enters into deep meditation, during which time a member of the assembly reiterates in verse the principal themes of the text. Only afterward does the Buddha withdraw from his absorption and begin to preach the real *Lotus* and the *Vajrasamādhi*. As perhaps we may expect, neither of these preliminary texts is attested anywhere in Indian sources. The titles are fabrications, intended to suggest to the reader that there is a vast store of Mahāyāna sūtras as yet unavailable in the world of men. In fact, the existence of such titles was itself a catalyst for textual production. The preliminary scripture mentioned in the *Lotus*, the *Sūtra of Immeasurable Doctrine* (*Wu-liang-i ching*), was eventually written in China, fulfilling its destiny as a known, circulating text.[45] If East Asian Buddhists had shown sufficient ini-

---

[45] *Wu-liang-i ching*, *T* 276.9.384a–389b. The translation is said to have taken place in 481 and is attributed to Dharmāgatayaśas (*Ku-chin i-ching t'u-chi* 4, *T* 2151.55.363b13). Ogiwara Unrai and Ōchō Enichi have made strong cases for its Chinese origin, however, based on stylistic evidence, unusual transliterations and translations of terms, and peculiar hierarchical arrangements of Indian doctrinal concepts. There are also problems in the biography of the alleged translator (this is his only attributed translation), and peculiar events in the transmission of the text, which suggest that attempts have been made to hide its spurious provenance by

tiative, the *Vajrasamādhi*'s preliminary scripture, *Single taste . . . Inspiration of Original Enlightenment Sūtra*, might also have made it into print!

To show how closely the *Vajrasamādhi* mirrors the structure and phraseology of the *Lotus*'s prologue, I have placed their opening sections side by side in table 1.1.[46]

Why would the *Lotus Sūtra* have provided such a compelling model for an apocryphal text like the *Vajrasamādhi*? The *Lotus*, as is well known, was the focus of considerable scholarly investigation in East Asia, especially during fifth- and sixth-century China. Its eclectic tendencies were eminently suited to the syncretic approaches to doctrine pursued in many of the learned schools of sinitic Buddhism. As the East Asian tradition evolved, the *Lotus* comes to be most closely associated with the T'ien-t'ai school, but this association is rather more tenuous during the era considered here, not really crystallizing until Chan-jan's (711–782) time. While the Ch'an school retrospectively seeks to align itself with first the *Laṅkāvatāra* and later the *Diamond* sūtras, these alignments are not clear-cut until well into the eighth century. Throughout Ch'an's incipiency, it too drew often upon the insights of the *Lotus* to authenticate its own approach. In the *Hsiu-hsin yao-lun* (Treatise on the essentials of cultivating the mind), for example, a seminal document of the East Mountain faction of early Ch'an that will be considered later, its putative author, Hung-jen (601–674), states that "my instructions to you are based on the *Lotus Sūtra*."[47] The *Platform Sūtra*, presenting perhaps the quintessence of early and middle Ch'an doctrine, uses the *Lotus* as a text against

---

shrouding its origins in mystery. Mitomo Kenyō has sought to refute each of the major points made by Ogiwara and Ōchō in order to establish the sūtra's Indian origin; see his "*Muryōgikyō Indo senjutsu setsu*," pp. 1119–45. While Mitomo can provide controverting evidence to each specific point, his argument of Indian provenance is completely *ex silentio*. He does not provide any evidence that the sūtra ever circulated in India or that it was ever cited in Indian materials.

[46] For these passages, see *Miao-fa lien-hua ching*, T 262.9.1c–5b27; translation adapted from Leon Hurvitz, trans., *Scripture of the Lotus Blossom of the Fine Dharma*, pp. 3–22; and see *VS*, chaps. 1 and 2. For Wŏnhyo's discussion of the structural relationship between *VS* and the *Lotus*, see *KSGR* 1, p. 963a11–17. Chu-chen (*T'ung-tsung chi*, pp. 226b–227a) also notes the affinities between the *Lotus* and *VS*, going so far as to try to place *VS* within T'ien-t'ai's fivefold temporal taxonomy of the teachings. After discussing various theories concerning the placement of the text, he attempts to prove that the preaching of *VS* succeeded that of *Lotus Sūtra*—the *Lotus* being designed to excise the initial doubts and regrets of the congregation, *VS* instead directed toward those who had already completed all the *bhūmis*. Cf. the similar narrative structures in the openings to the apocryphal texts *Chan-ch'a shan-o yeh-pao ching* 1, T 839.17.901c; and *Yüan-chüeh ching*, T 842.17.913a–b.

[47] See the Korean edition, which bears the title *Ch'oesangsŭng-ron*, T 2011.48.378a20; cf. translation in McRae, p. 126.

TABLE 1.1
The Prologues to the *Lotus Sūtra* and the *Vajrasamādhi*

| *Lotus Sūtra* | *Vajrasamādhi Sūtra* |
|---|---|
| 1. **Thus I once heard.** | 1. **Thus I once heard.** |
| 2. **The Buddha was dwelling in the great city of Rājagṛha, on Mount Gṛdhrakūṭa, together with a great assembly of** twelve thousand **bhikṣus, all of whom were arhats. Their names were** . . . **Śāriputra, Mahāmaudgalyāyana,** . . . **Subhūti,** . . . **a great many such arhats as these.** . . . | 2. **The Buddha was dwelling in the great city of Rājagṛha, on Mount Gṛdhrakūṭa, together with a great assembly of** ten thousand **bhikṣus, all of whom** had attained the arhat path. **Their names were Śāriputra, Mahāmaudgalyāyana, Subhūti—there were many such arhats as these.** |
| 3. Furthermore, **there were** eighty thousand **bodhisattva-mahāsattvas,** . . . **and other bodhisattvas like these.** . . . | 3. Furthermore, **there were** two thousand **bodhisattva-mahāsattvas.** Their names were Haet'al Bodhisattva, Simwang Bodhisattva, Muju Bodhisattva, **and other bodhisattvas like these.** . . . |
| 4. [See section 7.] | 4. Furthermore, **there were** six hundred million **devas, dragons, yakṣas, gandharvas, aśuras, garuḍas, kinnaras, mahorāgas, humans, and nonhumans.** |
| 5. **At that time**, the World Honored One, **surrounded by the** fourfold **congregation**, showered with offerings, deferentially treated and revered, **preached a Mahāyāna sūtra on behalf of all** the bodhisattvas, **entitled** *The Immeasurable doctrine.* | 5. **At that time**, the Lord, **surrounded by the great congregation, preached a Mahāyāna sūtra on behalf of all** the great congregation, **entitled** *Practice of the single taste, truth, signless, nonproduction, certitude, edge of reality, and the inspiration of original enlightenment.* If one hears this sūtra or retains even one four-line verse [of it], this person will then access the stage of the Buddha's knowledge; he will be able to proselyte sentient beings with appropriate expedients and become the great spiritual mentor of all sentient beings. |
| 6. **After the Buddha had preached this sūtra, he folded his legs into full lotus position, and entered into** the Abode of the Immeasurable Doctrine **absorption, with his body and mind motionless.** | 6. **After the Buddha had preached this sūtra, he folded his legs into full lotus position, and entered into** the adamantine **absorption, with his body and mind motionless.** |

TABLE 1.1 (*cont.*)

| *Lotus Sūtra* | *Vajrasamādhi Sūtra* |
|---|---|
| 7. At that time, in the assembly, **there were . . . devas, dragons, yakṣas, gandharvas, aśuras, garuḍas, kinnaras, mahorāgas, humans, and nonhumans** . . . these great assemblies gained what they never had before. . . . | 7. [See section 4.] |
| 8. Thereupon, the bodhisattva Maitreya, **wishing to reiterate the meaning of this [sūtra that had just been preached]**, questioned with gāthās. . . . | 8. At that time there was a bhikṣu named Agada, in the congregation, who arose from his seat, joined his palms together, and genuflected in foreign fashion. **Wishing to reiterate the meaning of this [sūtra that had just been preached]**, he recited gāthās. . . . |
| 9. **Arising from** the serenity of **his samādhi**, the World Honored One addressed Śāriputra: "**The wisdom of all the buddhas** is profound and incalculable. The approaches to that wisdom are **difficult to comprehend and difficult to access. They are not something that are known or cognized by any of the śrāvakas and pratyekabuddhas.** | 9. **Arising from his samādhi**, the Lord then spoke these words, "**The** stage of **wisdom of all the buddhas** accesses the given nature of the real characteristic of dharmas. For this reason, [the buddhas'] expedients and superpowers are all inspired by signlessness. The explicit meaning of the one enlightenment is **difficult to comprehend and difficult to access. It is not something that is known or cognized by any adherents of the two vehicles [of śrāvakas and pratyekabuddhas]**; it may only be known by the buddhas and bodhisattvas. |

which to test a student's understanding.[48] The *Lotus* was finally a common focus of cultic and ritual activity in East Asia. For all these reasons, then, the author of the *Vajrasamādhi* had good cause to frame his text in such a way that it would compare with one of the most popular, and undeniably authentic, Indian scriptures ever translated into Chinese.

---

[48] See the story of Fa-ta being "turned by the *Lotus*," in Philip Yampolsky, trans., *The Platform Sūtra of the Sixth Patriarch*, sect. 42, pp. 165–68.

But if an indigenous sūtra like the *Vajrasamādhi* was to have any hope of entering the mainstream of East Asian Buddhism, it had first to gain the sanction of the arbiters of canonicity, the scriptural cataloguers. Without such sanction, few texts were able to overcome the onus of fraudulence, which was seen as threatening the bibliographical impeccability of Buddhism, if not the very viability of the tradition as a whole—either reason enough to blacklist the scripture and bar it from being entered into the canon. Let us, then, turn to the cataloguers' entries on the *Vajrasamādhi* as a way of exploring traditional views of the sūtra's pedigree.

## The *Vajrasamādhi* in the Chinese Catalogues

In any attempt to ascertain the dating, provenance, and authorship of a suspect scripture, it is to the Buddhist bibliographical catalogues that one must first turn. While the inherent critical limitations of such catalogues should be recognized,[49] when carefully used they can serve as an invaluable source of information on the spread and currency of a text in different dynastic periods and geographical regions. This examination of the treatment of the *Vajrasamādhi* in the catalogues will offer a particularly graphic example of the sort of information that may be gleaned from the catalogues, and especially of the ways in which that information can be used in evaluating traditional ascriptions about the origins of a sūtra.

The earliest reference known for a *Vajrasamādhi-sūtra* (*Chin-kang san-mei ching*) in East Asian catalogues appears in a section of Tao-an's *Tsung-li chung-ching mu-lu* (Comprehensive catalogue of all the scriptures): the *Liang-t'u i-ching lu* (Anomalous sūtras from the Liang region).[50] In this pioneering catalogue, completed in A.D. 374, the compiler, Tao-an (312–385), lists only sūtras he had perused himself at least once in his career; sūtras of unusual content or style that he knew to exist only in one region are listed under his classification of *i-ching* ("anomalous sūtras").[51] Based on this notice, we can

---

[49] See the discussion in Lewis R. Lancaster, Review of *Répertorie du Canon Bouddhique Sino-Japonais*, pp. 130–31. For an extensive analysis of the treatment of sinitic apocrypha in the Chinese catalogues, see Kyoko Tokuno, "The Evaluation of Indigenous Scriptures in Chinese Buddhist Bibliographical Catalogues."

[50] Tao-an's *Liang-t'u i-ching lu* is discussed by Hayashiya Tomojirō, *Kyōroku kenkyū*, pp. 414–16, and its contents are reconstructed on pp. 416–18. Liang-t'u is Liang-chou in Kansu province.

[51] Hayashiya, *Kyōroku kenkyū*, p. 414; noted also by Erik Zürcher, *The Buddhist Conquest of China*, vol. 1, p. 195. The term used here, *i-ching* ("anomalous scripture"; sometimes *ku-i ching* ["archaic anomalous scripture"]), refers to "peculiar" or "unusual" scriptures geographically

be sure of the existence of a one-*chüan* text entitled *Vajrasamādhi* during the latter part of the fourth century. However, as Tao-an's was only a regional catalogue, listing just works from those locales in which he had traveled personally, there is no information on the extent of the scripture's diffusion in other areas of China. However, since even Tao-an knew of the sūtra's existence in only the Liang region of northwestern China, its circulation may have been quite limited.

Tao-an's listing is picked up one century later by Seng-yu (445–518) in his *Ch'u san-tsang chi-chi* (A collection of notes concerning the translation of the tripiṭaka), which includes many sections lifted wholesale from Tao-an's catalogue. Because the *Vajrasamādhi* is not included in Seng-yu's list of extant works, we can only assume that he did not know personally of a copy of the sūtra circulating anywhere around his base of operations, the Chiang-nan area, just south of the Yangtze River. Since Seng-yu's catalogue was also a regional compilation covering only southern Chinese Buddhism, we cannot be absolutely certain that there was not a *Vajrasamādhi* in circulation somewhere in northern or western China at that time; however, Tao-an's implication that the text was available only in the far northwest, and the lack of any reference at all to the text in the south, certainly provide strong grounds for doubting the text's currency during the fifth century.[52]

The first attempt at a comprehensive catalogue covering all of China was *Chung-ching mu-lu*, compiled in 594 by Fa-ching (fl. late sixth century) and nineteen associates in a period of just over two months. This catalogue was compiled as a means of consolidating Sui dominion over China, by providing a record of the full range of Buddhist literature available in Chinese; this information was then to be used as the basis for a Sui edition of the Buddhist tripiṭaka, which would be disseminated throughout the empire. Fa-ching

---

restricted to one particular region of China (Hayashiya, pp. 414–15); and cf. Tao-an's definition of *ku-i*: "Although the text of the scripture is disorganized and has several lacunae, by examining the extant sections, the [identity of the] old and present [recensions] can be discerned" (*Ch'u san-tsang chi-chi* 3, *T* 2145.55.15b13–14). This term should be carefully distinguished from *i-ch'u* ("variant translation [lit., publication]"), which was used by Tao-an and his successors to refer to different Chinese translations of the same Sanskrit or Middle Indic original (*Chu san-tsang chi-chi* 3, *T* 2145.55.13c22); see the discussion by Antonino Forte, *Political Propaganda and Ideology in China*, p. 17.

[52] The noncomprehensiveness of Seng-yu's catalogue is discussed in Hayashiya, *Kyōroku Kenkyū*, pp. 144–45. This catalogue is usually considered to have been compiled between 494 and 497. It has been noted, however, that references in *Ch'u san-tsang chi-chi* indicate that at least some portions of it were not compiled until after 510; see Naitō Ryūo, "*Shutsu sanzō kishū* no senshū nenji ni tsuite," p. 163; and his subsequent article, "*Sōyū no chosaku katsudō*," p. 285, where he dates some materials to 515.

includes a listing for a *Vajrasamādhi* in his section on single-edition texts by anonymous translators (*tan-pen shih-i*), but he gives no information as to whether the text was then extant.[53] As Hayashiya Tomojirō has pointed out, Fa-ching, in his zeal for comprehensiveness, gave complete listings for all sūtras mentioned in previous catalogues as well as for scriptures that were actually extant at that time in Sui China; hence, extant and nonextant sūtras were included indiscriminately in the listings, and no separate section was set aside just for nonextant materials.[54] For this reason, we cannot be absolutely certain about the status of the text at the time of the compilation of this catalogue, though it does seem most probable that Fa-ching simply copied the reference to the sūtra directly from the entry in Tao-an's catalogue, which had been recorded in *Ch'u san-tsang chi-chi*.

Seng-yu's citation from Tao-an's catalogue is also quoted verbatim by Fei Ch'ang-fang (fl. late sixth century) in his *Li-tai san-pao chi* (Notes on the successive triratnas), another Sui attempt at a comprehensive catalogue, written in 597. Fei lived during a period of resurgent Taoist influence at the court and the ardent religious rivalries engendered thereby. In attempting to counter this burgeoning Taoist strength, Fei's catalogue deliberately distorted many textual references, falsely attributing to famous translators Buddhist texts that were then circulating as anonymous in order to give them more credibility. Although his ascriptions provided the basis for the attributions made in the later *K'ai-yüan shih-chiao lu*—from whence they entered the mainstream of the Chinese tradition—they are completely unreliable for determining dating or authorship.[55] His notice therefore offers little help in determining the currency of the *Vajrasamādhi* during his time.

Based on these notices in the catalogues of Seng-yu and Fei Ch'ang-fang, Chu-chen made the only attempt among the classical commentators to the *Vajrasamādhi* to determine the translator of the scripture. He proposes that Tao-an himself had rendered the *Vajrasamādhi* into Chinese: "Furthermore, based on the account in *[Li-tai] san-pao chi*, Tao-an of Fu Chien's [court, viz., the Former Ch'in dynasty] had also translated some twenty-four works of

[53] See Hayashiya, *Kyōroku kenkyū*, pp. 77–79. The *Fa-ching lu* reference states that "the above 123 sūtras [including *VS*] are all single edition [texts] by anonymous translators (*tan-pen shih-i*)"; (*T* 2146.55.121c14); Liebenthal (p. 349) mistranslates this entry to read "extant in a separate edition" and postulates that the text was still extant in the sixth century; this, as will be seen, is by no means certain.

[54] Hayashiya, *Kyōroku kenkyū*, pp. 77–78.

[55] The *Li-tai san-pao chi* is treated by Hayashiya (*Kyōroku kenkyū*, pp. 82–85), where he discusses the number of wrong attributions made in the catalogue; and pp. 151–52, where he calls attention to the uselessness of its bibliographical references in determining textual origins.

scripture. Moreover, according to Seng-yu, [the *Vajrasamādhi*] was first listed in Tao-an's *Liang-t'u i-ching [lu]*. Perforce, [*VS*] was translated by Tao-an."[56] From the previous catalogue listings, however, it is clear that Chu-chen's surmise can hardly be correct. There is no indication from any catalogue that Tao-an himself had made the *Vajrasamādhi* translation, and this conclusion hardly follows from the fact that the sūtra first appears in Tao-an's early listings. Despite Chu-chen's attempt to resolve some of the difficulties concerning the origins of the *Vajrasamādhi*, there are good reasons to reject his hypothesis out of hand.

Since the utility of Fa-ching's catalogue as a basis for a Sui edition of the tripiṭaka was considerably diminished by his indiscriminate listings of both extant and nonextant sūtras, still another catalogue that carefully distinguished the extant from the nonextant was compiled under Sui auspices in 602. This was *Chung-ching mu-lu* by Yen-ts'ung (557–610), a noted Chinese Sanskritist, historiographer, and cataloguer. Any doubts about the status of the *Vajrasamādhi* that might have remained from the catalogue entries of Fa-ching and Fei Ch'ang-fang are quickly allayed by Yen-ts'ung's work: here, the sūtra is listed among 378 nonextant texts (*ch'üeh-pen*) in a total of 610 fascicles.[57] Thanks to this reference, we are finally certain that the *Vajrasamādhi* was not in circulation anywhere in China at least by 602. In addition, since the only unequivocal reference to the existence of the text in earlier catalogues was in Tao-an's compilation, there is good reason to assume that the text had, in fact, dropped out of circulation sometime during the latter part of the fourth century.

The *Vajrasamādhi* remained nonextant through the end of the seventh century. In the 695 *Ta-Chou kan-ting chung-ching mu-lu* (The Great Chou [dynasty's] revised catalogue of all the scriptures), compiled during the reign of Wu Chao (r. 690–705)—and significantly, fully nine years after the death of Wŏnhyo, the first commentator to the sūtra—the *Vajrasamādhi* is still listed as lost. This catalogue, compiled from the combined information of seventy monks from around the country, was meant to be exhaustive and is noted for including in its entries every bit of available information—even spurious references from previous catalogues.[58] If this sūtra were extant in China at that time, the chance that it would have been missed by these diligent cata-

---

[56] Chu-chen, *T'ung-tsung chi* 1, p. 227c12–14.

[57] Hayashiya (*Kyōroku kenkyū*, p. 78) notes that Yen-ts'ung's *Chung-ching mu-lu* is a catalogue of exclusively extant works. *VS* and its categorization into the nonextant list appears at *T* 2147.55.175a25–26 and 176b28.

[58] See discussion in Hayashiya, *Kyōroku kenkyū*, pp. 94–100.

loguers is exceedingly slim at best. Wŏnhyo's exegesis of the sūtra, written just a few years before, had apparently not yet been transmitted to the mainland, and the *Vajrasamādhi* remained unknown in China. This assumption that the text was nonextant in China at least through 695, while it was known in Korea at least a decade before, is borne out by the fact that the text appears on the nonextant list in four other catalogues compiled between 602 and 695.[59]

The *Vajrasamādhi* dramatically reenters the Chinese catalogues some three centuries after its disappearance in China in *K'ai-yüan shih-chiao lu* (Catalogue in explanation of the teachings, compiled during the K'ai-yüan era), completed in 730 by Chih-sheng (658–740). (See table 1.2 for catalogue listings of the *Vajrasamādhi*.) The *Vajrasamādhi* is still listed as the product of an unknown translator of the Pei-Liang period (397–439), but the text known to Chih-sheng is cited as having been reconstructed from scattered folios (*shih-i p'ien-ju*).[60] Hayashiya Tomojirō was the first to note this anomaly concerning the listing of the *Vajrasamādhi* in the Chinese catalogues. Based on his pioneering research on translation terminology and techniques, he deduced that the *Vajrasamādhi* as it appeared in *K'ai-yüan lu*—the version extant today—could not have been composed before the time of Kumārajīva (344–413), because of the use of Buddhist technical equivalencies and transliterations that first appear only in Kumārajīva's translations. Hence, he concludes that the *Vajrasamādhi* appearing in Tao-an's late fourth-century catalogue and the sūtra by the same name listed in the eighth century could not have been the same text.[61] His deductions were confirmed by Mizuno who, however, was apparently unaware of Hayashiya's earlier conclusions.[62] The fact that the *Vajrasamādhi* is listed as nonextant in China through 695, reappearing as a "reconstructed" text only in 730, shows that the Koreans knew of the text several decades before the Chinese. We must take seriously the possibility that it is of Korean, not Chinese, provenance.

---

[59] The dates of the catalogues in table 1.2 follow Yabuki Keiki ("Tonkō shutsudo gigi kobutten ni tsuite," pp. 48–49) and Hayashiya (*Kyōroku Kenkyū*, pp. 13–15); these texts are listed according to their compilers' names or the reign periods in which they were published. Some of the dates are still open to investigation, as for the *Ch'u san-tsang chi-chi*.

[60] Discussed in Mizuno, pp. 37–38, and p. 38 n. 5, where he gives other examples of reconstructed texts. See also Hayashiya, *Kyōroku kenkyū*, p. 1078, and Kimura, "*Kongōzammaikyō*," p. 106.

Note also the use of *san-ching* in Tao-an's catalogue in *Ch'u san-tsang chi-chi* 3, *T* 2145.55.15b, which indicates that *i-ching* were often *san-ching*, "scattered," i.e., fragmentary, sūtras.

[61] Hayashiya, *Kyōroku kenkyū*, pp. 1078–79.

[62] Mizuno, pp. 37–38.

TABLE 1.2
Catalogue Entries for the *Vajrasamādhi-Sūtra*

| Catalog | Date | VS Extant? | Citation | Comments |
|---------|------|-----------|----------|----------|
| *Tao-an lu* | 374 | Yes | T 2145.55.18c6 | Anomalous *sūtra* from Liang-t'u; north only. |
| *Seng-yu lu* | 494–7 | no | T 2145.55.18c6 | Cites *Tao-an lu*; not extant in Chiang-nan. |
| *Fa-ching lu* | 594 | ? | T 2146.55.121a14 | Anonymous translator section; extant and non-extant texts cited together. |
| *Li-tai san-pao chi* | 597 | ? | T 2034.49.85a18 | Copies *Seng-yu* entry. |
| *Jen-shou lu* | 602 | no | T 2147.55.176b28 | Only extant works listed; cited as lost *sūtra*. |
| *Nei-tien lu* | 664 | ? | T 2149.55.256c4 | Cites *Tao-an lu* |
| *Ching-t'ai lu* | 666 | no | T 2148.55.214a29 | Cited as lost. |
| *Ku-chin i-ching t'u-chi* | n.d. | ? | T 2151.55.361a24 | Cites *Tao-an lu* |
| *Ta Chou lu* | 695 | no | T 2153.55.439c8 | Cited in anonymous translator section. |
| | | | .448a25 | Cited as lost. |
| | | | .450a21 | Cited as lost. |
| *K'ai-yüan lu* | 730 | yes | T 2154.55.522b14 | Cited as extant; two other sūtras mentioned with it are lost. |
| | | | .605b15 | Reconstructed text; anonymous translator. |
| | | | .667a22 | Cited as reconstructed text. |
| | | | .688c20 | In 27 folios; note Wonhyo's biography; in same wrapper with 23 other texts. |
| | | | .712b9 | Anonymous translator. |
| *K'ai-yüan lu lüeh-ch'u* | 730 | yes | T 2155.55.734b2 | Anonymous translator. |
| *Nara shakyō* | 737 | yes | *Nara shakyō* #611 | Manuscript copied in Japan in this year. |
| *Ch'en-yüan lu* | 800 | yes | T 2157.55.819a22 | |
| | | | .938c10 | |
| | | | .1006a8 | |
| | | | .1036b10 | |

Why would Chih-sheng have allowed the inclusion of the *Vajrasamādhi*, suspiciously reappearing after a three-hundred-year hiatus, in his listing of canonical texts? We can only presume that he believed the earlier *Vajrasamādhi* listed by Tao-an had been rediscovered. Its apparent recovery in Korea might have rendered the authenticity of this *Vajrasamādhi* that much more plausible to Chih-sheng: lost since the fourth century in China, the sūtra had continued to circulate in Korea whence, thanks to the international attention engendered by Wŏnhyo's commentary to the text, it finally made its way back to China. During Buddhism's tenure in Korea it becomes common for scriptures lost in China to be reintroduced via Korean editions.[63] Although the *Vajrasamādhi* would be the earliest known example of such reimportation, this therefore need not have been an unusual occurrence. The *Vajrasamādhi*'s associations with such an eminence as Wŏnhyo must also have been a plus in its favor. There is no unimpeachable evidence that the legends concerning Wŏnhyo's connection with the sūtra, which will be discussed in detail in the next chapter, developed before the tenth century. Nevertheless, the fact that Chih-sheng cites the text as "reconstructed" makes plausible the assumption that at least some elements of the legend were known to him. At any rate, Chih-sheng's bibliographical research suggested that a long-lost translated text had finally returned to circulation, apparently via a rare Korean recension; he remained oblivious to terminology in the text that could not have predated Kumārajīva, as well as to certain of its doctrinal elements, evocative of the *Awakening of Faith*, which were not current until the sixth century. For the author of the *Vajrasamādhi* it must also have been convenient to have a catalogue entry for an otherwise unknown sūtra, especially since the content of his composition would be readily adaptable to that title. Once the *K'ai-yüan lu* accepted the *Vajrasamādhi* as a translated sūtra, the text was thenceforth assured of remaining in the canon. The *Vajrasamādhi* had entered the mainstream of sinitic Buddhism, from which it was never to recede.

---

[63] For example, important T'ien-t'ai texts were reintroduced into China (Wu Yüeh) by Ch'egwan (d. 971) in 961; see *Fo-tsu t'ung-chi* 10, *T* 2035.49.206a–b, *ch.* 43. pp. 294c–295a; discussed in Edmund H. Worthy, Jr., "Diplomacy for Survival: Domestic and Foreign Relations of Wu Yüeh, 907–978," p. 36, and noted p. 44 n. 121. Ŭich'ŏn traveled to the Sung kingdom in 1085, taking along several lost works by Chih-yen (602–668), Fa-tsang (643–712), and Ch'eng-kuan (738–840), and stimulating thereby the resurgence of Hua-yen thought in China; see discussion in Cho Myŏnggi, *Koryŏ Taegak kuksa wa Ch'ŏnt'ae sasang*, pp. 13–14; Kamata Shigeo, *Chōsen bukkyō no tera to rekishi*, pp. 203–204. Of course, this movement was reciprocal, and many lost Korean works were also reintroduced from China as well. For other textual exchanges between Sung China and Koryŏ Korea, see Kim Sanggi, "Song-tae e issŏsŏ ŭi Koryŏ-pon ŭi yut'ong e taehayŏ," pp. 273–79.

Based on this evidence, it appears that, after centuries of obscurity, a *Vajrasamādhi-sūtra* began to circulate again in China sometime between 695 and 730. The big questions, of course, remain: from where? and under whose auspices? Apart from whatever inferences one can draw on the basis of textual evidence, the only extant information bearing on these questions appears in the hagiographies of Wŏnhyo, versions of which were written in both China and Korea. Wŏnhyo, who died in 686, wrote his commentary a minimum of nine years before the *Ta-Chou lu* entry stating that the *Vajrasamādhi* was still nonextant in China, and forty-four years before the sūtra's reappearance in Chinese catalogues in the *K'ai-yüan lu*. Based on such evidence as content, stylistic features, and textual citations, it is virtually indisputable that Wŏnhyo's commentary is authentic, and one must account for the fact that he obviously knew of the text several years before its reappearance in China. How was this possible? A number of interesting points concerning this question are raised in his hagiographies. The next chapter explores what these hagiographies might tell us about the provenance and dating of the *Vajrasamādhi*.

# THE HAGIOGRAPHIES OF THE KOREAN SCHOLIAST WŎNHYO: THE DATING AND PROVENANCE OF THE *VAJRASAMĀDHI*

If there were one man who could be said to embody in his own life and career the highest ideals of the Korean Buddhist tradition it would have to be Wŏnhyo (617–686). Wŏnhyo is widely recognized as having made some of the most seminal contributions to the development of a distinctively Korean approach to Buddhist theology and practice. His range of scholarly endeavor covered the whole gamut of East Asian Buddhist materials, from the Flower Garland (Hwaŏm/Hua-yen) to Mere-Representation (Yusik/Wei-shih) to the Pure Land (Chŏngt'o/Ching-t'u) school, and the some one hundred works attributed to this prolific author find no rivals among his fellow Korean exegetes.[1] Over twenty works ascribed to him are still extant today, giving us a solid body of material upon which to base an examination of his contributions to Buddhist philosophy in Korea and, indeed, throughout East Asia. Erudition aside, Wŏnhyo also made a vigorous personal commitment to disseminating Buddhism throughout his country, helping make Buddhism the bedrock of Unified Silla culture. The destiny of Buddhism in Korea was so intertwined with Wŏnhyo's vocation that he can with little exaggeration be considered the exemplar par excellence of Korean Buddhism. But in addition to Wŏnhyo's intrinsic importance to that tradition,

---

[1] For a comprehensive listing of works attributed to Wŏnhyo, see Tongguk taehakkyo Pulgyo munhwa yŏn'guso, ed., *Han'guk Pulgyo ch'ansul munhŏn ch'ongnok*, pp. 16–37. Sung Bae Park ("Wŏnhyo's Commentaries on the *Awakening of Faith in Mahāyāna*," pp. 64–70), expanding on the listings in Cho Myŏnggi (*Silla Pulgyo ŭi inyŏm kwa yŏksa*, pp. 97–102), has conveniently grouped 106 of Wŏnhyo's compositions into 15 textual categories. Cho Myŏnggi (ibid., pp. 103–22) has also given a valuable summary of each of the 25 extant works attributed to Wŏnhyo. A one-thousand-page collection of secondary studies in Korean, Japanese, and English on all aspects of Wŏnhyo's life and thought has recently appeared as *Wŏnhyo yŏn'gu nonch'ong: kŭ ch'ŏrhak kwa in'gan ŭi modŭn kŏt*, ed. Kim Chigyŏn. The book was compiled for free distribution and is extremely difficult to procure.

he is also the one historical person that legend ties most intimately to the composition of the *Vajrasamādhi*. It is for this reason that a treatment of his hagiographies looms large here.

In comparison to the broad knowledge of Wŏnhyo's theological stance, which I shall cover in more detail in the following chapter, surprisingly little is known of the man himself and the personal factors that may have contributed to his philosophical development. As is inevitably the case for personages separated by such distances from our own time, distinguishing biographical fact from hagiographical fancy is no mean challenge. Especially for a person of Wŏnhyo's stature, the sheer mass of legendary materials is initially imposing, if not ultimately overwhelming. This problem is exacerbated by the self-effacing penchant of Wŏnhyo in his own works—hardly unexpected in exegetical writing—which allows little of his own life to emerge.

Fortunately, recent research has shown that virtually all of our knowledge of Wŏnhyo's life derive from two sources: the *Sung Kao-seng chuan* (Biographies of eminent monks compiled during the Sung; hereafter *SKSC*) and the Koryŏ-period *Samguk yusa* (Memorabilia and mirabilia of the three kingdoms; hereafter *SGYS*).[2] The only other source is *Kosŏn-sa Sŏdang hwasang t'appi* (Stūpa inscription to the *Upādhyāya* Sŏdang of Kosŏn-sa), a cenotaph dedicated to Wŏnhyo that was rediscovered in 1914 in a stream bed near the ancient Silla capital of Kyŏngju.[3] This inscription would be extremely valuable were it not for its unfortunately fragmentary state. Even considering this disadvantage, its precise dating of Wŏnhyo's death and its mention of at least one of Wŏnhyo's works provide important corroboration for some of the statements appearing in the other biographies. While we must always

[2] Outlines of primary materials pertaining to Wŏnhyo's life can be found in Motoi Nobuo, "Shiragi Gangyō no denki ni tsuite," pp. 41–46; and Mizuno, pp. 39–41. Kim Yŏngt'ae has made an exhaustive study of primary sources and oral legends from the Kyŏngsang-do region relating to Wŏnhyo in his "Chŏn'gi wa sŏrhwa rŭl t'onghan Wŏnhyo yŏn'gu," pp. 33–76.

[3] *Kosŏn-sa Sŏdang hwasang t'appi*, in *Wŏnhyo taesa chŏnjip*, ed. Cho Myŏnggi, pp. 661–63. For accounts of the rediscovery of the text see Motoi, "Gangyō," pp. 33–34, and see p. 41 for a summary of the earlier Japanese scholarship concerning this inscription, much of which is unavailable in this country; note also Yi Chongik, "Wŏnhyo ŭi saengae wa sasang," p. 220; Sung Bae Park, "Wŏnhyo's Commentaries," p. 46. Additional fragments were recently discovered and published by Hwang Suyŏng, "Silla Sŏdang hwasang pi ŭi sinp'yŏn," pp. 1–6. An illustrated account of the lives of Wŏnhyo and his contemporary and friend, Ŭisang, depicting many of the events appearing in the biographies discussed herein, appears in the thirteenth-century Japanese illustrated scroll *Kegon engi emaki*; see Kameda Tsutomu, ed., *Kegon engi*. This scroll receives its most extensive treatment in any language in Karen Brock, "Tales of Gishō and Gangyō: Editor, Artist, and Audience in Japanese Picture Scrolls."

bear in mind that our view of Wŏnhyo and Silla Buddhism in *SKSC* and *SGYS* is reflected in a several-centuries-old speculum, there is independent confirmation for substantial portions of their accounts; indeed, both of their narratives reflect earlier accounts that, in several cases, probably do not far postdate Wŏnhyo's own lifetime.

An exhaustive treatment of Wŏnhyo's life would require considerably more space than would be relevant to the principal focus here on the *Vajrasamādhi*. Hence my overriding concern will instead be with the structure of, and topoi appearing in, the biographies themselves—that is, the way in which an eminent religious is treated by Buddhist biographers and the implications of the symbolism and imagery used therein, especially as these relate to the provenance of the *Vajrasamādhi*. At the same time, I shall examine any data suggested in the biographies that will help to clarify the major periods in Wŏnhyo's religious vocation. Wŏnhyo's central role in forging a distinctively Korean form of Buddhism accounts for why an examination of his life will help to illuminate something of the doctrinal outlook and social role of the Silla Buddhist ecclesia, offering some broad sense of the milieu within which the *Vajrasamādhi* may have been composed.

## The *Sung Kao-seng chuan* Hagiography and the Provenance of the *Vajrasamādhi*

The *Sung Kao-seng chuan* was compiled under imperial auspices by Tsanning (919–1001), the noted historiographer and Ch'an polemicist, between 982 and 988.[4] Its biography of Wŏnhyo, which draws heavily upon conventional biographical elements in presenting a stereotyped characterization of a religious figure, is a quintessential example of East Asian Buddhist hagiography.[5] Couched in thaumaturgy and theurgy, Buddhist hagiography was

---

[4] Tsan-ning's biography and writings are discussed in Chou Yi-liang, "Tantrism in China," pp. 248–51. His career receives a detailed treatment in Albert A. Dalia, "The 'Political Career' of the Buddhist Historian Tsan-ning," pp. 146–80. The *Sung Kao-seng chuan* has been summarized by Chan Hing-ho ("Ta Sung Kao-seng chuan," pp. 349–50). Tsan-ning's contribution to Buddhist historiography has been treated in Jan Yün-hua, "Buddhist Historiography in Sung China," pp. 362–64.

[5] Tsan-ning's account appears in *T'ang Hsin-lo-kuo Huang-lung-ssu Yüan-hsiao chuan* (Biography of Wŏnhyo [Break of Dawn] of Hwangnyong-sa [Yellow Dragon Monastery] in the T'ang Dominion of Silla), in *SKSC* 4, *T* 2061.50.730a6–b29. I have made a complete, annotated translation of the biography in my article "The Biographies of the Korean Monk Wŏnhyo." For general treatments of Buddhist hagiography in China and Korea, see Arthur F.

designed for the edification of the faithful and the proselytization of the un-
converted, not the imparting of biographical fact. Hagiography was ultimately a composite of a number of conflicting sentiments toward the subject, each of which had its own peculiar concerns: the life of the person
himself, the retained memories of him within the religious community, and
his value as a personification of certain spiritual ideals, cultural symbols, or
religious accomplishments. The paradigmatic elements present in sacred biography tend to interfere with attempts to reconstruct historically the
"facts" about important spiritual figures.

The *Sung Kao-seng chuan* is best treated as a successor to the Chinese Buddhist hagiographical tradition that started with Hui-chiao (497–554), in
which Buddhist biography was written to acculturate Buddhists and Buddhist ecclesiastical institutions to the indigenous civilization.[6] This feature
will be seen explicitly in what I hope to show is the major theme of *SKSC*'s
biography of Wŏnhyo: the scriptural authenticity of the *Vajrasamādhi*. Wŏnhyo's biography appears in the second section of the work on "Doctrinal
Exegetes" (*i-chieh*),[7] together with a number of other Korean scholiasts who
played important roles in the development of the learned schools of sinitic
Buddhism.

Tsan-ning's account opens with a few stereotyped encomiums about
Wŏnhyo's scholarly prowess before turning to a controversy among Wŏnhyo's peers concerning his participation in a *Jen-wang ching/Inwang-kyŏng*
(Book of benevolent kings) convocation, a sūtra–recitation ceremony that
was periodically convened during the Silla and Koryŏ dynasties for the protection of the kingdom.[8] Despite the opposition of the other elders, the Silla

---

Wright, "Biography and Hagiography: Hui-chiao's *Lives of Eminent Monks*," pp. 383–432, especially pp. 384–87; Jan Yün-hua, "Hui Chiao and His Works, a Reassessment," pp. 177–90;
and Peter H. Lee, trans., *Lives of Eminent Korean Monks*, introduction. For the biographical
genre in Chinese literature as a whole, see Denis Twitchett, "Problems of Chinese Biography,"
pp. 24–39, and Arthur F. Wright, "Values, Roles, and Personalities," esp. pp. 9–15.

[6] See discussion in Wright, "Biography and Hagiography," p. 385.

[7] See Tsan-ning's definition of the "doctrinal exegetes" category at *SKSC, T* 2061.50.710a.

[8] The "Hu-kuo p'in" (Protecting the kingdom chapter) of the *Jen-wang po-jo po-lo-mi ching*
(*T* 246.8.840a11–19) stipulates that whenever a country is faced with danger, one hundred images and one hundred seats are to be prepared, and monks of an equal number are to be invited
to recite and expound upon this sūtra; see Chou Yi-liang, "Tantrism in China," p. 296 n. 61;
Hong Yunsik, "Koryŏ Pulgyo ŭi sinang ŭirye," p. 664. See also Yoritomi Motohiro, "Gokoku
kyōten to iwareru mono: *Ninnōkyō* o megutte," pp. 45–62; Ninomiya Keinin, "Chōsen ni
okeru Ninnōkai no kaisetsu," pp. 155–63; Roger Leverrier, "Étude sur les rites bouddhiques a
l'époque du royaume de Koryŏ," pp. 61–72; and Buswell, *Korean Approach*, pp. 2, 71 n. 1, and
80 n. 85, for other references. For national-protection Buddhism and the central role of such

1. The *Jen-wang ching* convocation

2. Illness of the queen–consort

3. The Silla envoy is dispatched to T'ang China

4. A gaffer appears amid the waves

5. The envoy is escorted to the Dragon King's palace

6. The gate to the Dragon King's palace

7. Receiving the *Vajrasamādhi* from the Dragon King

8. Searching for Taean in the marketplace

9. Taean receives the *Vajrasamādhi*

10.   Taean collates the text of the *Vajrasamādhi*

11.   The newly collated *Vajrasamādhi*
is delivered to the Silla palace

12.   Wŏnhyo writes his commentary to the *Vajrasam*

13. Lackeys steal Wŏnhyo's commentary

14. Wŏnhyo rewrites his commentary

15. Wŏnhyo lectures on the *Vajrasamādhi*

king (who is unidentified) orders that Wŏnhyo be allowed to join. Sometime later, his queen-consort is stricken with a mysterious illness, which shamans say can be cured only if medicine is brought from overseas. An envoy is immediately dispatched to T'ang China; but while he is still en route across the sea an old man suddenly appears from out of the waves and leads him to the Dragon King's palace, where he has an audience with the king himself. The Dragon King informs the envoy that the illness of the Silla queen was merely a pretext to allow a previously unknown sūtra, the *Vajrasamādhi*, to be introduced to, and disseminated in, Korea. The king commands that, upon the envoy's return to Silla, the thirty-odd uncollated folios of the sūtra are to be put in order by the siddha Taean and expounded upon by Wŏnhyo. To ensure the scripture's safe return to Silla, the pages are wrapped in waxed paper and hidden inside the envoy's thigh.

Escorted back to the surface of the sea, the envoy reboards his ship and returns home, where he informs the Silla king of his miraculous journey. The king orders Taean to arrange the folios and sew them together into a bound volume, but Taean refuses to "cross the threshold of the royal palace," accepting the text only after it is brought to his own residence. Once Taean has completed the editing, Wŏnhyo is then commanded to write a commentary to the restored text and lecture on it at Hwangnyong-sa. However, just before Wŏnhyo's presentation, "menial lackeys" of his learned antagonists steal the newly written commentary. Delaying his lecture for three days, Wŏnhyo summarizes his exegesis in a shorter, three-fascicle version, called the "abbreviated commentary" (*lüeh-shu*; Kor. *yakso*). Before a large assembly, Wŏnhyo finally delivers his lecture, his erudition and wisdom humbling his previous opponents. (These events are illustrated in the thirteenth-century Japanese scroll *Kegon engi emaki* [Illustrated scroll of the history of the Kegon school]. See the photo insert.) Tsan-ning reports that both of these commentaries were still in circulation in Korea, but only the abbreviated version had been transmitted to China.[9] This latter exegesis was so

---

apocryphal sūtras as *Jen-wang ching* in its development, see Mochizuki Shinkō, *Bukkyō kyōten seiritsu shiron*, pp. 425–85; Rhi Ki-yong, "*Inwang panya-kyŏng* kwa hoguk Pulgyo," pp. 163–93.

[9] There is no evidence that the longer, "expanded" commentary was ever written; see my article "Did Wŏnhyo Write Two Versions of His *Kŭmgang sammaegyŏng-ron*?" The style of *KSGR* may have contributed to suspicions that there had at one time been a longer version of the treatise. Frequently in *KSGR*, Wŏnhyo abbreviates his treatment, referring the reader instead to other of his works for full explication. (This is, of course, an indication that *KSGR* postdates most of his other works, as I shall explore later.) In several spots as well, the commentary provides little more than the basic structure of his argument. This is somewhat unu-

highly regarded by the Chinese that a Trepiṭaka[10] (a "master of the canon") eventually changed its appellation from a "commentary" (*shu*; Kor. *so*) to an "exposition" (*lun*; Kor. *non*),[11] placing the composition on a par with śāstras written by the bodhisattva-exegetes of India.

Even a cursory perusal of this Chinese version of Wŏnhyo's biography suggests that attempts to ascertain biographical data about Wŏnhyo from it will likely prove disappointing. There is very little in Tsan-ning's account that can be considered to refer to Wŏnhyo the man. One cannot track down any information about Wŏnhyo's alleged acquaintance Taean, or even about a *Jen-wang ching* assembly that might have taken place during a time-frame to be relevant to this tale.[12] Wŏnhyo's life is constructed almost entirely of stereotypical biographical images drawn from the larger Sino-Indian Buddhist tradition. In the process the subject is spiritualized to such an extent

---

sual, given the penchant for detail that Wŏnhyo displays in major works like his commentary and autocommentary to the *Awakening of Faith*.

[10] The most probable candidate for this Trepiṭaka is the third Hua-yen patriarch Fa-tsang (643–712), who was widely referred to as *fan-ching ta-teh*, as his biography notes (*T'ang Ta-chien-fu-ssu ku-ssu-chu fan-ching ta-teh Fa-tsang ho-shang chuang*, *T* 2054.50.280c17). Fa-tsang is well known to have been familiar with Wŏnhyo's work and to have held him in great respect.

[11] The term *lun* (exposition) was generally reserved by Chinese translators for independent treatises and expositions presumed written by Indian bodhisattva-masters; translated from Sanskrit, such texts were accorded canonical status on a par with the scriptures attributed to the Buddha himself. Indigenous treatises on translated sūtras were usually given the appellation *shu* (Kor. *so*), "commentary," and had only semicanonical status. (It was the Korean cataloguer, Ŭich'ŏn, who first insisted on including such "commentaries" in the tripiṭaka.) Hence, conferring such a designation would have been equivalent to placing Wŏnhyo on a par with the bodhisattva-exegetes in the heartland of Buddhism—obviously a high honor. See also discussion in Kim Yŏngt'ae, "Wŏnhyo yŏn'gu," p. 31. Robert Shih's statement (*Biographies des moines éminents* [*Kao seng tchouan*] *de Houei-kiao*, p. 169) concerning the *Liang Kao-seng chuan* that *lun* refers to a Chinese composition is not necessarily valid for later texts; indeed, many of the interpretations of terms given by Shih in the appendix to his book do not pertain in post sixth-century materials.

[12] Chronologically, this *Jen-wang ching/Inwang-kyŏng* assembly would have to have occurred during the reign of either King Munmu (r. 661–681) or King Sinmun (r. 681–691). There is no solid evidence linking either of these two rulers, or anyone else for that matter, with the events depicted in this legend. Rhi Ki-yong ("*Inwang panya-kyŏng* kwa hoguk Pulgyo," p. 185) also notes that the date is unknown. Such national protection assemblies, which commonly used either *Jen-wang ching* or *Suvarṇaprabhāsottama-sūtra* (*Chin-kuang-ming ching*, *T* 664, *T* 665), were relatively common during the Silla period and virtually ubiquitous by the Koryŏ. None of the years during which such assemblies are recorded to have occurred, unfortunately, is within a range relevant to Wŏnhyo's life, and there are no other references to Korean *Inwang-kyŏng* assemblies in a *Kao-seng chuan* or a Korean historical record that might provide additional clues. Lacking any further evidence, one can only assume that the legend here extrapolates from other stories. For the dates of Silla national-protection ceremonies, see Kim Yŏngt'ae, "Silla Pulgyo sasang," pp. 113–15, and the annotation to my translation of Wŏnhyo's *SKSC* biography in "The Biographies of the Korean Monk Wŏnhyo."

that he is nearly dehumanized.[13] Expunged almost entirely is any semblance of the qualities that bring Wŏnhyo to life and reveal his basic humanity. We have here little more than generic biography, which is employed by Tsan-ning as a means of presenting the main concern of his account: the authen-tification of the *Vajrasamādhi*. It is this focus that apparently justifies Tsan-ning's inclusion of Wŏnhyo in his chapters on doctrinal exegetes (*i-chieh*), since the events related seem more appropriate to the theurgist (*shen-i*) sec-tions instead. In this overriding concern to legitimize the *Vajrasamādhi*, Wŏnhyo becomes a tool of the mythology, and any sense of him as an in-dividual is all but lost. Such problems demand that this hagiography be ap-proached as mythology or folklore and its significance examined in light of the indigenous culture and worldview. From such perspectives, however, the biography is rich with information, which will provide much that is relevant to ascertaining the provenance of the *Vajrasamādhi*.

Tsan-ning's story is unswerving in its focus on a single concern: the dis-covery of the *Vajrasamādhi*. Like much of folk literature, Tsan-ning's biog-raphy is "single-stranded," in that it makes no attempt to combine different stories and episodes into the complex narratives of more sophisticated fic-tional writing.[14] The structure of the biography itself also follows Axel Ol-rik's law governing folk tales of "Two to a Scene,"[15] in which no more than two characters will appear at a time in any one episode. Such pairs recur throughout the story: the king and the envoy he sends to T'ang, the envoy's meeting with the gaffer and, later, his audience with the Dragon King, Wŏnhyo's contact with the messenger, and so on. Wŏnhyo is brought into the story merely to serve as a vehicle for telling the tale of the recovery of the *Vajrasamādhi* from the depths of the Dragon King's palace. Since Wŏn-hyo wrote the first commentary to the *Vajrasamādhi*, it is no surprise that he comes to be associated with the reappearance of the text. But Wŏnhyo was apparently also sufficiently notorious in Korea, and perhaps throughout East Asia, as to afford a convenient peg upon which to hang the myth of the discovery of the *Vajrasamādhi*.[16]

Rather than biographical fact, what one finds instead is a plethora of folk-loric topoi, deriving from Korean, Chinese, and Indian sources. The sick-ness of a female member of the royal family, which prompted the trip lead-ing to the discovery of the *Vajrasamādhi*, is a common motif found in East

---

[13] See discussion in Reynolds and Capps, *The Biographical Process*, p. 3.

[14] See Axel Olrik, "Epic Laws of Folk Narrative," p. 137.

[15] Olrik, "Folk Narrative," pp. 134–35.

[16] Paraphrasing Lord Raglan's comments about why certain figures come to be associated with heroic events; see his *The Hero: A Study in Tradition, Myth, and Drama*, p. 214.

Asian miracle tales and figures prominently in Korean sources like *Samguk yusa*. Iryŏn, for example, tells the story of the mythic Ado *hwasang*, one of the first Koguryŏ missionaries to Silla, who is said to have cured the illness of one of King Mich'u's (r. 262–283) daughters in 264. Mukhoja, another early missionary in Silla, is claimed to have cured the illness of a princess of King Pŏphŭng in 528. *Samguk yusa* also includes the tale of a daughter of King Hyoso (r. 692–701), who, just a few years after Wŏnhyo's death, was stricken with an incurable illness that was healed only by the spells of the Tantric thaumaturge Hyet'ong (d.u.). During the same period in China, the Tantric master and translator Vajrabodhi (671–741) is said to have cured a similarly terminal illness that had afflicted the twenty-fifth daughter of Emperor Hsüan-tsung (r. 712–756).[17] Such convenient illnesses have parallels with the sicknesses often associated with shamanistic rebirth, which occur just prior to the reception of supernatural understanding.

Ko Ikchin has also suggested that one of the principal thrusts of Silla Buddhist ideology was to replace the indigenous shamanistic worldview, in which nature dominated humankind, with its Buddhist counterpart, in which man dominated nature.[18] The ineffectiveness of the native shamans in curing the illness of the queen-consort—while this Buddhist "talisman," a secret sūtra, succeeds—may adumbrate the entrenchment of Buddhism in the religious life of Silla and Shamanism's displacement from a position of political influence.

The thigh as a secret hiding place is a topos that appears frequently in Indian folklore and mythology.[19] Most often the thigh is cut open with a

[17] For the story of Mukhoja, see *Samguk sagi* 4, p. 78; *SGYS* 3, *T* 2039.49.986b7, hereafter cited only by page and column; and *Haedong kosŭng-chŏn, T* 2065.50.1017c–1018a (Peter H. Lee, trans., *Lives of Eminent Korean Monks*, pp. 49–56). For Ado *hwasang*, see *SGYS* 3, p. 986c1–3; and *Haedong kosŭng-chŏn, T* 2065.50.1017c–1018c (Lee, trans., pp. 49–56). For the thaumaturge Hyet'ong, see *SGYS* 5, pp. 1010c–1011b for the whole story, and specifically p. 1011a15 for reference to her illness; noted also in Inoue, "Chōsen bukkyō juyō," pp. 63–64. Hyet'ong was said to have been associated with Shan-wu-wei (Subhakarasiṃha; 637–735), the renowned esoteric master in China, who is also said to have traveled to the Dragon Palace, but from the deserts of Turfan no less! (*SKSC* 2, *T* 2061.50.715a; translated in Chou Yi-liang, "Tantrism in China," p. 262). Vajrabodhi's story appears in his biography in *SKSC* 1, *T* 2061.50.711b–712a, translated in Chou Yi-liang, "Tantrism," pp. 278–79. Other similar Korean stories are translated in *Korean Folk Tales*, ed. Chun Shin-yong. See especially "Bride's Island," where the illness of a spouse is said to be curable by a magical herb that grows only on a distant island (pp. 42–43; story analyzed on pp. 14–15); and "Princess Bari," where the king and queen become mysteriously ill and can only be cured by magical water from the Heavenly Kingdom (p. 100; analyzed p. 19).

[18] Ko Ikchin, "Han'guk kodae ŭi Pulgyo sasang," pp. 68–100.

[19] The thigh as a hiding place is listed as motif F1052 in Stith Thompson and Jonas Balys, *Oral Tales of India*.

knife and the item to be hidden sewn inside, with unguents applied or spells recited to restore the thigh to its original condition. Oral tales using his motif abound, as when a messenger hides a gift bottle of liquor inside his thigh.[20] Kota stories include a story of a woman hiding a sari inside the thigh, sewing it up, and then reciting a few spells to make it look as if nothing had happened.[21]

The theft of a sacred book—as one finds when Wŏnhyo's first commentary to the *Vajrasamādhi* is stolen by "lackeys" of his jealous rivals—is another common motif in Buddhist folklore, which is often used as a means of testing the resolve or understanding of the writer. According to Pali tradition, for example, Buddhaghosa's magnum opus, *Visuddhimagga* (Path of purification), was stolen twice by the King of the Gods, Sakka. By checking the final draft against the first two versions, Sakka was able to verify Buddhaghosa's complete consistency as an author and, by extension, the unimpeachableness of Sinhalese religious writings.[22] Even though the thieves in our story hardly have the same prestige as Sakka, their theft of his commentary to the *Vajrasamādhi* does present a similar type of test for Wŏnhyo. Here, however, the tale attests to Wŏnhyo's perseverance in the face of persecution and his determination to ensure that the message of the sūtra would not be lost.

But it is the larger structure of the *SKSC* story that reveals its true character as "monomyth," a universal pattern in sacred biography. Traditional biography is often used as a vehicle to explicate the mythic trials of heroic types, generally through three major stages: the separation of the subject from his community, his isolation and incumbent tribulations, and his eventual reinstatement in the community, often at a superior status.[23] In our story, Wŏnhyo's disenfranchisement from his community takes place at the time of the *Inwang-kyŏng* assembly. After undergoing successive struggles and adventures among the people—as in the Korean version of the story—

[20] Verrier Elwin, *Myths of Middle India*, p. 436.

[21] Story no. 23 in Murray B. Emeneau, *Kota Texts: Part Three*, and see the schematic analysis of the motif on p. 369.

[22] See Stanley Tambiah, *The Buddhist Saints of the Forest and the Cult of Amulets*, pp. 28–29.

[23] Joseph Campbell's description of "monomyth" (*The Hero with a Thousand Faces*, pp. 36ff) is one piece of his work that has withstood scholarly investigation; note the comments about the "sophisticated form" of Campbell's arguments and their universal applicability in Clyde Kluckhohn, "Recurrent Themes in Myths and Mythmaking," p. 167; see also the discussion in Reynolds and Capps, *The Biographical Process*, p. 17. For the heroic pattern in a Western cultural context, see Lord Raglan, *The Hero*, esp. pp. 174–75 for the twenty-two stages of this pattern in Greek and Roman mythology. For the related aretalogical pattern, see Hadas and Smith, *Heroes and Gods*, pp. 17–26.

he is called upon through supernatural intervention to work on a commentary to the *Vajrasamādhi*. The king appoints Wŏnhyo to lecture on the sūtra before a great assembly of Buddhists; his reputation redeemed, his previous opponents express contrition at their earlier hostility. Finally, Wŏnhyo exults in his redemption and publicly chides his earlier rivals.

What were the motives that might have prompted the creation of this story about Wŏnhyo and the *Vajrasamādhi*, which eventually found its way into Tsan-ning's account? As I have noted, Wŏnhyo himself all but vanishes in the weaving of the tale. But disregarding the theurgic aspects of the hagiography, a number of important clues about the sūtra's own origins are visible just beneath the surface.

Perhaps the most striking feature of the legend is the intimate association between Korea and the *Vajrasamādhi* from the moment of its "reappearance" in the world of humans. In Tsan-ning's version, an envoy from Korea first receives the text in scattered folios; an otherwise unknown Korean monk, Taean, is ordered to edit the text; the eminent Korean scholiast Wŏnhyo is commanded to popularize the text by writing a commentary on it. Wŏnhyo's role in disseminating the newly recovered sūtra is obviously central. The Dragon King decrees that it is Wŏnhyo who is to write a commentary to the sūtra and certifies that the text and its commentary will be a medicine (read: scripture) that can cure even the incurable. Here are obvious indications both of the importance of the *Vajrasamādhi* in Korea and of the major role Wŏnhyo's commentary to it was to play in Korean Buddhism. Significantly, neither China nor Chinese monks figure anywhere in this story: the sūtra is revealed through the direct intervention of the Dragon King before the Silla envoy is able even to reach the mainland. From the moment of its introduction, then, the *Vajrasamādhi* was addressed to at least an East Asian, if not a specifically Korean, audience. I do not believe, as Mizuno Kōgen has suggested,[24] that the role of the Dragon King in this legend requires that we go as far afield as Shan-tung or Liao-tung to locate the provenance of the text. Instead, it seems much more plausible that Tsan-ning testifies here that the text first "reappeared" (read: was first authored) in Korea through the instigation of Koreans. And Tsan-ning also gives us the opinion current at the time that the spiritual efficacy of the text these Koreans created surpassed all worldly products—hence, his statement that "the efficacy of the *agada* panacea of the Snowy Mountains [the Himalayas] does not surpass this [sūtra]."[25]

[24] Mizuno, p. 40.
[25] *SKSC* 4, *T* 2061.50.730b3–4.

In adopting the motif of the recovery of the sūtra from the scriptural repository of the Dragon King, the legend's author is drawing on two distinct stories: first, tales that circulated on the Indian subcontinent and thence throughout Asia concerning the recovery of the Mahāyāna scriptures from the Dragon Palace by Nāgārjuna (fl. ca. A.D. 150); and second, legends dating from the inception of Buddhism in Silla concerning the place of dragon and snake cults in the life of the people of the southeastern region of the peninsula.

The adoption of the dragon-palace motif is, from this first standpoint, an attempt to bring Korea into the fold of Buddhist macroculture, which was universally familiar with the legends of the recovery of Buddhist scriptures from the dragon palace.[26] One of the principal reasons for the telling of myth is as an "escape" from geographical or cultural isolation.[27] By demonstrating Korean contact with this palace, peninsular civilization was defined at least partially in terms of mainstream continental beliefs.

According to Chinese sailor's tradition, the Dragon King's palace was situated under a small island, located five to six days' journey east from Su-chou in Kiangsu province. Very high waves pounded the island so that no vessel could approach, but at high tide the island was inundated by water so that ships could pass. At night an eery red light shone above the spot to warn sailors away.[28]

---

[26] This would parallel the attempt to associate Korea with the Indian emperor Aśoka's establishment of stūpas throughout Asia; see Buswell, *Korean Approach*, pp. 72–73 n. 11.

[27] Cf. discussion in William R. Bascom, "Four Functions of Folklore," p. 290; and Wm. Hugh Jansen, "The Esoteric-Exoteric Factor in Folklore," p. 46.

[28] See M. W. de Visser, *The Dragon in China and Japan*, pp. 1–34; and Kondō Haruo, *Tōdai shōsetsu no kenkyū*, pp. 99–114, for a description of the dragon palace. The legend of the Dragon King (Nāgarāja) and his scriptural repository is also discussed in Edward Conze, *Buddhism: Its Essence and Development*, p. 124. Shizutani Masao, "Indo bukkyōshi to Nāga (tatsu)," pp. 131–46, also discusses the Indian background of Nāgas. For a traditional account of dragon faith and the dragon palace, see *Fan-i ming-i chi* 7, *T* 2131.54.1065c14–1066a1; and see Inoue, "Chōsen bukkyō juyō," p. 56. Chinese materials on ophidian worship are translated in Samuel Beal, *A Catena of Buddhist Scriptures from the Chinese*, pp. 415–23; E. T. C. Werner, *Myths and Legends of China*, pp. 210–17; Wolfram Eberhard, ed., *Folktales of China*, pp. 98–100, 151–56. Gisbert Combaz ("Masques et dragons en Asie," pp. 172–205) discusses the literature and symbolism of dragons in China; for dragon symbolism, see also Heinrich Zimmer, *Myths and Symbols in Indian Art and Civilization*, pp. 59–68. Tatsuzawa Toshiaki, "Chūgoku minzoku to ryūda no denshō," pp. 81–106, discusses the place of dragons in Chinese culture. Perhaps the most exhaustive treatment of ophidian worship and symbols appears in Balaji Mundkur, *The Cult of the Serpent: An Interdisciplinary Survey of Its Manifestations and Origins*, and see esp. p. 105 for China.

It is somewhat surprising that none of the East Asian recensions of such Dragon King stories predate the T'ang: there are no references to the dragon palace in the *Kao-seng chuan* of the

Korean associations with the Dragon King were many and varied. The monk Myŏngnang (d.u.), who was an acquaintance of Wŏnhyo, traveled to China in 632 and was invited to the Dragon King's palace during his return voyage in 635. His experience proved invaluable in the years following the fall of Paekche and Koguryŏ to the combined Silla and T'ang armies, when continued T'ang pressure to bring Silla under its dominion threatened the Korean kingdom's newly won independence. Through the intercession of Wŏnhyo's close friend Ŭisang, then studying in China under Chih-yen (602–668), the proposed T'ang plan for a massive sea invasion of Korea was made known in 670 to King Munmu (r. 661–680), the very same king who is later said to become a dragon protector himself. The king called a convocation of his vassals, who reported to the throne that Myŏngnang had recently returned from the dragon palace with esoteric spells. Myŏngnang was called in to advise the king and, thanks to his intercession, the T'ang invasion force was sunk by a typhoon.

After Ŭisang had returned to Korea and was in retreat in a cave near Naksan along the eastern seacoast, he is said to have received a "wish-fulfilling" (cintāmaṇi) gem from the Dragon of the Eastern Sea. In commemoration of the miracle, Ŭisang later built Naksan-sa on the mountain above the site, where Wŏnhyo is also reputed to have practiced.

During the reign of King Sŏngdŏk (r. 702–736), one generation after Wŏnhyo, Queen Suro visited the Dragon of the Eastern Sea, who had first appeared to her the day before as a gaffer. This relationship between Korea and the Dragon King is also noted in the later story of Poyang, who is said to have lived in the tenth century. Poyang was returning to Silla from China when the Dragon King of the Western Sea waylaid him and invited him to his palace. The Dragon King's son, Imok, accompanied Poyang back to Silla, where they played instrumental roles in the founding of the Koryŏ state.

This pervasive role of dragons in Korean folk tales is found also in Buddhist-influenced vernacular literature written in the native Korean orthography, han'gŭl. There are, for instance, many stories of filial sons who traveled to the dragon palace on their way to western China to get medicine for their ailing mothers or returned from an audience with the Dragon King with a wish-fulfilling gem that could benefit the masses. Hence, Koreans enthusiastically embraced this motif in many different strata of their litera-

---

Liang, only a handful in the *Hsü Kao-seng chuan* of the T'ang, while several appear in *SKSC*, including the story in this biography.

ture, in order to authenticate a variety of momentous events in the life of the nation.[29]

In addition to its obvious value in legitimating Korean pretensions to continental culture, however, this reference to the dragon palace legend would have served also to assuage Chinese doubts about the authenticity of the scripture. Such doubts could have been a major concern for the Koreans who must have introduced the sūtra to the mainland. Chinese skepticism would be alleviated through telling an explanatory tale validating the origins of the sūtra—authentication being one of the major forces behind the creation of myth.[30] Some aspects of the legend might well have been created with potential Chinese critics in mind. In China, the text of the *Vajrasamādhi* had not circulated for at least eight decades, and probably not since the time of Tao-an, fully five hundred years before. Wŏnhyo, although respected by his Chinese contemporaries in the nascent Hua-yen school, could very well have been challenged for this commentary, as interesting as it might have been: where had he obtained this text, unexpectedly reappearing after all those years in limbo? The Koreans bringing the scripture to China would have been hard-pressed for an answer. How better to deflect such controversy than to bring in the Dragon King—the figure so central to the appearance of the Indian Mahāyāna texts—through whose intercession the scripture was placed back in circulation and upon whose command Wŏnhyo was compelled to write his commentary? There would have been few easier ways to authenticate for East Asians a newly "discovered" scripture with canonical pretensions, as well as to nip in the bud whatever criticism might have been forthcoming about its human origins. Legends about mythic personages from inaccessible lands are difficult either to verify or to discount, and the Chinese rarely hesitated to accept such miracles of the faith. Especially for a lover of thaumaturgy like Tsan-ning,[31] this must have seemed a re-

[29] For Myŏngnang's associations with the Dragon King, see *SGYS* 2, p. 972b1–2, and *SGYS* 5, p. 1011a26–7; *SGYS* 5, 1011b7–c9; for his role in defeating the T'ang armies, see *SGYS* 2, p. 972b1–9. Ŭisang's contacts with the Dragon of the Eastern Sea are treated in *SGYS* 3, p. 996c2–14. Suro's visit to the same dragon is related in *SGYS* 2, p. 974a. For Poyang, see *SGYS* 4, p. 1003b–1004a; noted by Peter Lee, *Lives*, p. 77 n. 378. A summary of all the contacts between Korean monks and the Dragon King found in *SGYS* is given in Kim Yŏngt'ae, "Silla Pulgyo e issŏsŏ ŭi yongsin sasang," pp. 123–29. For the Dragon King in *han'gŭl* secular literature, see In Kwŏn-hwan, "Buddhist Preachings and their Korean Acculturation," p. 23. Translations of Korean stories about the Dragon King and his palace appear in Zŏng In-sŏb, *Folk Tales from Korea*, pp. 25–29, 103–105, 169–71.

[30] Note Bascom's comments ("Four Functions of Folklore," p. 292): "When . . . skepticism of an accepted pattern is expressed or doubts about it arise, whether it be sacred or secular, there is usually a myth or legend to validate it."

[31] Tsan-ning's interest in thaumaturgy is perhaps the major difference between *SKSC* and

markable tale, which more than accounted for any suspicions latent among the Chinese about the authenticity of this Korean recension.

Second, and even more provocatively, several elements in this legend strongly suggest that it was framed by its tellers with specifically Korean concerns in mind: in particular, to expedite the acceptance of the *Vajrasamādhi* in Silla by associating the story of its discovery with indigenous Korean ophidian cults. As the protective deities of water, snakes were common objects of worship in primitive agricultural societies, as of course was Silla in the centuries prior to Buddhism's official acceptance during King Pŏphŭng's reign. In China and northern Asia, dragons were also associated with water, and the thunder that was the precursor of storms represented the ferocious power of dragons.[32] As Silla embraced the alien cultures on its frontiers, its indigenous snake cults were eventually projected onto the dragon cults of China and northern Asia.[33] Dragons then came to be endowed with all of the power attributed indigenously to snakes, but considerably magnified in intensity and scope.[34]

Silla also knew of yellow dragons (*hwangnyong*), originally regional autochthonous deities, which also came to be associated with the snake gods of the water, becoming in the process protectors of both soil and water. Because of their affinities with foreign dragon cults and indigenous snake cults, yellow dragons came to be one of the most important popular deities in Silla, and their affiliations with Buddhism occur early on, in a story concerning the founding of Hwangnyong-sa,[35] the monastery where Wŏnhyo

---

its Chinese predecessors. This interest is attested by the fact that over 17 percent of the total biographies and one-third of the classified biographies in *SKSC* are of miracle-workers; see Yanagida Seizan, *Shoki Zenshū shisho no kenkyū*, p. 11 n. 10, noted by Whalen Lai, "T'an-ch'ien and the Early Ch'an Tradition," p. 66. Stanley Weinstein ("A Biographical Study of Tz'u-en," p. 147) has also contrasted the "absurdities" that clutter *SKSC* with the "far more conscientious Liang and T'ang Biographies of Eminent Priests."

[32] In China and northern Asia, thunder was considered to be indicative of the ferocious powers of dragons; see discussion in de Visser, *Dragon*, p. 42. De Visser also notes (p. 109) that dragons principally represented thunder but occasionally were considered to be water-spirits, like snakes. Dragons were associated both with storm and lightning and with wells and water in references from the Three Kingdoms period; see the passages collected in "Yongŏ i" (Oddities on dragons and fish) in *Munhŏn pigo*, *k*. 12, pp. 330–33. See also Shiratori Kiyoshi, "Rei to tatsu tono kankei o ronjite 'Lingism' no setsu on teishōsu," pp. 363–97, who treats the numinous qualities of dragons and their role as rain gods (pp. 373–74, 380).

[33] For Silla snake deities and their associations with north Asian dragon cults see Inoue, "Chōsen bukkyō juyō," pp. 53–54.

[34] A similar process is seen in China, where indigenous snake and python cults are appropriated by Buddhism. See Miyakawa Hisayuki, "Local Cults around Mount Lu at the Time of Sun En's Rebellion," pp. 85, 96–99.

[35] For treatments of yellow dragons, see de Visser, *Dragon*, pp. 64, 74, and Taira, "Sōsho,"

first lectured on the *Vajrasamādhi*. To complete the process of assimilation, the ophidian cults of Silla eventually merged with transplanted Mahāyāna beliefs in dragons as dharma-protectors to form the variety of state-protection Buddhism (*hoguk pulgyo*) peculiar to Silla. These events were occurring during the last years of Wŏnhyo's own life.

Such a synthesis between Buddhism and native cults was undoubtedly to the advantage of the new religion and helped to placate the opposition of the Silla nobility toward Buddhism. The Silla aristocracy seem to have accepted Buddhism initially more because of political exigencies than religious faith: Silla's annexation of the neighboring territories of Samhan and Kaya, and its absorption of peoples of different cultural backgrounds and tribal allegiances, were aided by the common ideology that Buddhism provided. As the drive toward peninsular unification intensified, the Silla aristocracy had still stronger incentives to embrace Buddhism. This acceptance was necessary both to create a national consensus among the new citizens of Silla and to mollify and eventually assimilate the leaders of the Koguryŏ and Paekche regions, who had accepted Buddhism long before. Since Buddhism also served as a vital conduit through which Chinese Confucian culture was introduced into the peninsula, the Silla acceptance of Buddhism closely paralleled the process whereby foreign tribes in China became sinicized. The importance of this mature form of dragon worship in Silla is attested by the number of legends concerning dragons and dragon palaces that appear in both Buddhist and secular literature from the Silla period, and even into the founding legend of the Koryŏ dynasty, while virtually nothing is recorded for Japan of the same era.[36]

This surge of interest in Mahāyāna Buddhism among the Silla aristocracy is reflected in the story concerning King Munmu, who died during the pe-

---

p. 73; for their importance in Silla Buddhism, and their relationship with Hwangnyong-sa, see Kim Yŏngt'ae, "Silla Pulgyo e issŏsŏ ŭi yongsin sasang," p. 130; Inoue, "Chōsen bukkyō juyō," p. 52; McClung, "The Founding of the Royal Dragon Monastery," pp. 69–80.

[36] Perhaps the most lucid discussion on indigenous snake and dragon cults in Korea and their assimilation with Buddhism appears in Inoue, "Chōsen bukkyō juyō," pp. 53–57, 85. The pioneering study on dragon worship in Korea was made by Mishina Akihide in 1931 and reprinted in Mishina, *Nissen shinwa densetsu no kenkyū*, pp. 263–303. The many and varied references to Silla dragon belief appearing in *SGYS* have been culled and discussed by Kim Yŏngt'ae, "Silla pulgyo ŭi yongsin sasang." The cult of the dragon (*miri*) in ancient Korea and its relation to early Maitreya (Mirŭk) worship is also discussed in Kwŏn Sangno, "Han'guk kodae sinang ŭi illan," pp. 81–108; Kwŏn surveys Chinese secular materials on dragons on pp. 85–86. Matsumae Takeshi ("Kodai Kanzoku no ryūda sūhai to ōken," pp. 53–68) treats the relationship between dragon belief and royal authority. For general discussions of Korean ophidian beliefs, see also Roger Leverrier, "Buddhism and Ancestral Religious Beliefs in Korea," pp. 38–39; and Peter Lee, trans., *Songs of Flying Dragons*, 109–13.

riod in which Wŏnhyo made many of his important contributions to Buddhist scholarship. In this well-known tale, Munmu swears that, after his death, he will become a sea dragon in order to protect both Silla and its state religion from foreign invaders.[37] In this vow was an early attempt to combine the protective power of Mahāyāna and the pacifying power of the dragon spirits of Silla. Through Munmu's oath, dragons came to be recognized as much more than regional protective deities and rapidly evolved into a national cult, guarding both the religion and the ruling house. Hence, the notion of state protection in Silla, which developed during Wŏnhyo's lifetime, was oriented around the two foci of indigenous snake cum dragon cults and Buddhism.

While there was some assimilation of indigenous cults into this alien religion, the Buddhist elements ultimately predominated. This is illustrated in the tale about the ca. 646 foundation of T'ongdo-sa by the Vinaya Master Chajang (608–686). To gain access to the location he had selected for building a monastery, Chajang had first to pacify through the power of the dharma nine dragons guarding the site. In this pacification, the relics (śarīra) of Śākyamuni Buddha, which Chajang had brought back from China, played a primary role. His success through using Buddhist paraphernalia indicates that, while Buddhism may have sought to merge with local cults, the foreign religion was assumed to provide protective power superior to that of the indigenous faiths. Buddhism thus came to play the principal role in guarding the fortunes of the kingdom.[38]

It is in this synthesis between Buddhism and native cults that one finds indications as to why the dragon story was used in relation to the *Vajrasamādhi* as well. For Silla Koreans of the last half of the seventh century, a sūtra would have been assured sympathetic attention if its appearance were associated with the guardian dragon of the sea. Hence, this legend was intended to validate to Silla Buddhists the authenticity of the scripture by associating it with a deity crucial to their own national fortunes.

The political symbolism of dragons in Silla society also provides further clarification as to why the Dragon King would have been introduced into

---

[37] *SGYS* 2, *T* 2039.49.972c3–4; *Samguk sagi* 7, p. 144. King Munmu's vow to be reborn as a state-protecting dragon after his death (681) would provide an interesting connection with the tale of the envoy's trip to the dragon palace; for this vow, see *SGYS* 2, p. 972c2–4; Yi Pyŏngdo and Kim Chaewŏn, *Han'guksa: kodae p'yŏn*, p. 690; Inoue, "Chōsen bukkyō juyō," pp. 52ff.; Rogers, "*P'yŏnnyŏn T'ongnok*: The Foundation Legend of the Koryŏ State," pp. 25–26 n. 34. The scriptural antecedents for the role of dragon-spirits in the protection of the dharma are given in Kim Yŏngt'ae, "Silla pulgyo ŭi yongsin sasang," pp. 136–44.

[38] The story appears in *SGYS* 3, p. 998b–c.

the story. Korean sources distinguish two distinct types of dragons: state-protection dragons, as exemplified in the story of King Munmu; and a latent frontier type, representing provincial magnates along the eastern seacoast who were frequently at odds with the monarchy in Kyŏngju.[39] A similar theme of political defiance is found for dragons from the Western Sea,[40] from where of course the *Vajrasamādhi* was recovered. Given that Silla political control had already been established throughout the peninsula by the time the sūtra was "rediscovered," the Dragon King of the West's role in revealing the text could thus symbolize the *Vajrasamādhi*'s challenge to the authority of the entrenched doctrinal schools of the Silla capital of Kyŏngju. The role of the mysterious siddha Taean in editing the *Vajrasamādhi* is particularly telling in this regard. Taean's contempt for the court—and, by extension, for the court-supported Buddhism of the capital—is implicit in his refusal to enter the palace to receive the sūtra. This antagonism between the redactor of the *Vajrasamādhi* and the orthodox scholastic schools of the capital adumbrates the milieu in which the sūtra first appeared. It also suggests the "frontier" quality of the *Vajrasamādhi*, especially considering that its putative author will be claimed to have had difficulties in presenting his message in Silla and ultimately went into retirement, as will be seen in chapter 4. Indeed, early Korean Sŏn, the Buddhist faction from which our author hailed, initially established itself in locales far from the capital of Kyŏngju. Hence, two different but complementary symbols unique to Silla culture are brought out in this Chinese tale about the Dragon King.

The challenge to the doctrinal schools of the Silla capital intimated in this story also suggests a further reason why the legend about the discovery of the *Vajrasamādhi* is an attempt to confront Silla realities. This reason is raised in a different context—but with remarkably parallel significance—by Michael Rogers in his provocative study of the legend of Chakchegŏn, the ancestor of the Koryŏ founding family.[41] Chakchegŏn, reputedly fathered by then crown prince Su-tsung of T'ang China (r. 756–762) during a trip to Korea around 753, had decided to visit his father but gave up his quest while en route over the Yellow Sea. After being thrown overboard and visiting the

---

[39] Yi Usŏng, "*Samguk yusa* sojae Ch'ŏyong sŏrhwa ŭi ilbunsŏk," pp. 89–127; discussed in Rogers, "*P'yŏnnyŏn T'ongnok*," pp. 25–26 n. 34. Based on all the *SGYS* stories in which dragons appear, Kim Yŏngt'ae ("Silla pulgyo ŭi yongsin sasang," p. 145) has distinguished three main types of dragon-spirits in Silla: sea dragons; pool, spring, and well dragons; and autochthonous dragons. He does not attempt to draw out the implications of these differences, however.

[40] Rogers, "*P'yŏnnyŏn T'ongnok*," pp. 25–26.

[41] Ibid., pp. 8–10, translating *Koryŏ-sa*, k. 1, pp. 7b16ff.

Dragon King of the Western Sea, Chakchegŏn finally returned home ca. 769. As Rogers notes, his return to Korea without continuing on to see the T'ang emperor signified the compelling need of Koreans to repudiate T'ang suzerainty over their native land: "Chakchegŏn's conduct unequivocally affirms Koryŏ's cultural self-sufficiency."[42] A similar theme occurs in this story of the *Vajrasamādhi*. The author of the legend demonstrates Korea's "cultural self-sufficiency" in the Buddhist arena as well by isolating the discovery (or authorship) of the *Vajrasamādhi* from the doctrinal schools of Kyŏngju, with their close Chinese connections. Thus, the envoy from the Silla court abandons his quest to confer with T'ang medical experts and returns straight home with a text—the *Vajrasamādhi*—conferred directly from the guardian spirit of Silla.

Walter Liebenthal has suggested that the Koreans who must first have told this legend were trying to protect Wŏnhyo from disrepute for having commented upon a spurious sūtra.[43] There are some indications in the hagiography that Wŏnhyo's associations with the *Vajrasamādhi* were controversial from the moment of the text's appearance. This disputation was carried even to the point that Wŏnhyo's opponents—blatantly jealous of the attention he was receiving from the royal family on account of the text—would stoop to petty theft in order to remove its commentary (if not the sūtra itself) from circulation. But I am not convinced that such indications suggest the decision to comment on the sūtra was an embarrassment to either Wŏnhyo or his fellow Koreans. That the *Vajrasamādhi* was to be expounded upon had not raised the ire of Wŏnhyo's antagonists; it was rather that their despised adversary had received such a prestigious commission. Since Wŏnhyo knew of, and explicated, the sūtra several years before it was available in China, it seems more likely that the legend was instead created to counter possible Chinese charges that Wŏnhyo himself had forged the text.

Despite the fact that this legend drew upon common Silla literary themes, there is no explicit evidence that it was created out of a distinct need to counter possible rumors circulating in Korea surrounding the authenticity of the *Vajrasamādhi*. The mention of Wŏnhyo's role in popularizing the newly discovered sūtra is overwhelmingly positive. The Dragon King decrees that Wŏnhyo should write a commentary to the sūtra and certifies that the text (and presumably, the lectures Wŏnhyo would deliver) will be able to cure an otherwise incurable royal illness. Here are indications both of the importance of the text in Korea and of the significance of Wŏnhyo's com-

[42] Ibid., p. 44.
[43] Liebenthal, p. 359.

mentary to the Korean tradition; neither implies that there was any indigenous controversy over the scripture.

The *Kosŏn-sa Sŏdang hwasang t'appi*, the earliest extant account of Wŏnhyo's life, composed approximately one hundred years after his death, also makes no mention of the *Vajrasamādhi* itself or of any part of this legend surrounding Wŏnhyo's associations with the text. In this inscription, only two works are mentioned: *Simmun hwajaeng-ron* (Ten approaches to the reconciliation of doctrinal controversy) and (if my reading is correct) *Hwaŏm chongyo* (Thematic essentials of the *Avataṃsaka-sūtra*).[44] To Wŏnhyo's Silla contemporaries, these two works must have represented the quintessence of his thought: *Hwaŏm chongyo*, because the thought of that sūtra dominated philosophical speculation during the period; *Simmun hwajaeng-ron*, for its outline of the syncretic philosophy that was Wŏnhyo's major contribution to Korean Buddhist thought. Whatever controversy there might have been in Korea at that time surrounding the authenticity of the *Vajrasamādhi* was apparently not enough to warrant any reference to this legend in the inscription—presuming, that is, that the legend was already evolving. Although there are several differences in detail between the Chinese and Korean accounts of this event, Iryŏn's brief mention of the story comes straight from Tsan-ning. Hence, the legend seems to have gone full circle: transmitted from Korea to China, it was finally reintroduced into Korea through the *Sung Kao-seng chuan*.

A final factor that might have prompted these legends is the attempt to legitimize the *Vajrasamādhi*'s authenticity as a valid canonical description of the teachings of original and actualized enlightenments, as found in the *Awakening of Faith*. As I shall discuss in detail in the next chapter, Wŏnhyo sees in the sūtra the scriptural validation for this gnoseological theory, which was the foundation of some of the more innovative developments in sinitic Buddhist doctrine as well as his own soteriology. By retrieving the *Vajrasamādhi* from the same scriptural repository as the *Prajñāpāramitā-sūtra*s and so many other important Mahāyāna texts, the author of this legend is giving

---

[44] *Kosŏn-sa Sŏdang hwasang t'appi*, p. 661.10, 13. The *Simmun hwajaeng-ron* was originally in two *kwŏn* (*Sinp'yŏn chejong kyojang ch'ongnok* 3, *T* 2184.55.1177c19); only fragments are extant, for which see Cho Myŏnggi, ed., *Wŏnhyo taesa chŏnjip*, pp. 640–46. An attempt has been made to reconstruct the arguments that might have characterized each of the ten approaches in Yi Chongik, *Wŏnhyo ŭi kŭnbon sasang: Simmun hwajaeng-ron yŏn'gu*. Motoi ("Gangyō no denki," p. 36) notes only that the *Simmun hwajaeng-ron* is mentioned in this passage from the inscription; if my reading here is correct, however, there seems to be a reference to Wŏnhyo's *Hwaŏmgyŏng chongyo*, a nonextant work of unknown length that was later subsumed in Wŏnhyo's *Chinyŏk Hwaŏmgyŏng-so*; see the notice in Ŭich'ŏn's *Sinp'yŏn chejong kyojang ch'ongnok* 1, *T* 2184.55.1166b4, and *infra*, n. 65.

the *Vajrasamādhi*—and, by extension, the *Awakening of Faith*—the same pedigree and respectability as the canonical scriptures of the Sino-Indian tradition.

## The *Samguk Yusa* Hagiography and the Dating of the *Vajrasamādhi*

Wŏnhyo is mentioned prominently in several sections of *Samguk yusa*, a Korean miscellany compiled sometime during the thirteenth century by the Buddhist monk Iryŏn (1206–1289).[45] One of the major purposes of *SGYS* was to collect Korean Buddhist lore that had not been recorded in other historiographical collections. The only other systematic account of the Three Kingdoms period, *Samguk sagi* (Historical record of the three kingdoms), a Korean secular history written in 1145 by Kim Pusik (1075–1151), included only passing references to Buddhist personages or ceremonies. Wŏnhyo, for example, is given but a single line in the biography of his literatus son, Sŏl Ch'ong (d.u.). Hence, *SGYS* comes to be of perhaps inordinate importance in understanding the early evolution of Korean Buddhism.

Like Tsan-ning, Iryŏn has included Wŏnhyo's hagiography in his section on "Doctrinal Exegetes" (*ŭihae*). Unlike the various Chinese *Kao-seng chuan*s, however, the "Doctrinal Exegetes" section in *SGYS* was not explicitly concerned with praising the scholastic accomplishments of eminent monks, but instead with treating those monks as objects of popular faith. While the scholarly achievements of the monks treated in this section are mentioned first in their biographies, the accounts typically soon turn to descriptions of their thaumaturgic powers. The eccentricities of the "doctrinal exegetes" in *SGYS* are distinguished from those of the pure "theurgists" (*sini*) only because of this initial mention of their academic prowess.[46] *SGYS* presents just a modicum of the incumbent detail as to Wŏnhyo's ancestry, training, and honors, preferring instead to devote its account to exuberantly told tales of Wŏnhyo's debauchery and his exploits among the common people. By adopting such an approach, Iryŏn's compilation is lively, robust, even ribald on occasion.

---

[45] Wŏnhyo's main biography in *SGYS* appears in *Wŏnhyo pulgi* (Wŏnhyo, the unbridled), *SGYS* 5, p. 1006a7–b29. I have translated this biography in full in my article "The Biographies of Wŏnhyo."

[46] See Hong Yunsik, "*Samguk yusa* wa Pulgyo ŭirye," pp. 237–39.

While *SGYS* is broadly based upon such Chinese models as the *Kao-seng chuan*s or *Li-tai san-pao chi* (Record of the three treasures throughout successive dynasties),[47] Iryŏn shows somewhat more concern than his Chinese predecessors with drawing from a variety of materials, including local legend and lesser-known stories in *hyangjŏn*s (local biographies), to supplement his account. In Wŏnhyo's case, this penchant is especially apparent, perhaps due to the fact that Iryŏn hailed from Wŏnhyo's own native area and would have been familiar with regional tales concerning the eminent Silla sage.[48] Because of his interest in events presumed to have taken place during a person's life, Iryŏn is less apt than was Tsan-ning to turn flesh-and-blood individuals into simulacra of sacred power. Hence, this hagiography does seem more amenable than most to the reconstruction of biographical fact—provided of course that its account is carefully weighed against other extrinsic evidence, such as epigraphical materials, biographies of his contemporaries, secular histories, or text-critical evidence. A careful reading of the *SGYS* hagiography, as supplemented by the *SKSC* description of Wŏnhyo, the Kosŏn-sa inscription, and other relevant material, will provide some of the few clues about specific phases in Wŏnhyo's vocation, which will be crucial in dating the *Vajrasamādhi*.

Despite the apparently jumbled structure of Iryŏn's hagiography of Wŏnhyo, it is not refractory to analysis when examined carefully. After opening his biography with remarks about Wŏnhyo's ancestry and ancillary stories about Wŏnhyo's native region, Iryŏn excerpts selections from Wŏnhyo's *Hyangjŏn* (Local biography), which is otherwise nonextant. These begin with his liaison with the widowed princess of Prasine Palace and follow a rough chronological order: his affair, the conception and birth of his son, Sŏl Ch'ong, Wŏnhyo's return to lay status, and finally his religious mission among the people. After completing his recital of the *Hyangjŏn* legends, Iryŏn then seems to backtrack and, in the last major section of his hagiography, starts over with what looks to be an explicit attempt to outline the major periods in Wŏnhyo's life. This section opens with Wŏnhyo's birth and early years, followed by an exegetical period, which culminates in the composition of his *Hwaŏmgyŏng-so* (Commentary to the *Avataṃsaka-sūtra*; discussed *infra*). His proselytizing and eccentric stage follows, which he

---

[47] Gari Ledyard suggested to me the parallels between *Li-tai san-pao chi* and *SGYS*.

[48] Iryŏn came from Changsan (the old Amnyang-kun that is mentioned in Wŏnhyo's biography), which would help to account for his familiarity with the *Hyangjŏn* materials on Wŏnhyo. See Kim Pusik, *Samguk sagi*, k. 34, p. 539a; *Sinjung Tongguk yŏji sŭngnam*, k. 27, fol. 1a–b.

abandons to return to scholarship in order to write his commentary to the *Vajrasamādhi*. This section concludes with an account of Wŏnhyo's death and funeral.

Let me cite the passage in question from the *Samguk yusa* so that the periods Iryŏn is describing are clear.

[1]  The village of his birth was named Pulchi (Stage of Buddhahood); his monastery was called Ch'ogae (Initial Opening); he called himself Wŏnhyo (Break of Dawn), which refers to the first shining of the sun of buddhahood. [The name] "Wŏnhyo" is also the Silla pronunciation. People of his time all referred to him in the vernacular as Sidan (First Dawning).

[2]  When he resided at Punhwang Monastery preparing his *Hwaŏm-so*, he reached the fourth [fascicle of the commentary] on the *Shih hui-hsiang p'in* (Ten transferences chapter) and, having completed it, laid down his brush.

[3]  Furthermore, because of the reproach he had suffered,[49] he divided his body among the hundred pines.[50] Everyone considered his status and position to be that of the first stage (*chi*; Skt. *bhūmi*).[51]

---

[49]  As related in the *SKSC* biography, *T* 2061.50.730a17.

[50]  "Divided his body among the hundred pines" (*pun'gu ŏ paeksong*): The imagery here can be interpreted in two ways. First, Wŏnhyo's body was scattered about like the infinite number of needles of hundreds of pine trees; hence, he was very busy, by implication, with odious official duties (specifically a possible military appointment) that were antithetical to the transcendent lifestyle of a monk; see the interpretation in Yi Pyŏngdo, trans., *Samguk yusa*, p. 403 n. 6, and cf. Peter Lee, *Anthology of Korean Literature*, p. 33. This interpretation casts obvious aspersions on Wŏnhyo's activities. A more salutary interpretation, which I consider to be more plausible in the present context, is to construe this passage as an allusion to a bodhisattva's supernatural power (*abhijñā*) of displaying myriads of transformation bodies (nirmāṇakāya). As Iryŏn mentions elsewhere, just as Wŏnhyo's friend Nangji (d.u.) was able to ride the clouds to China, in the same way, "Wŏnhyo divided himself into a hundred bodies" (*SGYS* 5, p. 1015c15). Support for this interpretation appears in a passage in the *Daśabhūmika-sūtra* (*Shih-ti ching* 2, *T* 287.10.542b5) which refers to the ability of bodhisattvas on the first stage of the bodhisattva path, the *Pramuditābhūmi*, "to manifest a hundred transformation bodies," language that parallels the account here and that would seem to support a positive reading of the following assertion that Wŏnhyo was considered to be a person "of the first stage." This reading is corroborated in *Avataṃsaka-sūtra* (*Ta-fang-kuang fo hua-yen ching* 9, *T* 278.9.548b22); and see discussion in Yi Chongik, "Wŏnhyo ŭi saengae wa sasang," p. 218. Kim Yŏngt'ae ("Wŏnhyo yŏn'gu," pp. 71–72) also notes other mentions of Wŏnhyo as a bodhisattva, including an interlinear note in *SGYS* 3 (p. 987c27) in which Wŏnhyo (there, called by his monastery's name, Punhwang) is said to have been the transformation of the renowned Indian logician, Diṅnāga (ca. A.D. fifth century). The ultimate sense here seems to be that Wŏnhyo's unhindered practice allowed him to go anywhere without discrimination—even to the bars and brothels normally forbidden to virtuous people—so that he seemingly appeared everywhere, as if via transformation bodies.

[51]  Construing the precise referent of "first stage" is also somewhat problematic. The term can refer to the Dry-Wisdom stage (Kanhye-chi) of the bodhisattva path, a pejorative term

[4] Also, due to the inducement of the Dragon of the Sea, he received a royal command while on the road and wrote *[Kŭmgang] sammaegyŏng-so*. He placed his brushes and inkstone between the two horns of an ox; because of this, he was known as Kaksŭng (Horn Rider),[52] which also expressed the recondite purport of the two enlightenments—original (*pon'gak/pen-chüeh*) and actualized (*sigak/shih-chüeh*). Dharma Master Taean collated the folios and then pasted them together. This [arrangement] also was "knowing the sound and singing in harmony."

[5] After [Wŏnhyo] had entered quiescence, [Sŏl] Ch'ong crushed his remaining bones and cast them into a life-like image, which he enshrined at Punhwang Monastery—this in order to show reverence and affection and his intent [to mourn his father until] the ends of heaven. When Ch'ong prostrated beside it, the image suddenly turned its head [to look at him]; still today, it remains turned to the side.

A major difference between the *SKSC* and *SGYS* hagiographies, and the feature that most distinguishes Iryŏn's account from that of Tsan-ning, is the stress on Wŏnhyo himself found in *SGYS* and the biography's concern to recount as many of the tales still known about the events of his life. As the title chosen for this miscellany would lead us to expect, Iryŏn, with the slightest of pretexts, packs his account with any and probably all extant stories, no matter how remotely relevant. Such detail serves the important purpose of supplying a context to Wŏnhyo's life and provides a much stronger sense of the man than was conveyed in the Chinese hagiography. While space will not allow a detailed treatment of each major biographical event, I will at least be able here to sketch the relative chronology of important stages in Wŏnhyo's life, especially as they relate to the *Vajrasamādhi*, and make some general comments about Wŏnhyo's mature career. This material has

---

indicating an inferior state of understanding, which is characterized by conceptual knowledge, not transcendental realization. It is often referred to as the first of the ten *bhūmi*s of the expedient vehicle. Construed in this way, it would imply that because Wŏnhyo did not limit the places he frequented, as monks should, others considered him to be only an inferior Buddhist ("the first stage"). As I indicate in the preceding note, however, a positive reading is to be preferred.

[52] Kaksŭng (Horn Rider, or Horned Vehicle) is homophonous in Korean with Kaksŭng (Enlightenment Vehicle), the pun Iryŏn obviously intended. Peter Lee (*Anthology*, p. 53) assumes that the epithet refers to Wŏnhyo himself and translates the term as Horn Rider, which seems most plausible to me also. The referent of Horn Rider in the eulogy that follows does, however, seem somewhat ambiguous, and could support a reading of Horn Rider as referring either to the ox-cart itself ("Horned Vehicle") or to the text of the *Vajrasamādhi*. Kim Yŏngt'ae ("Wŏnhyo yŏn'gu," p. 63) suggests this reference is an allusion to the simile of the ox-cart in *Miao-fa-lien-hua ching*, *T* 262.9.13b.

important implications for Wŏnhyo's intellectual development and the relative dating of his works, which have heretofore gone unnoticed.

Iryŏn, as is known from other sections of his work, was quite concerned with chronological fidelity and often attempted to sort out contradicting dates.[53] Including the period of Wŏnhyo's early vocation and study when he made his two attempts to travel to China (which Iryŏn covers later in the biography of Wŏnhyo's colleague Ŭisang), Iryŏn divides Wŏnhyo's life into six distinct stages, which must be carefully distinguished if any chronological sense is to be made of the biography. If one were to attempt to assign dates to these periods, an admittedly imprecise enterprise, the following chronology might prove to be the most supportable:

I. Birth and adolescence (617–631);
II. Ordination and early vocation (ca. 632–661)
   a. First China trip (650)
   b. Second China trip (661)
III. Textual exegete (ca. 662–676)
   a. Birth of Sŏl Ch'ong (ca. 662)
   b. *Hwaŏmgyŏng-so* as final composition before his retirement (ca. 676)
IV. Proselytist among the people (ca. 677–684)
V. Return to scholarship (ca. 685)
   a. Writing of *KSGR*
VI. Death and funeral (686)[54]

There are problematic points in each of these major periods that cannot be dismissed lightly. While I cannot examine all such questions, I would like to allude briefly to a few points that have not previously received extensive treatment. To delimit the start of Wŏnhyo's exegetical career, I shall first turn to accounts of his alleged pilgrimages to the Chinese mainland.

[53] See, for example, *SGYS* 3, p. 997a10–11, where Iryŏn attempts to clarify the problematic chronological relationship between Wŏnhyo, Ŭisang, and Pŏmil (810–889). Iryŏn also attempts to reconcile the disparate chronologies of Mukhoja and Ado *hwasang* by postulating that Mukhoja was simply a nickname for Ado (*SGYS* 3, p. 986c.28), who probably arrived in Silla during the reign of King Nulchi (*SGYS* 3, p. 986c26–7); the four different theories on Ado's life are summarized in Lee, *Lives*, p. 6 and n. 29.

[54] Other attempts at a chronology of Wŏnhyo's career, such as those by Motoi Nobuo ("Gangyō no denki," pp. 50–51) and Sung Bae Park ("Wŏnhyo's Commentaries," p. 71), should be used cautiously. Motoi in particular has often interpolated dates for the events described in the *SKSC* and *SGYS* hagiographies without any apparent evidence.

*Wŏnhyo's Attempted China Trips and His Enlightenment Experience*

Of all of the events in Wŏnhyo's early religious career, perhaps none has captured the imagination of East Asian Buddhists more than the bizarre tale surrounding his attempted pilgrimages to China and his enlightenment. According to tradition, Wŏnhyo twice attempted to travel to the mainland to study with the renowed translator Hsüan-tsang (d. 664), who had returned to China in 648 after sixteen years in India. Surprisingly, however, there is little information on Wŏnhyo's attempted pilgrimages included in his own biographies, and the chronological schema given in his *SGYS* biography does not include these trips. This may be because they were covered in Wŏn-hyo's *Haengjang* (Account of conduct) (though this is never explicitly stated), or because they are mentioned in the biography of his companion, Ŭisang, which immediately follows in the miscellany. This is unfortunate, for it would have helped to establish Iryŏn's view of the relative chronological relationship between these journeys and the other events in Wŏnhyo's life.

There are also many discrepancies in the extant accounts of these trips. *SKSC*, for example, makes only brief reference to the first pilgrimage and completely ignores the second. Ŭisang's biographies also give conflicting information, for his biography in *SKSC* only mentions the latter journey via sea, while the *SGYS* account includes both. Although the dating of the trips varies in the different versions, based on other supporting documentation, it is now generally accepted that the first took place in 650 and the latter in 661.[55] In addition to their important chronological considerations, these stories are also worth considering because Wŏnhyo's experience of enlightenment is said to have taken place in the course of the second of these trips, obviously an important event in reconstructing his biography.

On Wŏnhyo's first journey with Ŭisang, the two pilgrims were supposedly arrested in Liao-tung by Koguryŏ border guards for espionage and imprisoned for several "weeks" (*hsün*; Kor. *sun*) before being repatriated to Silla.[56] Wŏnhyo's biography in *SKSC* refers to these events laconically as his "discrepant karma." Little more is known about this trip.

On their second trip, Ŭisang's biography relates that he and Wŏnhyo had traveled to a port in Paekche territory, where they intended to board a ship

---

[55] For a survey of these materials, see Kim Yŏngt'ae, "Wŏnhyo yŏn'gu," p. 52; cf. Peter Lee, "Fa-tsang and Ŭisang," p. 56.

[56] *SKSC* 4, *T* 2061.50.729a7–8. A *hsün* is actually a ten-day period.

for China. Caught in a heavy downpour, they were forced to spend the night in what they thought was an earthen sanctuary but which turned out in the morning's light to be an old tomb littered with skulls. Still trapped by the incessant rain, they had to pass still another night in the tomb, and before the night was up they were harassed by evil spirits. Wŏnhyo was profoundly moved by the experience and marveled:

> Dwelling overnight yesterday, I was content in what I thought was an earthen sanctuary. But staying overnight this evening, I am ghastly haunted by a host of demons. Hence, I learn that because thoughts arise, all types of dharmas arise; but once thoughts cease, a sanctuary and a tomb are not different. Furthermore, the three realms of existence are mind-alone; the myriads of dharmas are mere-representation. Apart from the mind there are no dharmas; it is futile to attempt to seek [those dharmas] elsewhere. I will not continue on to T'ang.[57]

Wŏnhyo then returned home and Ŭisang traveled alone to China.

*SGYS* claims that this second journey took place at the beginning of the Yung-hui era (650–655), but this is probably confusing it with their earlier trip to Liao-tung. However, the *SKSC* biography of Ŭisang only mentions this single journey via sea, and its dating of this trip as taking place in 669 is equally implausible, given that Ŭisang's teacher in China, Chih-yen, died in 668.[58] Adding to the mystery, the *SGYS* biography of Ŭisang never states that Wŏnhyo accompanied Ŭisang on the second trip. While this lacuna might be taken to indicate that the story and the account of Wŏnhyo's enlightenment experience included therein are actually apocryphal, it is more probable that because the subject of the biography is Ŭisang, not Wŏnhyo, there was no compelling need to mention the latter.

It is also significant that neither of these two records makes any mention of a widely known story of Wŏnhyo's enlightenment, which is ubiquitous in popular accounts of Wŏnhyo's life. In this tale, which has been traced to the twelfth-century *Shih-men Hung Chüeh-fan lin-chien lu*, after finally reach-

---

[57] *SKSC* 4, *T* 2061.50.729a12–15; translated in Hubert Durt, "La Biographie du Moine Coréen Ŭi-Sang d'après le Song Kao Seng Tchouan," pp. 415–16; and partially translated with discussion in Yi Chongik, "Wŏnhyo ŭi saengae," pp. 189–90; Sung Bae Park, "Wŏnhyo's Commentaries," pp. 48–53; Kim Yŏngt'ae, "Wŏnhyo yŏn'gu," p. 50. For the implications of this enlightenment experience, see Sung Bae Park, "On Wŏnhyo's Enlightenment," pp. 470–467 [sic]; Yi Chongik, "Wŏnhyo ŭi saengae," pp. 190–91.

[58] Peter Lee, "Fa-tsang and Ŭisang," p. 56 n. 8.

ing China, Wŏnhyo first traveled among famous mountain temples before setting out alone on a backroad. Forced to call a halt to his journey because of darkness, he stayed overnight in a cave. Overcome by thirst, Wŏnhyo was able to find a small spring of water in the cave, from which he drank with his hand until he was completely satisfied. Upon waking in the morning, however, he discovered to his profound disgust that what he had thought was sweet spring water was actually rank water stagnating in a skull. Realizing that it was only his mind that created the distinction between satisfying refreshment and revolting spectacle, he was immediately enlightened to the truth that all dharmas are created by the mind alone, and he returned to Silla.[59] This story seems to be an adaptation of the *SKSC* legend; and, given that it is not corroborated in any other accounts, it should be disregarded in any serious evaluation of Wŏnhyo's career.

### Wŏnhyo as Textual Exegete and Proselytist

I would now like to move to a discussion of the chronology of Wŏnhyo's exegetical and proselytizing periods and how these relate to his return to scholarship. Establishing the relative chronology of these three periods is of utmost relevance to *SKSC*'s hagiography and its account of the recovery of the *Vajrasamādhi*; it also covers the mature phase of Wŏnhyo's career. In these sections as well one finds a graphic illustration of the ways in which hagiographical evidence, as supplemented by documentation from other sources, can yield implicit historical information about the wider contexts of a subject's life.

The continuity in both style and content apparent in most of Wŏnhyo's exegetical works suggests that they were written in succession, with little break between compositions. While this is not to say that all of the hundred or so works in some two hundred fascicles attributed to Wŏnhyo are authentic,[60] Wŏnhyo's authorship of the majority of these twenty-some extant

---

[59] *Shih-men Hung Chüeh-fan lin-chien lu*, *ZZ* 2b, 21, 4, 295a, from whence it entered into secondary accounts; see Kim Yŏngt'ae, "Wŏnhyo yŏn'gu," p. 53.

[60] Etani Ryūkai ("Shiragi Gangyō no *Yūshin anrakudō* wa gisaku ka," pp. 16–23), for example, has raised doubts concerning Wŏnhyo's authorship of *Yusim allak-to*. Among the five principal reasons for his suspicions are the dearth of catalogue entries for the text until the Kamakura period, its quotation of passages from two works not translated until after 713, and the similarities between its first half and another of Wŏnhyo's works, the *Muryangsu chongyo* (Thematic essentials of the *Amitābha-sūtra*), leading Etani to suspect that *Yusim* is simply reedited

compositions is unquestioned. Since Wŏnhyo was so determined to travel to China to enhance his knowledge of Indian Buddhist scholarship under the tutelage of the Hsüan-tsang, it seems reasonable to presume that he would not have felt himself competent to write most of these commentaries before his attempted pilgrimages.[61] Hence, most of his scholarship probably post-dates his return in 661 from his second attempt to travel to the mainland.

Political events on the peninsula at the time provide some information that may help us to sort out the dates of his exegetical period, as well as to clarify when Wŏnhyo might have left on his subsequent proselytizing mission among the people. Even after the fall of Koguryŏ in 668, peace still did not reign on the peninsula. In 675–676, Silla itself was invaded by the combined armies of T'ang soldiers and Paekche mercenaries, which would have made extensive travel difficult, if not impossible. Hence, if Wŏnhyo actually did go on tour to "sing and dance his way through a thousand villages and a myriad hamlets,"[62] as the *SGYS* biography states, this could probably not have occurred until after the withdrawal of the T'ang forces in 676. If so, Wŏnhyo would have had approximately fifteen years, from 661 to about 676, to complete most of his commentaries. The only date of which I am aware for any of Wŏnhyo's writings appears in the postface to his *P'an pir-yang-ron*, which states that it was written by Wŏnhyo in 671, seventh month, sixteenth day (August 25, 671), at Haengmyŏng-sa.[63] This date converges nicely with the chronological scheme I propose here.

Although our present state of knowledge does not allow us to ascertain much about the respective composition dates of most of Wŏnhyo's works, there are some indications that the *SGYS* biography is attempting to provide some chronological clarification for two of his most influential works: his *Chinyŏk Hwaŏmgyŏng-so* (Commentary to the Chin translation of the *Avataṃsaka-sūtra*) and *KSGR*. Against all previous scholarly opinion, I believe Iryŏn's conclusion is that *Hwaŏmgyŏng-so* was the last work Wŏnhyo wrote before his departure to proselytize among the people; an extraordinary series of events later prompted him, however, to return one final time

---

excerpts from that treatise. A periphrastic translation of this treatise appears in Leo Lee, *Le maître Wôn-hyo de Sil-la du VIIè siècle: Sa vie, ses écrits, son apostolat*, pp. 61–88.

[61] See discussion in Kim Yŏngt'ae, "Wŏnhyo yŏn'gu," p. 56.

[62] *SGYS* 2, p. 1006b14.

[63] Edited by Kim Chigyŏn and included in Cho Myŏnggi, ed., *Wŏnhyo chŏnjip*, pp. 674, 683; summarized in Cho Myŏnggi, *Silla Pulgyo ŭi inyŏm kwa yŏksa*, p. 120. The monastery name is clearly Haengmyŏng-sa in the original manuscript, not the Chuhaeng-sa given in the edited text.

to scholarship before his death in 686 to write *KSGR*, his commentary to the newly recovered *Vajrasamādhi*. Unlike Tsan-ning, who is content with his role as a purveyor of legends, Iryŏn thus seems to be attempting in this latter portion of his hagiography to bring some chronological sense to Wŏnhyo's life. In the section from his *SGYS* biography cited above, Iryŏn takes up Wŏnhyo's life near its end, starting with period III.b, the events that took place from the time that he retired from scholarship, with the completion of his *Hwaŏmgyŏng-so*; continuing with IV, his travels among the people, proselytizing with popular songs and gnomic verses; to v.a, a brief mention of the circumstances that led to writing *KSGR*, apparently his final composition; and culminating with VI, his death and funeral. Most scholars have presumed that Wŏnhyo wrote *KSGR* ca. 665, around the time of the *Inwang-kyŏng* assembly mentioned in the *SKSC* account (which I have shown to be actually undatable); later, as the final event in his life, Wŏnhyo then started his *Hwaŏmgyŏng-so*, but dropped it unfinished and went into retirement.[64] But a close reading of the *SGYS* story suggests instead that Iryŏn was attempting to place Wŏnhyo's retirement *prior* to the writing of *KSGR*. As I noted previously, Iryŏn shows throughout his miscellany a concern with chronological fidelity. Indeed, the listing of events in Wŏnhyo's life that he gives in the last section of his biography seems explicitly chronological. Iryŏn also remarked in the biography that he did not intend to duplicate information on Wŏnhyo already given in *SKSC*; hence, he was probably not simply appending to the end of his account a synopsis of Tsan-ning's story of the discovery of the *Vajrasamādhi*.

In Iryŏn's account, Wŏnhyo seems to have gone into voluntary retirement from his scholarly activities even before completing his *Hwaŏmgyŏng-so*, perhaps intended to be his magnum opus given the importance of the *Avataṃsaka-sūtra* at that time in Silla Buddhism.[65] The implication here is

[64] Mizuno, p. 40. Motoi Nobuo ("Gangyō no denki," p. 51), Rhi Ki-yong (*Kŭmgang sammaegyŏng-ron*, p. 331), Etani Ryūkai ("Shiragi Gangyō no *Yūshin anrakudō*," p. 19), and Kim Yŏngt'ae ("Wŏnhyo yŏn'gu," p. 59) all accept that *Hwaŏmgyŏng-so* was Wŏnhyo's last work.

[65] Only the preface and fascicle three (to the "Ju-lai kuang-ming-chüeh p'in") of Wŏnhyo's *Chinyŏk Hwaŏmgyŏng-so* are extant; the fragments are published in *T* 2757.85.234c–236a, and Cho Myŏnggi, *Wŏnhyo taesa chŏnjip*, pp. 647–53. The text is first listed, though without comment, in the Japanese Kegon catalogue, *Kegonshū shōsho byō immyōroku* (*T* 2177.55.1133a19), compiled in 914 by Enchō (d.u.). Ŭich'ŏn lists it in his 1090 catalogue, *Sinp'yŏn chejong kyojang ch'ongnok* (*T* 2184.55.1166b4), as a ten-*kwŏn* work. His interlinear note adds: "Originally this [text] was in eight *kwŏn*. Now, its fifth *kwŏn* has been expanded [*kae*, lit., opened up, divided] and [Wŏnhyo's Hwaŏmgyŏng] *chongyo* combined with it, to make [a total of] ten *kwŏn*." For Wŏnhyo's Hwaŏm thought, see especially Kim Hyŏnghŭi, "Hyŏnjon ch'anso–rŭl t'onghae pon Wŏnhyo ŭi *Hwaŏm-kyŏng* kwan"; Chang Wŏn'gyu, "Hwaŏm kyohak wansŏnggi ŭi sasang

that Wŏnhyo had judged his exegetical and scholarly career to be at a close; he had nothing more to say to the theologians and was content to go "on the road" among the people. Although no date is known for his *Hwaŏmgyŏng-so*, if Wŏnhyo had ten years as a proselytist before his death, it can be tentatively assumed that the commentary was completed sometime around 676.

One curious note about the reference to the *Hwaŏmgyŏng-so* is that Iryŏn says (sect. 2), "he reached the fourth [fascicle? (*kwŏn*) of the commentary] on the *Shih hui-hsiang p'in* (Ten transferences chapter) and, having completed it, laid down his brush." Since neither bibliographical entries nor Wŏnhyo's preface to *Hwaŏmgyŏng-so* give any information as to the structure of this commentary (such an outline would have appeared in the opening lines of the nonextant first fascicle of the commentary, judging from the approach Wŏnhyo adopts in other exegeses), one is left to assume that by "fourth" here is meant the fourth *kwŏn* of the commentary, and that the commentary was originally in four *kwŏn*, not the eight or ten that Ŭich'ŏn's scriptural catalogue mentioned. One of the meanings of the term "laid down his brush" (*chŏlp'il*) is to stop or to interrupt one's writing,[66] which could imply that Wŏnhyo gave up writing the treatise before it was finished. Potentially significant is the possible relationship between the *Shih hui-hsiang p'in* (Ten transferences chapter), which is concerned with the transfer of merit from the bodhisattva to unenlightened beings, and his immediately succeeding departure to proselytize among the people: Wŏnhyo's reading of this chapter may have inspired him to leave behind his commentarial career for active missionary work.[67] While Wŏnhyo traveled, Iryŏn says that he danced with a gourd, which he named Unhindered (Muae), after a passage in the *Avataṃsaka-sūtra*.[68] This name also suggests that Wŏnhyo had already worked on the *Avataṃsaka-sūtra* before he entered his proselytizing period. When cou-

yŏn'gu," pp. 11–26; Kim Ingsŏk, *Hwaŏm-hak kaeron*, pp. 19–22; Kim Chigyŏn, "Silla Hwaŏm-hak ŭi kyebo wa sasang," pp. 39–41; Kim Chigyŏn, "Silla Hwaŏmhak ŭi churyu ko," pp. 263–65; Koh Ik-jin, "Wŏnhyo's Hua-yen Thought," pp. 30–33. For a general discussion of the importance of the *Avataṃsaka-sūtra* in Korean Buddhism, see, for example, Kim Chigyŏn, "Silla Hwaŏmhak ŭi churyu ko," pp. 257–58; Kim Ingsŏk, *Hwaŏm-hak*, pp. 17–87.

[66] "Laid down his brush" (*chŏlp'il*) can refer to either a final calligraphy done before death or superior calligraphic abilities. In the present context, however, it seems most plausible to take it in the sense of "to interrupt one's writing," a meaning found in *Ch'un-ch'iu* (*Shih san-ching chu-shu* ed., vol. 6), ch. 59, fol. 11a3.

[67] Cf. Yi Chongik, "Wŏnhyo ŭi saengae," p. 194.

[68] The passage from the *Hua-yen ching*, "all unhindered men leave birth and death along a single path," appears at *Ta-fang-kuang fo hua-yen ching* 5, *T* 278.9.429a19; and *Ta-fang-kuang fo hua-yen ching* 13, *T* 279.10.68c13.

pled with the following statement that Wŏnhyo received a royal command to compose a commentary to the *Vajrasamādhi* "while on the road," the implication is that Wŏnhyo went into itinerant retirement after either completing or interrupting his writing of *Hwaŏmgyŏng-so*, only to return to scholarship to compose his *KSGR*. However, since there is no implication in any source that Wŏnhyo's *Hwaŏmgyŏng-so* ever circulated in an unfinished state, it seems safer to assume that the commentary was probably complete in four *kwŏn*, and subsequently redivided into double that number sometime before Ŭich'ŏn's time, a common occurrence with East Asian books.

Regardless of whether Wŏnhyo gave up writing the *Hwaŏmgyŏng-so* before its completion, however, it seems virtually certain that he retired to a life of disseminating the dharma among the people some years before his death. Although this period would have been primarily devoted to popular sermons and didactic teaching, it is probable that he composed some of his songs and short tracts dealing with faith and moral discipline at this time, as Sung Bae Park has suggested.[69] All the evidence, then, indicates that Wŏnhyo's main exegetical efforts preceded his proselytizing stage.

After perhaps a decade spent traveling among the peasantry, another event intervened that took Wŏnhyo away from his missionary vocation and compelled him to return to the mainstream of Silla scholastic life: the "appearance" of the *Vajrasamādhi*. Wŏnhyo was obviously fascinated by the text, enough to convince him to suspend his travels and return to writing, apparently for this one last time—and, again, not once, but twice, if one follows Tsan-ning's version of the legend. Because of certain teachings in the *Vajrasamādhi* that demand knowledge of nascent movements in Chinese Ch'an Buddhism, Wŏnhyo could not have been the writer of the *Vajrasamādhi*. I will propose an authorship candidate later who would have had the requisite knowledge of Chinese developments. But recognizing the problems of passage between the mainland and Silla during the period preceding the fall of Koguryŏ in 668—as Wŏnhyo's own experiences with Koguryŏ border guards illustrate—it is doubtful that this man could have returned to Silla before that date. Hence, the *Vajrasamādhi* was apparently composed in Korea sometime between 668 and 685, and more plausibly toward the latter of the two dates. This dating is supported by the fact that the *Vajrasamādhi* is neither quoted nor cited in any of Wŏnhyo's other compositions, even though his commentary to the sūtra quotes extensively from the full range

[69] Sung Bae Park, "Wŏnhyo's Commentaries," p. 71.

of texts he had consulted in earlier writings.[70] For a scripture as obviously important to Wŏnhyo as was the *Vajrasamādhi*, it is difficult, if not impossible, to imagine that he would not at least have referred to it in one of his earlier works if the text had been available to him. It is therefore safe to date the composition of the *Vajrasamādhi* to a time after the completion of all Wŏnhyo's other works and, from the hagiographical accounts, to sometime between the composition of *Hwaŏmgyŏng-so* and his death. Hence, although Iryŏn's account of these three final periods in Wŏnhyo's life is quite terse, its information is corroborated by other biographical, textual, and historical evidence.

The parallels between the *SKSC*'s redaction of the discovery of the *Vajrasamādhi* and the earlier-mentioned legend of Chakchegŏn provide a prudent reason for Iryŏn to truncate the story so radically. The *Vajrasamādhi* legend was strikingly similar to the account concerning the ancestry of the Koryŏ ruling family, mentioned above, and there must have been implicit political liabilities in casting aspersions on the authenticity of the royal genealogy. To avoid any such conflict (his excuse being that he did not need to repeat stories already covered in *SKSC*), Iryŏn passed quickly over the event, apparently assuming that it was easily available to whomever might wish to read it in the politically uncompromising Chinese record.

By the same token too, the involvement of Wŏnhyo, retrospectively viewed during the Koryŏ as the most renowned figure of Unified Silla Buddhism, might have compelled Iryŏn to relate the story in less controversial fashion; for even in Tsan-ning's account the role given to Taean in the reconstruction of the scripture is carefully differentiated from Wŏnhyo's responsibility for popularizing it. Iryŏn has gone one step further, by telling the legend so that any and all suspicions about the provenance of the *Vajrasamādhi* are carefully expunged. Iryŏn limits his remarks to the statement that the Dragon King ordered Wŏnhyo to write a commentary to the scripture—suggesting divine intervention in the ideas expressed in the commentary, not necessarily in the sūtra itself. The obviously apocryphal origins of the *Vajrasamādhi* in Tsan-ning's version of the legend may have been a sensitive issue to Koryŏ Koreans. By separating Wŏnhyo from any question about the composition of the text, Iryŏn has kept Wŏnhyo's reputation unblemished; the person closest to the questionable manuscript folios is the otherwise unknown Taean.

---

[70] See the convenient chart of Wŏnhyo's extant works and the texts they cite in Rhi Kiyong, "Kyŏngjŏn ŭi nat'anan Wŏnhyo ŭi tokch'angsŏng," pp. 220–23.

But what did Wŏnhyo see in the *Vajrasamādhi* that was so enticing to him intellectually? Its teachings apparently offered a message certain to appeal to Silla Buddhists, enough so that Wŏnhyo would be lured out of retirement to write what would be his last major commentary, *KSGR*. The next chapter considers the doctrinal teachings of the *Vajrasamādhi* and examine the contributions the sūtra made to East Asian Buddhist philosophy.

CHAPTER THREE

# THE DOCTRINAL TEACHINGS
# OF THE *VAJRASĀMADHI*

The Acculturation of Buddhism to East Asia

The Buddhist tradition that evolved in East Asia was a synthesis of ideas
drawn from imported Indian and Central Asian Buddhism, combined with
indigenous religious, philosophical, and cultural traits. India and East Asia
are separated by immense geographical, cultural, and linguistic gulfs, which
were not easily bridged. A creative process spanning several centuries was
required to narrow the gap separating the two cultures and to bring the alien
religion of Buddhism within the purview of indigenous intellectual discourse. This assimilation was made all the more difficult by the sheer size of
the Buddhist scriptural corpus, and the different languages from which
those texts had to be translated: Sanskrit, Middle Indic, and the several Indo-
European dialects of Central Asia and the Takla Makhan basin, Sogdian and
Khotanese among them. As an open canon with relatively liberal standards
for the inclusion of new material, the Buddhist tripiṭaka had grown to include hundreds of texts, in thousands of volumes, by the time it began to be
transmitted to East Asia. In the last quarter of the fourth century, when the
first Buddhist scriptural catalogue was made by Tao-an, the Chinese had
already to come to grips with some 561 texts in 786 volumes.[1] By the early
part of the eighth century, just a few decades after the composition of the
*Vajrasamādhi*, the canon had grown many times larger, to some 2,278 texts
in 7,056 volumes.[2]

---

[1] To this number can be added twenty-six apocryphal scriptures and twenty-four treatises
by Tao-an himself, giving a total of 611 texts. See Hayashiya, *Kyōroku kenkyū*, p. 47.

[2] *K'ai-yüan shih-chiao lu* 1, *T* 2154.55.477a; this includes all texts cited in the catalogue,
including biographies, indigenous commentaries, and apocryphal scriptures. Of this total, only
1,076 texts in 5,048 volumes appear in listings of texts actually entered into the canon (*Ju-tsang
lu*); see the notice at *ch*. 19, *T* 2154.55.680a–b.

But compounding these linguistic and translation problems were the disparate messages of its texts. In addition to discovering early on the split in Buddhism between the Mahāyāna (the "Great Vehicle") and the Śrāvakayāna (which the Mahāyāna pejoratively termed the "Lesser Vehicle," or Hīnayāna), East Asians also learned that Mahāyāna itself included a number of learned "schools" and practice traditions, the approaches and premises of which seemed at times to be all but antithetical to one another. Resolving these eristic conflicts occupied much of the attention of Buddhist exegetes during the Sui and T'ang periods.

By the sixth and seventh centuries, Chinese Buddhists were well on their way toward developing hermeneutical taxonomies—what the Chinese termed p'an-chiao (Kor. pan'gyo), or "analyzing the teachings"—that would bring order to these variant materials and show how they all could collaborate in the common goal of liberation. What is striking in these maturing sinitic interpretations of Buddhism is the emphasis they place on what they considered the kataphasis of the Yogācāra and Tathāgatagarbha systems, rather than the apophasis of the Madhyamaka school. Whereas early Chinese Buddhists had been attracted by the sheer novelty of the Madhyamaka ideology of emptiness (śūnyavāda), by the sixth century the cynosure of Buddhist scholarship had shifted from emptiness to immanence.[3] To show how pervasive this tendency was in China, even Chi-tsang (549–623), the principal exponent of the Chinese Madhyamaka school (the "Three Treatises" or San-lun school), incorporated the Buddha-nature doctrine into his doctrinal system.[4] This new focus is reflected in the subordination of Prajñāpāramitā and Madhyamaka literature to more explicitly Tathāgatagarbha teachings in these indigenous doctrinal taxonomies. T'ien-t'ai classifications, for example, typically place the Mahāparinirvāṇa-sūtra, a scripture renowned in East Asia for proclaiming the inherence of the buddha-nature in all beings, above the Prajñāpāramitā.[5] In the Hua-yen taxonomy, the Prajñāpāramitā was considered to be merely the incipient (shih) stage of Mahāyāna, just a step above the maligned Hīnayāna, and was succeeded by the final (chung) Mahāyāna teachings of Tathāgatagarbha. But the teachings of

[3] For a compelling exposition of the Chinese critique of Madhyamaka, see Robert M. Gimello, "Apophatic and Kataphatic Discourse in Mahāyāna: A Chinese View," pp. 117–36.

[4] See Kamata Shigeo, Chūgoku bukkyō shisōshi kenkyū, pp. 31–46; Aaron Koseki, "Prajñāpāramitā and the Buddhahood of the Non-Sentient World: The San-lun Assimilation of Buddha-Nature and Middle Path Doctrine," pp. 16–33.

[5] See discussion in David W. Chappell, ed., Masao Ichishima, comp., T'ien-t'ai Buddhism: An Outline of the Fourfold Teachings, pp. 30–40, and diagram p. 35.

the *Avataṃsaka-sūtra*, Hua-yen claimed, represented the full perfection of Buddhism by being beyond all distinctions and thus epitomized the consummate unity (*yüan*) of the religion.[6] Besides their polemical purpose, such classifications also sought to bring harmony to the teachings and helped to instill in Chinese adherents a syncretic perspective on Buddhism.

This taxonomical concern was no less ardent in Korea. Wŏnhyo also developed his own scriptural hermeneutic, which classified Buddhist texts in terms adapted from the *Awakening of Faith*. Wŏnhyo's taxonomy of the teachings will be covered in more detail later, but for now let it suffice to say that it subordinates Prajñāpāramitā literature to the *Nirvāṇa* and *Avataṃsaka* sūtras and finally places the more syncretic teachings of the *Laṅkāvatāra-sūtra* and *Awakening of Faith* at its apex. This ordering illustrates Wŏnhyo's penchant for approaches to doctrinal study that were synchronic rather than diachronic and that would serve to synthesize the variations in the many schools of Buddhism. In his own country and era, Wŏnhyo's most popular and best-known work seems to have been his *Simmun hwajaeng-ron*, a short essay that advocated an ecumenical perspective on Buddhist doctrine. Hence, the Koreans were as interested as the Chinese in developing all-encompassing systems of Buddhist thought that would reconcile the presumed differences they saw in the teachings.

The scriptural taxonomies explored by thinkers of this period raise in turn a whole set of complementary issues, such as the correct number and classification of the different types of consciousness, several variations of which were presented in Buddhist texts. This controversy related to a number of wider and more fundamental issues in Buddhist ontology and soteriology, such as whether the mind was inherently pure or defiled, or whether enlightenment was intrinsic or extrinsic to the mind—in many ways the Buddhist analogue of the Mencius/Hsün-tzu debate in indigenous Chinese philosophy over whether human nature was inherently good or evil.[7] Resolving these issues would have enormous implications for the sinitic Buddhist worldview and the soteriological stratagems the tradition would adopt.

The mature East Asian schools that formed during the sixth and seventh centuries rejected what they perceived as the world-renouncing tendencies of the so-called Hīnayāna branch of Indian Buddhism. In its stead, they fa-

---

[6] For the traditional Hua-yen taxonomy, see Ming-wood Liu, "The *P'an-chiao* System of the Hua-yen School in Chinese Buddhism," pp. 10–47.

[7] See Whalen Lai's discussion in "The Pure and the Impure: The Mencian Problematik in Chinese Buddhism," esp. p. 305.

vored the basic humaneness of Mahāyāna, as enunciated in its clarion call of compassion toward and liberation for everyone, not merely an elite cadre of religious specialists. Tathāgatagarbha thought, based on the inherence of enlightenment in all sentient beings, would be used to justify this ideal of universal salvation. At the same time, the East Asians demanded a workable program for pursuing this ideal. If enlightenment was to be truly accessible to all types of people—cenobites and laypeople alike—some way had to be found to make it coextensive with ordinary life. The East Asians would eventually go so far as to claim that the mundane world was itself the ground of enlightenment. Spiritual attainment thus need not be envisaged as a state of otherworldly transcendence, but as the realization of the multivalent web of interrelationships connecting the individual to his environment and his fellow man—what the Hua-yen school would term the "unimpeded interpenetration of all phenomena" (shih-shih wu-ai). True bodhisattva action on behalf of all beings could then mean simply fulfilling one's social obligations and filial duties, without demanding that the individual abandon his place in the world. In this wise, enlightenment was made accessible in the here and now, without requiring that the adept complete an elaborate regimen of learning and meditation. Rather, living an examined life could be sufficient in itself to reveal instantly the enlightened purity at one's noetic core—the notion of "sudden enlightenment" (tun-wu) that would inspire so many of the East Asian schools of Buddhism.

Written during the late decades of the seventh century, the Vajrasamādhi presents one cross-section of the debates concerning philosophy and practice occurring at this crucial juncture in the evolution of the indigenous schools of sinitic Buddhism. This sūtra will have much to tell us concerning the theoretical uses of the seminal notions of tathāgatagarbha and amalavijñāna ("immaculate consciousness") in East Asian Buddhism, and particularly about their soteriological roles. The interest of its author in the notion of vajrasamādhi will be seen as an attempt to reveal the praxis aspects of tathāgatagarbha and amalavijñāna, transforming them from abstract philosophical theories into pragmatic tools of practice. The author of the Vajrasamādhi, too, like many indigenous Buddhist thinkers, was also attempting to find a way to bring together the different teachings of Buddhism into a coherent whole, which could be both consistent philosophically as well as viable in practice. The syncretic orientation of the text seems to have attracted the interest of the Silla Koreans, and especially Wŏnhyo. I seek in this chapter to place the innovations made in the Vajrasamādhi in the context of the ongoing debates concerning ontology and soteriology then taking place in East

Asian Buddhism. Because of space considerations, I will be content to provide only the modicum of background necessary to clarify the perspectives
of the *Vajrasamādhi* and the contributions it makes to these debates.

## Tathāgatagarbha and the Immanence of Enlightenment

Perhaps most prominent among the reasons for the *Vajrasamādhi*'s renown
in East Asian Buddhism has been its treatment of the concept of tathāgatagarbha (womb [or embryo] of buddhahood). This feature of the text has
attracted considerable attention from traditional Buddhist exegetes as well
as contemporary scholars.[8]

Tathāgatagarbha proposes to explain how it is possible for ordinary, deluded beings to attain what they presume to be the rarified state of enlightenment. Its explanation for this achievement is less a solution than a disso-
lution: Tathāgatagarbha thought seeks to skirt the issue entirely by denying
the reality of ignorance, positing instead that the mind is intrinsically luminous but dulled by adventitious defilements.[9] Since defilements remain forever extrinsic to the mind's true, enlightened nature, the individual has actually never been deluded at all; that presumption of ignorance is nothing
more than a mistaken belief produced by unsystematic attention (*ayoniśomanaskāra*). Enlightenment therefore involves nothing more than relinquish-

---

[8] Among modern scholars, Takasaki Jikidō in his pioneering survey of Indian Tathāgatagarbha literature notes that the treatment of this theory in sinitic apocryphal texts, specifically
*Awakening of Faith* and *VS*, is one area that still remains to be explored. See Takasaki Jikidō,
*Nyoraizō shisō no keisei*, p. 774. For the varying analyses of the Sanskrit compound tathāgatagarbha, see David Seyfort Ruegg, *La Théorie du Tathāgatagarbha et du Gotra*, pp. 507–14.
Ruegg's study, while extremely valuable, draws almost exclusively on Sanskrit sources and
their Tibetan commentarial interpretations, which are not always relevant to East Asian developments.

[9] In this regard, tathāgatagarbha builds on an ancient strand in Buddhist thought, of which
the locus classicus is the oft-quoted statement in *Aṅguttara-nikāya* 1.10: "The mind, oh monks,
is luminous but defiled by adventitious defilements" (*pabhassaraṃ idaṃ bhikkhave cittaṃ, tañ ca
kho āgantukehi upakkilesehi upakkiliṭṭhaṃ*). While this passage is discussed in much of the relevant
secondary literature, its implications for Buddhist spiritual cultivation are brought out best in
two fascinating books by Bhikkhu Ñāṇananda, which deserve wider recognition: *Concept and
Reality in Early Buddhist Thought*, esp. p. 58; and *The Magic of the Mind: An Exposition of the
Kalākārāma Sutta*, pp. 83ff. Similar passages can also be found in other Mahāyāna materials.
The *Aṣṭasāhasrikāprajñāpāramitā-sūtra* (1.5) says, for example, "When a Bodhisattva courses in
perfect wisdom and develops it, he should so train himself so that he does not pride himself on
that thought of enlightenment. That thought is no thought, since in its essential original nature
thought is transparently luminous." See Edward Conze, trans., *The Perfection of Wisdom in Eight
Thousand Lines and Its Verse Summary*, p. 84.

ing one's misperception that one is ignorant and accepting one's true state;[10] there need be no complex procedures or curricula to follow—no mārga or *tao*, such as are taught in most schools of Buddhism. Tathāgatagarbha thought as it evolved in East Asia thus provides the ontological justification for the Mahāyāna ideal of universal salvation, as well as the theoretical underpinnings for a viable subitist approach to enlightenment. It is for these reasons that Tathāgatagarbha thought proved to be immensely popular with sinitic exegetes.

Tathāgatagarbha's exclusive focus on the reality of enlightenment, however, leads to near-total neglect of the equally compelling problem of the origin of ignorance. If the mind is inherently enlightened, as Tathāgatagarbha doctrine claims, then whence does ignorance arise? Or, to phrase the question in slightly different terms, if the mind is inherently pure, then why would it ever come to appear as if tainted by the defilements? This problem is the Buddhist parallel of the issue of theodicy, which is so compelling in monotheistic religions: that is, how to justify the goodness and omnipotence of God in the face of apparently intractable or unwarranted suffering. To allay this tension between enlightenment and nonenlightenment in Buddhism, some explanation of the process by which enlightened beings come to conceive themselves as deluded had to be found. The problem of the origin of ignorance is addressed in a second major Mahāyāna philosophy of mind: the ālayavijñāna (storehouse consciousness) doctrine of the Yogācāra school. Yogācāra posited that the mind served as a repository of all of one's past experiences, both unwholesome and wholesome. This "storehouse" was considered to be an eighth type of consciousness, which "stored" the seeds (*bīja*) of both defilement and purity. Given the Buddhist abhorrence of any philosophical concept resembling a first cause, the religion has typically treated ignorance as having no beginning, though it may be brought to an end (in enlightenment). Hence, left untrained, following its own inveterate tendencies, the mind would forever tend toward unwholesomeness; thus its "storehouse" has a veritable infinity of time to collect an infinity of impure seeds. These seeds would have to be removed to produce the total purity that is enlightenment. To effect this change, the individual must be instructed in the necessity of cultivating constructive types of action, so as to

---

[10] See Takasaki, trans., *Ratnagotravibhāga*, pp. 22–23. A number of Tathāgatagarbha sūtras and śāstras state that enlightenment, or the absolute aspect of existence (*paramārtha*), is accessible only through faith (*adhimukti*); see David Seyfort Ruegg, "On the Knowability and Expressibility of Absolute Reality in Buddhism," pp. 495–89 [*sic*].

begin producing the wholesome seeds that would sanitize the mind *cum* storehouse.

The ālayavijñāna theory thus posits that mental purity is not innate: that process of decontamination begins outside the mind, by "hearing the dharma"—that is, learning about religious praxis. The mind in the Yogācāra system is incapable of generating its own deliverance, as Tathāgatagarbha presumed: enlightenment instead involved a radical transformation of the mind through an external catalyst, so that all the seeds of defilement are eventually removed and the mind remains filled exclusively with pure seeds. This could involve a long, tedious process of practice; indeed, the standard mārga outlined in the *Yogācārabhūmi-śāstra* was said to take three *asaṃkhye-yakalpa*s (incalculable eons) to complete—the Buddhist euphemism for an infinity.[11] One can sympathize with the East Asians who wondered whether this system held out any real hope of ever achieving enlightenment. The diametrical opposition between these two Mahāyāna philosophies of mind may be schematized as follows:

| Tathāgatagarbha | Ālayavijñāna |
|---|---|
| origin of enlightenment | origin of ignorance |
| enlightenment intrinsic | enlightenment extrinsic |
| mind innately pure | mind innately impure |
| defilements extrinsic | defilements intrinsic |

Buddhism was thus faced with two radically different perspectives on Mahāyāna ontology and soteriology and two variant solutions to the Problematik of defilement and purity. How was this philosophical dilemma to be resolved?

Initial, unsystematic attempts at reconciling these two theories are made in a few early Indian Mahāyāna texts. The *Laṅkāvatāra-sūtra*, for example, explicitly equates the two by saying that "the ālayavijñāna is called the tathāgatagarbha."[12] According to the *Laṅkāvatāra*'s analysis, the ālayavijñāna as

---

[11] The different issues addressed by these two philosophies of mind were first discussed by D. T. Suzuki in his *Studies in the Laṅkāvatāra Sūtra*, pp. 261ff. There he describes the cause of the wholesome, and thus the pure aspect of the mind, as tathāgatagarbha, the cause of the unwholesome, and thus impurity, as ālayavijñāna. My characterization in this section of this philosophical Problematik in sinitic Mahāyāna thought is drawn from Peter N. Gregory, "The Problem of Theodicy in the *Awakening of Faith*," pp. 63–78, and Robert Gimello, "Chih-yen (602–668) and the Foundations of Hua-yen Buddhism," pp. 212–77.

[12] *Ju Leng-ch'ieh ching* 7, *T* 671.16.556b29–c1; cf. Suzuki, trans., *Laṅkāvatāra Sūtra*, p. 190.

tathāgatagarbha is originally pure and catalyzes the production of all wholesome actions, while the tathāgatagarbha as ālayavijñāna serves as the storehouse of unwholesome impulses (vāsanā) and is thus defiled. Hence, "the
tathāgatagarbha is the cause for both the wholesome and the unwholesome;
therefore it can serve as the cause for birth and death in the six destinies."[13]
Even though the mind as tathāgatagarbha may be innately pure, it is so obscured by the conceptualizing tendencies of mind (parikalpa) and the attachment to the things of the mundane world (abhiniveśa) that the hapless individual mistakenly believes he in truth is defiled. The false impressions
created by that fundamental perceptual error are retained, that is, "stored,"
in the ālayavijñāna. It is through a transformation (parāvṛtti) of one's perception that this deception is corrected and the innate purity and integrality of
the tathāgatagarbha restored. Such a transformation principally involves
abandoning the inveterate tendency to perceive things always from the point
of view of oneself—what the Buddhists term the ego-conceit (asmimāna).
Finally reinstated to its originally pristine state, the mind is now known in
its pure guise as tathāgatagarbha and transcends the dichotomy between
production and extinction that governs the workings of the mundane
world.[14] The Laṅkāvatāra thus accepts the Yogācāra solution to the origin of
ignorance while nevertheless positing that that origin was nothing more
than a false construct, in keeping with Tathāgatagarbha theory.

It was, however, in East Asia that the most sustained attempts to synthesize these two disparate philosophies of mind were made. East Asian Buddhists seem to have been especially attracted to the tathāgatagarbha concept
because of its potential for justifying philosophically their concern with the
immanence of enlightenment.[15] Thus, while Tathāgatagarbha thought never
developed into a full-blown school in Indian Mahāyāna, it was at the core of
most of the sinitic schools of Buddhism, from Hua-yen to Ch'an. Elaborations of this strand of Mahāyāna are also found in many sinitic apocryphal
compositions—especially the Awakening of Faith, probably composed during the third quarter of the sixth century, and the Vajrasamādhi. Because of

---

See also the discussion in Shimizu Yōkō, "Nyūryōgakyō no shiki no sansōsetsu ni tsuite:
nyōraizō to arayashiki no dōshi o megutte," pp. 162–63.

[13] Ju Leng-ch'ieh ching 7, T 671.16.556b23–24; see Suzuki, trans., Laṅkāvatāra Sūtra, p. 190.
The six destinies are gods, aśuras, humans, animals, hungry ghosts, and hell denizens.

[14] For the soteriological process of the Laṅkāvatāra-sūtra, see Suzuki, trans., Laṅkāvatāra
Sūtra, pp. 190–92, Studies, pp. 182–86, and cf. pp. 105–106; see also Ju Leng-ch'ieh ching 7, T
671.16.556b–557a.

[15] For a discussion of this characteristic of the sinicized schools of Buddhism, see Gimello,
"Chih-yen," pp. 93–119.

the importance to the *Vajrasamādhi* of ideas that first appear in the *Awakening of Faith*, it is worth examining briefly that treatise's solution to the ālaya-vijñāna/tathāgatagarbha problem.

The *Awakening of Faith* attempts to merge Tathāgatagarbha and Yogācāra thought by positing that the one mind may be bifurcated for heuristic purposes into two aspects: the true-thusness (*chen-ju*; Kor. *chinyŏ*) and production-and-extinction (*sheng-mieh*; Kor. *saengmyŏl*) aspects, corresponding respectively to ultimate (*paramārtha*) and conventional (*saṃvṛti*) truths, or the unconditioned (*asaṃskṛta*) and conditioned (*saṃskṛta*) realms. Thusness (tathatā) is in turn also twofold: empty of either self-nature or defilements, but also full of the myriads of wholesome qualities that comprise enlightenment.[16] This characterization of the absolute aspect of mind as being both empty and full is a clear indication that true thusness is construed as the equivalent of the tathāgatagarbha, for which a similar distinction is also known from Indian scriptures.[17] This same equation of thusness and tathāgatagarbha is also drawn in the main Indian treatise on Tathāgatagarbha thought, *Ratnagotravibhāga*, where tainted thusness (*samalā tathatā*) is tathāgatagarbha while untainted thusness (*nirmalā tathatā*) is the realization of the dharmakāya.[18]

In addition to being simply thus, however, the one mind is also said to be subject to "production and extinction," one of the ways in which the Chinese translated the Indian term saṃsāra, the ordinary realm that is subject to continual life and death. This conventional aspect is the ālayavijñāna, which *Awakening of Faith* defines as "the intersection (*ho-ho*) of that which is not subject to production and extinction [the absolute] with that which is subject to production and extinction [the phenomenal, in such a way that] they are neither one nor different."[19] But because *Awakening of Faith* states explicitly that "the production-and-extinction aspect of mind [=ālaya-vijñāna] exists on the basis of the tathāgatagarbha,"[20] conventional states of mind always retain the potential to be transformed into the absolute mind of true thusness. This transformation takes place through a process of actualization of enlightenment (*shih-chüeh*; Kor. *sigak*)—undertaking religious

---

[16] *Ch'i-hsin lun*, T 1666.32.576a24–26; Hakeda, trans., *Awakening of Faith*, p. 34.

[17] See, for example, *Sheng-man ching* (*Śrīmālādevīsiṃhanāda-sūtra*), T 353.12.221c16–18; Wayman and Wayman, trans., *Lion's Roar*, p. 99.

[18] Takasaki, trans., *Ratnagotravibhāga*, p. 187; cf. *Chiu-ching i-sheng pao-hsing lun* 2, T 1611.31.827a1–4.

[19] *Ch'i-hsin lun*, T 1666.32.576b8–9; after Gregory's translation in "Theodicy," p. 73.

[20] *Ch'i-hsin lun*, T 1666.32.576b8.

cultivation, specifically calmness and insight meditation (*chih-kuan*; Kor. *chigwan*; Skt. *śamatha-vipaśyanā*), and no-thought (*wu-nien*; Kor. *munyŏm*) practice. At the completion of this actualization process, however, one realizes that the enlightenment one has achieved through practice is in fact identical to the enlightened dharmakāya that has always been innate—what the text terms "original enlightenment" (*pen-chüeh*; Kor. *pon'gak*). The difference between these two types of enlightenment is but a matter of perception: the innate luminosity and purity of the tathāgatagarbha and dharmakāya are seen as "original" (viz., "intrinsic") by the saints, but as something that must be "actualized" by the ordinary person.

The *Awakening of Faith*'s uses of tathāgatagarbha and ālayavijñāna differ somewhat from those found in Indian materials. Tathāgatagarbha, as seen previously, would typically be construed as more concerned with soteriological issues—the possibility of enlightenment. The *Awakening of Faith*, however, gives it more of an ontological bent: tathāgatagarbha is the singular reality of absolute existence as seen by both the deluded individual (viz., as tathāgatagarbha) and the enlightened saint (viz., as dharmakāya). In an Indian Buddhist context, the ālayavijñāna is usually more concerned with issues of ontology, since it provides the justification for the individual's existence in the world of saṃsāra. But in the *Awakening of Faith* the ālayavijñāna is instead treated soteriologically as original and actualized enlightenment. Hence, the convergences between tathāgatagarbha and ālayavijñāna in the *Awakening of Faith* ultimately force the collapse of ontology into soteriology: mastery of the conventional production-and-extinction realm ( = ālayavijñāna) through the actualization of enlightenment leads back full circle to the original enlightenment that is absolute thusness ( = tathāgatagarbha).[21] In turn, soteriology is given an ontological grounding not found in Indian Tathāgatagarbha theory, providing a means of justifying the sinitic view that the ordinary world could serve as the ground of enlightenment.

When the deluded sentient being finally completes the process of actualizing his enlightenment, he finds that his ordinary state of mind is nothing more than his intrinsic enlightenment that has always been present. Just as from the absolute standpoint of the saint the potential for enlightenment represented by the tathāgatagarbha is seen in its full glory as dharmakāya, from the conventional standpoint of the ordinary person the state of saṃsāra

---

[21] My analysis here of the synthesis created in *Awakening of Faith* between tathāgatagarbha and ālayavijñāna is inspired by Peter Gregory's "The Problem of Theodicy in the *Awakening of Faith*," though my placement of the various categories differs slightly.

is "revisioned" through the process of actualization of enlightenment until it is seen in its full glory as nirvāṇa. This hermeneutic allows the author of the *Awakening of Faith* to merge the teachings of tathāgatagarbha and ālayavijñāna: "The mind, though pure in its self nature from the beginning [=true-thusness aspect, or tathāgatagarbha], is accompanied by ignorance [=production-and-extinction aspect, or ālayavijñāna]."[22] The relationship between these two aspects of mind in *Awakening of Faith* is diagrammed in figure 3.1.

The *Awakening of Faith*'s treatment of tathāgatagarbha and ālayavijñāna was extremely influential in the composition of the *Vajrasamādhi*. Written approximately one century before the sūtra, we know that *Awakening of Faith* influenced the *Vajrasamādhi*, not vice versa. But the traditional exegetes were unaware of this chronology and regarded the *Vajrasamādhi* as the scriptural source of the one-mind/two-aspects hermeneutic outlined in the *Awakening of Faith*. This scenario was eminently plausible to the East Asian commentators, since śāstras like the *Awakening of Faith* were considered to be the elaboration of ideas originally preached by the Buddha in the sūtras. Wŏnhyo located the source of this hermeneutic in the following passage in chapter 2 of the *Vajrasamādhi*: "The nature of the mind of sentient beings is originally void and calm. The essence of the mind that is void and calm is free from form and characteristics."[23] In his exegesis of this passage, Wŏnhyo interprets "void and calm" as the one mind, "the mind of sentient beings" as the production-and-extinction aspect, and "free from form and characteristics" as the true-thusness aspect. But because the production-and-extinction aspect is that through which the true-thusness aspect is revealed, the *Vajrasamādhi* says that "the nature of the mind of sentient beings is originally void and calm." However, Wŏnhyo clarifies, "the essences of those two aspects are nondual and, therefore, they are both nothing more than the dharma of the one mind."[24] This "dharma of the one mind," which is the tathāgatagarbha, is then said to be "calm and motionless"—characteristics identical to those attributed to the vajrasamādhi, the special absorption after which the text is named.[25] Wŏnhyo finally sees the sūtra culminating in a thoroughgoing fusion of all Buddhist teachings in the tathāgatagarbha,[26] il-

22 *Ch'i-hsin lun*, T 1666.32.577c2–3; Hakeda, trans., p. 50.
23 *VS*, chap. 2, after n. 12.
24 *KSGR* 1, p. 966a4–9.
25 For the passages see respectively *VS*, chap. 2, after n. 15; *VS*, chap. 1, before n. 3.
26 *KSGR* 1, p. 963c8.

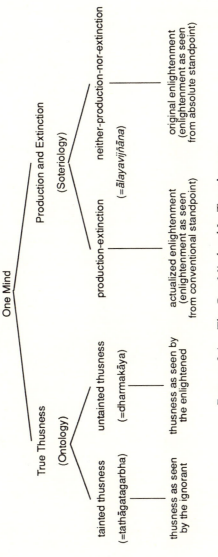

FIGURE 3.1.    The One Mind and Its Two Aspects

lustrating that he considered Tathāgatagarbha thought to be the very core of the text.

Wŏnhyo similarly found in chapter 4 of the *Vajrasamādhi* the scriptural basis for the *Awakening of Faith*'s crucial twofold gnoseology of "original enlightenment" and "actualized enlightenment":

> The original enlightenment of each and every sentient being is constantly enlightening all sentient beings by means of that one enlightenment, prompting them all to regain their original enlightenment. They become enlightened to the fact that all the affective consciousnesses are void, calm, and unproduced.[27]

In Wŏnhyo's interpretation,

> This passage gives a thorough elucidation of the two kinds of enlightenments: original and actualized. "The original enlightenment of each and every sentient being" is the meaning of original enlightenment. "They become enlightened to the fact that all the affective consciousnesses are void, calm, and unproduced" is the meaning of actualized enlightenment. This [juxtaposition of phrases] elucidates the fact that the actualized enlightenment is in fact identical to the original enlightenment."[28]

It is also interesting to note that Wŏnhyo has managed to find actualized enlightenment in the *Vajrasamādhi*, even though the term, while perhaps implicit in the above passage, is never explicitly mentioned anywhere. When a text served their purposes, East Asian exegetes often displayed an uncanny ability to find what they needed, no matter how vague the reference. Even given this caveat, it is clear that the *Vajrasamādhi* contained enough points of

---

[27] *VS*, chap. 4, at n. 33. Original enlightenment, in fact, is an indigenous Chinese term, which appears in sūtra literature only in sinitic apocrypha; Lewis Lancaster, "Buddhist Apocryphal Words."

[28] *KSGR* 2, 978a23–26; cf. Chu-chen, *T'ung-tsung chi*, pp. 256d–257a. Yüan-ch'eng (*Chu-chieh* 2, p. 199b13–16) takes a somewhat different tack to this passage: "Because the previous fifth, sixth, and seventh consciousnesses are [marked by] mundane characteristics, they are affective consciousnesses. The eighth consciousness then contains both the mundane and transcendental. The ninth consciousness alone is transcendental. This passage means that one transmutes these mundane affective consciousnesses so that they access the transcendental pure nature." Yüan-ch'eng's reading of this passage is an apparent attempt to resurrect the southern Ti-lun school's bifurcation of the ālayavijñāna into both pure and impure aspects. This reading cannot be supported by *VS*, however, since in the following exchange Muju Bodhisattva states unequivocally that all eight consciousnesses are mundane ("Each and every one of the eight consciousnesses all arise conditioned by the sense spheres").

resonance with the *Awakening of Faith* to evoke for Wŏnhyo that śāstra's distinctive teachings. Given the telling Tathāgatagarbha orientation of both texts, it should come as no surprise that Wŏnhyo would view them as having a single pedigree.

The nonduality of the original and actualized enlightenments, such as was posited in the *Awakening of Faith*, is also upheld in the *Vajrasamādhi*. A passage elsewhere in the fourth chapter states:

> When one is enlightened to the fact that thoughts are unproduced, one's mind becomes calm and serene. That is the inspiration of original enlightenment. That inspiration is motionless.[29]

Wŏnhyo tells us in his exegesis:

> "That is the inspiration of original enlightenment" [expresses] the understanding that there is no difference between actualized enlightenment and original enlightenment. As a śāstra [*Awakening of Faith*] states, "If there is a person who gains no-thought, he then knows the characteristics of the mind—its production, duration, decay, and extinction—because these [four characteristics] are all equal in [the state of] no-thought. And yet, in fact, there is no difference between the actualized enlightenment [and the state of original enlightenment that is realized through this attainment of no-thought]. This is because, when these four characteristics exist [i.e., function] in succession, they do not operate independently [because they each can be defined only in reference to each other]. They are originally equal and are identical to the one enlightenment."[30]
>
> Comment: [The statement] "in fact, there is no difference between the actualized enlightenment . . ." explains the passage in the *Vajrasamādhi* that this "is the inspiration of original enlightenment." "When these four characteristics exist in succession, they do not operate independently. They are originally equal . . .": this explains the passage in this sūtra "that inspiration is motionless."[31]

Wŏnhyo also perceives in chapter 2 the antecedents of original and actualized enlightenments in two different perspectives the *Vajrasamādhi* advocates toward the voidness of all phenomena. The *Vajrasamādhi* says:

[29] *VS*, chap. 4, after n. 47.
[30] For the relevant passage, see *Ch'i-hsin lun*, *T* 1666.32.576c1–4; Hakeda, trans., *Awakening*, p. 40.
[31] *KSGR* 2, p. 982a2–10.

It enables all those sentient beings to leave behind mind and self, for both mind and self are originally void and calm. If they attain voidness of mind, then that mind will not illusorily project anything. Free from all illusory projections, they will then attain nonproduction.[32]

Wŏnhyo explicates this process in terms of the original and actualized enlightenments. The first part of the passage, "if they attain voidness of mind, then that mind will not illusorily project anything," refers to original enlightenment.

When one penetrates to the fact that the mind and self are void, one straightaway obtains the void and calm mind of original enlightenment. This void and calm mind originally leaves behind the clinging subject, and because the clinging subject is left behind, there are fundamentally no illusory projections. No illusory projections means that there is no more deception or falsity.

Actualized enlightenment is described in the passage "free from illusory projections, they will then attain nonproduction."

When one gains this void and calm mind of original enlightenment, the discriminations [wrought by] the clinging subject are no longer produced. This is because, in accordance with the mental state that is thereby achieved, there are no longer any illusory projections. . . . In this wise, the unproduced state of mind achieved via actualized [enlightenment] corresponds to that principle which is originally void, calm, and unmodifiable.[33]

The *Vajrasamādhi*'s analysis of tathāgatagarbha also recalls a distinction the *Awakening of Faith* makes between the calm, unchanging essence of the mind (*t'i*; Kor. *ch'e*) and its active, adaptable functioning (*yung*; Kor. *yong*). In chapter 7, the tathāgatagarbha is equated with the "original edge of reality" (*pon silche/pen shih-chi*) that is beyond all distinctions—the equivalent of original enlightenment, or the essence. But tathāgatagarbha is also the active functioning of that original enlightenment—the "beneficial power of that fundamental faculty"—which induces the adept to access his inherent enlightenment. By completing three types of practice, the cultivator is certain to "access the tathāgatagarbha." Accessing the tathāgatagarbha brings in

---

[32] *VS*, chap. 2, at n. 12.
[33] *KSGR* 1, p. 965c3–21.

turn four kinds of knowledge: fixed knowledge, which accords with thusness; adaptable knowledge, which applies the appropriate expedients necessary to overcome defilements; nirvāṇic knowledge, which overcomes sensory attachments; and ultimate knowledge, which perfects the path. Once the cultivator is adept at applying these four types of knowledge, he is then able to make use of "three great matters": recognition of the mutual interfusion of the internal consciousnesses with the external sensory realms; a special type of absorption of mind, the analytical suppression (*pratisaṃkhyā-nirodha*), which is accessible only to the enlightened; and the ability to cultivate concentration and wisdom in conjunction with the altruistic aspiration of compassion, ensuring that his practice will be to the benefit of both himself and others. The tathāgatagarbha is thus both the "original edge of reality" that is beyond cultivation (= essence), as well as the specific types of wisdom and mystical talents that are the byproducts of enlightenment (= function). In its description of this sequence, however, the *Vajrasamādhi* notes that "accessing the tathāgatagarbha has no access point; it is like [the enigmatic way in which] a sprout matures into a fruit."[34] This caveat ensures that the student will not mistakenly presume that the realization of the immanence of enlightenment is a gradualistic process. Rather, actualization of enlightenment is as ineffable as original enlightenment: both are nondual, in the same way that essence and function are reduced to one in *Awakening of Faith*. Hence, original and actualized enlightenments are both subsumed in the tathāgatagarbha.

The *Vajrasamādhi* also continues the tendency seen previously in *Laṅkā-vatāra-sūtra* and *Awakening of Faith* to synthesize tathāgatagarbha with ālayavijñāna. The *Awakening of Faith*'s transformation of ālayavijñāna into the true thusness that is tathāgatagarbha is broached in the concluding verse to chapter 7: "Transmuting both the subject and object of clinging,/ He accesses the tathāgatagarbha."[35] "Subject" here may be construed as the ālayavijñāna, the basis for the mistaken belief that there is a perceiving self, while "object" would refer to the myriad of sensory objects into which the world is differentiated by the affective consciousnesses. Once both ālayavijñāna and the sense realms are "transformed" or "evolved" (*parivṛtti*) back

---

[34] This paragraph is a synopsis of *VS*, chap. 7, between n. 113 and n. 118. For the *t'i-yung* distinction in *Awakening of Faith*, see *Ch'i-hsin lun*, *T* 1666.32.575c; Hakeda, trans., *Awakening*, pp. 29–30. For Wŏnhyo's use of this distinction in explicating the treatise see Sung Bae Park, "A Comparative Study of Wŏnhyo and Fa-tsang on the Ta-Ch'eng Ch'i-Hsin Lun," pp. 579–97.

[35] *VS*, chap. 7, after n. 127.

into the natural purity of the mind, the adept will find his original enlightenment restored to its innate condition ("he accesses the tathāgatagarbha").[36]

The most precise description of the *Vajrasamādhi*'s interpretation of tathāgatagarbha appears not in the eponymous seventh chapter, but instead in
chapter 2, "The Practice of Nonproduction": "The tathāgatagarbha is that
characteristic of discriminative awareness, subject to production and extinction, which conceals the principle (*i/li*) so that it is not made manifest. The
nature of the tathāgatagarbha is calm and motionless."[37] This terse yet co-
gent definition alludes to one of the major aspects of tathāgatagarbha: that
of "concealment" (*saṃdhi/abhisaṃdhi*; *yin-fu*). Concealment refers to the second of the ten meanings of tathāgatagarbha given in *Fo-hsing lun* (Exposition
of the buddha-nature), a treatise on Tathāgatagarbha thought traditionally
ascribed to the Indian exegete Vasubandhu, but perhaps composed in China.
There, tathāgatagarbha is described as "that store (*garbha*) which conceals
and covers."[38] As "Vasubandhu" explains:

> The second meaning, "that store which conceals and covers over (*yin-fu*),"
> means that because *the tathāgata conceals himself so that he does not appear* (Ch.
> *tzu-yin pu-hsien*; Kor. *chaŭn purhyŏn*) [emphasis added], it can be called a
> "store." . . . Before the tathāgata-nature comes to reside on the path, it is
> concealed and covered over by the defilements, so that sentient beings cannot
> see it. Hence, it is called a "store."[39]

"Vasubandhu"'s description here implies two different connotations of concealment: first, the tathāgatagarbha as an active agent of liberation, secreting
itself away within the minds of sentient beings so as to motivate them soteriologically; and second, tathāgatagarbha in its more passive sense as concealed, and thus obscured, by the defilements. It is the passive denotation
that is most commonly seen in Tathāgatagarbha literature, from the earliest

[36] This process is discussed in detail in Takasaki, *Nyōraizō shisō*, pp. 196, 770–71. My treatment here is suggested by Wŏnhyo's rather laconic exegesis on this passage; see *KSGR* 3, p.
1001a12–13. Chu-chen's analysis is slightly different. He takes the object as the "dharma of
calm extinction" and the subject as the "mind of nirvāṇa." *T'ung-tsung chi* 10, p. 285c.

[37] *VS*, chap. 2, before n. 16. Wŏnhyo takes the first half of the definition ("that characteristic of discriminative awareness, subject to production and extinction") as the void tathāgatagarbha and the second half ("conceals the principle so that it is not made manifest") as the
nonvoid tathāgatagarbha. *KSGR* 1, p. 969a10–13.

[38] *Fo-hsing lun* 2, *T* 1610.31.795c24; for the problem of its authorship of *Fo-hsing lun*, see
Takasaki, *Ratnagotravibhāga*, p. 47.

[39] *Fo-hsing lun* 2, *T* 1610.31.796a19–20, 23–25.

stratum onward.[40] In the *Vajrasamādhi*, however, the interpretation tends toward a more active presentation. There the tathāgatagarbha is said to function not as the hapless object that is hidden, but instead as the active agent that conceals the "principle" ( = dharmakāya). As the concealer, tathāgatagarbha thus works at revealing that principle to the adept through the process of actualizing his enlightenment, as seen previously.

Wording most clearly evocative of the *Vajrasamādhi*'s active aspect of the tathāgatagarbha is found in Wŏnhyo's commentary to the *Awakening of Faith*. Wŏnhyo's own description of this aspect states: "It is in this aspect [of production and extinction] that the nature of the tathāgata *is concealed and not made manifest* [emphasis added]. This is called the tathāgatagarbha."[41] This passage differs from that found in the *Vajrasamādhi* by a single, homophonous logograph: for Wŏnhyo's "is concealed and not made manifest" (*ŭn i purhyŏn*) *VS* gives instead "conceals the principle so that it is not made manifest" (*ŭni purhyŏn*). This strong similarity intimates that the author may have been trying to appeal directly to the wording of Wŏnhyo's authoritative commentary in constructing his text, perhaps suggesting that Silla scholiasts, if not Wŏnhyo himself, were the target audience of *VS*.

The second half of the *Vajrasamādhi*'s definition of tathāgatagarbha as "subject to production and extinction" also resonates with a number of other Tathāgatagarbha texts. The *Śrīmālā* says, for example, "Production and extinction [ = saṃsāra] depends on the tathāgatagarbha. . . . Because there is a tathāgatagarbha, it is said that there is production and extinction."[42] *Laṅkāvatāra-sūtra* remarks, "If there were no such thing as a tathāgatagarbha-ālayavijñāna there would be no production and no extinction."[43] But it is *Awakening of Faith* once again that is closest to the language of our text: "Depending on the tathāgatagarbha there exists the mind that is subject to

---

[40] The seminal text of the doctrine, the *Tathāgatagarbha-sūtra*, for example, says, "All sentient beings have the tathāgatagarbha . . . which is covered over and hidden (*fu-pi*) by all the defilements." See *Ta-fang-teng ju-lai-tsang ching*, *T* 666.16.457c25–26. Another early Tathāgatagarbha scripture, *Śrīmālādevīsiṃhanāda-sūtra*, offers a similar interpretation of tathāgatagarbha: "this dharmakāya of the tathāgata when not free from the store of defilement (*avinirmuktakleśakośa*) is referred to as the tathāgatagarbha." See *Sheng-man ching*, *T* 353.12.221c11; rendering by Wayman and Wayman, trans., *Lion's Roar*, p. 98. This passage, of course, need not imply that dharmakāya and tathāgatagarbha are identical; rather both should be viewed instead as variant aspects of the unitary thusness, where defiled thusness is tathāgatagarbha and undefiled thusness dharmakāya. See Wayman and Wayman, trans., *Lion's Roar*, p. 98 n. 83.

[41] *Kisillon-so* 1, *T* 1844.44.206c19–20.

[42] *Sheng-man ching*, *T* 353.12.104b.

[43] *Ju Leng-ch'ieh ching*, 556c28–29, cf. Suzuki, trans., *Laṅkāvatāra Sūtra*, p. 192.

production and extinction."[44] Indeed, the *Vajrasamādhi*'s description of tathāgatagarbha as "a discriminative knowledge subject to production and extinction" seems remarkably parallel to the *Awakening of Faith*, wherein discriminative thought is said to create the false distinctions between dharmas
that the ordinary person perceives, creating in turn production and extinction.[45]

The pedigree of the *Vajrasamādhi* as a Tathāgatagarbha text is clearly established by these obvious affinities with the established literature of that
branch of Mahāyāna thought. A major advance the sūtra makes in treating
the concept is its attempt to bring together more passive descriptions of the
tathāgatagarbha as obscured by discriminative thought, with explicit references to it as an active agent that conceals the principle. Tathāgatagarbha in
the *Vajrasamādhi* is clearly not a benign force, submissively acquiescing to
the vagaries of defilements and discrimination; it instead secrets itself away
inside ignorance and taints so as to beckon the benighted, ordinary person
toward enlightenment. The clarification the *Vajrasamādhi* provides concerning the soteriological function of tathāgatagarbha, and especially its relationship to original and actualized enlightenments, is helpful too for understanding the East Asian penchant to see enlightenment as immanent in ordinary
life. But it is in the nexus the *Vajrasamādhi* creates between the tathāgatagarbha and two related concepts—amalavijñāna and vajrasamādhi—that its
principal contribution to Tathāgatagarbha thought is found.

## Amalavijñāna and the Innate Purity of Mind

A concept in the *Vajrasamādhi* closely related to tathāgatagarbha is that of a
ninth mode of consciousness beyond the eight ordinarily posited by the Yogācāra school. This is the so-called immaculate consciousness, or amalavijñāna. The doctrinal issues raised in treating amalavijñāna are closely akin
to those discussed in relation to tathāgatagarbha. With amalavijñāna, however, the emphasis is not so much on the dichotomy of ignorance and enlightenment as on its corollary of impurity and purity. Amalavijñāna stands
in much the same relationship to ālayavijñāna as did the tathāgatagarbha and
may be viewed as the intrusion of Tathāgatagarbha thought into the Yogācāra classification of consciousness. Such classifications were matters of

[44]  *Ch'i-hsin lun,*  T 1666.32.576b8.
[45]  See *Ch'i-hsin lun,*  T 1666.32.576a9–10.

considerable controversy in East Asian Buddhism,[46] especially between the northern and southern branches of the Chinese Ti-lun school, and the later She-lun (Mahāyānasaṃgraha) and Fa-hsiang (Yogācāra) schools. The *Vajrasamādhi* provides one of the more trenchant interpretations of the amalavijñāna, and its account is valuable for understanding the connections East Asians drew between Tathāgatagarbha and Yogācāra thought. Let me first outline briefly the development of the amalavijñāna doctrine before turning to the contributions of the *Vajrasamādhi* proper.[47]

The theory of amalavijñāna derives from debates within the so–called idealist branch of Mahāyāna philosophy concerning the nature of the mind as well as the relationship between the subjective realm of consciousness and the objective realms of the senses. The *Daśabhūmika-sūtra*, translated in the fifth century, had stated that the world was nothing more than a projection of the mind (*cittamātram idam yad idam traidhātukam*).[48] The significance of this position was first explored in Vasubandhu's commentary to this sūtra, the *Shih-ti-ching lun* (\**Daśabhūmikasūtrôpadeśa*), commonly known in East Asia by its abbreviated titled, *Ti-lun*, from which the school that emphasized its exegesis derived its name. It was through the *Ti-lun* that the Chinese were introduced to the quintessential concept in the Yogācāra analysis of mind: the ālayavijñāna, the repository within consciousness of the seeds that produced the objective world.

Controversies soon arose, however, over the nature of the ālayavijñāna, which led in turn to debates over the actual number of consciousnesses and their correct classification. Such controversies began in large part because of internal inconsistencies in the *Ti-lun*'s own analysis of the ālayavijñāna. In some places, Vasubandhu suggests that the ālayavijñāna is the tainted source from which saṃsāra, with all its defilements, arises.[49] Elsewhere, he implies

[46] In the context of *VS*, one of the more insightful struggles with these different taxonomies of consciousness appears in Chih-yen's (602–668) *Hua-yen wu-shih yao wen-ta* 1, *T* 1869.45.522c–523a. Chih-yen, writing around the same time *VS* is composed and drawing from many of the same sources, suggests that tathāgatagarbha can be described with reference to either an eight- or nine-consciousness taxonomy (p. 522c24–25).

[47] My account of the significance of these issues is especially indebted to Robert Gimello, "Chih-yen," pp. 212–28, 313–28. Gimello's work is arguably the most insightful and erudite treatment of the sinicization of Buddhist thought to appear in any language. Some of the same material is covered also in Diana Paul, *Philosophy of Mind in Sixth-Century China*, pp. 46–71.

[48] See *Shih-ti ching T* 286.10.514c26; *Shih-ti ching lun, T* 1522.26.169a15. See also Gimello, "Chih-yen," p. 291, for further references to Chinese sources and Sanskrit textual variants. Cf. the parallel passage in *Ch'i-hsin lun, T* 1666.32.576a5, Hakeda, trans., *Awakening of Faith*, p. 31.

[49] "Name and form arise in conjunction with the ālayavijñāna." *Shih-ti ching lun* 3, *T* 1522.26.142b13; Gimello, "Chih-yen," p. 287.

instead that thusness (tathatā) and the *ālaya* are coextensive, suggesting that the ālayavijñāna is fundamentally pure.[50] Determining the nature of the āla-yavijñāna would in turn affect the status of the world evolved from that storehouse: is the world produced by a tainted ālayavijñāna, and thus intrin-sically defiled?; or is it transformed from pristine thusness instead, and thus instrinsically pure? Answering these questions was made all the more diffi-cult by the support for both positions found in other Yogācāra-oriented scriptures translated around the same time as the *Daśabhūmika*, such as the *Saṃdhinirmocana-sūtra* (*T* 675) and the *Laṅkāvatāra-sūtra* (*T* 671).

Chinese exegetes in the Ti-lun school fervently debated the nature of the ālayavijñāna. The northern branch of the Ti-lun school, deriving from teachers with Yogācāra predilections, is usually depicted as taking the posi-tion that the ālayavijñāna is fundamentally impure: it is a tainted source that produces only defiled dharmas. This view that the ālayavijñāna is intrinsi-cally corrupted later becomes emblematic of the Chinese Yogācāra, or Fa-hsiang, teachings of Hsüan-tsang and K'uei-chi (632–682). In distinction to this position was that of the southern branch of the Ti-lun school, deriving from scholars who had affinities with Tathāgatagarbha thought. While our knowledge of the views of the southern scholiasts is far from adequate, they seem to have placed the ālayavijñāna as the last of a sevenfold schema of consciousness, interpreting it as a combination of both pure and impure ele-ments. Ālayavijñāna in their view was considered to be the functioning (*yung*) of thusness itself and thus pure; but the ālaya was subject to the same law of conditioned origination as were both the "evolutionary" or "trans-formed" sensory consciousnesses (*chüan-shih*) and all worldly objects, and therefore it could also be considered impure as well.[51] In this issue of purity versus impurity, the philosophical debate over the nature of the ālayavijñāna intersects with the strong partiality East Asian exegetes were already dis-playing toward Tathāgatagarbha thought. The debate thus focusses not solely on the nature of the ālayavijñāna, but also on the nexus between āla-yavijñāna and the tathāgatagarbha, as well as the possible implications of any such interrelationship in developing a viable praxis.

---

[50] E.g., "[The eighth-stage bodhisattva] abides well in the suchness of the ālayavijñāna"; *Shih-ti-ching lun* 10, *T* 1522.26.180a20. See the characterization of the ramifications of this de-bate over the nature of ālayavijñāna in Stanley Weinstein, "The Concept of *Ālaya-vijñāna* in Pre-T'ang Chinese Buddhism," p. 39; Gimello, "Chih-yen," p. 291.

[51] My account of the varying sectarian positions on the ālayavijñāna is indebted to Gimello, "Chih-yen," pp. 294–97, Weinstein, "*Ālaya-vijñāna*," pp. 40–43; Paul, *Philosophy of Mind*, pp. 46–52; and Walter Liebenthal, "New Light on the Mahāyāna Śraddhotpāda Śāstra," pp. 157, 209.

A striking advance in resolving these issues was made by Paramārtha (499–569), an important Indian translator of many seminal works on Yogācāra, Tathāgatagarbha, and Abhidharma philosophy. In his personal writings, Paramārtha condemned the ālayavijñāna as being fundamentally impure, positing instead that only a ninth mode of consciousness—which he termed the amalavijñāna or "immaculate consciousness"—was pure.[52] The most sustained analysis of the amalavijñāna is made in the She-lun school, an exegetical school that formed around a reading of Paramārtha's translation of Asaṅga's *Mahāyānasaṃgraha* (*She Ta-sheng lun*).

Although present scholarly consensus accepts that the concept of amalavijñāna derives from Paramārtha,[53] there is still considerable controversy as to what its Indian antecedents, if any, may have been. David Ruegg has suggested possible parallels between amalavijñāna and the notion of immaculate gnosis (*amalajñāna*) found in the Tathāgatagarbha treatise, *Ratnagotravibhāga*, which calls that gnosis stable (*dhruva*), tranquil (*śiva*), eternal (*śāśvata*), and immutable (*acyuta*).[54] Wŏnch'ŭk (613–695), a Korean expatriate disciple of Hsüan-tsang and a contemporary of the author of the *Vajrasamādhi*, suggests an Indian Vijñānavāda pedigree through Paramārtha in his *Chieh-shen-mi*

---

[52] See Chan-jan's account of Paramārtha's role in developing the amalavijñāna concept in *Chih-kuan chüan-hsing ch'uan-hung chüeh* 3a, *T* 1912.46.221c2–9; quoted in Paul, *Philosophy of Mind*, p. 70. It is principally in an anthology of Paramārtha's own works, the *Wu-hsiang lun*, that the amalavijñāna is treated; see Paul, p. 94. For a convenient survey of the theory of amalavijñāna as attributed to Paramārtha, see Paul, pp. 6–7, 108–11, 160; and for background on the controversy within Chinese Yogācāra concerning the various schemes of consciousnesses, see Paul, pp. 46–71, summarizing the work of Yūki Reimon, Fukaura Seibun, and Sakaino Kōyō (for which see pp. 196–97 n. 55). Other summaries of amalavijñāna doctrine appear in Ruegg, *Tathāgatagarbha*, pp. 439–44, and Eric Frauwallner, "Amalavijñānam und Ālaya-vijñānam," pp. 148–59. Perhaps the most complete treatment of the meaning and significance of the amalavijñāna is found in Fukaura Seibun, *Yuishikigaku kenkyū*, vol. 1, pp. 188–228. For other sources, and Walter Liebenthal's thoughts on the topic with reference to *VS*, see Liebenthal, pp. 368–69n.

[53] This view that amalavijñāna was the innovation of Paramārtha has been challenged by Yūki Reimon. Yūki suggests instead that the nine-consciousness schema derives instead from a passage in the *Laṅkāvatāra-sūtra*, which Ching-ying Hui-yüan used to justify a taxonomy of either eight or nine consciousnesses: "One can also theorize that there are nine [consciousnesses]. This is because the 'Sagāthākam chapter' of the *Laṅkāvatāra-sūtra* states, 'The eight or nine types of consciousness are like waves on water.' " *Ta-sheng i chang* 3, *T* 1851.44.530c8–9; for the *Laṅka* citation see *Ju Leng-ch'ieh ching* 9, *T* 671.16.565b21; Suzuki, trans., *Laṅkāvatāra Sūtra*, p. 227. See discussion in Yūki Reimon, "Shina Yuishiki gakushijō ni okeru Ryōgashi no chii," pp. 29, 37–42; and see Weinstein, "Ālaya-vijñāna," pp. 47 and 50 n. 41; Takamine Ryō-shū, *Kegon shisōshi*, pp. 121–23. For general background on the controversy, see Yoshifumi Ueda, "Two Main Streams of Thought in Yogācāra Philosophy," pp. 155–65; and Paul, *Philosophy of Mind*, pp. 196–97 n. 55, who rejects Yūki's argument.

[54] See discussion in Ruegg, *Tathāgatagarbha*, pp. 440–44, citing *Ratnagotravibhāga* ii.26 (Takasaki, trans., p. 321).

*ching shu* (Kor. *Haesimmilgyŏng-so*; Commentary to the *Saṃdhinirmocāna-sū-tra*): "According to the school of Sthiramati, the ninth *amala*-consciousness is essentially thusness. As object, it is tathatā and the edge of reality (*bhūta-koṭi*); as subject, it is amalavijñāna and original enlightenment."[55] Since Para-mārtha is presumed to have been a disciple of Sthiramati, it may be that he was taught something at least akin to the idea of amalavijñāna during his studies in India. But there is no Sanskrit or Middle Indic source that would clinch the Indian provenance of the term, and Wŏnch'ŭk may simply have been extrapolating an Indian origin for the concept based on his knowledge of Paramārtha's heritage.

Paramārtha's conception of amalavijñāna ultimately derives from Tathā-gatagarbha thought, which similarly emphasizes the inherent purity of the mind.[56] Paramārtha used amalavijñāna synonymously with the more con-ventional Yogācāra concept of *pariniṣpanna*, the "perfected nature" of con-sciousness, indicating that amalavijñāna was to be equated with the absolute reality of thusness (tathatā).[57] Amalavijñāna was therefore construed as the very basis of all eight consciousnesses, including the ālayavijñāna. Ālaya-vijñāna was conceived instead as merely a provisional description of the mind, which had meaning only in distinction to the other seven delusory consciousnesses. While ālayavijñāna served both to counter the mistaken be-lief that those consciousnesses existed in reality and to account for the arising of ignorance and defilements in the world, amalavijñāna was instead truth itself and was realized once the mistaken belief in the reality of the ālaya-vijñāna was corrected.[58] The ālayavijñāna may be the source of defilement and the ontological ground of saṃsāric existence, but knowledge of it would not conduce to enlightenment. The amalavijñāna, conversely, may have had no explicit ontological role, but it did serve as the principal catalyst of lib-eration.[59] One sees from this account that amalavijñāna and tathāgatagarbha

---

[55] *Chieh-shen-mi ching shu*, ZZ 34.360c7–11; translation adapted from Gimello, "Chih-yen," p. 313; see discussion in Takamine, *Kegon shisōshi*, pp. 90ff. It was through this commentary, which was one of the first exegetical texts translated into Tibetan, that the Tibetans also came to recognize the theory of nine consciousnesses as being ascribed to Paramārtha. See discussion in Inaba Shōju, "On Chos-grub's Translation of the *Chieh-shên-mi-ching-shu*," pp. 110–11.

[56] For the Tathāgatagarbha influence on amalavijñāna, see Gimello, "Chih-yen," pp. 323–28; Paul, *Philosophy of Mind*, pp. 143–45; and Liebenthal, p. 373 with reference to *VS* in specific.

[57] "The perfect nature is precisely the amalavijñāna"; *Chüan-shih lun*, T 1587.31.62c19; translated, and implications discussed, in Gimello, "Chih-yen," p. 323; see also Paul, *Philosophy of Mind*, p. 160.

[58] "It is through counteracting (*tui-chih*) the ālayavijñāna that one realizes amalavijñāna." *Chüeh-ting-tsang lun*, T 1584.30.1020b; cited in Gimello, "Chih-yen," p. 326.

[59] "The ālayavijñāna is the root of all defilements but does not serve as the root of the at-

occupied virtually the same position vis-à-vis the ālayavijñāna. By equating amalavijñāna with *pariniṣpanna* in his discussion of the nature of consciousness, Paramārtha places the tathāgatagarbha at the hierarchical apex of his philosophy of mind. Conceptually, amalavijñāna provides a means of synthesizing these two philosophical filiations of Mahāyāna: as "immaculate," amalavijñāna emulates the Tathāgatagarbha's emphasis on the innate purity of the mind; but as a form of "consciousness," it could be placed within the Yogācāra compartmentalization of the mind as a ninth mode of consciousness. This analysis thence became the hallmark of the She-lun school.

Ching-ying Hui-yüan (523–592), the main disciple of Fa-shang (495–580) in the southern Ti-lun lineage, drew on Paramārtha's insights to synthesize the variant positions of the Ti-lun and She-lun schools, which emphasized respectively the importance of the ālaya and amala vijñānas.[60] While essentially equating the two, Hui-yüan, following Paramārtha, is able to distinguish them by saying that ālayavijñāna is true only in distinction to the illusory seven consciousnesses that precede it in the taxonomy; but amalavijñāna, as the basis of enlightenment, is true in and of itself. Thus, "the sole truth is but one: that is, the originally pure amalavijñāna."[61] But Hui-yüan goes much farther than had Paramārtha in coopting for the amalavijñāna the ālayavijñāna's role as the ontological substratum of all existence. Hui-yüan notes, for example, that "the mind's characteristic of true thusness is precisely the ninth consciousness, because the ninth consciousness is the essence of all dharmas."[62] Thus, by the end of the sixth century, the amalavijñāna no longer carried principally soteriological overtones but had assumed the ālayavijñāna's ontological role as well.

The use of amalavijñāna in synthesizing variant tendencies in Mahāyāna philosophy is particularly prominent in the *Vajrasamādhi*. All commentators to the sūtra have drawn attention to the pronounced syncretic focus of the text, and amalavijñāna serves many of the same purposes in the *Vajrasamādhi* as it did in the She-lun school, such as resolving the perceived differences between tathāgatagarbha and ālayavijñāna.

In traditional exegesis the *Vajrasamādhi* was often presumed to have been

---

tainment of the noble path. It is the amalavijñāna that serves as the support of that noble path." *Chueh-ting-tsang lun*, *T* 1584.30.1020b; translated in Gimello, "Chih-yen," p. 326.

[60] See Weinstein, "*Ālaya-vijñāna*," pp. 44ff; Gimello, "Chih-yen," pp. 328–35; Paul, *Philosophy of Mind*, pp. 52–64, 68.

[61] *Ta-sheng i chang* 3, *T* 1851.44.530c11–14, cited in Gimello, "Chih-yen," p. 335.

[62] Hui-yüan, *Ta-sheng ch'i-hsin lun i-shu* 1a, *T* 1843.44.179a21–22; noted in Gimello, "Chih-yen," p. 335.

the scriptural source of the concept of amalavijñāna. Wŏnhyo in fact states explicitly that Paramārtha derived the theory of a ninth consciousness from the following passage in chapter 4:

"Lord! Through what inspiring transmutation may one transmute all the affective consciousnesses of sentient beings so that they access the amala[vijñāna]?"
"All the buddhas, the tathāgatas, constantly transmute all the consciousnesses by means of the one enlightenment so that they will access the amala."[63]

Wŏnhyo says in explanation,

"All the affective consciousnesses" are precisely the eight consciousnesses. "Amala" is the ninth consciousness. The Trepiṭaka Paramārtha's theory of the ninth consciousness is based upon this passage [in the Vajrasamādhi].[64]

The same claim is found in the Sŏk Mahayŏn-ron (Exegesis of the Mahāyāna), an eighth-century apocryphal commentary to the Awakening of Faith, attributed to a Korean monk named Wŏlch'ung (d.u.).[65] But nowhere in his own works does Paramārtha ever cite the Vajrasamādhi, and it remains controversial, as seen previously, that it even was Paramārtha who coined the term amalavijñāna. At the very least, we now know that it was impossible that the Vajrasamādhi could have influenced Paramārtha, since the sūtra was composed some one hundred years after his death.

Given the centrality of amalavijñāna in medieval Buddhist intellectual discourse, it is probably inevitable that the concept would appear in a text that partially catered to scholastic interests. The Vajrasamādhi, however, has little sustained treatment of amalavijñāna itself, or of its relationship with ālayavijñāna and tathāgatagarbha, such as one might expect if the author's intent were solely to resolve sectarian controversies over the concept; instead, they seek to orient the discussion toward matters involving actual practice. If rather jejune from a learned standpoint, the text's analysis of amalavijñāna

---

[63]  VS, chap. 4, at n. 32.
[64]  KSGR 2, p. 978a6–8; this has been noted by Ko Ikchin, p. 229 and n. 21.
[65]  Sŏk Mahayŏn-ron, T 1668.32.611c23–27. Sŏk Mahayŏn-ron (Ch. Shih Mo-ho-yen lun; T 1668) is attributed to Nāgārjuna and was alleged to have been translated by Vṛddhimata (d.u.) et al., sometime after A.D. 401. The authenticity of the treatise is discussed by Mochizuki (Kyōten seiritsu, pp. 651–70), who concludes that it was written in Korea sometime between 720 and 779, apparently by Wŏlch'ung.

will have important implications for understanding the doctrinal underpinnings of Ch'an meditation.

The *Vajrasamādhi* displays some ambivalence as to the respective nature of the ālaya and amala vijñānas. In chapter 4, the *Vajrasamādhi* portrays all the consciousnesses, up through and including the eighth, as being defiled. These are called "affective consciousnesses" that must be "constantly transmuted so that they will access the *amala*." Whatever special status other texts might accord the ālayavijñāna as the ground of existence, the *Vajrasamādhi* nevertheless relegates it to the same level as the delusory consciousnesses: it is subject to discrimination and thus inextricably bound up with the mundane world of the senses.[66] This judgment shares close affinities with the She-lun position on the nature of consciousness, which rejected the ālayavijñāna as impure.

Elsewhere, however, the *Vajrasamādhi* is rather less clear-cut concerning the ālayavijñāna's defiled nature. In chapter 5, for example, the eighth and ninth consciousnesses are treated in almost identical terms, both becoming "limpid" and "pure" once the mind is freed from its dichotomizing tendencies (*punbyŏl/fen-pieh*; *vikalpa*). After the outflows (*āsrava*) from the ālayavijñāna are stemmed, all discrimination will vanish and the bodhisattva will realize the voidness of dharmas. Through such nondiscriminative wisdom (*mubunbyŏl-chi/wu-fen-pieh chih*; *nirvikalpajñāna*), taints are abandoned and the bodhisattva realizes original enlightenment, which is the amalavijñāna. Because the ālayavijñāna is then no longer swayed by sensory experiences, the sixth and seventh consciousnesses, which process those perceptions and interpret them in terms of self, will never arise again either.[67] None of the sectarian perspectives outlined previously on the nature of the mind seems quite to correspond to what one finds here. If anything, we are closest to the *Awakening of Faith*'s interpretation of ālayavijñāna and tathāgatagarbha, in which the ordinary world is conceived as the ground of both ignorance and enlightenment.

Wŏnhyo's exegesis treats these two deepest forms of consciousness in terms of the She-lun school's analysis. He explicitly calls the penultimate eighth consciousness the basis of the outflows and equates the ninth consciousness with the original enlightenment, following a tautology drawn in

---

[66] "Each and every one of the eight consciousnesses is produced conditioned by the sense realms." *VS*, chap. 4, at n. 34.

[67] *VS*, chap. 5, at n. 82. My interpretation follows *KSGR* 2, p. 989b22–26.

the *Vajrasamādhi* itself.[68] Looking back at the ambiguous passages in the *Vajrasamādhi* in the light of Wŏnhyo's treatment, we see that amalavijñāna *cum* original enlightenment is the force that renders enlightenment accessible. As chapter 4 says, "The original enlightenment of each and every sentient being is constantly enlightening all sentient beings . . . , prompting them all to regain their original enlightenment."[69] Wŏnhyo also notes in his *Kisillon pyŏlgi* (Autocommentary to the *Awakening of Faith*) that "because of the influence of original enlightenment, [deluded thoughts] come to have a modicum of enlightened function (*kagyong/chüeh-yung*)."[70] The amalavijñāna as original enlightenment is therefore constantly acting on sentient beings, exerting a beneficial influence that ultimately will prompt those beings to rediscover their inherent enlightenment. This treatment of amalavijñāna as the catalyst of enlightenment corresponds to the active interpretation of the tathāgatagarbha followed elsewhere in the *Vajrasamādhi*.

The *Vajrasamādhi*'s discussion of amalavijñāna supports the view that this concept has its antecedents in Tathāgatagarbha, rather than Yogācāra, thought.[71] It also confirms the close association between amalavijñāna and the tathāgatagarbha that was such an important factor in Paramārtha's writings and in the She-lun analysis of consciousness. But the *Vajrasamādhi* is most concerned with the soteriological, rather than ontological, import of the term. These implications are brought out more fully in a passage in chapter 6, where the author incorporates the theory of amalavijñāna into his comprehensive mārga schema, similar to that which is in the Hwaŏm/Hua-yen school.

> True thusness has voidness as its nature. As its nature is void, its knowledge is empyreal, incinerating all the fetters. In an equipoised and balanced manner, the three stages of equal enlightenment (*tŭnggak/teng-chüeh*) and the three bodies of sublime enlightenment (*myogak/miao-chüeh*) shine brilliantly in the ninth consciousness so that there are no shadows.[72]

The treatment of the amalavijñāna here in terms of equal and sublime enlightenments is closely allied to that found in another Chinese apocryphon, the *P'u-sa ying-lo pen-yeh ching* (Book of the original actions that adorn the

---

[68] "Original enlightenment is exactly the amalavijñāna"; *KSGR* 2, 978a20.

[69] *VS*, chap. 4, at n. 33.

[70] *Kisillon pyŏlgi* 1, *T* 1845.44.230a19–21.

[71] Liebenthal, p. 373, first broached this suggestion with reference to *VS*.

[72] *VS*, chap. 6, at n. 96.

bodhisattva).[73] Our text, like that indigenous sūtra, attempts to synthesize the variant mārga schemata presented in translated Buddhist texts into a comprehensive regimen, which culminates in the two levels of enlightenment: equal and sublime, which the *Ying-lo ching* calls the Immaculate Stage (*wu-kou ti*; *amalabhūmi?*) and Sublime-training Stage (*miao-hsüeh ti*).[74] By treating amalavijñāna in terms of specific soteriological stages, the *Vajrasamādhi* raises the discussion of that consciousness beyond mere psychological abstraction to concrete religious praxis.

Wŏnhyo's exegesis of this passage makes associations between these two final stages of the mārga and the ālaya and amala *vijñāna*s, helping to clarify in the process the relationship between those two modes of consciousness:

> The prior level of equal enlightenment still involves the fountainhead of the mind that has yet to exhaust production and extinction; hence, it involves the eighth consciousness. Arriving now at sublime enlightenment, production and extinction are forever left behind, and one returns to the fountainhead of the one mind of original enlightenment. Thus he accesses the brightness and purity inherent in the ninth consciousness. . . . Now, returning to the fountainhead of the mind, that original substance becomes one's essence and, due to this, all "shadows"—all characteristics—become extinct.[75]

The correlation the *Vajrasamādhi* makes between amalavijñāna and the mārga shows that the idea of an immaculate form of consciousness was not merely an abstract psychological concept, but a concrete soteriological tool—the motivating force that renders ordinary people capable of enlightenment. Like the tathāgatagarbha, amalavijñāna was not primarily intended to explain why a person mistakenly believes himself to be deluded (i.e., to function as the origin of ignorance), or to serve as the ground of existence (i.e., to play an ontological role)—two of the ways in which East Asian exegetes had employed the ālayavijñāna concept. Once amalavijñāna was actualized, the student would learn that it has always been present, subtly influencing the individual—that is, it was original enlightenment. This clarification of the soteriological implications of this ninth mode of con-

---

[73] *P'u-sa ying-lo pen-yeh ching*, *T* 1485.24.1012c27–1013a9. For the Chinese provenance of this text, see Mochizuki, *Bukkyō kyōten*, pp. 471–84.

[74] See *P'u-sa ying-lo pen-yeh ching* 2, *T* 1485.24.1017a3, 1010b278, 1022b13; cited in Liebenthal, p. 362 n. 1.

[75] KSGR 3, 995c25–27; and cf. Chu-chen, *T'ung-tsung chi* 9, p. 277c; Yüan-ch'eng, *Chu-chieh* 2, p. 212a–b.

sciousness may be the most important innovation in the *Vajrasamādhi*'s treatment of both amalavijñāna and tathāgatagarbha.

But the author does not stop merely at demonstrating the soteriological import of amalavijñāna or explaining how it relates to stages on the mārga. He ultimately seeks to show its pragmatic utility, by relating amalavijñāna to a specific meditative technique that will bring about its re-cognition. This is the practice of no-thought (*munyŏm/wu-nien*), which is described as the "benefit" or "inspiration" (*i/li*—that is, the practical application or functioning—of original enlightenment *cum* amalavijñāna.

> "How can one prompt those sentient beings not to give rise to a single thought?" "One should prompt those sentient beings to sit with their minds and spirits calm, abiding in the adamantine stage. Once thoughts are tranquillized so that nothing is produced, the mind will be constantly calm and serene. This is what is meant by the absence of even a single thought." Muju Bodhisattva said, "This is inconceivable. When one is enlightened to the fact that thoughts are unproduced, one's mind becomes calm and serene. That is the inspiration of original enlightenment."[76]

The step the author takes here begins to suggest that there are implications in the *Vajrasamādhi*'s treatment of amalavijñāna and tathāgatagarbha that go beyond the scholastic controversies summarized earlier concerning the nature of the mind. The notion that enlightenment is immanent in the mundane world—the quintessence of sinitic Buddhist doctrine—ultimately fostered the evolution of new meditation techniques, such as no-thought, which have no direct analogues in Indian Buddhism.[77] The placement of this section on no-thought is also suggestive, in that it comes just before chapter 5 of the *Vajrasamādhi*, where most of the major Ch'an elements occur. Given the nascent Ch'an doctrines found in the *Vajrasamādhi*, which will be explored in the next chapter, there are indications here that the ontological and soteriological speculations current in seventh-century sinitic Buddhism contributed to the development of types of meditation that would come to be identified with Ch'an. Chu-chen's commentary to this passage draws out its resonances with sayings attributed to the legendary Ch'an patriarchs Bodhidharma, Seng-ts'an (d. 606?), and Hui-neng.[78] We know that no-thought was one of the principal practices of the early and middle Ch'an schools, and

---

[76] *VS*, chap. 4, at n. 47.

[77] See my discussion of this process in "*K'an-hua* Meditation," pp. 324–28.

[78] Chu-chen, *T'ung-tsung chi* 6, p. 260c.

some have suggested it may even have antecedents in the Northern school of the early Ch'an period.[79] The testimony of the sūtra now indicates that no-thought practice can be traced into the incipiency of Ch'an, at least a few decades before the emergence of the Northern school. The *Vajrasamādhi* therefore confirms the Tathāgatagarbha orientation not only of much sinitic Buddhist doctrine, but also of sinitic Buddhist practice, and specifically its Ch'an forms.

The importance to Ch'an meditation of the concepts of tathāgatagarbha, amalavijñāna, and inherent enlightenment are brought out with greatest clarity in Chu-chen's commentary. Chu-chen relates amalavijñāna to a concept that becomes of seminal importance in more mature phases of Ch'an: "counterillumination" (*panjo/fan-chao* or *hoegwang panjo/hui-kuang fan-chao*), a notion the *Vajrasamādhi* alludes to elsewhere in chapter 4 as "reversion of the spirit" (*hoesin/hui-shen*).[80] In this new, uniquely Chinese description of the process by which meditative development occurs, the innate enlightenment of the mind is said to be naturally luminous, shining ever outward and allowing beings to become aware of their external world. This natural quality of luminosity is what is meant by "sentience," the one characteristic common to all "sentient" beings, and the very fact that beings are conscious is proof ipso facto that they are inherently enlightened. If the meditator can turn this radiance emanating from his mind back toward its source, he would rediscover that luminous core of the mind and become instantly enlightened. As Chu-chen explains: "One does not know that this [amala-vijñāna] is a thing with which one is originally endowed; it is not something obtained from without. Sentient beings, who are composed of five skandhas [aggregates of existence], originally are endowed with the immaculate and pure nature. Now the one enlightenment transforms all the consciousnesses so that they access the pure nature. . . . The word 'access' means to 'look back on the fount' (*fan-yüan k'an*; Kor. *panwŏn kan*)."[81] Chu-chen here is drawing on the Yogācāra concept of *āśrayaparāvṛtti*—the transformation of consciousness through the intercession of an external stimuli—but giving it an introspective twist. He instead sees the catalyst for this transformation of mind coming not from without but from within, deep inside the innermost recesses of each individual's enlightened identity. This is the "inspiration" of

[79] See McRae, p. 223.

[80] *VS*, chap. 4, before n. 41. For the role of *fan-chao* in Ch'an meditation, see my article "Chinul's Systematization of Chinese Meditative Techniques in Korean Sŏn Buddhism," pp. 213–16.

[81] Chu-chen, *T'ung-tsung chi* 6, p. 260a8–11.

original enlightenment, which is working always on the individual, encouraging him toward his enlightenment.

Counterillumination and, in turn, the theoretical underpinnings of Ch'an meditation therefore seem to derive from this sinitic analysis of mind. In that all types of meditation foster an interiorization that will ultimately lead back to the source of mind itself, each in some sense involves counterillumination. The *Vajrasamādhi*'s treatment here thus suggests that features characteristic of Ch'an thought and practice in its mature phases are present already in its incipiency and owe their inspiration to the doctrinal matrix represented by sinitic Tathāgatagarbha thought.

## The Meaning of "Vajrasamādhi":
## The Practical Implications of Innate Enlightenment

The fact that the sūtra is entitled after the vajrasamādhi (*kŭmgang sammae/ chin-kang san-mei*), or "adamantine absorption," may derive as well from its emphasis on tathāgatagarbha and amalavijñāna. I noted in chapter 1 that the appearance of an otherwise unknown *Vajrasamādhi-sūtra* in the catalogues may have tempted the author to co-opt this title for his own composition, thus ensuring its instant legitimacy. But this "matter of convenience" may not have been the only reason. The notion of vajrasamādhi occupied a seminal place in the scriptural materials from which the author drew many of his ideas. The *Mahāparinirvāṇa-sūtra*, a proto-Tathāgatagarbha text, includes extensive references to vajrasamādhi, as will be seen in the following discussion. The *Laṅkāvatāra-sūtra*, the scripture that makes arguably the earliest reference to a ninth consciousness, draws almost a tautology between vajrasamādhi, calmness and tranquillity of mind, the "other shore" of nirvāṇa, the *tathāgatakāya* ( = dharmakāya), and the nirmāṇakāyas of the tathāgatas.[82] The vajrasamādhi is therefore closely allied with the Tathāgatagarbha-amalavijñāna constellation of ideals that is so central to the sūtra.

The term vajrasamādhi is synonymous with, and often simply an alternate translation of, the *vajropamasamādhi* or "adamant-like samādhi," a term central to both Sarvāstivādin and Mahāyāna accounts of soteriology. To simplify a complicated series of steps that are not relevant to the discussion here, the Sarvāstivādins conceived of *vajropamasamādhi* as a meditative ab-

---

[82] Bodhiruci's translation of *Ju Leng-ch'ieh ching* 2, *T* 671.16.522c; cf. Suzuki's translation from the Sanskrit, which is rather different, in *Laṅkāvatāra Sūtra*, p. 38.

sorption achieved toward the end of the path of cultivation, or *bhāvanāmārga*, which catalyzed the final experience of enlightenment, or bodhi. Overcoming all the emotional fetters was necessary in order for the adept to experience arhatship, the state of enlightenment that is catalyzed by radical non-attachment. This process of abandonment (*prahāṇa*) was initiated by this special kind of meditative absorption, which could destroy even the subtlest and most persistent of fetters, just as adamant or diamond could shatter even the hardest of minerals. With their destruction, the adept then knew that those fetters were gone forever (*kṣayajñāna*), an experience that was in some cases followed by knowledge of nonproduction (*anutpādajñāna*)—that the fetters would never arise again. *Vajropamasamādhi* was thus the factor that initiated final transcendence, or nirvāṇa.[83]

The consummate ability of the vajrasamādhi in its Śrāvakayāna interpretation to defend against any and all obstacles to cultivation is illustrated in a tale about Śāriputra, one of the Buddha's two main disciples, which appears in the *Ekottarāgama*. While Śāriputra was cultivating the vajrasamādhi, it is said, he was attacked by a demon, who struck him viciously over the head. Completely unaware of what had happened to him, he eventually withdrew from his samādhi and came before the Buddha, who had learned of the assault. The Buddha asked him whether he was in pain, to which Śāriputra replied that he was fine, but that his head did indeed hurt a little. The Buddha then told him about the demon, who, the Buddha marveled, was so powerful that had he similarly struck Mt. Sumeru, the mountain would have crumbled. But the power of the vajrasamādhi had protected Śāriputra so that no injury could befall him. In the same way, other bhikṣus who gain the vajrasamādhi become impervious to flood, conflagration, or war.[84] This story apparently excited the imaginations of sixth-century Chinese, for it is excerpted in the earliest Chinese Buddhist collectanea, *Ching-lü i-hsiang* (Oddities from the sūtra and vinaya), compiled in 516.[85]

A transitional role for *vajropamasamādhi* similar to that found in the Sarvāstivāda school is seen also in Mahāyāna interpretations of the term. The *bhāvanāmārga* in one Mahāyāna scheme continues through the ten stages (*bhūmi*) of the bodhisattva path, at the culmination of which the bodhisattva approaches buddhahood itself. This final stage of the path was termed the

---

[83] For discussion on the Sarvāstivādin treatment of *vajropamasamādhi*, see Herbert B. Guenther, *Philosophy and Psychology in the Abhidharma*, pp. 228–29, summarizing *Abhidharma-kośabhāṣya* vi.44–45.

[84] *Tseng-i a-han ching* 45, *T* 125.2.793a–c for the story.

[85] *Ching-lü i-hsiang*, *T* 2121.53.70c–71b.

*niṣṭhāmārga*, and was initiated by the *vajropamasamādhi*.[86] *Vajropamasamādhi* in this system thus leads to the same experience of *kṣaya* and *anutpāda* jñānas noted previously for the Sarvāstivāda program.[87] One of many alternate Mahāyāna schemata is found in Bodhiruci's translation of the *Laṅkāvatāra-sūtra*, where the vajrasamādhi is achieved after the bodhisattva has entered the first of the ten *bhūmi*s: "when a bodhisattva attains the first *bhūmi*, the Joyful, he realizes the clear gate of the hundreds of vajrasamādhis, . . . sur-passes all the stages of the śrāvakas and pratyekabuddhas, and abides in the home of the tathāgatas, the realm of true thusness."[88] Hence, the vajrasa-mādhi transforms the adept from a follower of the two inferior vehicles of the śrāvakas and pratyekabuddhas to a kinsman of the buddhas themselves.

This sense that vajrasamādhi augurs the achievement of buddhahood, with all its unique qualities and superlative powers, is found frequently in sūtras of explicitly Mahāyāna pedigree. The *Mahāprajñāpāramitā-sūtra* treats the vajrasamādhi as the catalyst for the attainment of *sarvajñatā* (all-knowl-edge).[89] Elsewhere the Prajñāpāramitā literature notes that the intractable-ness of the vajrasamādhi works like adamant to break the Buddha free from his physical bonds so that he can attain liberation and thereby aid all sentient beings.[90]

This close association between vajrasamādhi and the achievement of bud-dhahood frequently implies that the vajrasamādhi is a special type of samā-dhi that is accessible only to, and specially reserved for, the buddhas.[91] This

---

[86] Cf. *Ta-chih-tu lun* 23, *T* 1509.25.235a15–16: "Once he completes the ten *bhūmi*s, he sits at the *bodhimaṇḍa* and gains the vajrasamādhi." A series of four sets of practices that lead to vajrasamādhi are given at *Ta-fang-teng ta-chi ching* (*Mahāsaṃnipāta-sūtra*) 12, *T* 397.13.83a2–16. The connection between vajrasamādhi and the mārga is also made prominently in the *P'u-sa ying-lo pen-yeh ching*, as the numerous citations in Wŏnhyo's *KSGR* attest; see, for example, *KSGR* 3, 993c19–20, where Wŏnhyo cites the text to illustrate the soteriological stage at which vajrasamādhi occurs; and *KSGR* 3, p. 994c, where vajrasamādhi is shown to be the culmination of thousands of samādhis, achieved by one who dwells on the equal-enlightenment stage.

[87] Following the account in *Abhidharmasamuccaya*, pp. 76ff; summarized in Guenther, *Abhidharma*, pp. 245–46.

[88] *Ju Leng-ch'ieh ching* (*Laṅkāvatāra-sūtra*) 7, *T* 671.16.557c10–12; cf. Suzuki, trans., *Laṅkā-vatāra Sūtra*, p. 196.

[89] Cf. *Mo-ho po-jo po-lo-mi ching* 22, *T* 223.8.381a. See also " 'The Buddha said: one who has already gained the vajrasamādhi gains *sarvajña*.' " *Fang-kuang po-jo ching* (*Pañcaviṃśatisāhas-rikāprajñāpāramitā-sūtra*) 2, *T* 221.8.9b22–23.

[90] "Ānanda. When the Tathāgata entered nirvāṇa, he entered [first] the vajrasamādhi and pulverized this physical body as if it were a mustard seed." *Lien-hua-mien ching* 1, *T* 386.12.1071a17–18. A similar quote appears in the *Fang-kuang po-jo ching* 7, *T* 221.8.53c25–27. See also *Ta-chih-tu lun* 15, *T* 1509.25.173c3, ch. 59, pp. 480a24–25, 481a21.

[91] See *Kuang-po yen-ching pu-t'ui-chuan-lun ching* (*Avaivartikacakra-sūtra*) 1, *T* 268.9.257a3.

association seems to have been especially strong in sinitic apocryphal scriptures. One example is the *Wu-shang-i ching* (Book of the supreme basis), an important Tathāgatagarbha text that may have been written by someone from Paramārtha's coterie of disciples, perhaps even Paramārtha himself, to justify his amalgamation of the Tathāgatagarbha and Yogācāra systems. It says that "the tathāgatas alone attain vajrasamādhi."[92] The *Jen-wang ching* (Book of benevolent kings), an apocryphal scripture with Prajñāpāramitā affinities, also states that "the buddhas and the tenth-*bhūmi* bodhisattvas both employ the acquiescence to calm extinction (*chi-mieh jen*) in order to access the vajrasamādhi."[93] The prologue to the *Vajrasamādhi* opens with the Buddha entering into that eponymous absorption, a scene found also in other scriptures.[94] The *Vajrasamādhi*'s description there of the vajrasamādhi as being a state wherein both body and mind are motionless is also corroborated in other sūtras, where the vajrasamādhi is described as the perfect stillness achieved through realizing the truth of voidness.[95] Our sūtra's description of vajrasamādhi as "unmoving" (*pudong/pu-tung*; Skt. *acala*) is noteworthy, since immobility was also considered to be one of the characteristics of the amalavijñāna.[96] This reference is one of the first explicit suggestions of the affinities between the two ideas. Throughout much of Mahāyāna literature, then, vajrasamādhi was considered to be the consummation of the cultivation of samādhi;[97] but it was a kind of samādhi that had soteriological

[92] *Wu-shang-i ching*, *T* 669.16.475c10. On the Chinese origins of this text, see Takasaki, *Ratnagotravibhāga*, p. 52. The vajrasamādhi is mentioned in association with *sarvajñatā* and buddhahood in the apocryphal *P'u-sa ying-lo pen-yeh ching* 9, *T* 656.16.80b15.

[93] *Jen-wang po-jo po-lo-mi ching* 1, *T* 245.8.826c21–22; discussed in Chih-i's commentary, *Jen-wang hu-kuo po-jo ching shu* 4, *T* 1705.33.271a; and in Chi-tsang's commentary, *Jen-wang po-jo ching shu* 3, *T* 1707.33.330b–c.

[94] See, for example, *P'u-sa ts'ung Tou-shu-t'ien chiang shen-mu-t'ai shuo kuang-p'u ching* 1, *T* 384.12.1015c5–6.

[95] "Mañjuśrī. In your chamber, sit straight with your body held erect and, with mind motionless, recollect the realms of the buddhas. Realizing for yourself the dharma of voidness, you gain the vajrasamādhi." *Pu-t'ui-chuan fa-lun ching* 1, *T* 267.9.228c5–7. A similar sense of vajrasamādhi as being a state in which all dharmas are in perfect equanimity is also found in the *Shih-hsiang po-jo po-lo-mi ching*, *T* 240.8.776b9–10; and *Kuang-tsan ching* 6, *T* 222.8.190c25–26: "When one abides in this absorption, all is equal, and nothing can harm one." See also Hui-yüan, *Ta-sheng i chang* 16, *T* 1851.44.786b29–c1, who treats vajrasamādhi as equanimity of mind.

[96] See Chih-i's *Chin-kuang-ming ching hsüan-i* 1, *T* 1783.39.4a12–13. This passage is cited also in the Sung dynasty Buddhist lexicon, *Fan-i ming-i chi* 6, *T* 2131.54.1158c18.

[97] As the *Pañcaviṃśati* says, "There is no other samādhi that can possibly match abiding in this samādhi." *Fang-kuang po-jo ching* 4, *T* 221.8.23b28–29. Note also: "They praise the vajrasamādhi as surpassing all samādhis." *Pu-t'ui-chuan fa-lun ching* 2, *T* 267.9.234b2–3. "Wŏnhyo's

implications that far surpassed all other aspects of the dharma, including the concept of voidness, the trainings in *śīla*, samādhi, and prajñā, and even liberation itself.[98] One scholar-monk even went so far as to say that vajrasamādhi *is* enlightenment.[99]

The vajrasamādhi is sometimes treated in conjunction with a sudden approach to enlightenment, which ultimately comes to occupy such an important spot in the East Asian Buddhist tradition. In the *Prajñāpāramitā* and *Mahāratnakūṭa* sūtras, the vajrasamādhi is listed as one of the samādhis that can quickly lead to the attainment of the complete, perfect enlightenment of buddhahood (*anuttarasamyaksaṃbodhi*),[100] while elsewhere it is said to prompt the adept to "leap to the eighth *bhūmi*," the stage of buddhahood according to an early mārga scheme.[101] The affinity of the vajrasamādhi with subitist soteriologies has antecedents in early Indian thought, since even the *Abhidharmamahāvibhāṣā* notes that some Ābhidharmikas had proposed that the *vajropamasamādhi* brings about the instantaneous eradication of all the defilements and thence sudden enlightenment.[102] A similar function of vajrasamādhi is mentioned in the *Ta-sheng ju-tao tz'u-ti* (Mahāyāna program for accessing the path) by the Fa-hsiang scholar Chih-chou (679–723), written

---

hagiographer, Iryŏn, also brings out this sense of vajrasamādhi as being the preeminent form of samādhi when he calls it "the hub of samādhi" (*SGYS*, p. 1006b2).

[98] *Kuang-tsan ching* 5, *T* 222.8.181b3–8.

[99] Pu-k'ung (Amoghavajra; 704–774), *Chin-kang-ting ching ta yu-ch'ieh pi-mi hsin-ti fa-men i-chüeh* 1, *T* 1798.39.809a14.

[100] "A bodhisattva-*mahāsattva* who cultivates these samādhis will quickly attain *anuttarasamyaksaṃbodhi*." *Mo-ho po-jo po-lo-mi ching* (*Mahāprajñāpāramitā-sūtra*) 3, *T* 223.8.237c. "This bodhisattva-*mahāsattva* . . . perfects the abiding in the *vajropamasamādhi*, and uses the wisdom that comes into accordance in one thought-moment (*i-nien hsiang-ying hui*) to attain *anuttarasamyaksaṃbodhi*"; *Mo-ho po-jo po-lo-mi ching* 3, *T* 223.8.408b18–19; *Ta-chih-tu lun* 92, *T* 1509.25.708b15; *ch.* 86, p. 662b3; *Ta-pao-chi ching* (*Mahāratnakūṭa*) 111, *T* 310.11.628c21–22. See also *Fang-kuang po-jo ching* 2, *T* 221.8.16b. The vajrasamādhi is also described as catalyzing the transition from bodhisattvahood to buddhahood in *Shan-hai-hui p'u-sa ching* (*T* 2891.85.1406b19–25), a Chinese apocryphon written no later than 695.

[101] *P'u-sa ying-lo pen-yeh ching* 8, *T* 656.16.79c18.

[102] "Some have this grasping: When the *vajropamasamādhi* appears, it suddenly eradicates all the defilements of the three realms of existence that may be cut off by insight and cultivation. All the stages before those can only subdue them, and cannot yet cut of all the outflows. Like the śramaṇas [who advocate] such sudden eradication, these [people] advocate sudden enlightenment (*tun-chüeh*) and attainment of the *aśaikṣaphala*. This is like waking from a dream: one suddenly abandons one's torpor and lassitude." *A-pi-ta-mo ta-pi-p'o-sha lun* (*Abhidharmamahāvibhāṣā*) 90; *T* 1545.27.465c. Whalen Lai has also argued that the Sarvāstivāda manual *Abhidharmahṛdaya* exerted critical influence in the evolution of Tao-sheng's (ca. 360–434) theory of sudden enlightenment; see Lai, "Tao-sheng's Theory of Sudden Enlightenment Re-examined," pp. 174–77.

in the same period during which the *Vajrasamādhi* was composed. He notes, "Once one has completed the ten *bhūmi*s and the *vajropamasamādhi* appears, in an instant (*kṣaṇa*) all the defilements that have arisen in the three realms of existence are simultaneously eradicated and one gains right enlightenment."[103] Given the Ch'an affinities in our sūtra, the use of vajrasamādhi in its title may thus be one of the first, albeit tentative, adumbrations of the Ch'an concern with subitism that would be proclaimed so strongly a few decades later in the *Platform Sūtra*.

The closest links between vajrasamādhi and Tathāgatagarbha doctrine are drawn in the *Mahāparinirvāṇa-sūtra*.[104] The *Nirvāṇa Sūtra* is best known for teaching the inherence of the buddha-nature in all sentient beings, a precursor of the Tathāgatagarbha doctrine. But it also includes one of the most extensive exegeses of the vajrasamādhi in Mahāyāna literature and closely associates this absorption with seeing the buddha-nature and achieving *anuttarasamyaksaṃbodhi*.[105] "Peaceful abiding" (*an-chu*) in vajrasamādhi brings a number of special talents that are exclusive to the bodhisattva. These include the ability "to eradicate all the defilements of all sentient beings in a single instant of thought and transmogrify his body like a buddha so that its numbers are immeasurable, pervading all the buddha lands of the ten directions, which are like the sands of the Ganges."[106] Perhaps the most important effect of abiding in the vajrasamādhi, however, is that it produces an expansive vision of all dharmas in which the bodhisattva

sees in the distance all the dharmas, none of which are unclear, just as a person who ascends a tall mountain sees in the distance all directions, all of which are clear.[107] . . . He sees that all dharmas are without obstructions, as if he were seeing an *āmalaka* [myrobalan] fruit in the palm of his hand. . . . Abid-

---

[103] *Ta-sheng ju-tao tz'u-ti, T* 1864.45.464b7–9.

[104] Unless otherwise indicated, all the passages from the *Mahāparinirvāṇa-sūtra* cited in the following paragraphs are from *Ta pan-nieh-p'an ching* 24, *T* 374.12.509b–510b.

[105] *Ta pan-nieh-p'an ching* 2, *T* 374.12.372b1–2; and see *Ta pan-nieh-p'an ching* 1, *T* 375.12.611c24–26.

[106] The *Ta-chih-tu lun* also notes that "abiding in the vajrasamādhi destroys all defilements" (*chüan* 62, *T* 1509.25.497c9), brings "liberation of the mind" (*ch.* 84, p. 649b9) and the "unimpeded liberation of all the buddhas" (*ch.* 40, 350b20).

[107] This metaphor from the *Nirvāṇa Sūtra* is adapted by the apocryphal *Jen-wang ching* 2, *T* 246.8.842c2–3, suggesting the strong influence of the *Nirvāṇa Sūtra* over many indigenous sinitic compositions; the metaphor is discussed in Yen-shou's (904–975) *Tsung-ching lu* 30, *T* 2016.48.594b. This metaphor is often used in East Asian Buddhism as an analogy for the soteriological program of gradual cultivation/gradual awakening; see Buswell, *Korean Approach*, pp. 287–88, translating Ch'eng-kuan and Chinul.

ing in [the vajrasamādhi], he is able to dominate [lit., to destroy and scatter]
all those dharmas. . . . Wherever adamant strikes, there is nothing that is not
shattered, and yet that adamant is not marred. So too is it with vajrasamādhi:
there are none of those dharmas that it strikes which is not shattered, and yet
that samādhi is in no way marred.[108]

This perfect control over the dharmas is possible only because the meditator absorbed in the vajrasamādhi does not become attached to their external characteristics. Rather, he notes their essence—their voidness—and thus
keeps his mind in a state that is completely beyond discrimination:

Although he sees sentient beings, from the beginning his mind knows no sign
of "sentient being." . . . Although he perceives day and night, he knows no
sign of day and night. Although he sees everything, he knows no sign of
"everything." Although he sees all defilements and bonds, he also knows no
sign of defilement. Although he perceives the holy eightfold path, he knows
no such sign. Although he sees bodhi, he knows no such sign. Although he
perceives nirvāṇa, he knows no such sign. Why is this? Oh son of good family. It is because all dharmas are originally signless. Because of the power of
this samādhi, the bodhisattva sees that all dharmas are originally signless.

The apocryphal *Fan-wang ching* (Book of Brahmā's net) also makes a similar claim, when it declares that "once all signs are extinguished one gains
the approach of the vajrasamādhi. One accesses both the gate of all-embracing practices and the stage that is void and equanimous."[109] This same sense
of utter nonattachment toward all dharmas is to be applied even to the practices of the bodhisattva, for "the vajrasamādhi allows the bodhisattva to destroy all the defilements after cultivating, but without ever thinking that
there is a self who can sunder those bonds. . . . Although the vajrasamādhi
can destroy all the defilements, from the first he does not think, 'I will destroy them.' " Like so much of Mahāyāna literature, then, the *Nirvāṇa Sūtra*
treats the vajrasamādhi as the apex of samādhi, a claim the text backs up, as
it does with so many of its teachings, with numerous similes.[110]

---

[108] Similar passages concerning the control the vajrasamādhi brings to all dharmas can be
found also in *Pei-hua ching* (*Karuṇāpuṇḍarīka*) 8, *T* 157.8.221b13–14: "There is the vajrasamādhi.
One who enters this samādhi, completely penetrates all dharmas . . . and does not see even the
subtlest of obstacles."

[109] *Fan-wang ching* 1, *T* 1848.24.1000b6–7.

[110] "Oh son of good family. Just as among all gems diamond is preeminent, so too is it for
the bodhisattva who attains vajrasamādhi: among all samādhis it is supreme. Why is this? A

The meaning and significance of the vajrasamādhi were of considerable concern in East Asian exegetical writings. The most extensive analysis of the vajrasamādhi by a Chinese scholiast was made by Ching-ying Hui-yüan in his magnum opus, *Ta-sheng i chang* (Encyclopedia of Mahāyāna). His treatment there is valuable for gleaning the nuances the term carried among Sui and T'ang exegetes sympathetic to Tathāgatagarbha thought. Hui-yüan assumed that vajrasamādhi derived from the *Nirvāṇa Sūtra*.[111] He analyzes the vajra in vajrasamādhi as meaning "true realization" and says that it has as its essential nature "true consciousness," which he defines as

the eighth consciousness (*hsin*), the tathāgatagarbha. . . . The original nature of this mind of the true consciousness is pure, but because it conceals the meaning of voidness, it consequently becomes maculated and tainted. If one cleans away these false taints, the mind, purified, will shine radiantly. This radiantly bright, pure wisdom will realize the original thusness of dharmas, and not perceive even a single dharma that can produce false conceptions. Because no falsity arises, it is able to remove benighted delusion, and will not be affected by deluded obstacles. Hence, it is called vajra.[112]

Among the several possible analyses of its characteristics, Hui-yüan notes that vajrasamādhi leads to four kinds of knowledge, including knowledge of the absolute tathāgatagarbha.[113] One of the more interesting features of Hui-yüan's treatment is his statement that a bodhisattva's initial entry into the tenth *bhūmi* brings the attainment of immaculate samādhi (*li-kou san-mei*),

bodhisattva-*mahāsattva* who cultivates this samādhi wields power over each and every samādhi. My good man. It is just as all petty kings pledge allegiance to a cakravartin [wheel-turning emperor]. So too is it with all samādhis: they all pay allegiance to the vajrasamādhi. . . . It is that which all samādhis honor and respect. . . . Oh son of good family. It is like this: One should know that a man on the banks of a great sea has already availed himself of the water of the rivers, springs, and ponds. So too is it with a bodhisattva-*mahāsattva*. If he cultivates in this wise the vajrasamādhi, one should know that he has already cultivated all the samādhis." *Ta-pan-nien-p'an ching* 24, *T* 374.12.509c. See also the *Karuṇāpuṇḍarīka-sūtra*, where it is said that the vajrasamādhi is the supreme samādhi that can destroy all others; *Pei-hua ching* 8, *T* 157.3.220c8–9; *Ta-sheng pei fen-t'o-li ching* 7, *T* 158.3.278b1.

[111] *Ta-sheng i chang* 9, *T* 1851.44.637c16; Hui-yüan's exegesis of the term vajrasamādhi appears on pp. 637c–41a.

[112] *Ta-sheng i chang* 9, *T* 1851.44.638b.

[113] "One, knowledge of worldly truths, which is awareness of worldly events and characteristics. Two, knowledge of absolute truth, which is awareness of the voidness of all dharmas. Three, knowledge of the one reality, which is knowledge that nothing either exists or does not exist. Four, knowledge of the *dharmadhātu*, that is, awareness of the distinctions in the *dharma-dhātu* aspect of the true and real tathāgatagarbha." *Ta-sheng i chang* 9, *T* 1851.44.639b25–28; for this whole section see pp. 638b–39b.

which, like vajrasamādhi, can destroy all obstacles to enlightenment.[114] The association he draws between vajrasamādhi and an "immaculate samādhi" would have immediately suggested to a Chinese reader the amalavijñāna. A similar affinity is also seen in the connection drawn between the vajrasamādhi and the Immaculate Stage (wu-kou ti) in the apocryphal P'u-sa ying-lo pen-yeh ching.[115] Hence, it is clear that, by the late sixth century, East Asian scholiasts were treating the vajrasamādhi as the meditative analogue of the more scholastic terms tathāgatagarbha and amalavijñāna, if not the type of samādhi that was specifically intended to induce realization of the tathāgatagarbha.[116]

The associations of the vajrasamādhi with this same tathāgatagarbha/amalavijñāna cross-section of ideas is brought out in analyses of the term in the writings of other learned scholars of the period, especially authors associated with the T'ien-t'ai, San-lun, and early Ch'an schools. Many of the same themes found in the sūtra literature are reiterated by such renowned thinkers as Chih-i, the T'ien-t'ai exegete, and Chi-tsang, the systematizer of the San-lun or Madhyamaka school. Chih-i, for example, remarks that "one who wishes to realize supreme, sublime enlightenment must first access the vajrasamādhi; then all the buddhadharmas will appear before him."[117] Chi-tsang notes that "only the tathāgatas access the vajrasamādhi, for the power of that transcendent path can destroy this physical body,"[118] suggesting, as had many sūtras, that vajrasamādhi was the exclusive provenance of the buddhas. Wŏnhyo considers the essence (ch'e/t'i) of vajrasamādhi to be the edge of reality (bhūtakoṭi), or enlightenment itself, and its function (yong/yung) to be the destruction of any and all obstacles to that enlightenment. Wŏnhyo states that the vajrasamādhi "realizes the principle and probes the fountain-

---

[114] Ta-sheng i chang 9, T 1851.44.639c. This function of vajrasamādhi is brought out by Tzu-hsüan (d.1038), a Sung dynasty Hua-yen exegete: "Once the vajropamasamādhi appears, it destroys the obstacles to the buddha-bhūmi and one thence accesses sublime enlightenment." Shou-leng-yen i-shu chu-ching 8-2, T 1799.39.932b8–9.

[115] P'u-sa ying-lo pen-yeh ching 2, T 1485.24.1018b9–10.

[116] Although deriving from a later period, Tzu-hsüan also mentions the role of the vajrasamādhi in realizing the tathāgatagarbha: "Through the power that comes from [seeing all dharmas] as illusory, he infuses his cultivation with the wisdoms of learning, reflection, and cultivation and achieves the vajrasamādhi. He is then able to destroy the beginningless subtle ignorance, and completely realize the essence of the tathāgatagarbha." Shou-leng-yen i-shu chu-ching 6-2, T 1799.39.903c23–25.

[117] Shih ch'an po-lo-mi tz'u-ti fa-men 1a, T 1916.46.476c23–24. Cf. the statement in the Wei-mo ching shu (ch. 6, T 2772.85.420b14–15): "By the time one reaches the final mind of the ten bhūmis, the vajrasamādhi intimately produces the meritorious qualities of buddhahood."

[118] Fa-hua hsüan-lun 9, T 1720.34.434c5–6.

head [of the mind]," language that immediately recalls the *Vajrasamādhi*'s description of the tathāgatagarbha. Wŏnhyo also attempts to show that vajrasamādhi allows other soteriological stratagems to function optimally, free from any impediments to their operation, by revealing that all samādhis are devoid of own-nature (*niḥsvabhāva*).[119] Hence, the preponderance of evidence suggests that, within the sinitic tradition, the vajrasamādhi was regarded as one of the principal soteriological weapons in the Buddhist spiritual arsenal, which was closely tied to the revelation of the realm of buddhahood.

Given the broad attention the concept of vajrasamādhi received in scholastic writings of the sixth and seventh centuries, it is no surprise that it is also treated extensively in literature from the beginnings of Ch'an. There seems to have been two reasons for this attention. First, vajrasamādhi was often regarded within the Chinese tradition to be the quintessence of samādhi, if not even the consummation of dhyānapāramitā itself, as the preceptive *Yu-p'o-sai chieh ching* (*Upāsakaśīla-sūtra*) had said;[120] for a school like Ch'an that claimed to be the principal bastion of meditative expertise, it is to be expected that it would have been attracted to this type of samādhi and would have sought to make it its own. Second, vajrasamādhi had important resonances with the notion of intrinsic enlightenment, which was so central to the maturing sinitic doctrinal approach, including Ch'an. Ch'an praxis was founded upon the notion of "seeing the nature" (*kyŏnsŏng/chien-hsing*), the nature being for our purposes equivalent to tathāgatagarbha or amala-vijñāna, and the vajrasamādhi thus could have been interpreted as the type of samādhi that produced this vision.

This burgeoning Ch'an interest in vajrasamādhi is attested by the term's appearance in writings attributed to Tao-hsin and Hung-jen, the Ch'an adepts most closely associated with the thought of the *Vajrasamādhi*, as will be seen in the next chapter. The section on Tao-hsin in *Leng-ch'ieh shih-tzu chi* (Record of masters and disciples of the *Laṅkā[vatāra]*) has a lengthy passage in which the vajrasamādhi is mentioned prominently in connection with the idea of seeing (*k'an*; Kor. *kan*) the buddha-nature:

One then sees that this sort of mind is identical to the Tathāgata's body of the true dharma-nature. It is also called the right dharma, buddha-nature, the real-nature and the edge of reality of all dharmas, the pure land, bodhi, vajra-

---

[119] *KSGR* 1, p. 961c.
[120] See the statement in *Yu-p'o-sai chieh ching* (*Upāsakaśīla-sūtra*) 4, *T* 1488.24.1054a5–6.

samādhi, original enlightenment, and so on. It is also called the realm of nir-vāṇa, prajñā, and so on. While its names may be infinite, they all have the same exact essence.[121]

The vajrasamādhi as the culmination of the process of practice is also re-ferred to in the *Hsiu-hsin yao-lun* (alt. *Ch'oesangsüng-ron*), attributed to Tao-hsin's successor, Hung-jen. There vajrasamādhi is said to be engendered by eradicating the delusion of personal possession,[122] which would initiate the experience of nonattachment that is nirvāṇa, as seen previously in the sūtra literature.

The vajrasamādhi is often associated with another type of samādhi, which also comes to occupy an important place in the indigenous exegetical and practice tradition, and particularly in Ch'an. This is the *śūraṃgamasamādhi*, or "heroic-march absorption." As the *Nirvāṇa Sūtra* notes in a famous pas-sage that is frequently quoted in the commentarial literature:

> Furthermore, my good man, the buddha-nature is precisely the *śūraṃgama-samādhi*. That nature is like clarified ghee, and it is precisely the mother of all the buddhas. It is through the power of the *śūraṃgamasamādhi* that you are prompted to have the permanence, bliss, selfhood, and purity of all the bud-dhas. All sentient beings possess this *śūraṃgamasamādhi*; but because they don't cultivate, they can't see it. Therefore they are unable to attain *anuttara-samyaksaṃbodhi*.
>
> My good man. The *śūraṃgamasamādhi* has five names. The first is *śūraṃ-gamasamādhi*. The second is prajñāpāramitā. The third is vajrasamādhi. The fourth is the lion's roar samādhi. The fifth is buddha-nature. Each of these names comes from its particular function.[123]

This connection between the vajra and *śūraṃgama* samādhis[124] is particularly compelling when one considers that the *Vajrasamādhi* and *Shou-leng-yen ching* (*Śūraṃgamasamādhi-sūtra*), which like the *Vajrasamādhi* takes its name from an important samādhi, are two of the sinitic apocryphal scriptures most in-fluential in the Ch'an school. The *Shou-leng-yen ching* is alleged to have been

---

[121] *Leng-ch'ieh shih-tzu chi, T* 2837.85.1287a17–20.

[122] *Ch'oesangsüng-ron, T* 2011.48.378c25–26; cf. the translation in McRae, p. 130, made from his new edition in his appendix, p. 12.

[123] *Ta pan-nieh-p'an ching* 27, *T* 374.12.524c18–25; cf. 26, 534a20–21, where the vajra and *śūraṃgama* samādhis are associated. This passage has received much attention in Chinese exe-getical writing: see, for example, Chih-i's *Wei-mo-ching lüeh-shu* 9, *T* 1778.38.684a5ff; and I-hsing's *Ta-p'i-lou-che-na ch'eng-fo ching shu* 6, *T* 1796.39.645c12ff.

[124] See also the discussion in Chi-tsang's *Jen-wang po-jo ching shu* 1, *T* 1707.33.319a.

translated in A.D. 705 by the otherwise-unknown Pāramiti (alt. Pramiti), but it is generally presumed to be an indigenous Chinese composition, displaying considerable influence from the *Awakening of Faith*.[125] Still another related text is the *Yüan-chüeh ching*, or *Book of Consummate Enlightenment*. The translation of this sūtra is said to have been done by Buddhatrāta in 793, but it is now known to have been composed in China in the last decade of the seventh century, only a few years after the writing of the *Vajrasamādhi*.[126] The Ch'an affinities with each of these scriptures are well documented, and they are all cited extensively in Ch'an exegetical works written in support of the school's distinctive positions. All three derive from a similar philosophical milieu, founded on Tathāgatagarbha thought and based principally on the *Awakening of Faith*.

The theme constantly reiterated in both translated and apocryphal sūtras as well as indigenous commentarial literature was that vajrasamādhi was the culmination of the development in samādhi, if not of all of Buddhist spiritual culture. The conceptual jump the *Vajrasamādhi* seeks to make is to claim that vajrasamādhi does not merely consummate Buddhist praxis, but in fact *subsumes* it. This inference is made by Wŏnhyo, who notes that vajrasamādhi "brings into operation the functioning of all other samādhis, in the same way that polishing a precious gem can make it functional [as jewelry, etc.]."[127] The vajrasamādhi thus becomes another example of the fundamental synthetic interests of the sūtra. And it draws on a wide-ranging debate concerning soteriological processes and their ontological underpinnings then taking place in sinitic Buddhism.

## The *Vajrasamādhi*'s Message to Silla Buddhists

Previous sections have mapped out the contours of the philosophical terrain covered in the *Vajrasamādhi*. It has been seen that Tathāgatagarbha/amala-vijñāna thought, with a strong praxis orientation, is the most prominent feature of the sūtra. Given these various doctrinal elements, what message did the *Vajrasamādhi* convey to the Silla Buddhists who would have first had

---

[125] See Mochizuki, *Bukkyō kyōten*, pp. 493–509. Ronald Epstein has tried to prove the Indian provenance of the text in his dissertation, "The *Śūraṅgama-sūtra* with Tripiṭaka Master Hsüan-hua's Commentary *An Elementary Explanation of Its General Meaning*: A Preliminary Study and Partial Translation." I find his argument unconvincing.

[126] See Mochizuki, *Bukkyō kyōten*, pp. 509–19.

[127] *KSGR* 1, p. 961c8.

contact with the scripture? Wŏnhyo's exegesis of the scripture in his commentary *Kŭmgang sammaegyŏng-ron* (*KSGR*) is a good place to search for answers. Among the traditional commentators, Wŏnhyo made arguably the most exhaustive and insightful study of the text. He seems also to have been most enthralled personally by the *Vajrasamādhi*—so much so that he would come out of retirement to write one final work. In Wŏnhyo's treatment, two concerns are foremost, which one would do well to keep in mind in assessing the possible reasons for the composition of the text in Korea: first, its utility in resolving the internal divisions renting what was perceived to be the pristine harmony of the Buddhadharma; and second, the close connection Wŏnhyo saw between its synthetic outlook and actual religious praxis.

As Korean scholars are wont to point out, Silla Buddhism was a syncretic, or, perhaps better, an "ecumenical" tradition (what the Koreans call *t'ong pulgyo*, or "comprehensive Buddhism"). While this view is repeated so perfunctorily in Korean scholarship as to suggest stereotypy, a glance at the writings produced by Silla Buddhist exegetes does, to a large extent, bear it out. Extant works written during the early decades of the Unified Silla dynasty, as well as catalogue listings of nonextant works, show that Wŏnhyo and his contemporaries were actively exploring the whole gamut of Buddhist philosophical materials, from Madhyamaka to Yogācāra to Pure Land, and attempting to integrate the viewpoints of these different teachings into an all-inclusive perspective on Buddhist thought and practice. Wŏnhyo states, for example, in the preface to his *Simmun hwajaeng-ron* that his intent is to harmonize all the variant descriptions in Buddhist texts concerning the original "consummate sound" (*wŏnsŏng*/*yüan-sheng*) of the Buddha's teaching—variations causing controversies that threatened to obscure the fundamental consistency of the religion's message.[128] A similar ecumenical refrain pervades most of Wŏnhyo's works, especially his commentaries to *Awakening of Faith* and the *Vajrasamādhi*. This refrain so inspired the Silla intellectual community that "syncretism" became the watchword of Korean Buddhism from Wŏnhyo's time onward.

Pak Chonghong first suggested that one of the specific goals of Wŏnhyo's syncretic philosophy was to resolve what he perceived as a bifurcation in Mahāyāna Buddhist philosophy: the *śūnyavāda* of the Madhyamaka and the

---

[128] *Simmun hwajaeng-ron*, in Cho Myŏnggi, ed., *Wŏnhyo chŏnjip*, p. 640; this is quoted also in *Kosŏn-sa Sŏdang hwasang t'appi*, in *Wŏnhyo chŏnjip*, p. 661, translated in part in Park, "Wŏnhyo's Commentaries," p. 74.

*vijñaptimātra* ("mere-representation") of the Yogācāra.[129] Wŏnhyo's major effort toward this resolution was made in one of his most influential works, *Taesŭng kisillon-so* (Commentary to the *Awakening of Faith*).[130] There, Wŏnhyo draws on the innovative explication of Tathāgatagarbha doctrine in that treatise to outline a possible reconciliation.[131] He presumes the one mind (the tathāgatagarbha) to be the ontological ground of two fundamental qualities: first, true thusness (representing Madhyamaka), and second, production-and-extinction (representing Yogācāra). These same two aspects are then said to be fundamental to the tripartite scriptural taxonomy Wŏnhyo provides in his *Kisillon-so*, which clarifies the preeminent place Tathāgatagarbha scriptures hold in his interpretation of Buddhism. The first level, represented by the Perfection of Wisdom (Prajñāpāramitā) scriptures, explains the absolute aspect of existence, or true thusness, that is, that which is indefeasible and immutable. The second level, as found in such texts as the *Nirvāṇa Sūtra* and the *Avataṃsaka-sūtra*, details the conventional nature of the world—the principle of production-and-extinction—which is governed by causal processes. These two levels, which are all but diametrically opposed, are amalgamated in the third level of the teachings: the approach that is adaptable (*suyŏn/sui-yüan*; lit., "in accord with conditions") and yet motionless,[132] where both true thusness and production-and-extinction are interfused. This level is represented by the synthetic teaching found in such texts as the *Laṅkāvatāra-sūtra* and the *Awakening of Faith*, where the tathāgatagarbha concept is used to synthesize variant Buddhist doctrines into comprehensive systems of thought. Although Wŏnhyo does not mention the *Vajrasamādhi* in connection with this taxonomy, it is clear that he would have placed the sūtra in the third and highest level of his classification.[133] As an

---

[129] Pak Chonghong, *Han'guk sasang sa: Pulgyo sasang p'yŏn*, pp. 85–106; Yi Chongik, "Wŏnhyo ŭi saengae wa sasang," pp. 221–26; Sung Bae Park, "Wŏnhyo's Commentaries," pp. 50–53. For the syncretic focus of Wŏnhyo's thought, see Kim Unhak, "Wŏnhyo ŭi hwajaeng sasang," pp. 173–82; Yi Chongik, *Wŏnhyo ŭi kŭnbon sasang*; and for accessible general surveys, see Rhi Ki-yong, "Wŏnhyo and His Thought," pp. 4–9, and Hong Jung-Shik [Hong Chŏngsik], "The Thought and Life of Wŏnhyo," pp. 15–30.

[130] *T* 1844/1845.44.202a–39c. There are a number of Korean vernacular translations, of which Rhi Ki-yong's is the best; see Rhi Ki-yong, *Han'guk ŭi Pulgyo sasang*, pp. 29–137, and his study of the text, *Wŏnhyo sasang*. Sung Bae Park has translated a portion of the text in his "Wŏnhyo's Commentaries," pp. 120–85.

[131] See Takamine Ryōshū, *Kegon shisōshi*, pp. 190–93, discussing both the *Kisillon-so* and *KSGR*.

[132] *Taesŭng kisillon pyŏlgi*, *T* 1845.44.227c23–228a2; noted in Park, "Wŏnhyo's Commentaries," pp. 182 and 248 n. 203.

[133] Despite these close links between the *Vajrasamādhi* and *Awakening of Faith*, Wŏnhyo

aside here, it may be noted that in *Kisillon-so* Wǒnhyo intimates that the *Laṅkāvatāra* is the sūtra source for the ideas presented in the *Awakening of Faith*; in *KSGR*, however, he sees the *Vajrasamādhi* instead as that source.

One of the best summaries of Wǒnhyo's syncretic concern appears in his *Yǒlban-kyǒng chongyo* (Thematic essentials of the *Nirvāṇa Sūtra*):

> The myriads of meritorious qualities of the stage of buddhahood have, in brief, two aspects. If you first abandon the characteristics [of true thusness and production-and-extinction], and return to the aspect of the one mind [the tathāgatagarbha, then] all meritorious characteristics will be the same as the *dharmadhātu*. . . . If you rely on the aspect in which these myriads of meritorious qualities are perfected through [the fact that they arise from] the nature, there will be none of the meritorious qualities of either body or mind with which you will not be fully endowed. . . . Although there are these two aspects, they are free from any sign of differentiation. For this reason, all theories are free from any limitations [i.e., any theory is valid].[134]

For Wǒnhyo, then, both the Madhyamaka apophasis as well as the Yogācāra kataphasis were equally valid descriptions of reality, accurately describing one aspect of the process of causation.[135] But it was only the Tathāgatagarbha doctrine that could effect a truly syncretic vision in which both of these descriptive approaches could function symbiotically for the benefit of the Buddhist practitioner.

As has been seen, one of the principal treatises that provided scriptural justification for such a syncretic attitude was the *Awakening of Faith*, perhaps the most important text in the development of Korean Buddhism in general and Unified Silla Buddhism in particular. Wǒnhyo's exegesis of the *Vajrasamādhi* suggests a possible motive behind the composition of the scripture in Korea: to appeal to intrinsic Silla interest in a sūtra that would legitimate the views presented in that treatise. Many Silla and T'ang commentators, including Wǒnhyo, considered the *Awakening of Faith* to be an ideal vehicle for amalgamating the various tendencies within Mahāyāna philosophy.[136]

---

does not include the *Vajrasamādhi* in this taxonomy. This omission lends further support to my argument in chapter 2 that Wǒnhyo was unfamiliar with the *Vajrasamādhi* at the time he wrote his *Kisillon-so*.

[134] *Yǒlban-kyǒng chongyo*, *T* 1769.38.245b15–19; noted also by Ko Ikchin, p. 226.

[135] For this use of apophasis and kataphasis in a Chinese Buddhist rhetorical context, see Robert Gimello, "Apophatic and Kataphatic Discourse in Mahāyāna," pp. 117–36.

[136] The syncretic nature of *Ta-sheng ch'i-hsin lun* has been discussed by Takamine Ryōshū, *Kegon shisōshi*, pp. 140–45; Rhi Ki-yong (Yi Kiyǒng), *Wǒnhyo sasang: segye kwan*, pp. 23–27; and cf. Kashiwagi Hiroo, *Daijō kishinron no kenkyū*, pp. 427–66.

But the *Awakening of Faith* was just a śāstra and, consequently, a nonultimate description of reality (*neyārtha*), which was potentially subject to challenge. Clearly, Silla Buddhists, and Wŏnhyo in particular, would have welcomed a sūtra—a definitive (*nitārtha*) scripture spoken by the Buddha himself—that would support the positions of *Awakening of Faith* and, by extension, the philosophical outlook of their entire tradition. Whoever the author of the *Vajrasamādhi* was, the tack his composition took shows that he was aware of the sensibilities of the scholastic climate of the time, if not actually in contact with, or a part of, the Silla academic coterie.[137]

But resolving this philosophical conflict scholastically was apparently not enough for Wŏnhyo. As seen in his biographies, Wŏnhyo also advocated and acted out in person a faith-oriented approach to practice, which would help to fix this syncretic vision in the minds of Buddhist followers. Several of Wŏnhyo's works are concerned with Pure Land scriptures and recitation of the Buddha's name;[138] hence, it cannot be denied that religious praxis was any less important to Wŏnhyo than theological exegesis. It is interesting to note in this connection that even in his Pure Land writings, Wŏnhyo follows the same hermeneutic he forged in his *Kisillon-so*, basing his descriptions of Pure Land practice on the one mind and its two aspects.[139]

I believe that it was these two concerns—resolving the philosophical conflict inherent in the Buddhist church of his day, and establishing a firm praxis foundation for his ecumenical vision—that prompted Wŏnhyo to renounce his retirement and work one final time on a commentary to the sūtra. Wŏnhyo appears to have seen in the *Vajrasamādhi* the ideal vehicle for amalga-

---

[137] See Kimura, "*Kongōzammaikyō*," p. 116. Han Kidu (*Silla Sŏn*, p. 23) has gone as far as to suggest that precisely because of the Ch'an/Sŏn elements in Wŏnhyo's *KSGR* (and thus by extension in *VS*, as will be discussed in detail in the following pages), "I believe that there was a thorough understanding of Sŏn thought among the Silla intelligentsia and that Sŏn was practiced in association with the scholastic teachings." Han does not, however, give any indication as to how these Buddhist scholiasts working on the peninsula would have come into contact with Sŏn, a movement with little currency even on the Chinese mainland at that time. Given that Wŏnhyo himself shows no signs of recognizing the Sŏn origins of some of the doctrines found in *VS*, I think that this surmise may be safely dismissed.

[138] These are listed in Tongguk taehakkyo, ed., *Han'guk Pulgyo ch'ongnok*, pp. 20–37, nos. 16, 17, 18, 19, 20, 25, 26, 44, 79, 80, 84, 85, 86. For Wŏnhyo's works on Pure Land, see the survey in Kim Kangmo, "Shiragi Gangyō no bungakukan," pp. 124–30; see also Minamoto Hiroyuki, "Shiragi Jōdokyō no tokushoku," pp. 294–307; Etani Ryūkai, "Shiragi Gangyō no Jōdokyō shisō," pp. 71–92; An Kyehyŏn, *Silla Chŏngt'ogyo sasangsa yŏn'gu*, pp. 11–68; Matsubayashi Kōshi, "Shiragi Jōdokyō no ichikōsatsu: Gangyō no Jōdokyō shisō o megutte," pp. 196–98.

[139] See discussion in Ko Ikchin, p. 254.

mating the syncretic principle he explores in *Kisillon-so* and *Simmun hwa-jaeng-ron* with this practice orientation that was so important to him personally. Wŏnhyo's commentary to the *Vajrasamādhi* employs many of the same sources used in writing his *Kisillon-so*; and like that earlier treatise—as indeed so much of his writing—*KSGR* too draws from the analysis of the one mind and its two aspects. In *KSGR*, however, Wŏnhyo moves in a slightly different direction and focuses his hermeneutical structure on the "contemplation practice that has but a single taste" (*ilmi kwanhaeng/i-wei kuan-hsing*). This "single taste" is an ancient metaphor used in Buddhist texts to describe the overriding soteriological import of the Buddhist teachings. The locus classicus for the term appears in the Pali *Cullavagga*: "As the vast ocean, oh monks, is impregnated with a single taste, the taste of salt, so too, monks, is my Dharma and Vinaya impregnated with but a single taste, the taste of liberation."[140] His explication of each chapter of the *Vajrasamādhi* is made in terms of a particular type of meditative practice, finally culminating in this "single-taste" contemplation. Wŏnhyo summarizes his approach to the text succinctly in the preface to his commentary, where he clarifies the progressive relationship that pertains between the different chapters of the scripture.

> The practice of nonproduction arcanely harmonizes with the signless. The signless dharmas correspondingly become the inspiration of original [enlightenment]. Since this inspiration is the original inspiration and yet is gainless, it does not waver from the edge of reality. Since this limit is the edge of reality and yet is distinct from the nature, the true limit is also void. All the buddhas, the tathāgatas, are stored therein and all bodhisattvas accordingly access it. Thus, reference is made to accessing the tathāgatagarbha. These are the principal ideas of each of the six chapters [of the main body of this sūtra].
>
> In the approach to contemplation [outlined in this sūtra], there are six practices established, from initial resolute faith through equal enlightenment. When the six practices are completed, the ninth consciousness appears via an evolutionary process. The manifestation of this immaculate consciousness (*amalavijñāna*) is the pure *dharmadhātu*. The other eight consciousnesses evolve into the four wisdoms. Once these five dharmas are perfected, one is then furnished with the three bodies [of buddhahood]. In this wise, cause and fruition are not separate from phenomenal objects and wisdom. Since phenomenal objects and wisdom are free from duality, they have only a single

---

[140] See *Cullavagga* ix.14; for "single taste," see also *Chieh-shen-mi ching* (*Sandhinirmocana-sūtra*) 1, *T* 676.16.692a25.

taste. Thus, the contemplation practice that has but a single taste is considered to be the theme of this sūtra.[141]

Hence, while employing the same philosophical principles used in his *Ki-sillon-so*, Wŏnhyo has tried in *KSGR* to extend their import into the realm of actual practice. The major step Wŏnhyo takes in his commentary, and the fundamental contribution it thus makes to Korean Buddhist philosophy, is to correlate this "contemplation practice that has a single taste" with the tathāgatagarbha. In so doing, Wŏnhyo fuses his ontological outlook with his view toward praxis, synthesizing around this contemplation practice the various intellectual and religious currents then prominent in Silla Buddhism.

As further substantiation for this interpretation, in his opening comments to the second prologue section of the *Vajrasamādhi*, Wŏnhyo gives four different hermeneutical schemata via which to examine the sūtra, each of which culminates in "the essence of the one-mind tathāgatagarbha," or "the fountainhead of the tathāgatagarbha that has a single taste."[142] The second of these analyses is the most compelling.

The beginningless churnings of all deluded thoughts ordinarily result from nothing more than the affliction of discrimination, which derives from clinging to signs. Now, wishing to reverse this churning in order to return to the fountainhead, one must first negate all these signs. It is for this reason that [the sūtra] first explains the contemplation of the signless dharma.

But while all these signs may have been annihilated, if one conserves the mind that contemplates (*yak chon kwansim/jo ts'un kwan-hsin*), then the mind that contemplates will continue to arise and one will not experience original enlightenment. Consequently, one must annihilate the arising of the mind. Therefore, this second chapter [of the main body of the text] illumines the practice of nonproduction.

Once one's practice produces nothing, one then experiences original enlightenment. Drawing from this [experience], one transforms beings and prompts them to gain the original inspiration. Hence, this third chapter elucidates the aspect of the inspiration of original enlightenment.

If, while relying on original enlightenment, one therewith inspires sentient beings, then those sentient beings in fact can leave behind falsity and access reality. Therefore, the fourth chapter elucidates the approach to the edge of reality.

[141] *KSGR* 1, p. 961a–b.
[142] *KSGR* 1, p. 963c18–19, 21–22. Ko Ikchin (pp. 241 and 243) gives convenient charts outlining these different schemes.

One's internal practice is in fact signless and unproduced. External proselytism is in fact the original inspiration's accessing of reality. In this wise, the two types of benefit [of oneself and others] are replete with the myriads of spiritual practices. These all derive from the true nature and all conform to true voidness. Consequently, the fifth chapter elucidates the voidness of the true nature.

Relying on this true nature, the myriads of spiritual practices are perfected. One accesses the tathāgatagarbha's fountainhead that has a single taste. Therefore, the sixth chapter illumines the tathāgatagarbha.

Since one has returned to the fountainhead of the mind, one then has nothing more to do (*musoŭi/wu-so-wei*). As there is nothing more to do, there is nothing that has not been done. Hence, it is said that these six chapters therewith incorporate all the Mahāyāna.[143]

In Wǒnhyo's interpretation of the *Vajrasamādhi*, then, each chapter describes one aspect of the path toward accessing the tathāgatagarbha, which "includes completely all approaches [to dharma] and shows that they are equally of the same one taste."[144] In assessing the possible reasons for the composition of the *Vajrasamādhi* in Silla Korea, one would thus do well to keep in mind this close connection Wǒnhyo saw between its syncretic philosophical outlook and its all-encompassing praxis.

But there was something more to the doctrinal teachings of the *Vajrasamādhi* that even the perspicacious Wǒnhyo and his Silla colleagues missed. Some of its teachings, which they assumed derived from Indian sūtras or śāstras, actually had quite another source, of which they could not have known; and their ignorance of the real pedigree of those teachings left them totally oblivious to one of the *Vajrasamādhi*'s major agendas. That alternate source was a new indigenous movement within Chinese Buddhism, then in its incipiency on the mainland, which was just making its way to Korea. It was Ch'an.

---

[143] *KSGR* 1, p. 963c9–20.
[144] *KSGR* 1, p. 963c25–26.

CHAPTER FOUR

# CH'AN ELEMENTS
# IN THE *VAJRASAMĀDHI*: EVIDENCE
# FOR THE AUTHORSHIP OF THE SŪTRA

The principal inspiration the *Vajrasamādhi* gave Wŏnhyo was the link it could help forge between religious ideology and practice. There is one school of sinitic Buddhism, in particular, that is closely identified with such interests: Ch'an, or Sŏn, as it is known in Korea. Wŏnhyo, who did not complete either of his two attempted pilgrimages to China, had no way of knowing of this school, which was only in its nascency in the latter part of the seventh century, when the sūtra was written. The advantage of hindsight allows us now, however, to see several distinct Ch'an influences in the *Vajrasamādhi*, especially in chapter 5, "Approaching the Edge of Reality." These include references both to the "two accesses" (*iip/erh-ju*) soteriological schema attributed to Bodhidharma and to the "guarding the one" (*suil/shou-i*) or "guarding the mind" (*susim/shou-hsin*) contemplative approach of the East Mountain school of Tao-hsin and Hung-jen. Wŏnhyo of course could not have known the pedigree of these teachings. But could it be that, in his focus on the contemplative (*kwanhaeng/kuan-hsing*) implications of the *Vajrasamādhi*, Wŏnhyo has given us a key to unlock the problem of the authorship of the text?

Ch'an Influences in the *Vajrasamādhi*

*Ch'an and the Sinicization of Meditation*

No school of Buddhism developed in a vacuum, isolated from the philosophical and praxis currents buffeting its contemporaries. This is true even for the Ch'an school, which has most vehemently claimed its independence from the rest of the Buddhist tradition. The previous chapter demonstrated that the author of the *Vajrasamādhi* was certainly familiar with the scholastic controversies that helped to mature the indigenous doctrinal schools of East Asian Buddhism. But the Ch'an elements in the text show too that he was aware of new movements in sinitic Buddhism that would ultimately evolve into a full-fledged Ch'an "school."

We have already noted the East Asian penchant for subitist soteriologies, in which enlightenment was made accessible through a "re-visioning" of one's ordinary perceptual processes. But if this subitism was to take practical form, specific meditative techniques had to be developed that would catalyze this instantaneous awakening. In adopting the name "Meditation" (*ch'an*; dhyāna) for itself, Ch'an was laying claim to a special niche in East Asian Buddhism: it would be the school most concerned with creating new, truly sinitic, methods of contemplation. This adaptation of Buddhist meditation to East Asian cultural sensibilities began with the T'ien-t'ai school, but the most protracted experiments took place in Ch'an. This process would culminate in the Sung dynasty, when Ch'an developed the mature techniques of "public cases" (*kung-an*; Kor. *kongan*) and "critical phrases" (*hua-t'ou*; Kor. *hwadu*), which are quintessentially, and exclusively, the provenance of the Ch'an school.[1] But these experiments had already begun in earnest by the time the *Vajrasamādhi* was written; indeed, the sūtra provides some of the earliest documentation available of the practices attributed to two of the earliest figures in the school, Bodhidharma and Tao-hsin.

It was inevitable that meditation would come within the purview of the same process of sinicization that was spurring doctrinal innovation in East Asian Buddhism. Buddhism had always valued a pragmatic approach to religion, in which its teachings were claimed to have been conceived through, and their truths attested by, explicit meditative programs. Because of the inseparable connection in Buddhism among its ontological views, soteriological regimens, and meditative techniques, change occurring in one area would invariably have an impact on the others. This is precisely what was occurring in sixth- and seventh-century East Asia. I have already discussed some aspects of the doctrinal evolution then occurring in sinitic Buddhism and how these are reflected in the *Vajrasamādhi*. But the sūtra also provides evidence concerning related meditative innovations. These innovations will be the focus of this chapter.

Despite the Ch'an elements appearing in this sūtra, the *Vajrasamādhi* can

---

[1] I discuss the evolution of these mature Ch'an meditative techniques in my article "*K'an-hua* Meditation," esp. pp. 343–56.

hardly be considered an apologia, since only a relatively small portion of the text involves ideas that could have been identified as exclusively Ch'an. But this weighting in itself tells us something important about the school. Despite the claim it eventually makes of being a "separate transmission outside the teachings," Ch'an's early adepts were well aware of the issues and problems debated within the scholastic traditions of East Asian Buddhism, if not central figures themselves in those debates. Ch'an advocates were certainly acquainted with the specifics of the debate then raging between Ti-lun and She-lun advocates over the nature of the mind. Ch'an adherents mentioned in the biography of Hui-k'o (ca. 485–593), the putative second patriarch of Ch'an, were said, for example, to have based their teachings on the *She-lun*,[2] and the *Ti-lun* is cited in early Ch'an writings attributed to both Hui-k'o and Hung-jen.[3] Hence, there is evidence to support affinities between these learned traditions of Mahāyāna and early Ch'an.[4] Indeed, based on the testimony of the *Vajrasamādhi*, one may go so far as to claim that the Ch'an Problematik was framed by the same controversy then occupying sinitic Buddhist philosophers.

Even the legends Ch'an later tells about the school's putative founder, Bodhidharma,[5] hardly suggest a school isolated from the mainstream of the Chinese tradition. The earliest work of the Ch'an school, *Erh-ju ssu-hsing lun* (Treatise on the two accesses and four practices), which is ascribed to Bodhidharma, proclaims in its opening lines that one of its two principal soteriologies is to "awaken to the source by relying on the teachings."[6] Ch'an often seems to place as much emphasis on Tathāgatagarbha thought as that seen in the writings belonging to the learned traditions of Chinese Buddhism.[7] Bodhidharma is said, for example, to have initiated the Ch'an trans-

[2] See the notice in the biography of Fa-ch'ung (589–665?), *Hsü Kao-seng chuan* 25, *T* 2060.50.366b20, translated in McRae, p. 26.

[3] See Hui-k'o's biography in *Leng-ch'ieh shih-tzu chi*, *T* 2837.85.1285c3; *Hsiu-hsin yao lun*, *T* 2011.48.377a21, translated in McRae, pp. 121–22. It should be noted, however, that this quotation does not appear in any known recension of the *Ti-lun*; see Yanagida, *Shoki no Zenshi*, vol. 1, p. 152; noted in McRae, p. 313 n. 42, who suggests that the *Leng-ch'ieh shih-tzu chi* citation is taken from the *Hsiu-hsin yao lun*.

[4] See discussion in Kamata Shigeo and Ueyama Shunpei, *Bukkyō no shisō VII (Chūgoku Zen)*, p. 113; Yanagida Seizan, *Shoki no Zenshi*, vol. 2, pp. 152ff; Suzuki Daisetsu, *Zen shisōshi kenkyū*, pp. 304ff; Jorgensen, *"Long Scroll*," p. 94.

[5] See the discussion in Bernard Faure, "Bodhidharma as Textual and Religious Paradigm," pp. 187–98.

[6] I use the edition of *Erh-ju ssu-hsing lun* included in Yanagida Seizan, trans., *Daruma no goroku*, here p. 31. Cf. *Hsü Kao-seng chuan*, *T* 2060.50.551c8. This passage is cited in Ching-chüeh's *Leng-ch'ieh shih-tzu chi*, *T* 2837.85.1285a12.

[7] Hattori Masaaki has gone so far as to suggest that Ch'an in fact derives from the Tathā-

mission in China by handing down the *Laṅkāvatāra-sūtra*,[8] one of the first texts to use the tathāgatagarbha concept synthetically, a use that is also prominent in the Chinese doctrinal systems. The career of *Erh-ju ssu-hsing lun*'s redactor, T'an-lin (fl. 506–574), is particularly striking in the context of the larger concern with the philosophical origins of Ch'an. Besides being an assistant to a number of Indian translators, T'an-lin is also said to have lectured upon, and written commentaries to, the *Śrīmālā* and *Nirvāṇa* sutras, both texts dealing with Tathāgatagarbha doctrine.[9] Indeed, if T'an-lin's doctrinal interests were in any way representative of those of his Chinese contemporaries associated with Ch'an, we have a graphic example of the seminal role played by the tathāgatagarbha theory in Ch'an's early evolution. The author of the *Vajrasamādhi* too seems to have been particularly attracted to Tathāgatagarbha thought and it occupies a central place in the teachings of the scripture, even lending its name to the seventh chapter. But by combining Ch'an and doctrinal elements in the same text, the *Vajrasamādhi* provides invaluable information concerning both the Tathāgatagarbha underpinnings of Ch'an praxis and the ideological milieu out of which Ch'an evolved. This synthesis will reveal once more the strong affinities that pertain between the different schools of sinitic Buddhism.

## The Two-Accesses Soteriological Schema

By far the most celebrated section of the *Vajrasamādhi* is chapter 5's treatment of the two accesses of principle (*iip/li-ju*) and practice (*haengnip/hsing-ju*). This dichotomy occupies a vital place in the early evolution of Ch'an doctrine, for it is the general rubric from which is constructed Bodhidharma's *Erh-ju ssu-hsing lun* (Treatise on the two accesses and four practices). This treatise is generally regarded as the earliest work with an explicitly Ch'an pedigree, and probably the only of the many works ascribed to Bodhidharma that has the slightest chance of being in any way associated with him. The first modern scholar to discover the affinity between *Erh-ju ssu-*

gatagarbha strand in Indian Buddhist thought; see his "Zen to Indo bukkyō," pp. 509–24, esp. p. 520.

    [8] See the biography of Hui-k'o in *Hsü Kao-seng chuan* 16, *T* 2060.50.552b20–22. Although the Northern school tried to authenticate this connection between early Ch'an and the *Laṅkā-vatāra-sūtra* by compiling a history of the "masters and disciples of the Laṅkāvatāra" (*Leng-ch'ieh shih-tzu chi*; *T* 2837), the connection remains tenuous; see McRae, pp. 90–91.

    [9] See Tao-hsüan's *Hsü Kao-seng chuan* 16, *T* 2060.50.552b17 and 431c25, in the biography of Hui-k'o; Liebenthal, pp. 351–55, and pp. 384–85 for a table of T'an-lin's translations; McRae, pp. 23–24.

*hsing lun* and this section of the *Vajrasamādhi* was Hayashi Taiun, who proposed that the *Vajrasamādhi* was the scriptural source for this distinctive teaching of Bodhidharma.[10] (To give credit where credit is due, I should note that the Ch'ing commentator Chu-chen had made the same observation long before.[11]) Hayashi's hypothesis prompted a series of studies that sought to determine the relationship between the two texts.[12] These culminated in the research of Mizuno Kōgen, who conclusively demonstrated that the *Vajrasamādhi*'s account of the two accesses was copied from the Bodhidharma text, not vice versa.[13] This radical theory revolutionized our view of the *Vajrasamādhi* and suggested for the first time that the very authenticity of the sūtra itself was now in question. Clearly, too, the affinities between the two texts would thenceforth figure importantly in any attempt to ascertain the dating and authorship of the *Vajrasamādhi*.

The *Erh-ju ssu-hsing lun* is a treatise with a complicated textual history.[14] The text is certainly not of Indian provenance, since it includes passages lifted verbatim from earlier Chinese translations of both sūtra and śāstra literature. The present scholarly consensus is that the treatise was written by T'an-lin, a close associate of Bodhidharma's successor, Hui-k'o. The extent to which the text reflects Bodhidharma's actual teachings is purely speculative, though it does not require a great leap of imagination to presume that it might constitute T'an-lin's presentation of, at least, Hui-k'o's knowledge of Bodhidharma's thought. By the middle of the seventh century, only a few decades before the *Vajrasamādhi* was written, *Erh-ju ssu-hsing lun* was circulating under Bodhidharma's name and from that point on was regarded as the principal statement of his teachings. Ancillary materials attributed to

[10] Hayashi Taiun, "Bodaidarumaden no kenkyū," pp. 62–72.

[11] Chu-chen, after giving the text of the *Erh-ju ssu-hsing lun* in his commentary to the two-accesses section of *VS*, notes that "this teaching of the first patriarch was established on the basis of this sūtra [*VS*]." *T'ung-tsung chi* 7, p. 264b9–10.

[12] These include studies by such prominent scholars as Suzuki Daisetsu, "Daruma no Zenbō to shisō oyobi sono ta"; and Paul Demiéville, *Le concile de Lhasa*, p. 54 n. 2.

[13] Mizuno, pp. 51ff; see also discussion in Liebenthal (pp. 349–56) and Han Kidu (*Silla Sŏn*, pp. 29–31).

[14] For a lengthy discussion of the textual history of *Erh-ju ssu-hsing lun*, drawing on much of the relevant Japanese scholarship, see Jorgensen, "*Long Scroll*," pp. 359–62, 377–78. The text has been expertly translated and annotated by Yanagida Seizan, *Daruma no goroku*. Annotated English translations of *Erh-ju ssu-hsing lun*, with most of its supplementary materials, appear in McRae, pp. 102–106, and Jorgensen, "*Long Scroll*," pp. 239–358. The text has recently been rendered into French in Bernard Faure, *Le Traité de Bodhidharma*. The Tibetan translation of *Erh-ju ssu-hsing lun* has been studied by Okimoto Katsumi, "Chibetto yaku *Ninyūshigyōron* ni tsuite," pp. 999–92 (sic).

Bodhidharma's disciples continued to be appended to the treatise perhaps as late as the 680s, but the structure of the text was fairly well standardized in the period with which we are concerned here.

The term "access" (*ip/ju*), which figures so prominently in the treatise, is often used in Chinese compounds to render Sanskrit terms expressing entry into such higher reaches of Buddhist spirituality as samādhi (*ju-ting*; *samādhipraviṣṭa*); *samāpatti*, or attainment (*ju-kuan*; *samāpanna*); *niyāmāvakrānti*, or the certitude of attaining enlightenment (*ju cheng-ting wei*); and even nirvāṇa (*ju nieh-p'an*; *parinirvṛta*).[15] "Access" was sometimes itself equivalent to dhyāna in sinitic apocrypha, a usage found in the sixth-century *Tsui-miao-sheng ting ching* (Book of the most sublime and supreme dhyāna).[16] The term is frequently found in Chinese scholastic and Ch'an texts in the compound "to access the path" (*ju-tao*), the virtual equivalent of enlightenment, or bodhi. It is this compound that apparently inspired the description of the path found in the apocryphal *P'u-sa ying-lo pen-yeh ching* as a "teaching of the six accesses" (*liu-ju fa-men*). There, the accesses correspond to six basic levels of the mārga: the ten abidings, ten practices, ten transferences, ten *bhūmi*s, immaculate *bhūmi*, and sublime-enlightenment *bhūmi*. In addition, the *Ying-lo ching* also includes a preliminary level of the mārga—the ten faiths—preceding the formal initiation to the bodhisattva path that occurs at the first stage of the ten abidings.[17] These levels closely parallel the *Vajrasamādhi*'s division of the mārga into "six practices" (*yukhaeng/liu-hsing*), which are listed following the discussion on the two accesses: the ten faiths, ten abid-

[15] For listings of such compounds, see Hirakawa Akira et al., eds., *Index to the Abhidharma-kośabhāṣya*, part 2, pp. 368–69, ad loc.

[16] The *Tsui-miao-sheng ting ching* appears first in catalogues in 594. The scripture, which sought to synthesize variant theories about contemplation practice current during the late sixth century, calls *ju* the equivalent of the third dhyāna. See the study and edition of the Tun-huang recension of the scripture in the appendix to Sekiguchi Shindai, *Tendai shikan no kenkyū*, pp. 379–402; for the passage in question, see p. 399.

[17] For these six levels, see *P'u-sa ying-lo pen-yeh ching*, T 1485.24.1022b13–14 (which uses the term *liu-ju fa-men* for them), 1010b25, and 1017a5; the ten faiths are listed at p. 1011c2–8. Elsewhere, these six levels are expanded as "forty-two teachings to be clearly contemplated, which serve as the causes and fruitions of sagacity and sainthood"; p. 1022b4. When combined with the ten levels of faith, this expanded listing would provide the fifty-two total stages that would become *de rigueur* in the Hua-yen school's explication of the mārga. For a detailed study of the mārga schema of the *Ying-lo ching* and its impact on the Chinese Taoist tradition, see Stephen R. Bokenkamp, "Stages of Transcendence in Taoism." For a discussion of this sixfold schema as it is systematized in the Hua-yen school, see Buswell, *Korean Approach*, pp. 50–52. On the apocryphalness of the *Ying-lo ching*, see Mochizuki Shinkō, *Bukkyō kyōten seiritsu shiron*, pp. 471–84.

ings, ten practices, ten transferences, ten *bhūmi*s, and equal enlightenment.[18] The juxtaposition of "access" and "practice" in these two indigenous sūtras suggests the fluidity in the connotations of the two terms, a feature noticed by Wŏnhyo in his commentary to this section, which will be discussed below.

The term "access of principle" is not, however, attested in any translations of Indian or Serindian materials, and it seems to be an indigenous Chinese concept. Some of the closest parallels to "access of principle" as used in the Bodhidharma text and the *Vajrasamādhi* are found in the works of Tao-sheng (d. 434), one of the most creative exegetes in the early Chinese church. In his remarks concerning the *Vimalakīrtinirdeśa*'s reference to voidness itself being void, Tao-sheng uses the phrase "gain awakening by availing oneself of the principle," in which principle is construed as the equivalent of voidness.[19] In his commentary to the *Nirvāṇa Sūtra*, Tao-sheng describes principle in a way that is evocative of some of the specific terminology that will be used later in *Erh-ju ssu-hsing lun*: "Now, the true principle is natural and awakening is also in arcane accordance with it. The true principle is free from deviation; so how could awakening prompt any change? That unchanging essence is pellucid and ever radiant. It becomes perverted merely through ignorance, so that events are then no longer in your control. If you can restrain seeking, you will then turn away from ignorance and return to the ultimate. Once you have returned to the ultimate and gained the root, [the principle] will be just like it was at its nascency."[20]

The *Erh-ju ssu-hsing lun*'s account of the two accesses is quoted in Tao-hsüan's (596–667) biography of Bodhidharma, which appears in his *Hsü Kao-seng chuan* (Supplement to the biographies of eminent monks), compiled ca. 649, about a century and a half after the presumed date of Bodhidharma's death, and some thirty years before the composition of the *Vajrasamādhi*.[21] This citation is the terminus ad quem for Bodhidharma's connection to the teaching and proof that the *Vajrasamādhi* was not its source. But as with so many other doctrines in Ch'an, this idea need not

---

[18] *VS*, chap. 5, before n. 70.

[19] As quoted in Seng-chao's *Chu Wei-mo-chieh ching* 5, *T* 1775.38.373a21; cited in Yanagida, *Daruma no goroku*, p. 37; Jorgensen, "*Long Scroll*," p. 243 n. 1.

[20] *Ta-pan-nieh-p'an ching chi-chieh* 1, *T* 1763.37.377b10–13; rendering adapted from Walter Liebenthal, "A Biography of Tao-sheng," p. 245. This passage is cited in Yanagida, *Daruma no goroku*, p. 39; and Jorgensen, "*Long Scroll*," p. 244.

[21] *Hsü Kao-seng chuan* 61, *T* 2060.50.551c; the different versions of the schema are quoted and compared in Mizuno, pp. 51–52; cf. p. 34. Material continued to be added to this anthology until Tao-hsüan's death in 667.

have been the sole domain of any single school or teacher of Ch'an. Indeed, Tao-hsüan's association of this doctrine with Bodhidharma might well have clinched its traditional ascription to the first patriarch of Ch'an.[22]

Table 4.1 will help clarify the close affinities in the accounts of the two accesses in *Erh-ju ssu-hsing lun* and the *Vajrasamādhi*, especially the access of principle.[23] To summarize, the first access, the access of principle, suggests a passive, but nonetheless direct, approach to spiritual training, in which the adept need merely realize that each and every person is endowed with the buddha-nature—that is, all have the capacity for enlightenment. The means proposed to affect this salvation is simply to have the student deny his mistaken view that he is deluded and have "deep faith" instead in the fact of his enlightenment. As T'an-lin mentions in his preface to *Erh-ju ssu-hsing lun*, the intent of this access is to bring about "pacification of mind" (*an-hsin*), a term used also in the *Vajrasamādhi*, which may alternatively be called "wall contemplation" (*pi-kuan*). Given the emphasis on the immanence of enlightenment, along with faith as the primary catalyst of realization, one can see that the access of principle shares profound affinities with Tathāgatagarbha thought. The description in section 5, where the true nature is said to be "obscured by adventitious sense-objects," is in fact taken verbatim from the *Laṅkāvatāra-sūtra*'s treatment of the tathāgatagarbha: "Although this tathāgatagarbha *cum* ālayavijñāna . . . is pure in its own-nature, it is *obscured by adventitious sense-objects.*"[24] On the basis of this earliest text of Ch'an, then, the Ch'an Problematik is clearly framed by the doctrinal and praxis orientations of mainstream sinitic Buddhism.

The account of the "access of practice" in the *Vajrasamādhi* shares few affinities with *Erh-ju ssu-hsing lun*. There are no specific correspondences in the accounts of the two texts, though there are some implicit similarities of perspective. The *Vajrasamādhi* describes the access of practice as the endeavor to keep the mind completely undisturbed, by ignoring all such dichotomies as self and others, clinging and rejection, and so forth. The detached perspective developed thereby leaves the mind open to a state beyond all dis-

[22] The tendency for doctrines to float freely between different factions, only later to be ascribed to some eminent past figure, is seen, for example, in the *Platform sūtra*. See discussion in Carl Bielefeldt and Lewis Lancaster, "T'an Ching (Platform Scripture)," pp. 200–201, summarizing Yanagida's views, for which see Yanagida Seizan, *Shoki Zenshū shisho*, pp. 148–212, 253–78.

[23] *Erh-ju ssu-hsing lun*, Yanagida, trans., *Daruma no goroku*, pp. 31–32. The passage from *VS* appears in chap. 5, after n. 64.

[24] *Leng-ch'ieh-a-po-to-lo pao ching*, 4, *T* 670.16.510c1–2; cf. Suzuki, trans., *Laṅkāvatāra Sūtra*, p. 192.

TABLE 4.1
The Treatment of the "Two Accesses" in *Erh-ju ssu-hsing lun* and the *Vajrasamādhi*

| *Erh-ju ssu-hsing lun* | *Vajrasamādhi-sūtra* |
|---|---|
| 1. Now there are many pathways by which to access the path, but essentially we can say **there are** but **two** types. | 1. **There are two** accesses: |
| 2. **The first is the access of principle; the second is the access of practice**. | 2. **the first is** called **the access of principle; the second is** called **the access of practice**. |
| 3. **Access of principle means** to awaken to the source of doctrine (*tsung*) by relying on the teaching. | 3. **Access of principle means** |
| 4. **One has deep faith that** living **beings**, whether ordinary persons or sages, have the same **true nature**. | 4. **one has deep faith that** sentient **beings** are not different from the **true nature**, and thus are neither identical nor counterpoised. |
| 5. [This true nature] is unable to appear clearly **merely** through being falsely **obscured by adventitious sense objects**. | 5. [This true nature] is **obscured** and obstructed **merely by adventitious sense objects**. |
| 6. If one abandons falsity and takes refuge in truth and **abides frozen in** wall **contemplation**, then **self** and **others, ordinary person** and **sage**, will be one and the same. | 6. Without either going or coming, one **abides frozen in** attentive **contemplation**. One contemplates according to truth that the buddha-nature is neither existent nor nonexistent. It is neither **self** nor **others** and is no different in either **ordinary person** or **sage**. |
| 7. **One abides firmly without wavering**, and is never again swayed by the written teachings. | 7. **One abides firmly without wavering** in the state of the adamantine mind, |
| 8. This is to be in arcane accordance with the principle, **free from discrimination, calm,** and **inactive**. | 8. **calm**, quiet, **inactive**, and **free from discrimination**. |
| 9. **This is called the access of principle**. | 9. **This is called the access of principle**. |

crimination, which can be neither accessed nor abandoned. That is the mind's natural state of purity.[25]

*Erh-ju ssu-hsing lun*'s account of the access of practice is considerably more detailed, dividing it into four specific types of cultivation. While it is not necessary to discuss each of these practices exhaustively, the progression they imply is worth explicating. The first stage, the practice of the requital of enmity (*pao-yüan hsing*), helps the student to control his reactions to unpleasant situations by instilling in him an awareness of the truth of karmic cause and effect: viz., that his suffering is merely the result of his previous enmity. The complementary practice that accords with conditions (*sui-yüan hsing*) reveals that pleasant situations too are but the reward of *karman* and encourages the student to remain indifferent to good as well as evil by understanding that there is no eternal soul (*anātman*). The practice of seeking nothing (*wu-so-chiu hsing*) creates a radical detachment from the things of the world by exposing to the student the truth of suffering and its proximate cause (i.e., craving). The final practice of according with the dharma (*ch'eng-fa hsing*) reveals the truth of emptiness, by which the adept comes to know the fundamental nonduality of all dharmas, rendering him able to perform any sort of practice (specifically the six pāramitās) without clinging to their individual characteristics. Tellingly, however, this consummate form of practice is said to reveal the "principle of the purity of the nature," which is accomplished through "resolute faith" (*adhimukti*). Hence, after leading the student through a progressive process of detachment—first to both suffering and pleasure, then to the causes of suffering, and finally to all things—the four practices ultimately converge with the access of principle's peculiar type of understanding and its principal soteriological technique of faith. The implication here is that the truth of Buddhism can be understood either directly without a progressive regimen (access of principle), or indirectly through a graduated series of steps (access of practice). In either case, however, the realization achieved is identical.

The eventual convergence of the access of practice with the access of principle is reminiscent of Chinese doctrinal taxonomies and anticipates the soteriological use of such taxonomies that will become common in Chinese Buddhism in the eighth and ninth centuries. In the four practices of the Bodhidharma text, there is a hierarchical progression of practices *cum* teachings, with each stage complementing the preceding practice and anticipating the practice that will follow. A similar progression is seen in Chih-i's (538–597)

---

[25] *VS*, chap. 5, before n. 67.

hermeneutical rubric of the "five flavors," which draws on the *Nirvāṇa Sū-tra*'s metaphor of the stages in the clarification of milk to describe the progressive profundity of various sūtras. In the same way that the cow produces milk, which is then clarified in turn into cream, curds, butter, and ghee, so too does the Buddha speak (1) the twelvefold division of the Hīnayāna canon, which is refined in turn into (2) the Hīnayāna sūtras, (3) the expanded (*vaipulya*) sūtras of the Mahāyāna, (4) the Prajñāpāramitā sūtras, and finally (5) the *Nirvāṇa Sūtra*, in which the doctrine of the buddha-nature is equated with ghee.[26] In this wise the ultimate insight of Buddhism presented to the Buddhist adept at the fifth level of the schema converges with the person of the Buddha himself who initiates the hermeneutical progression in the first place. We may also note Chih-i's placement of teachings aligned with Tathā-gatagarbha thought at the apex of his doctrinal taxonomy, a tendency repeated subsequently in the T'ien-t'ai school (see *infra*).

A hermeneutical hierarchy that even more closely parallels the treatment of the two accesses in *Erh-ju ssu-hsing lun* is that developed by Hui-kuan (363–443), a scholar most closely identified with *Nirvāṇa Sūtra* exegesis. Hui-kuan is said to have bifurcated the Buddha's doctrine into two broad categories: the sudden (*tun-chiao*) teachings, represented by the *Avataṃsaka-sūtra*, and the gradual (*chien-chiao*) teachings. The gradual teaching was then subdivided into five temporal periods, corresponding to (1) separate instructions given to followers of each of the three vehicles; (2) the teachings common to all three vehicles, viz., the Śūnyavāda teachings of the Prajñāpā-ramitā; (3) the critical teaching that exposed the fallacies in the Hīnayāna approach, which was represented by such texts as the *Vimalakīrtinirdeśa*; (4) the common destiny of the Mahāyāna, in which all three vehicles are merged together, as found in the *Lotus Sūtra*; and (5) the omnipresence of buddha-hood, as taught in the *Nirvāṇa Sūtra*.[27] The parallel in its logical structure with the two accesses of the Bodhidharma text is even more remarkable in that Hui-kuan describes the sudden teaching as that which "manifests the principle," implying that the gradual teaching is more concerned with progressive soteriological regimens.

[26] See the account in *Ta-pan-nieh-p'an ching* 13, *T* 375.12.690c28–691a6; translated in Neal Donner, "Sudden and Gradual Intimately Conjoined: Chih-i's T'ien-t'ai View," p. 209.

[27] See the excerpt from Hui-kuan's preface to his commentary on the *Nirvāṇa Sūtra*, which is no longer extant, in Chi-tsang's *San-lun hsüan-i*, *T* 1852.45.b4–14. This taxonomy is summarized in Leon Hurvitz, "Chih-I (538–597)," pp. 219–24, and discussed in Ōchō Enichi, "The Beginnings of Tenet Classification in China," pp. 91–94. See also the discussion of this taxonomy with reference to *Erh-ju ssu-hsing lun* in McRae, p. 343 n. 332.

Even in these two examples, one already sees anticipated the tendency for graduated programs to culminate in a final stage of insight that verifies the understanding that first catalyzed the process. The inspiration for this convergence of the beginning and end of training is the *Avataṃsaka-sūtra*'s renowned statement that the culmination of the path is identical to its inception: "When the thought of enlightenment is first aroused (*bodhicittotpāda*), right enlightenment is then achieved."[28] This correlation is brought out explicitly in the T'ien-t'ai school's temporal hierarchy of the teachings, which was systematized by Chan-jan (711–782) in the eighth century. In this taxonomy, the ultimate teaching of the dharma occurs first with (1) the direct enunciation of the *Avataṃsaka-sūtra*. Finding most people incapable of understanding this direct expression of truth, the Buddha decides to begin his dispensation over again with (2) the *Āgamas*, (3) the *vaipulya* sūtras, and (4) the Prajñāpāramitā sūtras. Only when the ability of sentient beings to understand his teachings has been sufficiently matured does the Buddha then teach the *Lotus* and *Nirvāṇa* sūtras, which are syntheses of the second, third, and fourth periods and which essentially duplicate the message presented first in the *Avataṃsaka*.[29] A similar logical progression is also seen in *Erh-ju ssu-hsing lun*, where the understanding perfected through the access of practice is identical to that finally achieved through the access of principle.

Neither *Erh-ju ssu-hsing lun* nor the *Vajrasamādhi* uses the terms sudden or gradual, as had Hui-kuan, to describe its soteriological approaches—testimony *ex silentio* that the sudden/gradual problem was not yet an issue in late-seventh-century Ch'an. Nevertheless it is easy to see how the single access of principle could be viewed as a more immediate approach to enlightenment than the four stages of the access of practice outlined in the Bodhidharma text. Hence, *Erh-ju ssu-hsing lun*'s description of Ch'an soteriology does seem to anticipate the eighth-century debate concerning subitism that would rage in Ch'an circles after Shen-hui's (684-758) polemical challenge to the primacy of the Northern school.

Even without using such terms, however, *Erh-ju ssu-hsing lun*'s description of the two accesses is still clearly soteriological in approach. Although the doctrinal taxonomies with which it most closely compares in structure were hermeneutical schemata, scriptural interpretation was not their sole function. Polemical considerations certainly played a part in ordering the

---

[28] *Hua-yen ching* 8, *T* 278.9.449c14; cf. *Hua-yen ching* 17, *T* 279.10.89a1–2.

[29] For the T'ien-t'ai temporal taxonomy see Hurvitz, "Chih-I," pp. 229–44, and Chappell, ed., *T'ien-t'ai*, pp. 53–67.

teachings, especially in the taxonomies that come to be characteristic of the mature Hua-yen and T'ien-t'ai schools.[30] But such taxonomies also were sometimes intended to have explicitly soteriological purposes. This new purpose is particularly pronounced in some of the taxonomies of Chih-yen (602–668) and, especially, Tsung-mi (780–841), which outline the specific levels of understanding through which the Buddhist votary evolves in the course of his career.[31] This is precisely the intent of *Erh-ju ssu-hsing lun*: to forge a "soteriological hermeneutic" that would provide the Ch'an student with either a direct expression of Buddhist insight in the access of principle or a progressive unfolding of that insight through the four practices. Regardless of which of the two accesses the student may favor, either will lead to the identical gnoseological experience.

What is important to notice about the *Erh-ju ssu-hsing lun*'s presentation of Ch'an is that, during its nascency in the middle of the seventh century, Ch'an is grappling with a similar complex of issues as were exegetes in the learned schools of medieval Chinese Buddhism. And the mode of analysis it used to develop solutions to these problems was virtually identical to that used by learned Chinese exegetes. Clearly, Ch'an as reflected in this treatise defines itself in terms drawn from the larger Problematik of the sinitic tradition as a whole; it has barely started the long process of developing its own unique rhetorical and pedagogical rubrics, its own distinctive terminology, and its own separate praxis agenda. It was these unique features that would eventually distinguish Ch'an as a fully independent school of Chinese Buddhism.

Wŏnhyo's discussion of these two accesses is interesting for gauging the reaction that Buddhist exegetes unfamiliar with the nascent Ch'an movement would have had to its soteriological strategies. Wŏnhyo's comments reveal that he was completely oblivious to the Ch'an origin of these two accesses. He treats them instead in the context of the *mārga* schemata of such sūtras as *Fan-wang ching* and *Jen-wang ching*, also sinitic apocrypha. Wŏnhyo regards the two accesses as part of a sequential soteriological program—the access of principle corresponding to the stages of the path prior to the *bhūmi*s, the access by practice to the ten *bhūmi*s and above. In Wŏnhyo's interpretation, however, it is the access of principle that involves progressive

---

[30] I have treated some of these polemical purposes, and Ch'an's reaction to them, in my article "Ch'an Hermeneutics: A Korean View," pp. 231–56.

[31] This will be a major theme of Peter Gregory's forthcoming book, tentatively entitled "Tsung-mi's Synthetic Vision." For Chih-yen's *Hua-yen ching nei-chang men teng-tsa k'ung-mu chang* 2, *T* 1870.45.556a–c, summarized in Gregory, "Tsung-mi," chap. 2.

development, while the access of practice is more direct—a plausible conclusion if one only knew of the *Vajrasamādhi* version, which does not divide the second access into four substages.

> "Access of principle": it is called "access of principle" because, while it involves resolute faith (*adhimukti*) that is in accordance with the principle, it has not yet matured into the kind of practice that leads to realization. It is positioned prior to the *bhūmis*. "Access of practice": it is called "access of practice" because it is cultivation that involves realization of the principle and thus accesses the practice of nonproduction. It takes place on the *bhūmis*.
>
> In the section on access of principle there are four distinct passages. From "deep faith" to "adventitious sense-objects" is the access of the ten faiths. "Not identical" is said, because while that which characterizes sentient beings may not differ from the true nature, it is not identical to it. They are "not counterpoised" because they are neither identical nor different.
>
> The second section "without either going or coming, one abides frozen in attentive contemplation" is the access of the ten abidings. Because one awakens to the fact that sentient beings are void, it is neither going nor coming. This is because one calms one's mind via this experience of the voidness of the personality, attentively examining the fact that the buddha-nature is neither going nor coming.
>
> The third section "contemplating according to truth that the buddha-nature is neither existent nor nonexistent" is the access of the ten practices. As one has already gained the voidness of dharmas, one relies on the experience of the voidness of dharmas and contemplates according to truth that the buddha-nature lacks neither the characteristics of dharmas [phenomenal reality] nor the nature of voidness [absolute truth].
>
> The fourth section, "It is neither self nor others and is no different in ordinary person or sage," explains the level of the ten transferences. As one has already gained the access of principle, self and others are balanced and void. Hence, the mind abides firmly, without retrogressing, like adamant. What the *Fan-wang ching* calls the ten adamants and the *Jen-wang ching* the ten firm minds are different designations for the ten transferences.[32]

The access of practice, in distinction, represents the actual moment of enlightenment itself in Wŏnhyo's interpretation. In this access, the "deep faith" in the immanence of enlightenment engendered through the access of principle is verified through direct experience. The student then continues on to work for the benefit of both oneself and others.

[32] *KSGR* 2, p. 985a19–985b3; for the sūtra passages to which Wŏnhyo alludes, see *Fan-wang ching, T* 1484.24.997c23–26, and *Jen-wang ching, T* 245.8.826c10.

This section [on the access of practice] explains the access to realization that takes place on the *bhūmi*s. "The mind has no bias or inclination" because the mind that is endowed with knowledge that accords with the principle is free from any mental disturbances, for the mind that experiences mental disturbances does not arise. "Its shadows are free from flux" because objects that accord with the principle remain separate from the three time-periods [of past, present, and future], for the shadows of the sense realms, which are continually in flux, never appear again. He does not seek anything, neither any worldly pleasures, nor even bodhi, the fruition of great nirvāṇa. Because he has penetrated to equanimity, which is free from this or that, he therefore is not buffeted by the "wind" of the sense-realms. This explains the access of practice that benefits oneself.

From "it rejects" onward is the practice that prompts others to this same access. Because he can leave behind all signs of person or dharmas by realizing the voidness of both, he can universally ferry across everyone. Although the mind is unproduced and free from any characteristics of objects, it nevertheless does not cling to that nature of calm extinction and never abandons any sentient being. It is for this reason that it is said, "it is free from either clinging or rejection." These two kinds of practices [i.e., to benefit both oneself and others] are called the access of practice.[33]

Wŏnhyo's interpretations of these two accesses shows that he did not presume that they heralded a new, even radical, form of Buddhism, but instead were variant renditions of soteriological regimens common in sinitic Buddhism. Their description may have diverged slightly from the models he knew in the sūtras, but not sufficiently so as to be regarded as aberrant. What Wŏnhyo and his fellow exegetes could not have known was that some of the sūtras that presented these comprehensive mārga schemata—such as the *Vajrasamādhi*—may have been written by Ch'an sympathizers precisely to provide such convergences.

*"Guarding the One" and Early Ch'an Meditation*

Another major, and potentially more provocative, Ch'an influence in the *Vajrasamādhi* is "guarding the one" (*suil/shou-i*) practice, which follows the discussion on the two accesses in chapter 5 of the sūtra. *Shou-i* is one of the earliest attempts by Ch'an adherents to frame the processes and practices of Buddhist meditation in terms drawn from the indigenous Chinese religious tradition. As will be seen, the philosophical insights that inspire the practice

[33] *KSGR* 2, p. 985b6–16.

of *shou-i* would have vital ramifications for the subsequent evolution of the Ch'an contemplative tradition.

"Guarding the one" is most closely associated with a faction of early Ch'an known as the "East Mountain dharma-gate," or Tung-shan fa-men. This appellation is typically reserved for the Ch'an descending from Tao-hsin and Hung-jen. Unfortunately, there are no extant works that can be proven to have been written by either man, and their teachings are known solely through accounts preserved in later Northern school doxographies[34]—an imprecise way of determining their approaches at best and plain misleading at worst. The *Vajrasamādhi*'s discussion of *shou-i* provides one of the few independent sources of corroboration about this distinctive East Mountain meditation technique—virtually the only one outside of Northern school materials, in fact. And since the *Vajrasamādhi* predates the Northern school anthologies by at least two decades, its account of *shou-i* is one of the earliest in all of Ch'an-oriented literature.

*Shou-i* is a term with a venerable history in the indigenous religious tradition of Taoism. One of its earliest resonances appears in section 10 of the *Lao-tzu*: "Can you keep the spirit and embrace the one (*pao-i*) without departing from them?" As the immediate byproduct of the Tao itself, which itself gave rise in turn to everything else in the universe, the one served as the interstice between the conventional world of men and the transcendent world of the Tao.[35] This pivotal position prompted Wang Pi (226–249) to construe the *Lao-tzu*'s injunction to remain true to the one as enabling a way of life in which all things would come naturally under the adept's control, without having to force their allegiance.[36] In the *Chuang-tzu*, the one is taken as referring to the natural balance that pertains between all opposites once

---

[34] The distinction between the two groups may, however, be more hypothetical than real, since members of what is now called the "Northern school" (Pei-tsung) actually referred to themselves contemporaneously as followers of the East Mountain teachings. This is even the case with Shen-hsiu (606?–706), the man most closely associated with the label "Northern school"; see the notice in *Leng-ch'ieh shih-tzu chi*, *T* 2837.85.1290b2; Yanagida, *Shoki no Zenshi*, vol. 1, p. 298; and see discussion in McRae, pp. 8–10. To show how ambiguous the appellation was, Tung-shan fa-men is used in a mid-eighth-century cenotaph to refer to the Ch'an movement as a whole, in distinction to the T'ien-t'ai school; see McRae, p. 9 and p. 275 n. 27.

[35] See the *Lao-tzu*, sections 10 and 42, for these two references; Ariane Rump and Wing-tsit Chan, trans., *Commentary on the Lao Tzu by Wang Pi*, pp. 29, 128.

[36] "The One is the true nature of man. It means that if you can always dwell in the eternal abode, embrace the One, keep the spirit clear, and are able never to depart from them, 'all things would submit spontaneously.' " Rump and Chan, *Wang Pi*, p. 29. A similar term in the *Lao-tzu* is *shou-chung* (lit., "guard the center"), which appears in sect. 5: "Much talk will, of course, come to a dead end. It is better to keep to the center (*shou-chung*)."

freed from human intervention and guarding that one as the way to bring about personal immortality: "I guard this unity (*shou-i*), abide in this harmony, and therefore I have kept myself alive for twelve hundred years, and never has my body suffered any decay."[37]

But this "one" was not merely an abstract, philosophical concept. The evolution of Taoism as an organized religious tradition saw its gradual hypostatization as a personal deity, the Supreme One (T'ai-i), or even a trinity, the Three Ones (San-i).[38] As a probable result of influence from the incoming Mahāyāna tradition, with its vast pantheons of buddhas, bodhisattvas, and celestial deities,[39] religious Taoists came to view their world as populated by a myriad of "heavenly worthies" (*t'ien-tsun*). These gods retained and passed down to progressively lower levels of heaven the highest truths of the Supreme Lord Lao (T'ai-shang Lao-chün), the deified Lao-tzu, until finally those truths became known to humans. But the Taoists did not insist that their adepts ascend to the most rarified levels of heaven to gain access to this knowledge of the Tao. Because the human body was considered to be the microcosmic counterpart of the macrocosmic universe, the heavenly gods were in fact present within one's own body. Such correspondences are drawn in considerable detail in Taoist texts, the skull, for example, being regarded as the vault of heaven; the two eyes as the sun and moon; the veins, the rivers of the world, and so on, ad infinitum. A total of some thirty-six thousand gods were calculated to be populating the body. Each of them was charged with guarding an allotted organ, joint, or bodily part against attack from baleful spirits or contaminating pneuma, which might cause those organs to malfunction and lead to death. Taoist visualization practice was intended to watch over those interior gods and ensure that they stayed in place, performing their guardianship; if the visualization were performed correctly, all the bodily organs would continue to function optimally, and the physical immortality that was the goal of Taoist practice would be assured.

But it would obviously be extremely difficult for even the most adept of meditators to keep watch over such a plethora of individual gods. The inevitable need to concentrate separately on each of those gods could lead to a neglect of the other gods and bring in turn physical disequilibrium and possibly death. Hence, the Taoists assumed that the anthropomorphized one,

---

[37] *Chuang-tzu*, chap. 11; Burton Watson, trans., *The Complete Works of Chuang-tzu*, p. 120.

[38] For the Three Ones, see Poul Anderson, *The Method of Holding the Three Ones: A Taoist Manual of Meditation of the Fourth Century A.D.*

[39] According to Henri Maspero, *Taoism and Chinese Religion*, p. 275.

the Supreme One, also dwelling within the body, had been assigned primary responsibility for supervising the disparate activities of all his underlings. Merely by keeping careful watch over this one chief god, then, the Taoist adept could ensure that the duties of all the other gods were properly discharged and the body in turn kept free from illness. This visualization technique, called "guarding the one," had become the principal form of Taoist meditation by the sixth century, and thus should have been known to Chinese Buddhists, and especially to early Ch'an adepts, who often had rather eclectic backgrounds.[40]

The first uses of the term shou-i in Buddhist materials appears in some of the earliest translations of Indian Buddhist meditative tracts, especially those made by An Shih-kao (312–385), the prolific Parthian translator. An often used the homophonous shou-i (guard mentality) to translate the quintessential Indian meditative concept of "mindfulness" (smṛti), its denotation of "guarding" or "protecting" being well suited to the Indian connotation of mindfulness as watching over one's actions and thoughts. Perhaps the earliest usage of the variant term "guarding the mind" (shou-hsin), which is often found in East Mountain materials associated with Hung-jen, appears in an anonymous sūtra from the Pei-Liang region, the Ta-ai-tao pi-ch'iu-ni ching (Sūtra of the bhikṣuṇī Great Love of the Path), supposedly translated ca. 412–439—the same period, interestingly enough, as the Vajrasamādhi was alleged to have been translated. In that sūtra, "guarding the mind" is listed as one of eight things one must protect in order to gain enlightenment: guarding the will (shou-chih), eyes, ears, nose, mouth, body, thoughts (shou-i), and mind (shou-hsin).[41] This list shows that "guarding" was equated with sensory restraint (saṃvara) or "guarding the sense-gates" (indriyeṣu gupta-dvaratā), which was the prerequisite to the full sensory withdrawal achieved during dhyāna.[42]

---

[40] For the interior pantheon of gods and their relation to shou-i, see Henri Maspero, Taoism and Chinese Religion, pp. 272–83. The definitive studies of shou-i practice in the Taoist tradition are Yoshioka Yoshitoyo's "Bukkyō no zenpō to Dōkyō no shuitsu," pp. 109–25, continued in his "Shoki Dōkyō no shuitsu shisō to bukkyō: tokuni Taiheikyō o chūshin toshite," pp. 61–82; both have been reprinted in volume 3 of Yoshioka's Bukkyō to Dōkyō, pp. 285–314, 315–351. Extensive treatment of shou-i practice in the Taoist tradition may be found also in Isabelle Robinet's Méditation taoïste, pp. 183–211. For the Chinese background to the shou-i practice of the East Mountain school, see Chappell, "Tao-hsin," pp. 99–100; McRae, pp. 138–40; Faure, "One-Practice Samādhi," pp. 112–14. Bernard Faure's "La volonté d'orthodoxie," pp. 858–72, provides a valuable philological examination of the term in both Buddhist and Taoist literature. For shou-i in VS, see Takamine Ryōshū, Kegon to Zen, pp. 151–56.

[41] Ta-ai-tao pi-ch'iu-ni ching 2, T 1478.24.951c27–29.

[42] The relationship between shou-i and dhyāna is also brought out in one of the earliest

Early Ch'an usages of *shou-i* are typically found in texts associated with the East Mountain faction of Tao-hsin and Hung-jen. The locus classicus is Tao-hsin's description of "guarding the one" appearing in his *Ju-tao an-hsin yao-fang-pien fa-men* (Instructions on essential expedients for calming the mind and accessing the path). This text, which seems never to have circulated independently in China, is embedded in one of the earliest Ch'an doxographies, the *Leng-ch'ieh shih-tzu chi* (Record of the masters and disciples of the *Laṅkā[vatāra]*), compiled by the Northern Ch'an adept Ching-chüeh (683–750?), and dated to around 713.[43] Tao-hsin ascribes the Buddhist usage of *shou-i* to Fu *ta-shih* (Fu Hsi; 497–569), a renowned layman of the early Buddhist tradition in China, who is said to have taught the practice of "guarding the one without wavering" (*shou-i pu-i*).[44] In his discussion of five methods for realizing that "the Buddha is in fact the mind" (*fo chi-shih hsin*), Tao-hsin gives as the fifth:

---

translated scriptures, where *shou-i* is related to dhyānapāramitā; see *Fo-shou p'u-sa nei-hsi liu po-lo-mi ching*, T 778.17.714b26–c1. The text illustrates the soteriological function of *shou-i* by noting that one should "guard the one and gain liberation" (*shou-i teh-tu*). This is a Latter Han translation by Yen Fo-t'iao (fl. 181–188), probably the first native Chinese translator.

[43] The date of the *Leng-ch'ieh shih-tzu chi* is still somewhat controversial. Chappell ("Tao-hsin," p. 94) summarizes the research of Yanagida and Yin-shun, who date the text respectively to 716 and 720. Elsewhere, Yanagida Seizan ("The *Li-Tai Fa-Pao Chi* and the Ch'an Doctrine of Sudden Awakening," p. 17) dates it less specifically to the early period of Hsüan-tsung (713–755). McRae (p. 120) suggests the period between 713 and 720. The text has been translated in Yanagida Seizan, *Shoki no Zenshi*, vol. 1. A complete French translation with extensive annotations appears in Faure, "La volonté d'orthodoxie." An English translation has been made by J. C. Cleary in *Zen Dawn: Early Zen Texts from Tun Huang*, pp. 17–78; an annotated English rendering is in preparation by Jeffrey Broughton.

The authenticity of the *Ju-tao an-hsin yao-fang-pien fa-men* is also uncertain. Chappell notes the consensus of opinion that the Tao-hsin section of *Leng-ch'ieh shih-tzu chi* presents the text of Tao-hsin's *Ju-tao an-hsin yao-fang-pien fa-men*; "Tao-hsin," pp. 95 and 105 n. 45, citing Yanagida Seizan and Yin-shun. Chappell himself ("Tao-hsin," p. 105 n. 43), however, seems more suspicious of Tao-hsin's text and suggests that the work and the ideas it outlines "may all be products of early eighth century re-interpretation." This is the view taken by McRae, pp. 119–20. For Tao-hsin and his traditional place in the evolution of Ch'an see Ui Hakuju, *Zenshūshi kenkyū*, vol. 3, pp. 81–90; Heinrich Dumoulin, *A History of Zen Buddhism*, pp. 77–79; Takamine, *Kegon to Zen*, pp. 162–68; Martin Collcutt, "The Early Ch'an Monastic Rule," p. 172. His biography appears in *Li-tai fa-pao chi*, T 2075.51.181c–182a (translated and discussed in Yanagida Seizan, *Shoki no Zenshu*, vol. 2, pp. 86–92); *Ching-teh ch'uan-teng lu* 3, T 2076.51.222b–c; *Hsü Kao-seng chuan* 20, T 2060.50.606b–c.

[44] For Fu Hsi, see Chappell, "Tao-hsin," p. 125 n. 42. Faure notes, however, that this term does not appear in any of Fu Hsi's extant works; "Volonté d'orthodoxie," pp. 858–72. A parallel phrase, "guard mentation without wavering" (*shou-i pu-i*) replacing the logograph "one" with that for "mentation," is found also in the *Chin-shu* (Book of the Chin dynasty; Ssu-pu pei-yao ed.), *ch.* 37, p. 18b (Ching Wang-leng annals). The *Chin-shu* was compiled in the middle of the seventh century during the reign of T'ang T'ai-tsung (r. 626–649).

Guard the one without wavering (*shou-i pu-i*). To remain unflagging amid activity and stillness can enable the practitioner to see clearly the buddha-nature and quickly access the approach of dhyāna. The sūtras are all filled with many different types of contemplative techniques. Great Master Fu alone advocated guarding the one without wavering.[45]

This practice was intended to reveal that all mental and physical phenomena were empty and tranquil and, in so doing, calm the ratiocinative processes that veiled the natural purity and quiescence of the mind.

> To "guard the one without wavering" means to be intent on viewing the one thing [the buddha-mind] with this void and pure eye. Without asking whether it is day or night, devote yourself to remaining constantly unmoving. Should the mind be about to gallop off, quickly work to rein it back in. It is just like a cord binding a bird's foot, which would hold the bird fast should it try to fly off. View the whole day through, unceasingly. Then, extinguished, the mind will become concentrated of itself.[46]

There is little unique in such a description of Buddhist meditation. Indeed, its conjunctions with Mahāyāna attitudes toward contemplative practice are vastly more compelling than the differences of terminology or emphasis might suggest. There is, however, one subtle difference that will ultimately prove extremely important: the East Mountain school's interpretation of *shou-i* neither demanded the preparatory steps, such as observing moral injunctions, that typically preceded formal meditation practice in Indian Buddhism nor posited that the practice of *shou-i* invariably evolved through a graduated series of stages.[47] The analogy provided for the soteriological process governing *shou-i* practice is that of an archer doing target practice: he should try over and over again to hit the bull's-eye until he can do it consistently and thence train to hit the shafts of all his previous arrows until they stack up one upon the other. This same analogy of archery training would be used subsequently by such pioneering Ch'an thinkers as Shen-hui and Tsung-mi to describe a subitist soteriological program.[48] In such an

---

[45] *Leng-ch'ieh shih-tzu chi, T* 2837.85.1288a20–22; this section has been translated in Chappell, "Tao-hsin," p. 114. There is some controversy as to the reading of the character for Fu here; for an alternate translation, see Cleary, *Zen Dawn*, p. 57.

[46] *Leng-ch'ieh shih-tzu chi, T* 2837.85.1288b16–20; cf. Chappell, "Tao-hsin," p. 116; McRae, p. 141; Cleary, *Zen Dawn*, p. 59.

[47] This is a point compellingly made in McRae, p. 143.

[48] More specifically, Tsung-mi, following Ch'eng-kuan, describes this as a sudden cultivation/gradual awakening schema. See my *Korean Approach*, p. 295, and Peter Gregory, "Sudden Enlightenment Followed by Gradual Cultivation," pp. 279–320.

approach, the adept need not complete a sequential series of steps before enlightenment is ultimately attained; instead, he is simply to undertake the same identical practice until it becomes completely natural, at which point enlightenment is spontaneously consummated. Tao-hsin describes it as "focusing the mind thought-moment after thought-moment, until [that concentration] continues thought after thought. Once [one's concentration] continues without respite, right mindfulness will be uninterrupted. Then right mindfulness will appear."[49] When Tao-hsin notes that *shou-i* is intended to bring about the immediate vision that one's own mind is itself buddha, he is suggesting that the student need not make himself enlightened, but should instead simply learn to allow his innate enlightenment to appear naturally. Hence, *shou-i* is one of the first statements of the Ch'an emphasis on subitism that would become its hallmark after the mid-eighth century. In adopting such a key concept from the indigenous Taoist tradition for its principal meditation technique, the East Mountain school may have been seeking to break free from the conceptual straitjacket of Indian meditative terminology, with its gradualistic overtones, and allow new, potentially innovative descriptions of Buddhist soteriology.[50]

The connection drawn between *shou-i* practice and faith in the *Ju-tao an-hsin fa-men* also has important implications for the ideological bases of Ch'an meditation. Tao-hsin states explicitly that *shou-i* produces faith, which in turn catalyzes the "access to awakening."[51] Faith, as seen in the preceding chapter, was the principal soteriological tool of the Tathāgatagarbha stratum of Mahāyāna literature. The Tathāgatagarbha premise that enlightenment was inherent in the mind of each and every sentient being led to the conclusion that one need only accept—that is, believe fully in—that claim in order to realize one's enlightenment. Tathāgatagarbha praxis as it was conceived in East Asian Buddhism thus results not in the person *becoming* enlightened (and thus changing his fundamental nature) but simply *being* enlightened (merely accepting that fundamental nature). The concept is therefore eminently, though not exclusively, suited to subitist interpretations.[52] *Shou-i* was intended to produce precisely the same sort of acceptance in the stu-

[49] *Leng-ch'ieh shih-tzu chi*, T 2837.85.1288c1–2; cf. Chappell, p. 116–17; McRae, p. 141.

[50] I have argued that this concern was the major impetus to the evolution of Ch'an meditation in my article "*K'an-hua* Meditation."

[51] "None who engender faith through relying on this practice [of *shou-i*] will be unable to gain access to the right principle of nonproduction." *Leng-ch'ieh shih-tzu chi*, T 2837.85.1288c24–1288a1; see Chappell, "Tao-hsin," p. 118.

[52] Note Luis Gómez's cautions about the multivalency of the term tathāgatagarbha in his article, "Purifying Gold: The Metaphor of Effort and Intuition in Buddhist Thought," pp. 94–96.

dent—as Tao-hsin notes, to realize that "buddha is in fact the mind." Hence, *shou-i* may be one of the first attempts within Ch'an to transform the Tathā-gatagarbha ideology into a practical contemplative technique. This tendency would persist throughout the subsequent evolution of Ch'an meditation, culminating ultimately in the *kanhwa/k'an-hua* ("observing the critical phrase"), or *kōan*, technique of the classical Lin-chi lineage.

More explicit information on the way in which this "guarding" was to be performed appears in *Hsiu-hsin yao-lun* (Essentials of cultivating the mind; alt. *Ch'oesangsŭng-ron*, Treatise on the supreme vehicle), attributed to Tao-hsin's successor, Hung-jen.[53] Instead of using *shou-i*—a term with heavy Taoist overtones that would have been known to any educated Chinese—to describe this practice, Hung-jen instead adopts *shou-hsin* (guarding the mind).

The pure minds of all sentient beings . . . are merely covered by the dark clouds of the mental disturbances, deluded thoughts, defilements, and all [wrong] views.[54] If one can merely guard the mind (*shou-hsin*) intently (*ning-jan*),[55] these deluded thoughts will not arise, and the nirvāṇa-dharma will naturally appear. . . .

[53] For the textual history of the *Hsiu-hsin yao-lun*, see McRae, pp. 309–12 n. 36. Tun-huang manuscripts of this text are extant, as well as a 1570 xylograph from Korea's Ansim-sa bearing the title *Ch'oesangsŭng-ron* (Ch. *Tsui-shang-sheng lun*). The Korean recension is reproduced in the *Taishō* tripiṭaka (*T* 2011.48.377a–379b). The attribution of the text to Hung-jen is doubtful; see Nukariya Kaiten, *Zengaku shisōshi*, pp. 371–74; Masunaga Reihō, "Shoki Zenshi to Dōgen zenshi no buppō," p. 65; Yanagida, *Shoki Zenshū*, pp. 85 n. 7, 416 n. 7, 466. Ch'üan An ("Wu-tsu Hung-jen ch'an-shih," p. 27) suggests that the text attempts to synthesize Bodhidharma's "wall contemplation" and Tao-hsin's "guarding the one" approaches; see also the discussion in Takamine, *Kegon to Zen*, pp. 168–72.

McRae (pp. 119–20) has argued that the *Hsiu-hsin yao lun*, attributed to Hung-jen, may have been written before Tao-hsin's *Ju-tao an-hsin yao fang-pien fa-men*. McRae (p. 120) dates the Tao-hsin text to within a decade or so of the *Leng-ch'ieh shih-tzu chi* (written ca. 713–716) and suggests that Hung-jen's work may represent a " 'lowest common denominator' of Ch'an theory around the year 700." I find his argument convincing for the final form of the works themselves, but I suspect that the practice of *shou-i*, commonly associated with Tao-hsin, is earlier than Hung-jen's *shou-hsin*. *Shou-hsin* looks to me like a reinterpretation of *shou-i* intended to expunge the inevitable Taoist implications of the latter term. The fact that *VS*, written before 686, uses *shou-i* also supports the view that *shou-i* is the earlier form of this teaching.

[54] This same passage appears with nearly identical wording in the biography of Hui-k'o in *Leng-ch'ieh shih-tzu chi*, *T* 2837.85.1285c10–12. It is possible that we see in this borrowing, as I shall bring out later in this chapter, another attempt to connect the lineages of Tao-hsin and Hung-jen with that of Bodhidharma and Hui-k'o.

[55] A parallel phrase in found in *Shih-ti i-chi* 1 (*T* 2758.85.237c21–24): "Since the bodhisatt-va's mind is generated by the principle of the dharma-nature, . . . it guards the one intently (*shou-i ning-jan*) and is not generated by conditions."

One should merely believe in the real truth and guard one's own original mind (*shou tzu pen-hsin*). For this reason, the *Vimalakīrtinirdeśa* says, "There is neither own-nature nor other-nature. A dharma that originally is unproduced is now unextinguished."[56] One who awakens [to this principle] then leaves behind the two extremes [of existence and nonexistence] and accesses the nondiscriminative wisdom.

One who understands this principle should merely know the essentials of the dharma in regard to practice. [Of these,] guarding the mind is foremost. This principle of guarding the mind is, then, the basis of nirvāṇa and the essential approach for accessing the path. It is the principal theme of the twelvefold division of the scriptures, and the patriarch of all the buddhas of the three time-periods.[57]

This entire treatise, in fact, is punctuated by such injunctions as "guard the mind," "guard one's original true mind" (*shou pen chen-hsin*), and so on, to the extent that there can be little doubt that the East Mountain school regarded *shou-i/shou-hsin* as its principal teaching.

The way in which *Hsiu-hsin yao lun* treats *shou-hsin* also adumbrates the underlying Tathāgatagarbha orientation of the East Mountain approach to practice. Hung-jen notes that "the essence of cultivating the path is to discern that one's own body and mind are originally pure, free from production and extinction, and beyond discrimination. The pure mind is perfect and complete in its self-nature—it is your original teacher."[58] This inherently pure self-nature is itself sufficient to act as both the catalyst and goal of liberation, paralleling the tathāgatagarbha's active soteriological role discussed in the preceding chapter. Perhaps the primary concern, then, of "guarding the mind" was to compel the student to remain constantly aware of the presence of the Buddha-nature in each and every moment of consciousness.[59]

If one maintains unflagging attention to the inherent luminosity of the mind, the discriminative thought that obscures that radiance will not recur and nirvāṇa will be achieved. This ability of "guarding" to counteract thought and illusion is brought out in a number of sinitic texts. The *Fa-kuan*

---

[56] *Wei-mo-chieh so-shuo ching* [*Vimalakīrtinirdeśa*], *T* 475.14.540b5–6.

[57] *Ch'oesangsŭng-ron*, *T* 2011.48.377a26–b2; 377c8–13; cf. McRae, pp. 122, 124.

[58] *Ch'oesangsŭng-ron*, *T* 2011.48.377a18–20; see McRae, p. 121.

[59] This sense of guarding as adhering to the primacy of the mind is adumbrated also in an early sūtra, the *Fa-kuan ching*, the translation of which is ascribed to Chu Fa-hu: "As worldly people are all attached to their bodies, they are as yet unable to abandon their bodies and guard mentality (*shou-i*)." *Fa-kuan ching*, *T* 611.15.240b26–27.

*ching* (Contemplating the dharma sūtra) notes that *shou-i* (guarding mental-ity) is a state achieved when thinking is eradicated: "To extinguish thoughts and rely on your own mentality is thence 'guarding mentality.' "[60] *Shou-i* is treated as the opposite of discriminative thought in an inscription attributed to an anonymous dharma master of the Chou dynasty (684–704), who would have been a near-contemporary of the author of the *Vajrasamādhi*: "Be without much ratiocination or much knowledge. Much knowledge and many activities are not as good as extinguishing thought. Much ratiocina-tion and many activities are not as good as guarding the one."[61] The *Pao-tsang lun* (Treatise on the precious storehouse), a Buddhist treatise attributed to the early Chinese Madhyamaka specialist Seng-chao (374–414), but prob-ably written between 730 and 815, illustrates how guarding the mind serves to reveal the illusory nature of the world, and thence bring an end to ratio-cination: "Everything is illusory, false, and unreal. [Once you] know the illusory as illusory, and guard truth and embrace the one (*shou-chen pao-i*), external things will not be defiled. Pure space, the Supreme One (T'ai-i)—how would they have deficiencies? Desert the mind and destroy thoughts; then the body will never suffer any illness. Once a single characteristic does not arise, all fortune and misfortune are obviated."[62]

*Hsiu-hsin yao lun* describes several different ways in which the actual prac-tice of "guarding the mind" was to be carried out. In general these involve freeing the mind from any fixed locus, either externally in the sensory realms, internally within the seat of consciousness, or anywhere in between. From this detached perspective, one was simply to view the usual flow of consciousness until the flunctuations of mind disappeared of their own ac-cord. The mind's natural purity and tranquillity would then be restored spontaneously without forcing that change upon it.[63] This sense that com-pelling the mind to change only creates resistance to the final acceptance of intrinsic enlightenment would become a common theme in later Ch'an teachings, especially those of the Hung-chou school of Ma-tsu Tao-i (709–

---

[60] *Fa-kuan ching, T* 611.15.241b21.

[61] *Chou Wei-pin sha-men wang-ming fa-shih hsi-hsin ming*, in *Tzu-men ching-hsün* 2, *T* 2023.48.1052a8–9.

[62] See *Pao-tsang lun, T* 1857.45.145a26–29. The *Pao-tsang lun* was actually written sometime between 700 and 815; see Kamata, *Chūgoku Kegon shisōshi no kenkyū*, pp. 375–401.

[63] See *Ch'oesangsŭng-ron, T* 2011.48.379a6–14; translated in McRae, pp. 130–31. See also Carl Bielefeldt's excellent synopsis of East Mountain meditation in his " 'Secret' of Zen Medi-tation," pp. 140–42. There is an interesting parallel here with Wang Pi's interpretation of *shou-i* as given in the opening paragraphs of this section.

788) with its emphasis on "spontaneity."[64] As with Tao-hsin's text, such descriptions of soteriology are particularly amenable to a subitist interpetation, since they can be construed not as involving any real modification in the quality of mind itself, but as simply a restoration of the mind's original state. Such techniques, then, do not involve any gradual transmutation of the mind and are equally appropriate for the rank beginner in spiritual practice as well as the most advanced of adepts. The focus in the East Mountain teachings on forms of meditation practice that are applicable to students at all stages of the path illustrates the "reductionistic" tendencies so typical in East Asian Buddhist meditation. Rather than seeing the goal of Buddhist practice as the sequential perfection of a series of steps, which finally culminate in the achievement of nirvāṇa, the East Mountain accounts instead reduce these many stages to a single overriding experience. This development will be important for evolving a style of meditation that was consistent in form and practice from beginning to end—the quintessence of the "sudden" style of meditation that becomes the Holy Grail of Ch'an.

The fifth chapter of the *Vajrasamādhi*, "Approaching the Edge of Reality," which includes the allusion to the two-accesses theory, follows with a discussion of *shou-i*.

> "Bodhisattva! [You should] urge those sentient beings to preserve the three and guard the one, in order to access the tathāgatadhyāna. Due to this concentrated absorption, their minds will come to be free of panting."
>
> Taeryŏk Bodhisattva asked, "What do you mean by 'preserve the three and guard the one, in order to access the tathāgatadhyāna'?"
>
> The Buddha replied, " 'Preserve the three' means to preserve the three liberations. 'Guard the one' means to guard the thusness of the one mind. 'Access the tathāgatadhyāna' means the noumenal contemplation on the thusness of the mind. Accessing such a state is in fact what is meant by approaching the edge of reality."[65]

The influence of the East Mountain teachings on this passage is difficult to deny. The gloss of *shou-i* as "guarding the thusness of the one mind" recalls especially the interpretation of "guarding" in Hung-jen's *Hsiu-hsin yao lun*, where the term is purged of some of its explicitly Taoist connotations by being reconceived as "guarding the mind" (*shou-hsin*). The *Vajrasamādhi*'s

---

[64] See the discussion in my "*K'an-hua* Meditation," pp. 338–41.

[65] *VS*, chap. 5, after n. 73. The three liberations are the śūnya, vajra, and prajñā *vimokṣa*s; *VS*, chap. 5, after n. 74.

interpretation of *shou-i* in terms of the "thusness of the mind" clarifies *shou-i*'s affinities with *shou-hsin* and, by extension, the affinities between the practices ascribed to Tao-hsin and Hung-jen. By interpreting "guarding the one" as "guarding the thusness of the one mind," the author of the *Vajrasamādhi* also brings out the Tathāgatagarbha antecedents of this form of practice, for, as seen in the previous chapter, one of the terms by which tathāgatagarbha was glossed was thusness (tathatā). This same connection is drawn also in the Hung-jen text, where the inherent purity of the mind is termed both "thusness" and "the buddha-nature of true thusness."[66]

The causal relationship the *Vajrasamādhi* draws between guarding the one and access of the tathāgatadhyāna is also indicative of the connection its makes between East Mountain practice and the ideology of the *Laṅkāvatāra-sūtra*, one of the principal scriptural inspirations of early Ch'an. The concept of tathāgatadhyāna, the last and most profound of the four types of dhyāna discussed in the *Laṅkāvatāra*,[67] also appears prominently in such Ch'an-oriented apocrypha as the *Vajrasamādhi* and *Śūraṃgama* sutras. In this dhyāna, the full noetic experience of enlightenment infuses the bodhisattva's active work on behalf of all beings, bringing about the perfect fusion of knowledge and conduct (*vidyācaraṇa*). By equating access to the tathāgatadhyāna with access to the *bhūtakoṭi*, the *Vajrasamādhi* seeks to show that Ch'an enlightenment involves seeing both the interconnection of wisdom and action and the nonduality of the conscious subject and the perceived object.

The connection between the *Laṅkāvatāra-sūtra* and the evolution of early Ch'an is still a debatable issue and has been openly challenged by some modern scholars, such as John McRae. Even McRae acknowledges, however, that while "there is no evidence that its contents had any particular impact on the development of the school . . . this scripture apparently had some kind of mysterious appeal to the followers of early Ch'an."[68] The evidence, however, seems to suggest something more concrete than a "mysterious appeal." The value for synthesizing Buddhist doctrine that the Chinese saw in the concepts of tathāgatagarbha and amalavijñāna was inspired by the *Laṅkāvatāra*, and to that extent the sūtra could have influenced the evolution of Ch'an. The *Erh-ju ssu-hsing lun* displays clear affinities with the *Laṅkāvatāra*,[69] and its putative author, Bodhidharma, is claimed to have initiated the

---

[66] *Ch'oesangsŭng-ron*, *T* 2011.48.377b5; McRae, p. 122.

[67] *Leng-ch'ieh ching* 2, *T* 670.16.492a22–24; cf. *Ta-sheng ju Leng-ch'ieh ching* 3, *T* 672.16.602a12; Suzuki, trans., *Laṅkāvatāra Sūtra*, pp. 85–86.

[68] McRae, p. 29.

[69] See Jorgensen, "*Long Scroll*," pp. 179–239, esp. pp. 232–33.

Ch'an transmission by passing that sūtra on to his successors. One of the earliest histories of the Ch'an school, *Leng-ch'ieh shih-tzu chi*, seemingly identifies Ch'an with the sūtra, but the case made by the record's author, Ching-chüeh, in support of this claim is hardly convincing.[70] Rather than trying to view Ch'an as a systematic reading of the *Laṅkāvatāra-sūtra*, in the same way that T'ien-t'ai claims to be of the *Lotus* or Hua-yen of the *Avataṃ-saka*, it is more accurate to say instead that Ch'an was inspired by similar religious concerns. Certainly the author of the *Vajrasamādhi* knew the sūtra, even if his doctrinal formulations more commonly drew from the *Awaken-ing of Faith* and other sinitic elaborations of the *Laṅkāvatāra*'s distinctive interpretation of Tathāgatagarbha thought, rather than directly from the scripture itself. Indeed, it is in such Ch'an-oriented apocrypha as the *Vajra-samādhi* and *Śūraṃgama* sūtras that the legacy of the *Laṅkāvatāra* is particu-larly pronounced.

The context within which the *Vajrasamādhi* describes *shou-i* practice pro-vides independent corroboration of later Northern school accounts of the East Mountain teachings. I have already pointed out the pronounced syn-cretic focus of the sūtra as a whole, as well as of its interpretation of *shou-i* practice in specific. The East Mountain teachings are also typically portrayed as having been broadly eclectic in spirit. This eclecticism is adumbrated by the sheer volume of citations included in Tao-hsin's *Ju-tao an-hsin fa-men*. Among the texts quoted by title in the treatise are such seminal scriptures to the East Asian tradition as the Śūnyavāda-aligned *Prajñāpāramitā* and *Vi-malakīrtinirdeśa* sūtras, the synthetic *Lotus Sūtra*, the "idealist" *Avataṃsaka*, *Nirvāṇa*, and *Laṅkāvatāra* sūtras, the principal Pure Land work, *Sukhāvatī-vyūha-sūtra*, as well as sinitic apocrypha like *Fo i-chiao ching* and *Fa-chü ching* (*\**Dharmapada*), and the indigenous Taoist texts *Lao-tzu* and *Chuang-tzu*. This wide range of materials supports David Chappell's characterization of Tao-hsin's thought as uniting "Pure Land, Yogācāra and Mādhyamika thinking in a typical act of Chinese syncretism by asserting that the Pure Land, Buddha-nature, the *tathāgatagarbha*, *nien-fo* [recitation of the Buddha's name], *nirvāṇa*, etc. are identical, while acknowledging that the methods of achieving this are endless."[71]

The affinities between Northern school accounts of Tao-hsin's teachings and the *Vajrasamādhi* are brought out also in a passage from the *Ju-tao an-hsin fa-men* that reads like a litany of the issues addressed in the *Vajrasamādhi*:

---

[70] See McRae, pp. 24–29, and 90–91 for a summary of the relevant scholarship.
[71] Chappell, "Tao-hsin," p. 98.

One immediately views that this sort of mind is in fact the body of the tathā-gata's real dharma-nature. It is also called the right dharma (*saddharma*). It is also called the buddha-nature. It is also called the real nature and edge of reality of all dharmas. It is also called the pure land. It is also called bodhi, vajrasamādhi, original enlightenment, and so forth. It is also called the nir-vāṇa-element (*nirvāṇadhātu*), prajñā, and so on. Although its names are countless, they share the same one essence.[72]

While it is still controversial whether the *Ju-tao an-hsin fa-men* as preserved in *Leng-ch'ieh shih-tzu chi* represents the authentic teachings of Tao-hsin him-self, it at least provides a retrospective account of the East Mountain teach-ings as they were understood in the early part of the eighth century. The *Vajrasamādhi*, which predates these Northern school accounts by a few dec-ades, corroborates in the terminology it employs and its general philosoph-ical outlook this account of Tao-hsin's teachings.[73] Although the evidence is admittedly indirect, the convergence of the two accounts is striking enough to suggest that the *Leng-ch'ieh shih-tzu chi*'s account provides an accurate sense of the thrust of the East Mountain teachings.

Further corroboration of the East Mountain affinities of *shou-i* practice appears in a remarkable passage from an anonymous sūtra quoted in the *Hua-yen chin-kuan ch'ao* (Notes to the embroidered cap of the *Avataṃsaka*), attributed to Tsung-mi's disciple Ch'uan-ao *ta-shih* (ca. ninth century).

As a sūtra states, "Fix the mind at one spot and there is nothing you cannot do. Bind the mind at one spot and you will be able to open the gate of wis-dom. *Guard the one without wavering* [emphasis added] and the spirit will not be distracted and the infinite numinosity will be sustained. When first train-ing in the inscrutable samādhi (*pu-ssu-i san-mei*), you fix the mind on a single condition. But after practicing for a long time, viewing the mind (*k'an-hsin*) will be perfected; then there will be no further characteristics of mind (*hsin-hsiang*) and one will always be in conformity with dhyāna. Because all char-acteristics of mind are then precisely no-mind, it is called the inscrutable samādhi."[74]

---

[72] *Leng-ch'ieh shih-tzu chi*, T 2837.85.1287a17–20.

[73] See Philip Yampolsky's statement ("Early Ch'an History," p. 5) that *VS* "reflects the status of this East Mountain school in the late seventh century."

[74] For the passage from the *Hua-yen chin-kuan ch'ao* in which this sūtra passage appears, see the *Pŏpkye toji ch'ongsu-rok* 2b, T 1887B.45.765c26–766a1. The *Hua-yen chin-kuan ch'ao* is no longer extant; it is cited in Ŭich'ŏn's scriptural catalogue (*Sinp'yŏn chejong kyojang ch'ongnok* 1, T 2184.55.1167b6) as being in four (alternatively two) fascicles. The text seems to have been an explanation (or perhaps an outline) of Ch'eng-kuan's massive *Ta-fang-kuang fo Hua-yen ching*

There are striking elements drawn from the early Ch'an tradition in this passage. The four-logograph phrase "guard the one without wavering" is the clarion call of the East Mountain teachings and especially of Tao-hsin. "Viewing the mind" is a practice that appears frequently in East Mountain/ Northern school materials. While "contemplating the mind" is treated somewhat ambivalently in materials attributed to Tao-hsin, the Northern school founder, Shen-hsiu (606?–706), devotes his first work, the *Kuan-hsin lun* (Treatise on contemplating the mind), to this practice. Shen-hsiu's comments in particular seem reminiscent of this sūtra's account, as for example, where he states that the mind that is viewed is "no-mind," and looking at that mind *cum* no-mind is vacuous, like looking into space.[75]

A suggestive piece of evidence of both the apocryphal character of this unnamed sūtra and its sectarian affiliations is the fact that the first line of the citation—"Fix the mind at one spot and there is nothing you cannot do"— is taken verbatim from the *Fo i-chiao ching* (Book of the bequeathed teachings of the Buddha), another Chinese apocryphon. This line from the *I-chiao ching* is cited frequently in Ch'an sources and appears in both Tao-hsin's *Ju-tao an-hsin yao-fang-pien fa-men* and Hung-jen's *Hsiu-hsin yao-lun*.[76] Such phrases were the common property of the East Asian Buddhist tradition and served as the basic building blocks of indigenous texual composition; it is not unusual that two different apocryphal texts would include the same passage. It is only in this text, however, that this phrase is directly tied to the practice of *shou-i*. Given the doctrinal context within which this phrase is placed, the East Mountain pedigree of this unknown scripture is strongly suggested. The *Vajrasamādhi* may thus not have been the only attempt made to cloak in sūtra guise the teachings of the East Mountain Ch'an school.

---

*shu* (*T* 1735); see Buswell, *Korean Approach*, p. 357 n. 134 for references. The *Pŏpkye toji ch'ongsu-rok* (Collected annotations to the *Chart of the Dharmadhātu*) is a late Koryŏ compilation of notes to Ŭisang's *Hwaŏm ilsŭng pŏpkye-to* (Chart of the Hua-yen one-vehicle *dharmadhātu*); *T* 1887A.45.711a–716a. Its author is unknown, but it certainly postdates the Koryŏ Hwaŏm exegete Kyunyŏ (923–973), who is quoted in the text; see Tongguk taehakkyo, ed., *Han'guk Pulgyo*, p. 161.

[75] See Faure, "The Concept of One-Practice Samādhi in Early Ch'an," pp. 114–16, for discussion. McRae (p. 119) dates the *Kuan-hsin lun* to ca. 675–700; for information on the text, see p. 325 n. 159; he discusses the text in detail, with several extensive excerpts, on pp. 198–209.

[76] *Fo i-chiao ching*, *T* 389.12.1111a20; cited in Tao-hsin's *Ju-tao an-hsin yao-fang-pien fa-men*, Chappell, "Tao-hsin," p. 116; Hung-jen's *Hsiu-hsin yao-lun*, *T* 2011.48.377c24–25; see also *Li-tai fa-pao chi*, *T* 2075.51.193a11–12. For the frequent Ch'an citation of this phrase, see Yanagida, *Shoki no Zenshi*, vol. 1, p. 245. For coverage of the apocryphal *Fo i-chiao ching*, and the equally spurious commentary to it attributed by tradition to Vasubandhu, see Mochizuki, *Bukkyō kyōten*, pp. 642–45.

Indeed, there are several such scriptures written during the early eighth century that have a pervasive Ch'an flavor; often too, they show the same orientation toward Tathāgatagarbha doctrine seen in the *Vajrasamādhi*. These include the *Ch'an-men ching* (Book of the Ch'an gate), *Shou-leng-yen ching*, *Fa-chü ching*, and *Fa-wang ching* (Book of the King of Dharma).[77] These affinities suggest that textual forgery may have been a common artifice for disseminating early Ch'an doctrine. Indeed, proselytization was one of the reasons Tao-hsüan cited in his *Ta T'ang nei-tien lu* (The great T'ang catalogue of Buddhist scriptures) for the composition of apocryphal scriptures.[78] The approach taken here for determining the provenance, dating, and authorship of the *Vajrasamādhi* may thus prove fruitful in exploring other indigenous sūtras with possible Ch'an affinities.

What would an East Asian scholiast sensitive to trends in the learned schools of Buddhism toward the end of the seventh century, but as yet oblivious to Ch'an, have made of the *Vajrasamādhi*'s references to *shou-i*? Wŏnhyo's interpretation of *shou-i* is framed in terms of the *Awakening of Faith*'s distinction between the one mind and its two aspects. He takes *shou-i* as emphasizing the absolute, true-thusness aspect, which brings about the disappearance of the conventional production-and-extinction aspect, and presumes that the practice derives from the *P'u-sa ying-lo pen-yeh ching*. Wŏnhyo asserts that *shou-i* is the meditation technique most appropriate to the level of the ten practices (*siphaeng/shih-hsing*), the third of the seven major divisions of the mārga (including the prerequisite stage of the ten faiths) outlined in the *Ying-lo ching*, which is accessed after the bodhisattva has already understood that he is inherently enlightened at the preceding level of the ten abidings.[79] Hence, "guarding the one" is principally concerned with pro-

---

[77] Of these, the *Ch'an-men ching* probably has the most immediate affinities with *VS*. *Ch'an-men ching* is a Chinese apocryphal scripture now known to have been written no later than 730, and probably between 695 and 701. The Stein manuscript from Tun-huang that Yabuki discovered includes a preface by Hui-kuang, which links the sūtra with the prominent Northern school teacher, P'u-chi (651–739). See Yabuki Keiki, *Meisha yoin kaisetsu*, part 2, pp. 289–93; Yanagida Seizan, *Shoki Zenshū*, pp. 311–12. The *Fa-chü ching* circulated at least by A.D. 645 and may have been composed by Ch'an adepts in the Bodhidharma line. It contains principally a summary of Prajñāpāramitā teachings, with few obvious Ch'an elements. *Fa-wang ching* was composed no later than 695, probably by someone within the Northern Ch'an lineage. It is strongly influenced by the *Ch'i-hsin lun* and the *Hua-yen ching* and incorporates a number of Taoist expressions into its presentation of Buddhism. See Okimoto Katsumi, "Zenshūshi ni okeru gikyō: *Hōōkyō* ni tsuite," pp. 27–61. For a survey of these and other related texts, see Okabe Kazuo, "Gigi kyōten," pp. 351–76.

[78] *Ta T'ang nei-tien lu* 1, T 2149.55.219b10.

[79] For the relevant passage, see *P'u-sa ying-lo pen-yeh ching*, T 1485.24.1014a2–6. See the previous discussion previously in this chapter for the mārga schema of the *Ying-lo ching*.

tecting the initial understanding of the tathāgatagarbha that initiates bodhi-sattvahood, in line with the treatment seen in the Hung-jen text. "There are two aspects," Wŏnhyo writes,

> to this dharma of the "one mind." Now, initially, one guards the true-thus-ness aspect of the mind, in order to subdue the power of the great dragon of ignorance, for ignorance is completely deluded about the thusness of the one mind. "Guard" in this context means that when the person accesses [that con-templation practice], he tranquilly guards the noetic experience of the one thusness, but when he withdraws [from that contemplation], he does not lose the mind that has a single taste. This is why it is called "guard the one." This is as explained in the "Ten Practices" section of the *Pen-yeh ching* . . . , where it is said that not losing the single taste of the Middle Way during all three time-periods is precisely what is meant by this contemplation's function of guarding the one. This contemplation takes place at the level of the ten prac-tices.[80]

The explicit tathāgatagarbha connotations of *shou-i* are also brought out in Chu-chen's interpretation. While Chu-chen, like Wŏnhyo, shows no awareness of the Ch'an origins of *shou-i*, he associates that practice with the counterillumination (*fan-chao*) technique adumbrated elsewhere in the *Vajra-samādhi*, described previously as Ch'an's pragmatic reworking of Tathāga-tagarbha thought. Chu-chen interprets both *shou-i* and *tsun-san* ("preserving the three") as types of dhyāna that bring about "calming of the mind" (*hsin-an*).

> To direct the thoughts is called "preserve." To protect the thoughts is called "guard." "Tathāgatadhyāna [means] to revert (*fan*) to the pure essence of one's own nature. To absorb the mind and look back is called "contempla-tion." "Noumenal contemplation on the thusness of the mind" [means] that, by means of the true principle of one's own nature, one looks back on the one mind's essence of true thusness.[81]

Chu-chen's correlation here of *shou-i* and *tsun-san* is a convenient entry-point to the latter concept. The term "preserve" or "conserve" (*chon/tsun*) is

[80] *KSGR* 2, p. 987c8–15. Elsewhere, Wŏnhyo refers to "guarding the thusness of the one mind" as a type of contemplation that involves realizing the voidness of dharmas. It occurs while the bodhisattva is involved in disseminating the teachings throughout the three realms of reality; *KSGR* 2, p. 988c24–26.

[81] Chu-chen, *T'ung-tsung chi*, p. 269a14–16; Chu-chen follows with an explication of the meaning of tathāgatadhyāna.

considerably less common in Buddhist contemplative literature than is "guard," and the *Vajrasamādhi*'s reference to preserving the three liberations seems to be unique. The logograph *tsun* is used in the Taoist tradition as a type of visualization or interiorization.[82] The term most often appears in Ch'an texts in conjunction with mind, yielding a compound that typically is pejorative in connotation. Tao-hsin's *Ju-tao fa-men*, for example, gives the following citation from the *Lao-tzu*: "Obscure and mysterious, within it is the essence." Tao-hsin critiques this perspective as follows: "Although outwardly he denies characteristics, inwardly he still preserves the mind."[83] The persistence of this sort of appraisal is attested by the similar criticism found in the Sung dynasty *kung-an* collection, *Wu-men kuan* (Gateless checkpoint), which states that "preserving the mind's clarity and tranquillity is the perverse Ch'an of silent illumination (*mo-chao hsieh* Ch'an)."[84] Wŏnhyo too criticizes "preserving the mind" as the inferior practice of the Hīnayāna:

> The two-vehicle adherents et al. grasp at dharmas and preserve the mind (*chonsim*); they postulate the existence of a mind subject to production and extinction, which is impermanent. Therefore one must extirpate production and extinction in order to extinguish this view that the mind is preserved. . . . If one does not cling to production or extinction, there perforce will be no preservation of the mind.[85]

The practice of "preserving the three" as advocated in the *Vajrasamādhi*, however, seems qualitatively different from its meaning in the compound "preserve the mind." In this sūtra it is instead intended to keep the mind free from all discrimination, whether between mind and objects, or between gain and loss, so that its innate purity will be restored and the awareness of the person's inherent buddhahood achieved.[86] Wŏnhyo correlates these three kinds of liberation that are preserved—which, as far as I have been able to ascertain, are unique to the *Vajrasamādhi*—with the three types of prajñā that contain eight liberations as outlined in the "Ten Abidings" section of *P'u-sa ying-lo pen-yeh ching*. In the *Ying-lo ching*, wisdom generated by learning (*śrutamayīprajñā*) renders unascertainable both internal and external de-

---

[82]  See Michel Strickmann, "On the Alchemy of T'ao Hung-ching," p. 128.

[83]  *Leng-ch'ieh shih-tzu chi*, *T* 2837.85.1289b4–5; see Chappell, "Tao-hsin," p. 120. The citation is from *Lao-tzu*, chap. 21.

[84]  *Wu-men kuan*, *T* 2005.48.299a29–b1.

[85]  *KSGR* 1, p. 966c18–25.

[86]  As *VS* points out, "Preservation is put into operation when mind and objects are nondual." *VS*, chap. 5, before n. 75.

ceptions; that is the first type of liberation. It corresponds to the void liberation of the *Vajrasamādhi*, for it contemplates voidness without rejecting any
sign of materiality. Wisdom gained through reflection (*cintamayīprajñā*) renders unascertainable the five skandhas and all external dharmas; that is the
second liberation. It correlates with the adamantine liberation, for it destroys all material dharmas as if it were adamant. Wisdom gained through
spiritual cultivation (*bhāvanāmayīprajñā*) reveals the voidness of materiality
and, indeed, all the five skandhas in a series of six separate liberations. These
all correspond to the *Vajrasamādhi*'s general designation of prajñā-libera-
tion.[87]

As Wŏnhyo explains, if the meditator practices without learning to preserve these three types of liberation, he will remain forever attached to the
mistaken views of personal identity and personal possession, which sustain
the separation between mind and objects. But by maturing his cultivation of
these three, he will be able to preserve his awareness of them consistently
without grasping at self and others, liking and disliking. This contemplation
begins at the level of the ten faiths and is perfected at the subsequent level of
the ten abidings, and thus initiates the entrance onto the formal bodhisattva
path.[88] It is therefore a practice appropriate to an earlier stage in spiritual
development than is *shou-i*, which Wŏnhyo placed subsequent to the ten
abidings.

*Shou-i* does not exhaust the resonances found in the *Vajrasamādhi* to East
Mountain/Northern school teachings. Another of the more important of
these is the notion of the nonproduction of dharmas (*wu-sheng fa*; *anutpatti-
kadharma*). The East Mountain faction is sometimes specifically glossed as
the "East Mountain's teaching of nonproduction" (Tung-shan *wu-sheng* fa-
men),[89] and we have seen already in Tao-hsin's treatment of *shou-i* that he
connected that style of contemplation with the principle of "nonproduction." The *Vajrasamādhi* creates an expansion in the scope of the term *ch'an*
(dhyāna) by making "nonproduction," rather than quietude and calmness of
mind, the true goal of dhyāna: "Know that the nature of dhyāna is free from
both agitation and calmness and you will immediately attain the [acceptance
of the] nonproduction [of dharmas] and the prajñā that produces nothing."[90]

---

[87] See *P'u-sa ying-lo pen-yeh ching*, *T* 1485.24.1013b7–11; Wŏnhyo's commentary appears at
*KSGR* 2, pp. 987c22–988a22. Cf. Yüan-ch'eng, *Chu-chieh* 3, p. 208a.

[88] *KSGR* 2, p. 988a25–b2.

[89] This usage is found in the biography of Tao-shun (d.u.), one of the major disciples of
Hung-jen. See *Hsü Kao-seng chuan* 8, *T* 2061.50.758a2–3. For a short biography of Tao-shun,
see McRae, p. 39.

[90] *VS*, chap. 3, after n. 28.

The sūtra also clarifies that nonproduction in such contexts means the "acceptance of the nonproduction of dharmas" (*anutpattikadharmakṣānti*), a Mahāyāna Buddhist technical term that, for our purposes, is the virtual equivalent of nirvāṇa.[91] In this wise, the *Vajrasamādhi* freed *ch'an* from its limiting role as a noetic exercise. As Ch'an, it was now allowed to evolve into a comprehensive ideology and religious system, which brought within reach the crowning achievement of Mahāyāna Buddhism.

The notion of nonproduction is the common property of Mahāyāna literature, and its appearance in the *Vajrasamādhi* would not be enough in itself to clinch the East Mountain origins of that teaching. But there is an additional piece of evidence suggesting just this: the interlocutor in the "Practice of Nonproduction" chapter is the bodhisattva Mind King (Simwang/Hsinwang). This bodhisattva is the subject of an eponymous *Book of the Mind King* (*Hsin-wang ching*), which is cited in the Hung-jen text. This sūtra is listed as an apocryphal scripture in the *K'ai-yüan shih-chiao lu* and is now known only through brief citations in Ch'an literature.[92] It seems to have circulated among the early Ch'an factions and may in fact be another of the several Ch'an-oriented apocrypha written during the late seventh to early eighth centuries.

A related notion in East Mountain materials is that of the nonactivation of mind (*hsin pu-ch'i*), which is associated with nonproduction in Hung-jen's *Hsiu-hsin yao lun*: "If you guard the mind clearly, then false thoughts will not be activated. This, then, is nonproduction. . . . Once you extinguish the thought of personal possession and abandon this body, you are certain to gain nonproduction."[93] This term nonactivation comes to be used in

[91] This clarification appears in *VS*, chap. 3, before n. 21. *Anutpattikadharmakṣānti* is described as the principal realization gleaned at the seventh *bhūmi* of the Mahāyāna *mārga*, when the bodhisattva is certain to complete the path to buddhahood, and replaces the four noble truths as the principal content of the bodhisattva's experience of enlightenment. Through such acquiescence or compliance, the bodhisattva is able to abandon all limiting views about the true nature of all dharmas and perceive directly their calm, quiescent quality. See Suzuki, *Studies in the Laṅkāvatāra*, pp. 125–27, 226–28; and Edward Conze, *Buddhist Thought in India*, pp. 221–22.

[92] The reference to the *Hsin-wang ching* appears in *Ch'oesangsŭng-ron*, *T* 2011.48.377c1; McRae, p. 124. A *Hsin-wang p'u-sa shuo t'ou-t'o ching* (Mind-king Bodhisattva explains the *dhuta* practices) is listed as an apocryphal sūtra in *Ta-Chou lu* (*T* 2153.55.473c25) and *K'ai-yüan shih-chiao lu* 18, *T* 2154.55.677b21. There is also a Tun-huang fragment that may correspond to this same text: *Fo wei Hsin-wang p'u-sa shuo t'ou-t'o ching* (*T* 2886.85.1401c–1403b); see discussion in Mizuno, p. 44 n. 3. For citations to this sūtra in the works of Shen-hui and Tsung-mi, see McRae, p. 316 n. 62.

[93] *Ch'oesangsŭng-ron*, *T* 2011.48.377b15–16; cf. McRae, p. 123; *Ch'oesangsŭng-ron*, *T* 2011.48.378b17–18; cf. McRae, p. 128.

Northern school literature to refer to a state of mind that is beyond all conceptual dualities, such as existence and nonexistence; it is made the virtual equivalent of the "true mind," or buddha-nature. Hence, as Shen-hsiu says, "to activate the mind for the briefest instant is to go counter to the Buddha-nature, to break the Bodhisattva Precepts. . . . Always guard the true mind by not activating body and mind."[94] The idea of "extinguish the thought of personal possession," which was mentioned above in *Hsiu-hsin yao lun*, is glossed elsewhere by Hung-jen as equivalent to the vajrasamādhi,[95] indicating the alignment among nonactivation, nonproduction, and vajrasamādhi. Following Shen-hsiu's description, one may add to this list the terms buddha-nature and guarding the mind (*shou-hsin*), all themes prominent in the *Vajrasamādhi*.

Finally, the distinctive Northern school notion of "contemplation of the mind" (*kuan-hsin*) is adumbrated in chapter 3 of the *Vajrasamādhi*, which draws a virtual tautology between contemplation of mind and mental purity. This tautology is a common theme in Northern school literature, as seen in the admonition in the *Wu fang-pien* (Five expedient means) to "view the mind as pure,"[96] or Shen-hsiu's simple statement of Northern school practice: "View purity at the locus of purity."[97] Although this practice of "viewing purity" is vehemently criticized in later Ch'an literature for hypostatizing the illusory bifurcation between pure and impure,[98] the *Vajrasamādhi* tries instead to relate it to the access of principle, giving the practice a much more salutary interpretation. This accommodating attitude toward a distinctive Northern school practice is still another indication of the antiquity of the *Vajrasamādhi* in Ch'an literature, showing that it was written before the pronounced split between the Northern and "Southern" schools.

*Linking the Bodhidharma and East Mountain Traditions*

Both the "access of principle" and "guarding the one" share a similar foundation in Tathāgatagarbha soteriology. This orientation is clear in the *Vajrasamādhi* rendition of those teachings, as well as in the texts of the *Erh-ju ssu-hsing lun* and *Ju-tao an-hsin fa-men*. While the access of principle was intended

---

[94] From Shen-hsiu's *Wu fang-pien*, as translated in McRae, pp. 172, 174.

[95] *Ch'oesangsüng-ron*, *T* 2011.48.378c25–26; cf. McRae, p. 130.

[96] Translated in McRae, p. 172.

[97] Noted in McRae, "Ox-Head School," p. 225.

[98] See the criticism of "viewing the mind and viewing purity" in *Platform Sūtra*, sect. 14, Yampolsky, trans., p. 137.

to catalyze enlightenment through resolute faith in the truth of one's inherent buddha-nature, guarding the one sought to encourage the student to
accept the overarching primacy of that buddha-nature in all of life. This
commonality of concern brought out in the *Vajrasamādhi*'s treatment of the
access of principle and guarding the one may in turn have suggested affinities
between the two factions of early Ch'an most associated with these techniques: the Bodhidharma line and the East Mountain lineage. Such associations would have been crucial in creating an unbroken line of transmission
from the Buddha to the patriarchs of India and China and finally through to
Ch'an masters of the first Ch'an schools.

The Ch'an tradition conceives itself as descending from an unbroken line
of transmission between Indian and Chinese patriarchs, which can ultimately be traced back to the Buddha himself. For a tradition that claimed
not to rely on the scriptural teachings of Buddhism, such a direct connection
with the person of the Buddha—and by extension with his own experience
of enlightenment—was vital to legitimate its approach. But this transmission is clearly a retrospective view of Ch'an's evolution and its stages were
still quite fluid in the period with which we are concerned. The first extant
account of such a transmission occurs in the funerary inscription to Fa-ju
(639–689), a follower of the East Mountain teachings, where Fa-ju is listed
as the successor to Bodhidharma, Hui-k'o, Seng-ts'an, Tao-hsin, and finally
Hung-jen.[99] A number of variant accounts of the Ch'an lineage are extant in
eighth-century transmission records, but the standard account ultimately
accepted by the tradition has Ch'an evolving in the same lineal descent from
Bodhidharma through to Hung-jen, at which point the succession shifts
wildly depending on the sectarian affiliations of the authors. In Tao-hsüan's
*Hsü kao-seng chuan* (compiled ca. 649), however, which includes the earliest
biographies of several of the men who come to be recognized as the patriarchs of Ch'an, there is no evidence whatsoever linking Bodhidharma and
Hui-k'o, the traditional first and second patriarchs, with Tao-hsin and
Hung-jen, the fourth and fifth patriarchs. Seng-ts'an, in fact, may have been
conjured up precisely to fill the gap between the second and fourth patriarchs and thus unify the bifurcation in the early Ch'an lineage.[100] Similarly,
one of the motives behind the composition of the *Vajrasamādhi* may have
been to provide scriptural support for the distinctive practices of Bodhi-

---

[99] For Fa-ju and his role in forging the Ch'an transmission theory, see McRae, pp. 43–44,
85–86.

[100] On the problematic historicity of Seng-ts'an, see McRae, pp. 30 and 280–81 n. 40.

dharma and Tao-hsin, the principal figures in the two main lineages of the nascent Ch'an tradition, and to create an implicit association between their separate lines.[101] In fact, the Ch'an references in the *Vajrasamādhi* provide the earliest adumbration of the connections between the Bodhidharma and Tao-hsin branches, predating the explicit ties made in both Fa-ju's cenotaph and the *Ch'uan fa-pao chi* (Record of the transmission of the dharma-treasure) of 710–712.[102]

The affinities between these two factions are suggested in the relationship the *Vajrasamādhi* draws in chapter 5 between the access of principle and guarding the one. After completing its account of the two accesses and the six stages of the path, the sūtra continues on to describe the problems faced by ordinary persons who wish to gain access to the *bhūtakoṭi*—the absolute, or the principle. The Buddha explains that preserving the three and guarding the one make possible such access. *Shou-i* is thus made the primary expedient applied during cultivation of the access of principle, in one sense subsuming the East Mountain teaching within the most direct of Bodhidharma's two accesses. Since the successful practitioner of *shou-i* "will complete all the *bhūmi*s and attain the bodhi of the buddhas," the *Vajrasamādhi* suggests that guarding the one is the practice undertaken on the four stages of the path preceding the *bhūmi*s.[103] This chapter can therefore be explicated as merging the meditative technique of *shou-i* into the larger soteriological framework of the two accesses, thus creating a comprehensive outline of Ch'an training. By forging a synthesis of the two accesses and *shou-i*, the *Vajrasamādhi*, by implication, associates the teachings of Bodhidharma with the East Mountain lineage. The structure of the *Vajrasamādhi*'s discussion of the variant Ch'an teachings, in which the two accesses precede the treatment of guarding the one, also suggests that its author was sensitive to the relative chronology of these two separate lines of transmission.

The extent to which the teachings of the Bodhidharma and East Mountain lines were presumed to differ can be gleaned from a stanza in *Hsin-hsin*

---

[101] Mizuno, p. 36 et passim; Yanagida, *Shoki Zenshū shisho*, p. 27; mentioned also in Kimura, "*Kongōzammaikyō*," p. 114, and Okabe Kazuo, "Gigi kyōten," p. 362; Yampolsky ("Early Ch'an History," p. 4) also refers to the theory and accepts the Chinese origin of *VS*.

[102] For the Ch'an lineage as portrayed in Fa-ju's epitaph and the *Ch'uan fa-pao chi*, see the discussion in McRae, pp. 85–88.

[103] For these passages, see *VS*, chap. 5, between nn. 70 and 77. Wŏnhyo's comments were extremely helpful to me in understanding the connection between these sections; see *KSGR*, pp. 987bff.

*ming* (Inscription on faith in mind), a terse outline of Ch'an doctrine ascribed to the Third Patriarch, Seng-ts'an, who traditionally is affiliated with the Bodhidharma/Hui-k'o line:

> The "two" exist because of the "one,"
> But also *don't guard the one* [emphasis added].
> When the one mind is not produced,
> The myriads of dharmas will be without fault.[104]

It is doubtful that this inscription has anything to do with Seng-ts'an, one of the many black holes that populate early Ch'an history. Nevertheless, it does illustrate the type of reaction later Ch'an schools—which looked for inspiration principally to the reputed founder of the sect, Bodhidharma—had against the East Mountain/Northern school teachings. Hence, at the very least, this gnome expresses the ongoing conflict implicit in the contrary perspectives of these two early factions of Ch'an.

This connection the *Vajrasamādhi* implies between the Bodhidharma/ Hui-k'o and Tao-hsin/Hung-jen lines is potentially crucial for establishing its authorship. While the *Vajrasamādhi* appears to maintain the chronological fidelity of the two factions, its attitude toward their representative practices differs rather dramatically. The sūtra's account of the two accesses is faithful to the teachings of the Bodhidharma text, in that they culminate in the realization of the *bhūtakoṭi*, which is "replete with all meritorious qualities."[105] This description, reminiscent of that given for the nonempty tathāgatagarbha, is indicative of the Tathāgatagarbha emphasis that is so common in early Ch'an. But as soon as the two accesses are introduced in the sūtra, they are immediately criticized as sustaining the dualism that drives the conditioned realm.[106] The bodhisattva must eventually realize that the mind has neither egress nor access and abandon the two accesses as being an unnecessary expedient. This is hardly a sympathetic account of the two accesses, given Ch'an's typically strident nondualism; indeed, the treatment foreshadows the later Ch'an antipathy toward progressive formulations of soteriological development. *Shou-i*, on the contrary, is the practice that allows di-

---

[104] *Hsin-hsin ming, T* 2010.48.376c5–6. *Hsin-hsin ming* is a work composed during the eighth century and falsely attributed to Seng-ts'an; see Chappell, "Tao-hsin," p. 103 n. 2; Nishitani Keiji and Yanagida Seizan, eds., *Zenke goroku II*, pp. 105–12. See Arthur Waley's translation in *Buddhist Texts Through the Ages*, ed. Edward Conze et al., pp. 295–98.

[105] *VS*, chap. 5, before n. 67.

[106] *VS*, chap. 5, before n. 64.

rect access to the tathāgatadhyāna, which is "the edge of reality [that] has neither egress nor access."[107] It cures the "panting of the mind," which sustains all dualities. Hence, the *Vajrasamādhi* ultimately subordinates the two accesses to *shou-i* practice. While its author may have replicated accurately the thought of the Bodhidharma text, he did not advocate its practice. And although his sūtra may suggest connections between the Tao-hsin/Hung-jen line and Bodhidharma, he is a partisan of the East Mountain teachings.

## Reductionistic Tendencies in Ch'an Soteriology and Praxis

It has been seen previously how the emphasis on Tathāgatagarbha thought in early Ch'an would eventually lead to subitist forms of soteriology. But such sudden forms of soteriology almost inevitably lead in turn to a reductionistic position toward praxis, in which there can be no specific practices advocated to lead to enlightenment. If, as sinitic Tathāgatagarbha ideology claimed, all one had to do to achieve enlightenment was simply to allow one's innate enlightenment to appear, then there was nothing concrete one could do to speed that process along except perhaps to have faith in that fact. Indeed, there was a real risk that the very purposes of Buddhist meditation could be undermined by the fundamental identity drawn between real enlightenment and apparent nonenlightenment. Ch'an's use of meditative techniques that drew their inspiration and rationale from Tathāgatagarbha thought ultimately would demand that Ch'an develop a soteriological method that actually was "no-method." Ch'an was positioning itself on the horns of a considerable dilemma: the self-styled "Meditation" school could not openly acknowledge the need for meditation.[108]

Such conclusions are drawn from virtually the inception of the Ch'an tradition. Tao-hsin's *Ju-tao an-hsin fa-men* notes, for example,

> The basis of our method [of cultivation] is no-method (*wu-fa*). From the beginning, what has been called the method is this method of no-method. This method, therefore, is not to be cultivated. This method of non-cultivation is the true and real method (*chen-shih fa*). . . . Therefore, based on this interpretation the real method is not practiced by cultivation.[109]

[107] *VS*, chap. 5, after n. 70.

[108] See Carl Bielefeldt's trenchant characterization of this predicament in his "The 'Secret' of Zen Meditation," pp. 143–44.

[109] *Leng-ch'ieh shih-tzu chi*, T 2837.85.1289a26–29; translation from Chappell, "Tao-hsin," p. 120.

The *Chüeh-kuan lun* (Treatise on the transcendence of cognition),[110] one of the principal texts of the Niu-t'ou (Oxhead) school, a distinct school of the middle Ch'an period that traces its own lineage back to Tao-hsin,[111] contains similarly explicit dismissals of the value of meditation, as seen in the following exchange:

> Question: "What should I do?" Answer: "You should do nothing."
> Question: "I understand this teaching now even less than before."
> Answer: "There truly is no understanding of the Dharma. Do not seek to understand it."[112]

The persistence of such views in Ch'an is indicated in the rejection of formal practices like sitting meditation (*tso-ch'an*) found in the *Liu-tsu t'an ching*, a middle Ch'an work some presume to have been compiled ca. 780 within the Oxhead lineage. "In this dharma-approach, all is unobstructed. 'Sitting' means that, externally, thoughts do not arise with reference to the sense-spheres. 'Meditation' means that, internally, one sees one's original nature without confusion."[113]

The "Practice of Nonproduction" chapter of the *Vajrasamādhi* is strikingly parallel in orientation to these early works of Ch'an. It provides arguably the earliest denunciation in Ch'an-aligned literature of the role of formal meditation practice in catalyzing enlightenment—and certainly one of the most eloquent. Complete nonattachment, the sūtra claims, is itself sufficient to generate the practice of nonproduction, but such nonattachment is not something that can be cultivated. In fact, forming the intention to cultivate will itself disturb the natural tranquillity of the mind, dulling its innate

---

[110] I use the translation of the title proposed by McRae, "Ox-Head School," p. 211. For the term middle Ch'an, as referring to the period following the six traditional patriarchs but before the development of the five schools of the mature Ch'an tradition (ca. early eighth to mid-ninth centuries), see Jan Yün-hua, "Tsung-mi: His Analysis of Ch'an Buddhism," p. 4; Buswell, *Korean Approach*, p. 39; and my "*K'an-hua* Meditation," pp. 327–28.

[111] See the discussion of this claim in McRae, "Ox-Head School," p. 204.

[112] *Chüeh-kuan lun* (Pelliot no. 2074, etc.); translation from McRae, "Ox-Head School," p. 213; various recensions of the texts are reproduced, with Japanese and English translations, in Tokiwa Gishin, trans., *A Dialogue on the Contemplation-Extinguished*. McRae, "Ox-Head School," pp. 206–17, demonstrates, however, that this traditional evaluation of the school is not completely correct, for the Oxhead school "was not entirely against the notion of meditative contemplation *per se*" (p. 216).

[113] *Liu-tsu t'an ching*, *T* 2007.48.339a3–5; cf. Yampolsky, trans., *Platform Sūtra*, p. 140; and see his discussion at p. 117. For the sectarian affiliation of the text see Bielefeldt and Lancaster, "T'an Ching," passim; the date is noted in McRae, "Ox-Head School," p. 218.

enlightenment. Correct practice does not require the cultivation of either samādhi or sitting-meditation; rather, it is when one has abandoned all semblance of intentional activity that the dhyāna of nonproduction will be achieved. As the Buddha remarks,

> "If these [consciousnesses] are already calm and extinct, the producing mind will not be produced and the mind will be constantly calm and extinct, without efficacy or function. . . . All will be calm and extinct, pure and nonabiding. *He need not access samādhi; he need not persist in sitting in dhyāna* [emphasis added]. This is nonproduction and freedom from practice."

Simwang Bodhisattva asked, "Dhyāna can suppress all agitation and allay all illusory distractions. Why this negation of dhyāna?"

The Buddha replied, "Bodhisattva! Dhyāna in fact is agitation. Being neither agitated nor concentrated is the dhyāna that produces nothing. The nature of dhyāna is to produce nothing; it has no characteristics of the dhyāna that does produce something. The nature of dhyāna is to linger nowhere; it leaves far behind the agitation caused by trying to linger in dhyāna. Know that the nature of dhyāna is free from both agitation and calmness and you will immediately attain the [acceptance of the] nonproduction [of dharmas] and the prajñā that produces nothing. But also do not rely on, or linger over, these. Because of this knowledge, the mind also will not be agitated. For this reason, you will attain the prajñāpāramitā that produces nothing."[114]

A similar sort of reductionism, bordering almost on antinomianism, is seen in the attitude toward the precepts found in the *Vajrasamādhi*. The *Vajrasamādhi* adopts the threefold classification of Buddhist moral codes found in Yogācāra-oriented literature, which is also followed in other sinitic apocrypha: "(1) the moral code that maintains both the discipline and the deportments; (2) the moral code that accumulates wholesome dharmas; (3) the moral code that aids all sentient beings."[115] But it is only the ignorant

---

[114] *VS*, chap. 3, after n. 28.

[115] *VS*, chap. 6, after n. 86. Their Sanskrit equivalents are (1) *saṃvaraśīla*; (2) *kuśaladharmasaṃgrāhaka*; (3) *sattvārthakriyā*. See *Yu-ch'ieh-shih ti lun* (*Yogācārabhūmi-śāstra*) 40, *T* 1579.30.511a15, and explication at pp. 511a–c. The first type helps to calm one's mind; the second to mature one's own *buddhadharmas*; and the third to mature other sentient beings; ibid., p. 523a2–4. This same division of the precepts appears in such Chinese apocryphal sūtras as *Chan-ch'a shan-o yeh-pao ching* 1 (*T* 839.17.904c7–8) and *P'u-sa ying-lo pen-yeh ching* (*T* 1485.24.1019b17). Liebenthal (p. 365 and cf. p. 380 n. 1) gives a useful comparative listing of other relevant citations; to his listings add *Ta-sheng chuang-yen ching lun* (*Mahāyānasūtrālaṃkāra-śāstra*) 8 (*T* 1604.31.630c13–14), which is the closest to the wording of *VS*; *Ta-sheng A-p'i-ta-mo tsa-chi lun* (*Abhidharmasamuccaya*) 12, *T* 1606.31.749c4–5; and cf. *Hua-yen ching* 27, *T* 279.10.149b22 and ch. 49, p. 258a22–23.

śramaṇa, who is evil, haughty, and distracted, who needs the precepts. The correct way to keep precepts is to realize that it is one's own discriminative thought that creates good and evil; hence, if the inherent quiescence and extinction of the mind are realized, the purpose of the precepts will automatically be fulfilled.[116] The bodhisattva who realizes the nonproduction of dharmas, and thus the inherent purity of the mind, has no need for the help that precepts provide—but he also is free from the subtle hindrance they can create in those who observe them. The conclusion the *Vajrasamādhi* reaches about precepts is that "the nature of the moral codes is equanimous and void; [the śrāvakas] who hold fast to them are deluded and confused."[117] Virtually the same analysis appears in Shen-hsiu's *Wu fang-pien*, a seminal Northern school treatise: "To activate the mind for the briefest instant is to go counter to the Buddha Nature, to break the Bodhisattva Precepts."[118]

The numerous allusions found in the *Vajrasamādhi* to the teachings of Ch'an—and especially those of the East Mountain faction—compel one to take into account such affinities in ascertaining the authorship of the text. Indeed, given the Korean provenance of the text, the possible role of a Korean adept of Ch'an in writing the scripture must now be seriously considered. What is known about the presence of Ch'an in Korea during this early period?

## Early Korean Sŏn and the Legend of Pŏmnang

The study of early Korean Ch'an—there, known as Sŏn—is hampered by a dearth of contemporary source materials. Nothing is extant from its alleged beginnings in the latter part of the seventh century. The earliest sources, all dating from the ninth century, are a few inscriptions honoring the subsequent founders of the "Nine Mountain Gates of Sŏn" (Kusan Sŏnmun), the Koryŏ appellation for this early Sŏn tradition.[119] Four of these were written

---

[116] *VS*, chap. 5, after n. 82; chap. 6, after n. 86.

[117] *VS*, chap. 5, after n. 82.

[118] *Wu fang-pien*, trans. McRae, p. 172.

[119] There is a burgeoning literature on the early Nine Mountains schools of Korean Sŏn. A collection of several of the most important Korean articles on the formation of early Sŏn has recently appeared in *Han'guk Pulgyo Sŏnmun ŭi hyŏngsŏngsa-chŏk yŏn'gu: Kusan Sŏnmun-ŭl chungsim-ŭro*, ed. Pulgyo hakhoe. Two eminent Korean buddhologists, Kim Yŏngt'ae ("Ogyo Kusan e taehayŏ," pp. 59–77) and Yi Chongik ("Han'guk Pulgyo chejongp'a sŏngnip ŭi yŏksachŏk koch'al," pp. 29–58), have debated the era during which the schools were founded, Kim suggesting an early Koryŏ date, Yi supporting the traditional mid- to late-Silla time of foun-

in China by the expatriate Ch'oe Ch'iwŏn (b. 857), that paragon of sinicized Silla belles-lettres, who held important posts in the T'ang bureaucracy. These inscriptions must be used with caution, however, since they are rife with Confucian, "Taoist," and even geomantic elements, which reflect contemporary concerns more than the thought of the figures they were intended to commemorate.[120] Since they also postdate the period they are recounting by at least a century, one must tread wearily in drawing definitive conclusions based on their accounts.

However inadequate the extant sources might be for developing a precise account of the early history of Ch'an in Korea, we know that Ch'an and Korea were inextricably interwoven from virtually the inception of the tradition. Korean monks living on the mainland participated in the early saṃghas that grew up around the first teachers in the Chinese schools, at times becoming leaders themselves. One of the earliest Korean monks known to have studied Ch'an in China was a certain Yang-chou Kao-li-seng Chih-teh (Kor. Yang-chu Koryŏ-sŭng Chidŏk). Chidŏk is included in a listing of ten principal disciples of Hung-jen in the early Northern school doxography, *Leng-ch'ieh jen-fa chi* (Record of the persons and teachings of the Laṅkā[vatāra]), compiled ca. 706 by Hsüan-tse (d.u.), a fellow student of Hung-jen's. This reference, as cited in *Leng-ch'ieh shih-tzu chi*, is the only notice to Chidŏk in either Chinese or Korean sources, and nothing more is known about him.[121] Given that he was said to have hailed from Yang-chou, however, he may have been a member of one of the Korean exile communities founded along the Chinese coastline from Shan-tung down to Yang-chou after the fall of Koguryŏ and Paekche. As mentioned previously, the Pao-t'ang and Ching-chung schools of early Ch'an, both centered in the

---

dation. Hŏ Hŭngsik ("Sŏnjong Kusan-mun kwa *Sŏnmun yech'am-mun* ŭi munjejŏm," pp. 104, 149, and passim) has definitively demonstrated that the term "Kusan" is not used until the Koryŏ. Summaries of the nine schools appears in Kwŏn Sangno, "Han'guk Sŏnjong yaksa," pp. 267–74; Yi Hŭisu, *T'och'ak-hwa kwajŏng esŏ pon Han'guk Pulgyo*, pp. 57–66; Minn Younggyu (Min Yŏnggyu), "Le bouddhisme Zen de Silla et de Koryŏ," pp. 48–52; and Henrik Sorensen, "The History and Doctrines of Early Korean Sŏn Buddhism." See also Buswell, *Korean Approach*, pp. 9–14 and, for further references to the schools, p. 78 n. 52; on pp. 10–11, I also include a chart of the nine schools.

[120] For Ch'oe Ch'iwŏn's four inscriptions, see Ch'oe Pyŏnghŏn, "Silla hadae Sŏnjong Kusanp'a ŭi sŏngnip," pp. 265–68. As Han Kidu notes (*Silla Sŏn*, pp. 8–9), despite their inadequacy as contemporary source material, they remain the principal documents for the early history of Sŏn on the peninsula and should not be ignored out of hand.

[121] For the passage from *Leng-ch'ieh jen-fa chi* that mentions Chidŏk, see Yanagida, *Shoki no Zenshi*, vol. 1, p. 298; Yanagida, *Shoki Zenshū Shisho*, pp. 33, 273; Han Kidu, *Silla Sŏn*, p. 132; Yampolsky, *Platform Sūtra*, pp. 16–17.

frontier region of Szechwan in southwestern China, claimed as their patriarch the Korean Ch'an adept Musang. Such early connections between Koreans and Ch'an made it likely that Ch'an would receive a speedy introduction to the peninsula.

The Korean tradition credits the Silla monk Pŏmnang (d.u.) with first
introducing Ch'an from China.[122] According to Ch'oe Ch'iwŏn's 893 inscription to Chisŏn Tohŏn (824–882), the founder of the Hŭiyang-san
school of early Korean Sŏn, Pŏmnang traveled to China sometime during
the reign of Queen Sŏndŏk (r. 632–646), where he studied the Ch'an teachings under the fourth patriarch of the school, Tao-hsin. Sometime later, he
returned to Korea to disseminate his new message of Ch'an. The account
suggests that Pŏmnang, frustrated with his public mission, ultimately withdrew into retirement where finally he was able to pass his teachings on in
secret to Sinhaeng (704–779). Sinhaeng's teachings were then transmitted to
the otherwise unknown Chunbŏm (d.u.) and Hyeŭn (d.u.), until they finally reached Chisŏn Tohŏn, who in 879 formally founded the Hŭiyang-san
school—generally regarded as the oldest of the Nine Mountains schools.
While the historicity of Ch'oe's account leaves much to be desired, one of
its results was to make Tohŏn the sixth-generation successor to Tao-hsin,
perhaps in imitation of the transmission of the Chinese Ch'an lineage to the
Sixth Patriarch, Hui-neng.

Pŏmnang, unfortunately, is another of those enigmatic figures found to
be so ubiquitous in the early Ch'an and Sŏn traditions. Ch'oe provides little
evidence that he knew anything at all about Pŏmnang, not even such basic
information as his native place or clan, let alone when he might have returned to Korea with the Ch'an teachings he had learned. And one of the
themes of the account—the frustrations Pŏmnang is alleged to have suffered
in his attempts to teach Sŏn—is a leitmotiv common in Ch'an hagiographical writing. The same thing is found in the narration of even Bodhidharma's
career, which claims that "the words he preached were difficult to fathom
and few were inspired by them."[123]

---

[122] This information appears in the memorial inscription to Chisŏn Tohŏn (774–850), *Yu
Tang Silla-kuk ko Hŭiyang-san Pongam-sa kyo si Chijŏng taesa Chŏkcho chi t'ap pimyŏng*, in Yi
Nŭnghwa, *Chosŏn Pulgyo t'ongsa*, vol. 1, p. 127.3–4; Chōsen sōtokufu, ed., *Chōsen kinseki sōran*,
vol. 1, pp. 90–91; and discussed in Ch'oe Pyŏnghŏn, "Silla Kusan ŭi sŏngnip," pp. 278–79; see
also Kim Yŏngt'ae, "Hŭiyang-san Sŏnp'ae ŭi sŏngnip kwa kŭ pŏpkye e taehayŏ," pp. 11–38;
Buswell, *Korean Approach*, pp. 9 and 78 n. 53. The inscription was composed by Ch'oe Ch'iwŏn
in 893, though the stele was not erected until 924; Ch'oe Pyŏnghŏn, "Silla Kusan ŭi sŏngnip,"
p. 266 n. 8.

[123] *Hsü Kao-seng chuan* 20, *T* 2060.50.596c10.

Furthermore, the evidence provided by Ch'oe Ch'iwŏn to support Pŏm-nang's existence and alleged career is extremely flimsy. Ch'oe attempts to corroborate Pŏmnang's tutelage under Tao-hsin by citing the following passage in Tu Cheng-lun's (574–ca. 658) cenotaph for Tao-hsin:

> According to the inscription composed by Palace Secretary (*chung-shu*) Tu Cheng-lun: "An extraordinary gentleman from a distant land, an eminent man from a foreign region, did not shrink from the dangerous trip and came to this auspicious spot. He took hold of the jewel [of Tao-hsin's teachings] and took refuge in it." Who was this if not the master [Pŏmnang]? But those who know do not talk about it. And furthermore, he hid in secret.[124]

This passage quite obviously says nothing about the nationality of this "extraordinary gentleman," let alone that he was Pŏmnang. Ch'oe here is trying to establish the pedigree of the indigenous Korean Sŏn tradition by connecting it with the eminent fourth patriarch of Chinese Ch'an. Similar retrospective connections were made as well by the Oxhead school of middle Ch'an, which sought to establish its own credentials by associating its founder, Fa-jung (594–657), with Tao-hsin. An even more obvious example of such an attempt at legitimacy is the case of the earliest Vietnamese school of Ch'an, which claims descent from Seng-ts'an—who did not exist.[125] Hence, Tu's reference in itself offers the flimsiest of support for the traditional claim that Pŏmnang trained in the East Mountain school under Tao-hsin.

Ch'oe may have made his startling claim about Pŏmnang's identity to authenticate Sinhaeng's lineage, one account of which is found in Sinhaeng's memorial stele, *Haedong ko Sinhaeng sŏnsa chi pi* (Cenotaph to the past Sŏn master Sinhaeng of Korea), written in 813 by Kim Hŏnjŏng (d.u.).[126] In this stele, which provides the earliest extant account of Sŏn history, Sinhaeng is said to have first trained for two years under the Vinaya master Unjŏng

---

[124] Yi Nŭnghwa, *T'ongsa*, vol. 1, p. 127 l. 4–5; *Chōsen kinseki sōran*, vol. 1, pp. 90–91. Tu Cheng-lun's inscription for Tao-hsin is no longer extant, but it is quoted in Ching-chüeh's *Leng-ch'ieh shih-tzu chi*, as well as in *Ch'uan fa-pao chi* (see translation in McRae, p. 263). Yanagida (*Shoki Zenshū shisho*, pp. 83–84) has suggested that the inscription is falsely ascribed to Tu and actually dates from the early eighth century.

[125] See Thich Thien-an, *Buddhism and Zen in Vietnam*, pp. 32–33.

[126] Chōsen sōtokufu, ed., *Chōsen kinseki sōran*, vol. 1, pp. 113–16. Ch'oe Ch'iwŏn's inscription to Tohŏn uses a different character to transcribe the first syllable of Sinhaeng's name, however, suggesting that his account may have been based on oral tradition, not on his reading of Sinhaeng's stele.

(d.u.) before departing to Mount Hogŏ, where Pŏmnang was then dwelling in retirement. There, after an intensive period of training, Pŏmnang "transmitted the lamp of prajñā" to Sinhaeng, sanctioning Sinhaeng as his successor. Sinhaeng subsequently meditated in the wilderness for three years before also undertaking the incumbent pilgrimage to China sometime during the reign of the T'ang emperor Su-tsung (756–762). Making his way to the T'ang capitals of Lo-yang and Ch'ang-an, Sinhaeng trained under Ta-chao Chih-k'ung (703–779), a disciple of P'u-chi (651–739), the Second Patriarch of the Northern Ch'an school. Sinhaeng's own teachings are thus claimed to have combined Pŏmnang's instructions, which ultimately derived from the Fourth Patriarch's East Mountain faction, with those of the Northern school.[127]

Over the following century, Sŏn training centers were established on eight other mountain sites.[128] Fully seven of these were founded by Korean successors in the Hung-chou school of the middle Ch'an period, which would eventually evolve into the Lin-chi school of classical Ch'an. The last school to develop, the Sumi-san school, was founded by a teacher in the lineage of Ch'ing-yüan Hsing-ssu (d. 740) that eventually matured into the Ts'ao-tung school. It was these sites that would become known as the Nine Mountains school of Korean Sŏn. As convenient as the term Nine Mountains is, it is a real misnomer considering the richness of the Sŏn tradition at this time, which was certainly more widespread than this rubric would suggest.

All of these early Sŏn schools were founded on the periphery of the Silla kingdom, far from the capital of Kyŏngju, and several of their founders came from important regional families. Most support for these schools also came from the local gentry. As just one of many such examples, the Sumi-san school was sponsored by Wang Kŏn (r. 918–943), the eventual founder of the Koryŏ dynasty, at what would become the new capital of Kaesŏng. Repeated power struggles during the eighth and early ninth centuries had seriously emasculated the power of the central government in Kyŏngju. By the middle of the ninth century, these political intrigues had so weakened the court that regional power centers emerged with growing economic

---

[127] Min Yŏnggyu has sought to use this evidence to prove that Nine Mountains Sŏn was based on the Northern, not the "Southern" school, a vast overstatement of Northern Ch'an influence in Korea. See his "Iryŏn ŭi Sŏn Pulgyo," pp. 2–9.

[128] From the extant Korean sources, the next Sŏn adept known to have entered China after Sinhaeng was Toŭi (d. 825), founder of the Kaji-san lineage, who traveled there in 784, some five decades later; see Buswell, *Korean Approach*, pp. 12–13.

strength. Garrisons stationed on the frontiers to guard the kingdom teamed with the local magnates to bring strong military power as well to these regional centers. It was during this decline of Silla, leading up to the reunification of the Korean peninsula under the Koryŏ banner in 936, that Sŏn developed.

The presence of Sŏn on the periphery of the Silla kingdom suggests the "frontier quality" of the Nine Mountains schools. To extend their religious influence wider would require competing with the Hwaŏm school, long entrenched at the seat of government in Kyŏngju. Despite the political disarray in the capital, the Hwaŏm school remained a potent force, providing continued ideological support to the centralized Silla autocracy and the nobility. Indeed, the writings of early Nine Mountains figures, such as Toŭi (d. 825) and Muyŏm (799–888), testify to the ideological battles fought between Sŏn advocates and Hwaŏm exegetes.[129] This placed Sŏn—and in turn the local gentry that supported it—in direct opposition to the old aristocracy in Kyŏngju.[130] One finds in the story of Taean's editing of the *Vajrasamādhi* a similar challenge to the authority of the court.

Lacking any contemporary information about the earliest Korean advocate of Sŏn—the man we know as Pŏmnang—one may tentatively attempt to deduce something about the nature of his teachings from examining what the tradition has to say about his eventual successor, Chisŏn Tohŏn.[131] I referred above to the variety of texts that are quoted in the Tao-hsin section of *Leng-ch'ieh shih-tzu chi*; presumably Tao-hsin's students would have been steeped in the same knowledge of doctrinal materials that influenced their teacher's own approach to practice. Now, the Hŭiyang-san school—which claims to be derivative of Tao-hsin—is considered to have been the most syncretic of all the Nine Mountains schools. Chisŏn, its founder, is said to have gone so far as to advocate a fusion of the three teachings of Buddhism, Taoism, and Confucianism.[132] This propensity tallies well with the eclecti-

---

[129] See ibid., pp. 12–14, for examples of these confrontations.

[130] Ki-Baik Lee's *A New History of Korea*, pp. 94–107, provides a convenient summary of the political background to the rise of Sŏn.

[131] The lineage is discussed in Han Kidu, *Silla Sŏn*, pp. 77–81; a chart of the lineage is given on p. 81. Pŏmnang's line later became associated with the Northern school of Ch'an via his disciple Sinhaeng (d. 779); see discussion in Buswell, *Korean Approach*, p. 9.

[132] His stele inscription states, for example, that "the mind amalgamates the tripartite teachings"; see discussion in Han Kidu, *Sŏn sasang*, pp. 78–79. Note, however, Ch'oe Pyŏnghŏn's comments ("Silla hadae Sŏnjong Kusanp'a ŭi sŏngnip," pp. 265–68), for possible qualifications to this statement.

cism noted previously for both Tao-hsin and the *Vajrasamādhi*, and perhaps of the earliest adepts of Sŏn in Korea.

In his treatment of the Nine Mountains schools, Han Kidu provides another significant clue as to the character of the Hŭiyang-san teachings. Han proposes that the nine sites be divided into two major branches: the Puk-san, or "Northern Mountain," group and the Nam-ak, or "Southern Marchmount," faction. The members of the northern group, comprising the Kaji-san, Sagul-san, Saja-san, and Sŏngju-san schools, were more conservative in their approaches to Sŏn, adhering closely to the teachings received from their Chinese masters in the Hung-chou line. The southern faction, which included the Hŭiyang-san, Pongnim-san, Tongni-san, and Sumi-san schools, was rather more eclectic in orientation, showing a willingness to adapt the teachings received on the mainland to indigenous Korean concerns. The Hŭiyang-san school, which is representative of this branch, is said to have tried to synthesize variant approaches to the Buddhist teachings into a comprehensive, syncretic system of Sŏn practice. This Nam-ak faction Han regards as having been most heavily influenced by the teachings of the Northern school of early Ch'an, which had its origins in the East Mountain lineage. Han believes that the Nam-ak approach, with its characteristic eclecticism, would become the mainstream of Korean Sŏn, culminating in the explicitly syncretic teachings of the later Koryŏ Sŏn monk Chinul (1158–1210).[133] While one may quibble with Han over the precise division of the Nine Mountains schools, his bifurcation is valuable heuristically for detailing the wider orientations of the early Sŏn schools of Silla. And these orientations will help determine the possible motivations behind the composition of the *Vajrasamādhi*.

## The Authorship Problem

The *Vajrasamādhi* appears in Korea sometime during the last quarter of the seventh century, and probably within a few years of Wŏnhyo's death in 686. As I mentioned in chapter 1, and will detail in the annotation to my translation of the *Vajrasamādhi*, there are a number of passages in the text that either resonate with or show the direct influence of a number of important Mahāyāna texts, both authentic, translated sūtras and suspected sinitic apocryphal compositions.[134] For the *Vajrasamādhi* to have been composed in Ko-

---

[133] See the discussion in Han Kidu, *Silla Sŏn*, pp. 128–38.

[134] For references to these textual sources see Mizuno, pp. 41–46; Liebenthal, pp. 361–77; Kimura, "*Kongōzammaikyō*," pp. 109–14.

rea around 686, it is necessary to show at the very least that these scriptures were available then on the peninsula, and preferably that they enjoyed the attention of contemporary Silla writers. Table 4.2 shows that not only were all of these texts in circulation in Korea by the middle of the seventh century, but Wŏnhyo himself had either written specific commentaries on most of these scriptures or at least quoted them in his writings.[135] Hence, the evidence gleaned through such textual influences on the *Vajrasamādhi* also does not conflict with its apparent Korean origin. Corroboration of these close connections between Silla and China is also offered by art historians. Jonathan Best has shown, for example, that by the last quarter of the seventh century there was no longer any time lag in the introduction of Buddhist artistic motifs from China into Silla. Hence, a Silla Buddhist in the 680s would have had access to Buddhist literary and artistic materials virtually simultaneous with their creation on the Chinese mainland.[136]

TABLE 4.2
Scriptures and Treatises Figuring as a Basis for the *Vajrasamādhi-Sūtra*

| Text | Taishō No. | Wŏnhyo's Writings on the Text |
|------|-----------|------------------------------|
| Saddharmapuṇḍarika-sūtra | T 262 | 3 works (#4,5,6,7) |
| Mahāparinirvāṇa-sūtra | T 374 | 2 works (#21, 22) |
| Avataṃsaka-sūtra | T 278 | 4 works (#9,10,11,12) |
| Laṅkāvatāra-sūtra | T 671 | 3 works (#30,21,32) |
| Mūlamadhyamakakārikā | T 1564 | 1 work (#51), and 4 others on Madhyamaka school (#47,48,49,50) |
| Hṛdaya-sūtra | T 251 | 1 work (#3) |
| Suvikrāntavikrāmiparipṛcchā | T 231 | none; two other works on Prajñāpāramitā (#1,2) |
| P'u-sa ying-lo pen-yeh ching | T 1485 | 1 work (#41) |
| Suvarṇaprabhāsottama-sūtra | T 664 | 1 work (#29) |
| Ta-sheng ch'i-hsin lun | T 1666 | 8 works (#68,69,70,71,72,73,74,75) |
| Mahāyānasaṃgraha | T 1593 | 3 works (#57,58,59) |
| Jen-wang ching | T 245 | quoted 27 times in various works |
| Mahāyānasūtrālaṅkāra | T 1604 | quoted 1 time |
| Dásabhūmika-sūtra | T 287 | quoted 4 times |
| Daśabhūmikasūtropadésa | T 1522 | quoted 5 times |

[135] The serial numbers for Wŏnhyo's works in table 4.2 are drawn from Tongguk taehakkyo pulgyo munhwa yŏn'guso, ed., *Han'guk pulgyo ch'ansul munhŏn ch'ongnok*, pp. 16–37; references to quotations in Wŏnhyo's commentaries are from the chart in Rhi Ki-yong, "Kyŏngjŏn," pp. 220–23.
[136] Jonathan Best, "Buddhism, Art and the Transforming Power of Faith in Early Korea."

But does the obviously close connection between Wŏnhyo and the *Vajra-samādhi* implicate him in the composition of the sūtra? I think not. Tsan-ning's statements that the Dragon King had specifically commanded that the text be commented upon by Wŏnhyo say nothing about any role played by Wŏnhyo personally in its compilation. Rather, it is only an indication of the extent of Wŏnhyo's fame at the time—that is to say, Wŏnhyo's knowledge and intellectual acumen were so renowned that he would have been singled out by the Dragon King for this special office. Taean, certainly, is directly implicated, but nothing is known about this phantom apart from this single reference in Wŏnhyo's hagiographies. Whoever the writer of the *Vajrasa-mādhi* was, the text was of such design that its importance would be readily apparent to Wŏnhyo. By gaining the patronage of this preeminent Silla scholiast and his coterie, the text would immediately have been accorded a measure of prestige and legitimacy. The author thus ensured that the *Vajra-samādhi*—with its surreptitious Sŏn message—would be brought into the mainstream of the Korean Buddhist tradition as a whole, where its overrid-ing syncretic focus would help vivify subsequent doctrinal development within the tradition.

It is clear from the remarks in his commentary that Wŏnhyo himself ac-cepted without reservation the authenticity of the sūtra; indeed, nowhere does he even broach any possibility to the contrary. As discussed in the pre-vious chapter, Wŏnhyo saw in the *Vajrasamādhi* the canonical basis of both the twofold gnoseological schema outlined in the *Awakening of Faith* and Paramārtha's theory of the amalavijñāna. The parallels Wŏnhyo drew be-tween the *Vajrasamādhi* and other texts that had been so central to the devel-opment of his own thought excited him so much that he voluntarily quit his retirement to return to writing and lecturing. Nevertheless, there is no inti-mation from Wŏnhyo's treatment of, or attitude toward, the text that he was in any way involved in its composition. The clinching piece of evidence, however, is that Wŏnhyo, who was unable to complete either of his two attempted pilgrimages to China, could not have known of the pedigree of the Ch'an passages that appear in the sūtra.

But what of the possibility that Wŏnhyo may have written the *Vajrasa-mādhi* to further his own syncretic vision, while incorporating unwittingly fragments of originally Ch'an materials that somehow had made their way to Korea? We know, after all, that there was a ready exchange of texts be-tween the peninsula and the mainland throughout Buddhism's history in East Asia. Treating Wŏnhyo as author would have been my alternative end-ing. While this scenario cannot be dismissed out of hand, the structure of the Ch'an sections in chapter 5 of the scripture belie it. There, the author gives a chronologically accurate presentation of the historical evolution of Ch'an thought, beginning with the two accesses of the Bodhidharma text and continuing on to the East Mountain doctrine of guarding the one. The odds that Wŏnhyo, who was completely oblivious to the Ch'an or Sŏn movements, could have been so uncannily precise in his chronology are slim at best. But what is more striking in this account is its polemical bent: the structure of the argument supports the teachings of the East Mountain school over those of the Bodhidharma lineage. What possible motive could Wŏnhyo have had for such apologetics when he knew nothing about the evolving Ch'an tradition?

But might Wŏnhyo not have learned about Ch'an from an early missionary, perhaps someone like Pŏmnang? This is pure speculation. There is no evidence from any source that Wŏnhyo had contacts with early Sŏn teachers, and no identification of Wŏnhyo with the Sŏn schools in later hagiographical records. Sŏn was the predominant school of Buddhism at the time that *Samguk yusa*, the main anthology concerning Three Kingdoms religion, was written, and there would have been distinct advantages to identifying Koryŏ Sŏn with Wŏnhyo—if such a claim were in any way tenable. The fact that no such identification is made suggests that the Koreans had no retained memory of Wŏnhyo's involvement with Sŏn. As enticing as the prospect may seem, Wŏnhyo is not our man.

The only other authorship possibility would be that the *Vajrasamādhi* was written in China and then introduced into Korea virtually simultaneous with its composition. There is no evidence, however, that the sūtra circulated in China until 730, when it was finally relisted in the *K'ai-yüan lu*. I have also mentioned that there were several related Ch'an-orientated apocrypha written in China between the late sixth and early eighth centuries, at around the same time as the *Vajrasamādhi*. These included such texts as the *Fa-wang ching*, *Hsin-wang ching*, and *Ch'an-men ching*, as well as some unnamed indigenous sūtras now known only in citations. These scriptures are also associated with the East Mountain/Northern school lineage and are cited in Ch'an anthologies, such as *Leng-ch'ieh shih-tzu chi*. If the *Vajrasamādhi* were composed in China, it would have been composed in the same religious milieu that spawned these other Ch'an apocrypha. But it had also to have been finished no later than 686, the year of Wŏnhyo's death, and probably a year or so earlier to give it time to make it to Korea; it therefore antedates these related texts, most of which are dated ca. 695–730. Why, then, is the *Vajrasamādhi* never cited in any Chinese sources associated with the East Mountain/Northern school line, such as the *Leng-ch'ieh shih-tzu chi*, which was written ca. 713–720? Diehard sinophiles might suggest that the nucleus of the sūtra was composed in China, the complete sūtra being re-dacted later in Korea. But this conjecture is completely hypothetical and, given the present state of our knowledge, utterly unfounded. While it is not categorically impossible that the *Vajrasamādhi* was composed on the Chinese mainland and then introduced to the Korean peninsula, there is absolutely no evidence even hinting at such a possibility. Sinocentrists could finally suggest the *Vajrasamādhi* was written by a Chinese Ch'an missionary work-ing in Korea—again a prospect for which there is not a shred of evidence. But even in that most speculative of cases the *Vajrasamādhi* would have been written in Korea, for a Korean audience, and would have to qualify as a Korean sūtra.

But if Wŏnhyo, or a Chinese, was not the author of the scripture, then who was? To be able to write the *Vajrasamādhi*, any candidate would, first, have had to be conversant with the principal texts of the sinitic Tathāgata-garbha tradition, especially the *Awakening of Faith* and the *Laṅkāvatāra-sūtra*. He also had to be familiar with the incipient Ch'an doctrines on the Chinese mainland and, more specifically, with the teachings of the East Mountain faction. And finally, he had to have been Korean. The dearth of historical sources from the Silla period makes it problematic to determine authorship directly. But it is here that the Ch'an elements in the *Vajrasamādhi* loom large. What can be said of the possibilities that an early Korean Sŏn adept may have written the *Vajrasamādhi*?

Given what is known of the traditional accounts of the evolution of Ko-rean Sŏn, the obvious candidate for authorship of the *Vajrasamādhi* would be Pŏmnang. Of the figures about whom we have any knowledge, only Pŏmnang is directly associated with Tao-hsin, the Ch'an master whose teachings appear so conspicuously in the *Vajrasamādhi*, and thus would have had the requisite knowledge of the East Mountain teachings necessary to write the sūtra. If Pŏmnang's own scholastic background were anything like that ascribed to Tao-hsin, he would also have had sufficient doctrinal under-standing to contextualize those Ch'an teachings within the Tathāgatagarbha framework employed in the *Vajrasamādhi*. And Pŏmnang was a Korean. He is also claimed to have begun proselytizing in Korea right around the time I have dated the *Vajrasamādhi*. While the date of Pŏmnang's repatriation is not given in the inscriptions, it is doubtful that he could have returned to Korea until sometime after 676. This is because travel across national boundaries would have been virtually impossible until after the consolidation of the Silla victory in the three-kingdoms unification wars, as was noted in Wŏnhyo's case as well. One can see how nicely this scenario of Pŏmnang as author converges with the provenance, dating, and religious milieu already established for the *Vajrasamādhi*.

One could also provide a viable motivation for Pŏmnang to have written the scripture. By the last quarter of the seventh century, Sŏn—and specifically the Sŏn of Tao-hsin's lineage, which was still looking for legitimacy on the Chinese mainland—may have been making its first inroads in Korea. As some of the inscriptions note, however, Korean Sŏn seems not to have been particularly successful in the early years of its tenure on the peninsula, the major attention of Silla Buddhists being on the scholastic schools. Toŭi's (d. 825) cenotaph states, for example: "People of his time only revered the teachings of the scriptures and cultivated contemplation methods that maintained the spirit (*chonsin*); they could not understand the unconditioned school [of Sŏn], which is free in all situations."[137] Pŏmnang himself was said to have "hid in secret" rather than continue trying to disseminate publicly his new teachings.[138] It is in this connection that the statement appearing in the *Sung Kao-seng chuan* biography of Wŏnhyo of Taean's refusal "to cross the threshold of the royal palace" is worth recalling. As I have noted, the Sŏn teachers of the Unified Silla period transmitted their teachings in virtual isolation from the centers of ecclesiastical power in the Silla capital of Kyŏngju. The antipathy Taean displays toward the royal palace—and, by extension, toward the scholastic schools that the court supported—may imply the antiestablishment (perhaps Sŏn?) affiliations of the person most closely associated with the "rediscovery" of the text. Given the antagonistic climate of the times, it is thus easy to imagine that someone like Pŏmnang could have composed a text—the *Vajrasamādhi*—that implicitly connected Tao-hsin's teachings with those of the legendary Ch'an patriarch, Bodhidharma, finally couching these Sŏn messages in a sūtra that incorporated not only allusions to many of the major trends in East Asian Mahāyāna philosophy but also to that doctrinal element so vital to Silla Buddhist scholasticism: the synthetic Tathāgatagarbha theory of the *Awakening of Faith*. Titled after a type of samādhi that was the focus of widespread attention in sinitic Buddhist scholasticism, the new sūtra could thus be portrayed as the reappear-

---

[137] *Silla-kuk Muju Kaji-san Porim-sa si Pojo sŏnsa yŏngt'ap pimyŏng*, by Kim Wŏn (d.u.); in Yi Nŭnghwa, *Chosŏn t'ongsa*, vol. 1, pp. 120.13–121.1; *Chōsen kinseki sōran*, vol. 1, p. 62.8–9; quoted in Buswell, *Korean Approach*, p. 78 n. 55.

[138] *Chijŏng taesa chi t'ap pimyŏng*, in Yi Nŭnghwa, *Chosŏn Pulgyo t'ongsa*, vol. 1, p. 127 l. 5.

ance of a text long out of circulation, thanks to the happy coincidence that a long-lost *Vajrasamādhi-sūtra* continued to be listed in Buddhist bibliographical catalogues. Such a text would have been sure to attract the immediate attention of influential scholiasts like Wŏnhyo, thereby ensuring that its underlying Sŏn message would be popularized, perhaps to an extent that this early Sŏn adept himself could never have hoped.

One must remember, however, that any connections of the Pŏmnang mentioned in ninth-century inscriptions with either Tao-hsin or the historical Nine Mountains schools are extremely tenuous. Even the associations drawn between Pŏmnang and Sinhaeng, his presumed successor, are questionable, given the pronounced differences in their dates. Since Sinhaeng was not born until 704, while Pŏmnang studied under Tao-hsin ca. 632–646, their student-master relationship is difficult to support chronologically. If Pŏmnang studied under Tao-hsin as an adult, he would have to have been born at the very latest in the 620s. Since Sinhaeng had studied with a Vinaya master for two years before meeting Pŏmnang, and thus was probably at least twenty, he could not have met Pŏmnang before perhaps 723. This would make Pŏmnang about a hundred years old when he first met Sinhaeng—not impossible, but highly improbable. This discrepancy has led Kwŏn Sangno to suggest that the Pŏmnang who studied with Tao-hsin could not be the same person who transmitted the Sŏn teachings to Sinhaeng.[139] Any identity we might thus claim between Pŏmnang and the author of the *Vajrasamādhi* is, finally, speculative.

Nevertheless, whoever the author may have been, he was familiar with the literature of the two major factions of the nascent Ch'an tradition, was sympathetic to the East Mountain school and specifically with the teachings most closely associated with Tao-hsin, not Hung-jen, and possessed a working knowledge of sinitic Tathāgatagarbha thought. These characteristics tally more closely with the attributes of the Pŏmnang of the inscriptions than with any other contemporary person I know of in Korea. Only Pŏmnang had the necessary background to write the text and the compelling motive for resorting to scriptural forgery. If the *Vajrasamādhi* were not written by Pŏmnang himself, then it must have been written by someone very much like him.

The three other names available by which one might refer to the author of the *Vajrasamādhi* are all more problematic than is Pŏmnang. Taean is strongly implicated in the "rediscovery" of the sūtra, but he is not associated

---

[139] Kwŏn Sangno, "Han'guk Sŏnjong yaksa," p. 266.

with Sŏn, and no claim is made that he ever traveled to China, where he could have learned of the Ch'an teachings of Tao-hsin. Chidŏk, the Korean monk named in Northern school records as a disciple of Hung-jen, is the only other Silla monk besides Pŏmnang who is presumed to have trained under East Mountain teachers and, thus, the only other Korean exposed to the doctrines so central to the *Vajrasamādhi*. Had Chidŏk returned to Korea he might have made a plausible candidate. There is no such evidence, however. Chidŏk is not even mentioned in passing in indigenous Sŏn materials and seems to have remained unknown in his native land. Sinhaeng might also have been a viable choice if his pilgrimage to China had taken place some forty years earlier than the middle of the eighth century. The depiction of Pŏmnang therefore tallies best with the characteristics of the person who could have authored the *Vajrasamādhi*. In the absence of any definitive evidence to the contrary, the author may be called "Pŏmnang," provided, of course, that one understands by this name not the paleographic Pŏmnang but instead a historical shell used to designate the person with the requisite background to compose the *Vajrasamādhi*. While perhaps not the completely satisfying conclusion one might like to this story, more than anyone else it is Pŏmnang who deserves the prize of authorship.

## The Legacy of the *Vajrasamādhi*

Soon after its composition, the *Vajrasamādhi* began to be used frequently in the writings of East Asian Buddhists of varying sectarian persuasions. Perhaps the earliest Chinese treatise to cite the *Vajrasamādhi* (anonymously, as is common in Chinese works) is *Hua-yen ching i-hai po-men* (A hundred approaches to the sea of meaning of the *Avataṃsaka-sūtra*) by the Hua-yen systematizer, Fa-tsang.[140] While the date of this treatise is unknown, it was probably written sometime during the early years of the eighth century.[141] Fa-tsang is well known to have been profoundly influenced by Wŏnhyo and had near immediate access through his Korean contacts to a number of Wŏnhyo's compositions; hence it is quite possible that Fa-tsang received the *Vajrasamādhi* from Korea, perhaps even learning of the sūtra through Wŏnhyo's commentary. Another early source in which the *Vajrasamādhi* appears

---

[140] *Hua-yen ching i-hai po-men*, *T* 1875.45.628c21–22 = *VS*, p. 371c13–14.
[141] See Yoshizu Yoshihide, "Hōzō-den no kenkyū," pp. 168–93, for the most recent study of Fa-tsang's life and works.

is the *Sŏk Mahayŏn-ron*, an apocryphal composition to the *Awakening of Faith*, which was composed probably in Korea in the middle of the eighth century. The *Vajrasamādhi* is said to be one of the ten major scriptures upon which that treatise is based; and indeed the sūtra's pervasive impact on that text lends credence to theories of the Korean origin of both of those compositions.[142]

But it is in works with explicit Ch'an affiliations that the most extensive use of the *Vajrasamādhi* is made. It is cited extensively, for example, in the *Li-tai fa-pao chi*,[143] a doxographic collection on the early Ch'an patriarchs, compiled ca. 774–781 in the Pao-t'ang school.[144] Provocatively, the *Vajrasamādhi* is quoted by title in the section of that record devoted to the Korean Ch'an adept Musang. While there is little chance that the *Li-tai fa-pao chi* can be accepted as a verbatim record of Musang's teachings, the fact that the *Vajrasamādhi* was assumed to have been known by him is suggestive of the Ch'an—and specifically the Korean Sŏn—affinities of the sūtra. It was probably under Pao-t'ang auspices that the *Vajrasamādhi* became known in Tibet: the sūtra was translated into Tibetan by at least the end of the eighth century, as is attested by its citation in works attributed to Vimalamitra, one of the founders of the Rñiṅ-ma school.[145] The *Vajrasamādhi* is also quoted in an anthology of Tun-huang Ch'an materials, which has been given the title *Shokyō yōshō* (Essentials of the sūtras), the contents of which are closely associated with the *Li-tai fa-pao chi*.[146] That compilation is dated sometime after 716—the date of Śubhakarasiṃha's (d. 735) arrival in China, an account of which appears in the text—but is more plausibly dated, I believe, to within a few years of the *Li-tai fa-pao chi*.[147] This appeal of the *Vajrasamādhi* to a predominantly Ch'an audience is indicated as well by the fact that, in later materials, it continues to be cited primarily in Ch'an works, such as those by Yen-shou (904–975), or in Hua-yen treatises by doctrinal exegetes

---

[142] The *VS* is quoted by title in *Sŏk Mahayŏn-ron* at *T* 1668.32.593c12, 603b3–5, 606a8–17, 611c23–27, 630a15–17, and passim.

[143] *Li-tai fa-pao chi*, *T* 2075.51.189b2 = *VS*, p. 369a23–24; *VS* is also cited at *T* 2075.51.189a6. For the importance of apocryphal sūtras in the *Li-tai fa-pao chi* and the Pao-t'ang school, see Jeffrey Broughton, "Early Ch'an Schools in Tibet," p. 57 n. 36.

[144] See Yanagida, *Shoki zenshū shisho*, pp. 223, 279, for discussion of this important text.

[145] See the discussion by Luis O. Gómez ("Indian Materials on the Doctrine of Sudden Enlightenment," pp. 430–32 n. 21) concerning the authenticity of this section in Vimalamitra's work where the passage from *VS* is quoted. As Gómez notes (p. 395), apocryphal scriptures, including *VS*, were used by the Chinese debaters at the Tibetan Council of Lhasa to support their radical positions.

[146] Yanagida, "*Li-tai fa-pao chi*," p. 37.

[147] I accept Mizuno Kōgen's dating given in "Gisaku no *Hokkukyō* ni tsuite," p. 20.

strongly influenced by Ch'an, such as Ch'eng-kuan (738–840) and Tsung-mi (780–841).[148] Indeed, the continued appeal of the *Vajrasamādhi* to a Ch'an audience is perhaps unsurprising, given that we now know it was written by a Sŏn sympathizer with covert polemical motives.

It is significant, however, that all such citations of the *Vajrasamādhi* date at least two decades after Wŏnhyo had already commented on the text. Some previous scholars have been led astray by a few cases where a *Chin-kang san-mei ching* is cited in pre-eighth-century texts—such as in Tao-hsüan's *Shih-men kui-ching i* (661) or Tao-shih's (d. 683) *Fa-yüan chu-lin* (668). These, however, all prove instead to be quotations from *Chin-kang san-mei pen-hsing ch'ing-ching pu-huai pu-mieh ching* (Sūtra on the original nature of the vajrasamādhi being pure, indefeasible, and nondeteriorating), a completely different sūtra, which the catalogues presume to have been translated sometime during the three Ch'in dynasties (350–431).[149] Hence, citations of the *Vajrasamādhi* in East Asian literature provide final testimony to the scenario about the Korean origin of the text.

## The Place of the *Vajrasamādhi* in the Evolution of Ch'an

Despite Ch'an's claim of being a unique branch of Buddhism utterly divorced from the rest of the tradition, the evidence marshalled in this study clearly belies it. However vigorous its subsequent protestations to the contrary, Ch'an evolved out of the same trends in Buddhist thought and practice that forged other sinitic schools of Buddhism, such as T'ien-t'ai and Hua-

---

[148] Extensive listings of citations from *VS* appearing in Ch'an works are given in Mizuno, "Gisaku no *Hokkukyō*," passim. These include Tsung-mi's *Yüan-chüeh ching lüeh-shu chu* (*T* 1795; four quotes) and *Ch'an-yüan chu-chüan-chi tou-hsü* (*T* 2015.48.405b = *VS*, p. 368a); and Yen-shou's *Tsung-ching lu* (*T* 2016, thirty quotes) and *Wan-shan t'ung-kuei chi* (*T* 2017; five quotes). *VS* citations in other Ch'an texts are also given in Chu-chen, *T'ung-tsung chi* 1, p. 228c11–16.

[149] *Fa-yüan chu-lin*, for example, cites a *Chin-kang san-mei ching* at *T* 2122.53.431a28–b1; but this is instead a citation from *Chin-kang san-mei pen-hsing ch'ing-ching pu-huai pu-mieh ching*, *T* 644.15.699a18–21, 25. Yanagida's claim (*Shoki Zenshū shisho*, p. 30 n. 13) that this quotation does not appear in either of the two *Vajrasamādhi-sūtra*s is incorrect, belying his suspicion that there were variant recensions of *VS*, which were finally standardized into the text as it is known today. This same passage is cited by Tao-hsüan in his *Shih-men kui-ching i* 2 (*T* 1896.45.868a29–b3) and attributed to *VS*; he, however, has probably taken the quotation from *Fa-yüan chu-lin*. Thus it certainly does not come from a *Chin-kang shang-wei ching*, presumed translated by Buddhaśānta ca. 520–539, which is cited in Tao-hsüan's *Hsü Kao-seng chuan* 1 (*T* 2060.50.429a11), as Yanagida (*Shoki Zenshū shisho*, p. 30 n. 13) and Kimura ("*Kongōzammaikyō*," p. 117 n. 39) had presumed.

yen. Ch'an thought is closely allied with texts that prompted the emphasis in Chinese Buddhism on the immanence of enlightenment and subitism, such as the *Laṅkāvatāra* and the *Awakening of Faith*. The syncretic orientation of those two texts—particularly their harmonization of the variant philosophies of mind represented by the ālaya and amala vijñānas through recourse to the tathāgatagarbha concept—is seen also in the *Vajrasamādhi*. This book has shown that Ch'an, too, was inspired by similar philosophical concerns and must be placed squarely within the doctrinal matrix of the broader sinitic Buddhist tradition. Ch'an is a radical reading of the Tathāgatagarbha ideal, intended to bring out explicitly its soteriological connotations. Ch'an as presented in this sūtra has begun to develop the soteriological emphasis that would eventually blossom as new forms of meditation. Along with its unique rhetoric and pedagogical styles, it is those new practices that would eventually distinguish Ch'an as an independent school of sinitic Buddhism. The doctrinal context within which Ch'an ideas are placed in the *Vajrasamādhi* therefore says much about the philosophical influences that helped shape the early Ch'an movement in China and Korea and hopefully something about the theological milieu out of which Ch'an evolved.

Pŏmnang's own motives in composing the *Vajrasamādhi* must be understood also as a response to the state of Buddhism in Silla in the latter half of the seventh century. The entrenched scholastic schools—especially Hwaŏm—of the capital of Kyŏngju wielded tremendous political and ecclesiastical influence, leaving little hope for the successful transplantation of a new school that as yet had little following even on the Chinese mainland. After his return from China and his tutelage under Tao-hsin, Pŏmnang probably had at least nine years—we cannot know more precisely—to attempt to proselytize in a Korea that was said to have remained stubbornly unreceptive to his new teachings. Becoming frustrated with the progress of his mission, Pŏmnang eventually resorted to textual forgery to bring attention to his message. Combining around a Tathāgatagarbha core a variety of doctrinal elements drawn from many different Mahāyāna traditions, Pŏmnang used his sūtra as a vehicle to present surreptitiously the new message of Ch'an—and specifically the Tao-hsin school of Ch'an—to what would otherwise have been an antagonistic audience. To counter possible aspersions about the suspicious origins of the scripture, Pŏmnang titled his new work the *Vajrasamādhi*, after a translated sūtra that had appeared in scriptural catalogues from almost the inception of Buddhism in East Asia but that was otherwise unknown and unavailable.

Given the preponderance of evidence raised here, claims of an Indian or

Chinese provenance for the *Vajrasamādhi* are no longer tenable. Indeed, the scenario presented for Sŏn authorship of the sūtra provides a compelling motive for its composition, which will have major implications for our understanding of the development of the Korean Buddhist tradition. The *Vajrasamādhi* now emerges as the earliest text of Korean Sŏn, antedating all other relevant documents by well over a century. It must be given a full accounting in any future treatment of the development of Korean Sŏn. But just as significantly, the *Vajrasamādhi* also turns out to be one of the oldest extant works of all of sinitic Ch'an. It predates the earliest works of the Northern Ch'an school by some three decades. The only Ch'an work that has to date been proven to be older is the *Erh-ju ssu-hsing lun*, attributed to the founder of Ch'an, Bodhidharma. The *Vajrasamādhi* also provides the only independent corroboration of the East Mountain teachings, which have heretofore been accessible only through later Northern school anthologies. Finally, the *Vajrasamādhi* provides an explicit example of the organicism of the East Asian Buddhist tradition, in which a sūtra composed in Korea was able to influence the evolution of Buddhism not only in the Chinese heartland, but also in regions as distant as Szechwan and Tibet.

Part Two

*Translation*

# THE *VAJRASAMĀDHI-SŪTRA* (*BOOK OF ADMANTINE ABSORPTION*)

*Translated by an Anonym*
*During the Northern Liang Dynasty*

Chapter One

# Prologue

[365c24]   Thus I once heard.[1] The Buddha was dwelling in the great city of King's House (Rājagṛha), on Mount Gṛdhrakūṭa (Vulture Peak), together with a great assembly of ten thousand bhikṣus [ordained mendicants], all of whom had attained the arhat path. Their names were Śāriputra, Mahā-maudgalyāyana, Subhūti—there were many arhats such as these. [366a]   Furthermore, there were two thousand bodhisattva-*mahāsattva*s [adepts intent on enlightenment]. Their names were Haet'al (Liberation; Skt. Vimukti) Bodhisattva, Simwang (Mind King; Skt. Cittarāja) Bodhisattva, Muju (Nonabiding; Skt. Apratiṣṭhita) Bodhisattva, and other bodhisattvas like these. Furthermore, there were eighty thousand elders (*gṛhapati*). Their names were Elder Pŏmhaeng (Chastity; Skt. Brahmacarya), Elder Taebŏm-haeng (Great Chastity; Mahābrahmacarya), Elder Jyotiṣka (Kor. Suje; Luminary), and other elders like these.[2] Furthermore, there were six hundred million devas, dragons, yakṣas [demons], *gandharva*s [demigod musicians], aśuras [titans], *garuḍa*s [mythical birds], *kinnara*s [half horses/half men], *mahorāga*s [great snakes], humans, and nonhumans.

At that time, the Lord, surrounded by the great congregation, preached a Mahāyāna sūtra on behalf of all the great congregation, entitled *Ilmi chinsil musang musaeng kyŏlchŏng silche pon'gangnihaeng* (Practice of the single taste, truth, signless, nonproduction, certitude, edge of reality, and the inspiration

---

[1] Typically, this stock opening to Buddhist texts is broken into two clauses: "Thus have I heard. Once . . ." (*evam mayā śrutam ekasmin samaye*). I translate it as a single clause, following Wŏnhyo's analysis; see *KSGR* 1, pp. 362c27–366a3. John Brough has advocated this same interpretation ("Thus Have I Heard . . . ," pp. 416–26), following the Tibetan commentarial tradition.

[2] As Mizuno (p. 42) has noted, these would be unusual personal names for Indians, and their use provides a significant clue of the East Asian origin of *VS*.

of original enlightenment). If one hears this sūtra or retains even one four-line verse of it, that person will then access the stage of the Buddha's knowledge; he will be able to proselyte sentient beings with appropriate expedients and become the great spiritual mentor (*kalyāṇamitra*) of all sentient beings.

After the Buddha had preached this sūtra, he folded his legs into full-lotus position and entered into the adamantine absorption (vajrasamādhi), with his body and mind motionless.

At that time there was a bhikṣu named Agada in the congregation, who arose from his seat, joined his palms together, and genuflected in foreign fashion [*hogwe*; with his right knee on the ground]. Wishing to reiterate[3] the meaning of this [sūtra that had just been preached], he recited gāthās:

> That Lord who is filled with great friendliness,
> His wisdom penetrates without obstruction.
> Intending to ferry across sentient beings on a vast scale,
> He has explained the meaning of the one truth.
> All this was accomplished via the path that has a single taste,[4]
> Never by means of the Hīnayāna.
> The meaning, "taste," and place of his sermon,
> All leave the unreal far behind.
> They access the stage of wisdom of all the buddhas,
> That decisive and true edge of reality (*bhūtakoṭi*).
> All the audience has transcended the world,
> There is no one who has not achieved liberation.
> All the innumerable bodhisattvas,
> Each ferry across all sentient beings.
> For the sake of the congregation, they question extensively and profoundly.
> Learning of the dharmas' characteristic of calm extinction,
> They access that place of certitude [of attaining enlightenment;
>     (*samyaktva)niyāmāvakrānti*].
> The Tathāgata, through his knowledge (*jñāna*) and expedients (*upāya*),
> Speaks so that [all beings] will be sure to access reality,
> All this is in accordance with the one vehicle,
> There are no extraneous tastes.
> In the same way that, soaked by a single rain,
> The multitudes of plants all grow verdantly.
> [So too], according to their natures, which are each discrete,
> Soaked by the dharma that has a single taste,

---

[3] Following the Koryŏ II/Taishō edition; *VS*, p. 366a13.
[4] The one vehicle of the buddhas, according to Wŏnhyo; *KSGR* 1, p. 963b16–17.

All things achieve complete fulfillment,
Just as if, soaked by a single rain,
All their bodhi sprouts were matured.[5]
Accessing the adamantine taste,
He realizes the meditative absorption [that knows] the true reality of
    dharmas.
He is certain to excise doubts and regrets,
And perfect the seal of the one dharma.

---

[5] Alluding to the famous simile of the rain of dharma that nurtures all living things. See
*Miao-fa lien-hua ching* (*Saddharmapuṇḍarīka-sūtra*) 3, *T* 262.9.19a–20b; Leon Hurvitz, trans., *Lo-tus*, pp. 101–103.

Chapter Two

# The Signless Dharma

[366b]   Arising from his samādhi, the Lord then spoke these words, "The stage of wisdom of all the buddhas accesses the given nature of the real characteristic of dharmas.[6] For this reason, [the buddhas'] expedients[7] and superpowers (abhijñā)[8] are all inspired by signlessness (alakṣaṇatva). The explicit meaning (nitārtha) of the one enlightenment[9] is difficult to comprehend and difficult to access. It is not something that is known or cognized by any adherents of the two vehicles [of śrāvakas and pratyekabuddhas]; it may only be known by the buddhas and bodhisattvas. All [the tathāgatas] explain the single taste [only] to those sentient beings who are capable of deliverance."

At that time, Haet'al Bodhisattva arose from his seat, joined his palms together, genuflected in foreign fashion, and addressed the Buddha: "Lord! After the Buddha's demise, the right dharma (saddharma) will vanish from the world and the semblance dharma (pratirūpakadharma) will linger on in the world.[10] During the final age of the dharma (saddharmavipralopa), sen-

---

[6] "The stage of wisdom of all the buddhas" refers to the wisdom that is produced by accessing the vajrasamādhi. Wŏnhyo interprets the "given nature" (kyŏlchŏng sŏng) as follows: "this real characteristic of dharmas is not produced by the buddhas; its nature is itself just so, regardless of whether there are buddhas or not." KSGR, p. 964b2–4.

[7] The expedient display of eight stereotypical events in any buddha's life (p'alsang pangp'yŏn), beginning with his descent from Tuṣita heaven, and culminating in parinirvāṇa; KSGR 1, p. 964b11–12.

[8] These are the six superpowers: magical powers; divine ear; telepathy; divine eye; recollection of former existences; knowledge of the extinction of the outflows. KSGR 1, p. 964b12.

[9] Wŏnhyo glosses "the explicit meaning of the one enlightenment" as the one mind, original enlightenment, or the tathāgatagarbha. KSGR 1, p. 964b19–20.

[10] Wŏnhyo construes this passage as referring to VS's audience. The preceding expanded (vaipulya) sūtra was intended for the period of saddharma, while VS is directed at the needs of beings in the semblance-dharma age. KSGR 1, p. 964c19–21. Actually VS here jumbles the transition period of pratirūpakadharma and the final age of saddharmavipralopa. For a survey of

tient beings [who are tainted by] the five turbidities (*kaṣāya*)[11] will perform all types of evil actions and will transmigrate among the three realms of existence without respite. During that period, I beg that the Buddha, out of his friendliness and compassion, will proclaim for those later generations of sentient beings the single taste that is decisive and true, and prompt those sentient beings to achieve liberation together."

The Buddha said, "Oh son of good family! Feel free to ask me about the causes surrounding my appearance in the world. I wanted to proselyte sentient beings and to prompt those sentient beings to obtain the fruition [of enlightenment] that transcends the world. This one great matter [of a buddha's appearance in the world] is inconceivable, because it is performed out of great friendliness and great compassion. If I were not to respond [to your questions], then I would fall into niggardliness [for hoarding the dharma I have learned]. You should all listen attentively and carefully, and I will proclaim [the answers] for you.

"Oh son of good family! When you proselyte sentient beings, you should not conceive that proselytism either does or does not occur; such proselytism is great indeed! It enables all those sentient beings to leave behind mind and self, for both mind and self are originally void and calm.[12] If they attain voidness of mind, then that mind will not illusorily project anything. Free from all illusory projections, they will then attain nonproduction (*anutpatti*). The mind that does not produce anything derives from such nonprojection."

Haet'al Bodhisattva addressed the Buddha: "The nature of the mind of sentient beings is originally void and calm. The essence of the mind that is void and calm is free from materiality (*rūpa*) and characteristics (*lakṣaṇa*). How are we to cultivate and train so that we may obtain that mind which is originally void? I entreat the Buddha to proclaim this for us, out of his friendliness and compassion."

The Buddha replied, "Bodhisattva! All the characteristics of the mind

---

different Chinese Buddhist eschatological schemes, see David Chappell, "Early Forebodings of the Death of Buddhism," pp. 122–54.

[11] The five turbidities are five events that mark the gradual decay of the universe; they appear during the abiding period of an eon, or kalpa. (1) Turbidity of the kalpa, marking the beginning of the declining period of the kalpa; (2) turbidity of views, i.e., the wrong views of egoism, etc.; (3) turbidity of defilements; (4) turbidity of sentient beings, the decline in their behavior; (5) turbidity of the lifespan, or the decreasing length of life.

[12] " 'Self' means person; 'mind' means dharmas, because mind is the support and chief of all dharmas. At the time that one penetrates to the fact that all persons and dharmas are originally void, the signs at which one had grasped previously are not then produced. Therefore, both types of abandonment are simultaneously perfected." *KSGR* 1, p. 965b29–965c3.

originally have no origin. As they originally have no original locus, [the mind is] void and calm, producing nothing. If the mind produces nothing, it then accesses void calmness.[13] At that ground of the mind (*cittabhūmi*), where all is void and calm, one attains voidness of mind. Oh son of good family! The signless mind is free from both mind and self. It is the same with all the characteristics of dharmas."

Haet'al Bodhisattva addressed the Buddha: "Lord! If sentient beings have a conception of self [i.e., grasping at personality] or a conception of mind [i.e., grasping at dharmas], what dharma will awaken those sentient beings and prompt them to leave behind such fetters (*saṃyojana*)?"

The Buddha replied, "Oh son of good family! If there is someone who retains a conception of self, he should be encouraged to contemplate the twelvefold chain of causal conditioning (*pratītyasamutpāda*). The twelvefold chain of causal conditioning originally derives from cause and fruition. The production of cause and fruition is stimulated by the operation of the mind. But the mind does not exist, much less the body. If there is a person who conceives of a self, he should be encouraged to abandon his view [that the self] exists. If there is a person who conceives that there is no self, he should be encouraged to abandon his view [that the self] does not exist. If a person conceives that the mind can be produced, he should be encouraged to abandon [his view that] the nature [of the mind] is subject to production. If a person conceives that the mind can be extinguished, he should be encouraged to abandon [his view that] the nature [of the mind] is subject to extinction. Once these views about the nature are extinguished,   [366c]   he will immediately approach the edge of reality.[14] Why is this? Originally, production is not extinguished; originally, extinction is not produced. Both are nonextinct and unproduced, unproduced and nonextinct. It is just the same with the characteristics of all dharmas."

Haet'al Bodhisattva addressed the Buddha: "Lord! What view is extinguished when a sentient being perceives that a dharma is produced? What

[13] The equation drawn here between "nonproduction" (*anutpatti*) and "void calmness" (a synonym of nirvāṇa) is standard in the earliest stratum of Tathāgatagarbha materials. See William Grosnick, "Nonorigination and *Nirvāṇa* in the Early *Tathāgatagarbha* Literature," pp. 33–43.

[14] A relatively free rendering of a problematic passage, following the emendations introduced in the Yüan and Ming editions; *VS*, p. 366 nn. 13, 14. Wŏnhyo tortuously tries to wring some sense out of this passage by interpreting each statement as meaning its exact opposite. His understanding of the passage's import, however, ends up being quite close to these later emendations. See *KSGR* 1, p. 966c18–25.

view is extinguished when a sentient being perceives that a dharma ceases?"[15]

The Buddha replied, "Bodhisattva. When a sentient being perceives that a dharma is produced, this causes the extinction of the view of nonexistence. When he sees the extinction of a dharma, this causes the extinction of the view of existence. Once these views are extinguished, the true nonexistence of dharmas is achieved and he accesses certitude, where [the attainment of the state of] nonproduction is certain."

Haet'al Bodhisattva addressed the Buddha: "Lord! If a sentient being were encouraged to linger in the state of nonproduction, would that mean [he had achieved the acceptance of] the nonproduction [of dharmas; *anutpattika-(dharmakṣānti)*]?"

The Buddha replied, "Were one to linger in nonproduction, that would actually be producing something. Why is this? Only when one does not linger in nonproduction is it really nonproduction. Bodhisattva! If one produces nonproduction, production and extinction would therewith be produced. When production and extinction are both extinguished, production inherently would not be produced and the mind would be constantly void and calm; and that which is void and calm is nonabiding. Only the mind that does not abide anywhere is really unproduced."

Haet'al Bodhisattva addressed the Buddha: "If the mind does not abide anywhere, then what need is there for religious practice? [When the mind abides nowhere, is that then a state in which] there is still training left to complete (*śaikṣa*) or where no further training is necessary (*aśaikṣa*)?"

The Buddha replied, "Bodhisattva! The mind that is unproduced—that mind has neither egress nor access. It is the original tathāgatagarbha, whose nature is calm and motionless. It is neither subject to further training nor free from further training. When there is neither training nor nontraining— that then is the state where no further training is necessary. 'Training' means to ensure that there is no need for either training or not training."

Haet'al Bodhisattva addressed the Buddha: "How is it that the nature of the tathāgatagarbha is calm and motionless?"

The Buddha replied, "The tathāgatagarbha is that characteristic of discriminative awareness, subject to production and extinction, which conceals the principle so that it is not made manifest. This [is what is meant by the statement] 'the nature of the tathāgatagarbha is calm and motionless.' "

Haet'al Bodhisattva addressed the Buddha: "What is [meant by the state-

---

[15] This line is missing in the Wŏnhyo and K'ai-pao editions. *VS*, p. 366 n. 16.

ment] 'that characteristic of discriminative awareness [which is] subject to production and extinction'?"

The Buddha replied, "Bodhisattva! The principle is free from either acceptance or rejection. If there were acceptance or rejection, then all kinds of thoughts would be produced. The thousands of conceptions and myriad of mentations are marked by production and extinction.

"Bodhisattva! Contemplate the characteristics of the original nature [viz., the tathāgatagarbha] and the principle will become perfected in and of itself. The thousands of conceptions and myriad of mentations do not augment the principles of the path; they instead agitate [the mind] in vain so that one loses the original mind-king (*cittarāja*) [the one mind]. If there are neither conceptions nor mentations, then both production and extinction will vanish and, accordingly (*yathābhūta*), will not be produced. All [eight] consciousnesses will become peaceful and calm, the currents [*ogha*; of desire, existence, and ignorance] will not be produced, and the five dharmas will be purified. This is called the Mahāyāna.[16]

"Bodhisattva! By accessing the purity of the five dharmas, the mind becomes free from deception. Once deception has vanished, one immediately accesses the stage of the tathāgatas' own enlightened, sanctified knowledge. One who accesses this stage of wisdom is well aware that all things are unproduced from the beginning; and as he is aware that they originally are unproduced, he thence is free from deceptive conceptions."

Haet'al Bodhisattva addressed the Buddha: "Lord! One who is free from deceptive conceptions should have nothing that needs to be either tranquillized or brought to an end."[17]

The Buddha responded, "Bodhisattva! Deceptions are originally unproduced; hence, there are no deceptions that need to be brought to an end. By knowing that the mind is actually no-mind, there then is no mind that needs to be tranquillized. Once [the mind] is free from both differentiation and discrimination, the consciousnesses that manifest sensory objects are not

---

[16] Following Wǒnhyo's interpretation; *KSGR* 1, pp. 969b–970b. Wǒnhyo takes the five dharmas as the pure *dharmadhātu*, which derives from the ninth amalavijñāna, and the four wisdoms into which the other eight consciousnesses transmute; see *KSGR* 1, p. 970a28–b1. A different list appears in the *Laṅkāvatāra-sūtra* (Suzuki, trans., p. 194): name, form, discrimination, right knowledge, and thusness.

[17] As Wǒnhyo notes, the issue raised in this question is that someone who has realized the state of nonconceptualization would be unable to conceive either of any mental concept that needs to be controlled or of any conception of a person who actually performs such controlling. Such a position would imply that there was no such thing as actualized enlightenment—that is, a process of spiritual development by which enlightenment is achieved. *KSGR* 1, p. 970b26–28.

produced. When there is nothing produced that needs to be tranquillized, this then would be nontranquillization—but also *not* nontranquillization. [367a] Why is this? Because [true] tranquillization actually tranquillizes nothing."[18]

Haet'al Bodhisattva addressed the Buddha: "Lord! If tranquillization is nontranquillization, then tranquillization would be produced. How can you say it is unproduced?"

The Buddha replied, "Bodhisattva! At the moment when tranquillization occurs it is produced, but after it is tranquillized there is no further tranquillization necessary. One should not linger in either nontranquillization or a nonabiding state."

Haet'al Bodhisattva addressed the Buddha: "Lord! To what does the mind that produces nothing cling? What does it reject? In what characteristic of dharma does it linger?"

The Buddha replied, "The mind that produces nothing neither clings to anything nor rejects anything. It does not linger over either mind or dharmas."

Haet'al Bodhisattva addressed the Buddha: "What do you mean by saying 'it does not linger over either mind or dharmas'?"

The Buddha replied, "Not producing thoughts is what is meant by not lingering over the mind. Not producing dharmas is what is meant by not lingering over dharmas.

"Oh son of good family! If one does not produce [a conception of] either mind or dharmas, [the mind] will then have no support (*apratiṣṭhita*). Not lingering over any compounded thing (saṃskāra), the mind will be constantly void and calm, without any extraneous characteristics. It will be just like space, which is motionless and nonabiding, ungenerated and unproduced, and free from either that or this. Once one obtains the eye of the voidness of mind and the body of the voidness of dharmas, the five skandhas [aggregates of being] and the six sense-bases will all become void and calm.

"Oh son of good family! One who cultivates the dharma of voidness does not base himself on the three realms of existence and does not linger over the specific practices of the *Vinaya* [the discipline]. Pure and free from thoughts (*munyŏm*), he neither appropriates nor releases anything. His nature is the same as adamant, which is not pulverized even by the triratna [the three gems of the Buddha, Dharma, and Saṃgha]. His mind, emptied, is motionless and endowed with all the six pāramitās [perfections]."

---

[18] Cf. the parallel statement in *Hsin-hsin ming* (*T* 2010.48.376c25): "If motion is tranquillized, that is nontranquillization."

Haet'al Bodhisattva addressed the Buddha: "Lord! All the six pāramitās have characteristics. But are dharmas that have characteristics capable of inducing transcendence?"

The Buddha replied, "Oh son of good family! The six pāramitās of which I have spoken are signless and inactive (*muwi*). Why is this? If a person accesses [the essence of the mind] and forsakes desires (*kāmavītarāgya*), his mind will become constant and pure. Through his true speech, expedient devices, and original inspiration, he will inspire others. This is *dānapāramitā* [perfection of giving]. As his earnest thoughts are tenacious and intent, his mind is constantly unabiding, pure, and untainted and does not cling to the three realms. This is *śīlapāramitā* [perfection of morality]. Cultivating voidness and extricating himself from the fetters, he does not rely on any existing thing; he calms and quietens the three types of action [via body, speech, and mind] and does not linger in either body or mind. This is *kṣāntipāramitā* [perfection of patience]. Abandoning names and classifications, he overcomes the views of both voidness and existence and delves deeply into the voidness of the skandhas. This is *vīryāpāramitā* [perfection of vigor]. Abandoning completely void calmness [nirvāṇa], he does not linger in any type of voidness. The mind that subsists nowhere resides in great voidness.[19] This is dhyānapāramitā [perfection of meditation]. While the mind is free from all mental characteristics, it does not cling to vacuous voidness. While no compounded things are produced, one does not realize calm extinction. Where the mind has neither egress nor access, the nature is constantly in equilibrium. The edge of reality of all dharmas has the nature of certitude [of enlightenment]. One does not rely on any of the *bhūmi*s [the final ten stages of practice] and does not linger in wisdom. This is prajñāpāramitā [perfection of wisdom].

"Oh son of good family! Since all these six pāramitās gain the original inspiration and access the nature of certitude, they supernally transcend the world. This is unobstructed liberation.

"Oh son of good family! Dharmas that are marked in this way by liberation are all signless. To practice them is also to be free from both liberation and bondage. This is what is meant by liberation. Why is this? The characteristic of liberation   [367b]   is to be free from both characteristics and practices; it is motionless and undisturbed. It is calm and quiet nirvāṇa, but it also does not cling to the characteristics of nirvāṇa."

---

[19] Following Wŏnhyo; *KSGR* 1, p. 971c28. The Koryŏ II/Taishō recension reads instead: "The mind that subsists nowhere does not subsist in great voidness"; *VS*, p. 367a23.

Haet'al Bodhisattva heard these words. His mind greatly pleased and elated, he gained what he never had before (*adbhūta*). Wishing to proclaim the meaning and intent [of this sermon], he recited these gāthās:

That Lord who is replete in great enlightenment,
Has expounded the dharma for this congregation.
It has all been explained from the standpoint of the one vehicle,
Drawing nothing from the paths of either of the two vehicles.
The signless inspiration that has a single taste,
Is like great space,
In that there is nothing it does not embrace.
According to the differences in each of their natures,
All things gain the original locus.
To the extent that they abandon mind and self,
The one dharma is consummated.
All practices that involve identity and difference,
Gain the original inspiration,
And extirpate dualistic views.
One also neither lingers in, nor clings to, the realization,
Of that nirvāṇa which is calm and tranquil.
Accessing that place of certitude,
There are neither characteristics nor practices.
In that stage of calm extinction where the mind is void,
The calm, extinct mind is unproduced.
It is identical to the adamantine nature,
Which is not pulverized by the triratna.
Endowed with all six pāramitās,
One ferries across all sentient beings.
The Hīnayāna is never capable,
Of supernally transcending the three realms of existence.
The dharma seal that has a single taste,
Is perfected by the one vehicle.

At that time, the great congregation heard the exposition of these ideas. Their minds greatly pleased and elated, they were able to abandon [all conceptions of] mind and self. They accessed voidness and signlessness, which are broad and expansive, vacant and vast. All gained certitude, freeing themselves from the fetters and drying up the outflows [*āsrava*; of existence, nonexistence, and speculative views].[20]

[20] Wŏnhyo glosses these experiences as implying that the congregation accessed the path of vision (*darśanamārga*), the initiation into sagehood. *KSGR* 1, p. 973b6.

Chapter Three

# The Practice of Nonproduction

[367b20]  At that time Simwang Bodhisattva heard the Buddha's explanation of the dharma, which transcended the three realms of existence and was inconceivable. Arising from his seat he joined his palms together in supplication and asked in gāthās:

> The meaning of what the Tathāgata has said,
> Transcends the world and is free from characteristics,
> It enables all sentient beings,
> To complete the annihilation of the outflows.
> Eradicating the bonds and emptying both mind and self,
> This then will be [the state of] nonproduction.
> But how will one gain the acceptance of the nonproduction [of dharmas],
> If there is nothing that is produced?

At that time, the Buddha proclaimed to Simwang Bodhisattva: "Oh son of good family! The acceptance of the nonproduction of dharmas [means to realize that] dharmas are originally unproduced and that all practices produce nothing. As there is no way to practice this nonproduction, achieving the acceptance of nonproduction is in fact a deception."

Simwang Bodhisattva asked, "Lord! You say that 'achieving the acceptance of nonproduction is in fact a deception.'  [367c]  [But is the converse then true: that] nonachievement and nonacceptance perforce are not deceptions?"

The Buddha replied, "Not so. Why is this? If nonachievement and nonacceptance exist, then so would achievement. If achievement and acceptance[21] exist, then so would production. If achievement is produced,

---

[21] Following the Koryŏ II/Taishō edition. Both the Wŏnhyo and K'ai-pao recensions read *chu* ("abiding") for *in* ("acceptance") here; *VS*, p. 367 n. 8.

there then would exist dharmas that are the objects of that achievement. So both [achievement and acceptance] are deceptions."

Simwang Bodhisattva asked, "Lord! How is it that the mind may be free from either acceptance or production and yet not be deceived?"

The Buddha replied, "The mind that is free from both acceptance and production—that mind has neither form nor shape.[22] It is like heat [lit. the nature of fire], which, though latent in wood, cannot be found there. This is because the nature [of the mind] is fixed.[23] [Mind] is nothing more than a name and a word; its nature is unascertainable. Wishing to allude to this principle, [the buddhas] have provisionally named it [mind], but this name is unascertainable. This is also the case for the characteristics of the mind: their location cannot be found. If one knows that the mind is like this, the mind will then not produce anything.

"Oh son of good family! The nature and characteristics of the mind are like the *āmalaka* (myrobalan) fruit: they are not self-generated; they are not generated by some external agent; they are not produced in conjunction with something else; they are not produced in the absence of a cause for that production.[24] Why is this? Because these conditions [of production and extinction] alternate successively. These conditions are generated, but there is no production; these conditions decay, but there is no extinction. Whether hidden or made manifest, [nature and characteristics] are signless. Their fun-

---

[22] See Pao-chih's *Shih-ssu-k'o sung*, in *Ching-teh ch'uan-teng lu* 29, *T* 2076.51.451b5: "The mind-essence has neither form nor shape."

[23] For this simile, see *Kuang Po-lun pen*, *T* 1570.31.185b21–26, and chapter 8 *infra*. Wŏnhyo explains this simile as follows. Heat may be latent in wood, but that "heat" can never be isolated from "wood." In the same way innumerable dharmas may be latent inside the principle, but they cannot be isolated from that principle. While heat therefore may ultimately be unascertainable, we know that heat nevertheless exists; in the same way, while the vast numbers of wholesome qualities inherent in the principle may ultimately be unascertainable, the adept can draw upon them in his spiritual practice. *KSGR* 2, p. 974a18–23.

[24] The rendering of the last alternative follows Wŏnhyo's interpretation; *KSGR* 2, p. 974b9–11. Wŏnhyo interprets these four negations as follows: "As far as these four negations are concerned, because they [the fruits of the seeds] are dependent upon conditions [such as soil, water, and sunlight], 'they are not self-generated.' Because [the fruits grow from] their own seeds, 'they are not generated by some external agent.' Because they are inactive (*akarmaka*) [from an absolute standpoint], 'they do not arise in conjunction with something else.' And yet, because they do function, 'they are not produced in the absence of a cause for that production [lit., are not unproduced].' " *KSGR* 2, p. 974b4–6.

The myrobalan is used in *Mahāparinirvāṇa-sūtra* as a metaphor for the perfect clarity of insight that comes through accessing the vajrasamādhi. "If there is a bodhisattva who abides in this vajrasamādhi, he will see that all dharmas have no obstructions, just as if they were myrobalans in one's palm (*kāratalāmalakavat*)." *Ta-pan-nieh-p'an ching* 24, *T* 374.12.509c5–8, noted in Liebenthal, p. 371. For other references to the myrobalan in Buddhist literature, see Alex Wayman, "Notes on the Three Myrobalans," pp. 63–77.

damental principle is calm and extinct. There is no place where they abide, nor is there seen anything that abides, because their natures are fixed.

"This fixed nature is neither unitary nor different; neither evanescent nor permanent; it has neither access nor egress and is neither produced nor extinguished. It abandons all four of these alternatives (*catuṣkoṭi*), for the pathways of words and speech are eradicated (*ŏnŏdodan*).[25] This is the case as well for the unproduced nature of the mind: how can it be said that it is either produced or unproduced, either accepted or not accepted?

"If a person claims that the mind may either achieve [something] or abide [somewhere] and takes this as his [wrong] view, then he will not attain *anuttarasamyaksaṃbodhi* [complete, perfect enlightenment] and prajñā. This is the 'long night' [of saṃsāra]. One who has comprehended the mind-nature knows that the mind-nature is thus and that the nature is also thus. This is the practice of nonproduction."

Simwang Bodhisattva commented, "Lord! As the mind is originally thus, it will not produce such practices. As all practices are unproduced, there will be no practice that produces anything and this nonproduction will then not need to be practiced. This in fact is the practice of nonproduction."

The Buddha asked, "Oh son of good family! Can you realize the practice of nonproduction by not producing anything?"

Simwang Bodhisattva replied, "No. And why is this? In the actual practice of nonproduction, both nature and characteristics are void and calm. There is neither vision nor hearing; neither gain nor loss; neither words nor speech; neither cognition nor characteristics; neither clinging nor rejection. So how could one cling to this realization? If one clings to this realization, this would in fact serve [as the cause of] disputation and contention. Only when there is neither disputation nor contention is it the practice of nonproduction."

The Buddha said, "Have you attained *anuttarasamyaksaṃbodhi*?"[26]

Simwang Bodhisattva responded, "Lord! I am free from any attainment of *anuttarasamyaksaṃbodhi*. And why is this? The bodhi-nature has neither

[25] The locus classicus for this phrase is *Sutta-nipāta*, v.1076, describing the state of nirvāṇa: "There is no means of knowing him who has gone to rest,/ He has nothing that could be named./ When all dharmas are eradicated,/ All paths of speech are also eradicated" (*attan-gatassa na pamāṇam atthi; yena nam vajju, tam tassa n'atthi; sabbesu dhammesu samuhatesu; samuhata vādapathā pi sabbe ti*). For discussion of the significance of this verse, see Luis Gómez, "Proto-Mādhyamika in the Pāli Canon," p. 146, and for further references to the phrase in Sanskrit literature, p. 158 n. 5.

[26] For a similar exchange, cf. *Chin-kang po-jo po-lo-mi ching* [*Vajracchedikāprajñāpāramitā-sūtra*], T 235.8.749b11–15, and 751c20–27.

gain nor loss, neither attention nor cognition, for it is free from all differentiated characteristics. The pure nature actually exists in such nondiscrimination. This nature is free from any extraneous admixture [such as the dichotomies of production and extinction or subject and object]: it is free from words and speech; it neither exists nor does not exist; it is neither aware nor nescient.

"So too is this case for all the dharmas [training methods] that can be cultivated. Why is this? All dharmas and practices have no loci that can be found, because their natures are fixed.    [368a]    Originally, they are free from any semblance of attainment or nonattainment. So how can one attain *anuttarasamyaksaṃbodhi?*"

The Buddha replied, "So it is, so it is. As you have said, all of the activities of mind are nothing but signlessness; their essences are calm and unproduced. It is the same as well with each and every consciousness. Why is this? The eye and visual contact are both void and calm. [Visual] consciousness is also void and calm: it is free from any characteristic of agitation or motionlessness. Since it is free internally of the three feelings [*vedanā*; pain, pleasure, and neutral feeling], the three feelings are calm and extinct. So too is this the case for auditory, olfactory, gustatory, tactile, and mental [consciousnesses], as well as mind-consciousness, *mano[vijñāna]*,[27] and *ālaya* consciousness: as all of them are also unproduced, they are the mind that is calm and extinct and the mind that produces nothing.[28] But if one gives rise to the mind that is calm and extinct and the mind that produces nothing, this then would be practice that produces something, not the practice of nonproduction.

"Bodhisattva! Thus internally are generated three feelings, three karmic actions, and three moral restraints [of physical, verbal, and mental actions]. If these are already calm and extinct, the producing mind will not be pro-

---

[27] "Mental [consciousness]" (*ŭi*), "mind-consciousness" (*ŭisik*), and *manovijñāna* (*malna [sik]*) are actually the translations and transliteration of the same sixth consciousness (the *manovijñāna*), obvious indications that the author was not working from Sanskrit materials. Wŏnhyo tries to resolve the reiteration by specifying that both "mental" and "mind-consciousness" refer to the sixth consciousness—that consciousness being called *ŭi* (= memory) when it is past, *ŭisik* (mental consciousness) when it is present, and *sim* (mind) when it is future. *Manovijñāna* then refers instead to the seventh consciousness, the governing consciousness (*kliṣṭamanovijñāna*). See *KSGR* 2, p. 976a17–20.

[28] This passage, especially as it has been brought out in Wŏnhyo's interpretation, closely parallels statements concerning the meaning of nonproduction made by Ching-chüeh (683–750?), the Northern school adept who compiled *Leng-ch'ieh shih-tzu chi*, in his *Po-jo-hsin ching chu-chieh* (Annotation and explication of the *Heart Sūtra*): "Thus we know that all dharmas are tranquil and calm, unproduced and unextinguished." The text is reproduced in Yanagida, *Shoki Zenshū shisho*, p. 602.

duced and the mind will be constantly calm and extinct, without efficacy or function. He does not evince any characteristic of calm extinction; but he also does not insist on not corroborating [such a characteristic]. What is worth lingering in is the state of nonabiding, wherein is encoded (*ch'ongji*; *dhārayati*) signlessness. Then, there will be none of these three, such as the three feelings, and so forth, for all will be calm and extinct, pure and nonabiding. He need not access samādhi; he need not persist in sitting in dhyāna. This is nonproduction and freedom from practice."

Simwang Bodhisattva asked, "Dhyāna can suppress all agitation and allay all illusory distractions. Why this negation of dhyāna?"

The Buddha replied, "Bodhisattva! Dhyāna in fact is agitation. Being neither agitated nor concentrated is the dhyāna that produces nothing. The nature of dhyāna is to produce nothing; it has no characteristics of the dhyāna that does produce something. The nature of dhyāna is to linger nowhere; it leaves far behind the agitation caused by trying to linger in dhyāna. Know that the nature of dhyāna is free from both agitation and calmness and you will immediately attain the [acceptance of the] nonproduction [of dharmas] and the prajñā that produces nothing. But also do not rely on, or linger over, these. Because of this knowledge, the mind also will not be agitated. For this reason, you will attain the prajñāpāramitā that produces nothing."

Simwang Bodhisattva said, "Lord! The prajñā that produces nothing does not abide anywhere, and yet there is no place where it is not. The mind has no abiding place and there is no place where the mind can abide. When there is no abiding and no mind (*musim*), the mind will then abide in nonproduction. The mind that so abides is in fact abiding in nonproduction.

"Lord! The mind's practice of nonproduction is inconceivable. As it is inconceivable, it is both effable and ineffable."

The Buddha said, "So it is, so it is."

Simwang Bodhisattva heard these words and, praising its miraculousness, recited these gāthās:

That Lord who is replete in great knowledge,
Has explained extensively the dharma of nonproduction.
I have heard what has never been heard before,
Now has been explained what had yet to be explained.
Like the pure sweet dew,
That appears but once in a long while,
[So too is this dharma] difficult to encounter and difficult to imagine.
Difficult too is it to hear it,

It is the unsurpassed, excellent field of merit (*puṇyakṣetra*),
The supremely efficacious, sublime medicine.
It is in order to ferry across sentient beings,
That it has now been proclaimed.

At that time, all those in the congregation heard these words and attained the [acceptance of] the nonproduction [of dharmas] as well as the prajñā that produces nothing.

Chapter Four

# The Inspiration of Original Enlightenment[29]

[368b2]   At that time Muju Bodhisattva heard what the Buddha said about the single taste being true and inconceivable. From the distant past up to the present, [Muju] had drawn near to the tathāgatas' seats and listened to [the tathāgatas] carefully and with full attention. Accessing that pure, transparent place, his body and mind were motionless.[30]

At that time, the Buddha addressed Muju Bodhisattva: "Whence have you come? Where now have you arrived?"

Muju Bodhisattva replied, "Lord! I come from where there is no origin, and have now arrived where there is no origin."[31]

The Buddha said, "You originally came from nowhere and now you have also arrived nowhere. As you have gained the original inspiration (porri), which is inconceivable, you are a bodhisattva-mahāsattva."

---

[29] According to Wŏnhyo's exegesis, chapter 4 is concerned with the phenomenal, production-and-extinction aspect of the one mind's two aspects. The absolute, true-thusness aspect will be treated in the following chapter. See KSGR 2, p. 982b17–18.

[30] "Motionless" (acala) is not only the attribute of samādhi, as seen before in the sūtra with reference to the vajrasamādhi, but also a samādhi in its own right; see sources listed in Franklin Edgerton, Buddhist Hybrid Sanskrit Dictionary, p. 6 s.v. "acala."

[31] Wŏnhyo explains: "This explains [the process of practice] from the stage of an ordinary person (pṛthagjana) to the arrival at the stage of sanctity. When a person arrives at the stage of sanctity, he looks back on [his progress through] past and present. In the past, when he was at the stage of the ordinary person and first aroused his will [to practice and set out on the path], he himself believed that his own mind was originally free from production and motion, because the origin of production and motion can, ultimately, never be found. Now, once he has arrived at the stage of sanctity and has attained [the acceptance of] the nonproduction [of dharmas], he knows through realization that his own mind is originally unproduced, because an origin for such production cannot be found. Hence, he knows that he has first 'come from where there is no origin'; and the place where he has now arrived is also 'where there is no origin.' " KSGR 2, pp. 977b29–977c5.

Then, while emitting a great ray of light that pervaded the many thousands of world-systems, he recited gāthās:

How great you are, oh bodhisattva,
You who are replete in knowledge and wisdom.
Constantly by means of the original inspiration,
You inspire sentient beings.
In all the four postures [walking, standing, sitting, lying],
You constantly abide in the original inspiration,
Guiding all the classes of beings,
Without either coming or going.

At that time, Muju Bodhisattva addressed the Buddha: "Lord! Through what inspiring transmutation may one transmute all the affective consciousnesses of sentient beings so that they will access the *amala*[-*vijñāna*; immaculate consciousness]?"[32]

The Buddha replied, "All the buddhas, the tathāgatas, constantly transmute all the consciousnesses by means of the one enlightenment so that they will access the *amala*. Why is this? The original enlightenment[33] of each and every sentient being is constantly enlightening all sentient beings by means of that one enlightenment, prompting them all to regain their original enlightenment. They become enlightened to the fact that all the affective consciousnesses are void, calm, and unproduced. Why is this? It is a given that the original natures [of the eight consciousnesses] are originally motionless."

Muju Bodhisattva asked, "Each and every one[34] of the eight conscious-

[32] The affective consciousnesses refer to the eight consciousnesses, all of which are subject to the interplay of the defilements. Only the ninth consciousness, the amalavijñāna, is unaffected thereby, thus earning its designation as the "immaculate consciousness." Wŏnhyo presumes that this passage was the source for Paramārtha's theory of a ninth consciousness; *KSGR* 2, p. 978a7–8, and see discussion in part 1, chapter 3. The transcription *ammara* (Ch. *an-mo-lo*) for the Sanskrit word *amala* as used here, is generally described as being peculiar to the T'ien-t'ai tradition, and especially to Chih-i's (539–597) writings (see Mizuno, pp. 45–46; Liebenthal, p. 371 n. 1). It is not, however, exclusive to that tradition. The same transcription is found, for example, in Chinese Pure Land works (Ch'uan-teng's *Ching-t'u sheng wu-sheng lun*, *T* 1975.47.381c17), Ch'an materials (Yen-shou's *Tsung-ching lu* 90, *T* 2016.48.907b16), Korean Yogācāra commentaries (Tullyun's *Yugaron-ki* 13A, *T* 1828.42.605b22), and Japanese exegeses (Jōnen's *Gyōrinshō* 50, *T* 2409.76.352c7). The transcription is also used frequently in East Asian apocryphal compositions, such as at *Shou-leng-yen ching* 4, *T* 745.19.123c15. This rendering antedates Paramārtha's own works, which adopt the alternate *a-mo-lo*.

[33] Wŏnhyo glosses original enlightenment as the amalavijñāna; *KSGR* 2, p. 978a20.

[34] Wŏnhyo glosses *kail* as *ilch'e* ("each and every"). *KSGR* 2, p. 978b7. The Yüan and Ming editions have simply changed the following "eight" to *ch'e* to bring out the same sense; *VS*, p. 368b18, n. 13.

nesses is produced, conditioned by the sense realms. So how is it that they are motionless?"

The Buddha answered, "All the sense realms are originally void. All consciousnesses are originally void. Being void, their natures are not subject to conditions. So how are they produced by conditions?"

Muju Bodhisattva retorted, "If all the sense realms are void, then how can there be vision?

The Buddha replied, "Vision is in fact deceptive. Why so? All the myriad of existing things are unproduced and signless. Originally they have no names for themselves and are all void and calm. So too is this the case for all characteristics of dharmas. The bodies of all sentient beings are also just the same. And if even those bodies do not exist, then how much less so could vision!"

Muju Bodhisattva said, "If all sense realms are void, all bodies are void, and all consciousnesses are void, then enlightenment too must be void."

The Buddha replied, "Each and every enlightenment has a given nature that is neither destroyed nor annihilated. They are neither void nor nonvoid, for they are free from voidness or nonvoidness."

Muju Bodhisattva remarked, "It is the same too for all the sense realms. They are not marked by voidness and yet they must be so marked."

The Buddha assented, "So it is. The natures of all the sense realms are originally fixed. The bases of those fixed natures are not located anywhere."

Muju Bodhisattva said, "Enlightenment is also the same: it is not located anywhere."   [368c]

The Buddha assented, "So it is. Because enlightenment has no locus, it is pure. As it is pure, it is free from [any semblance of such a limiting concept as] enlightenment. As material things have no locus, they are pure. As they are pure, they are free from [any such limiting concept] as materiality."

Muju Bodhisattva remarked, "The mind and the visual consciousness as well are similarly inconceivable."

The Buddha said, "Yes, the mind and the visual consciousness as well are similarly inconceivable. Why is this? Materiality has no location; it is pure and nameless. It does not intrude into the internal [sense-bases]. The visual [base] has no location; it is pure and sightless. It does not go out into the external [sense objects]. The mind has no location; it is pure and unsurpassed, and has no place where it is produced. Consciousness has no location; it is pure and motionless, not distinguished by conditions. Its nature is entirely void and calm. That nature is free from any semblance of enlightenment, but if one becomes enlightened [that nature too] will then be enlightened [completing the process of actualizing enlightenment].

"Oh son of good family! Once one awakens to the knowledge that there is no enlightenment,[35] all the consciousnesses then access [enlightenment]. Why is this? At the stage of adamantine knowledge, the path leading to liberation (*vimuktimārga*) is eradicated. Once it is eradicated, you access the nonabiding stage [of sublime enlightenment] where there is neither egress nor access, that stage of certitude where the mind has no locus. That stage is pure, like transparent beryl[36] [representing the great, perfect mirror wisdom (*ādarśanajñāna*)]. That nature is constantly in equilibrium, like the great earth [representing the impartial wisdom (*samatājñāna*)]. Enlightened, sublime, contemplative examination [representing the subsequently obtained wisdom (*pratyavekṣaṇājñāna*)] is like the effulgence of the sun of wisdom.[37] [One's ability to] inspire [others] is perfected and one gains original [enlightenment]; this is like the great rain of dharma [representing the wisdom that has accomplished what was to be done (*kṛtyānuṣṭhānajñāna*)]. Accessing this knowledge is accessing the buddhas' stage of knowledge [the sublime enlightenment where these four types of wisdom are perfected]. For one who has accessed this stage of knowledge, none of the consciousnesses is produced."[38]

Muju Bodhisattva said, "The Tathāgata has explained that the sanctified dynamism of the one enlightenment and the stage of [sublime enlightenment where] the four vast wisdoms [are perfected] are in fact the enlightened

---

[35] Following Rhi Ki-yong's interpretation in *Kŭmgang sammaegyŏng-ron*, p. 143. Wŏnhyo clarifies that this realization refers to the wisdom produced by the actualized enlightenment. *KSGR* 2, p. 979a27–28.

[36] In Buddhist texts, the nominal binom *yuri* (Ch. *liu-li*) should be translated as "beryl," from Pali *veluriyam*, not the more common rendering of "glass." See Edward Schafer, "Combined Supplements to *Mathews*," s.v. "liu-li."

[37] Cf. the description of *pratyavekṣaṇājñāna* in *Ch'eng wei-shih lun* 10, *T* 1585.31.56a21–25.

[38] Wŏnhyo interprets this paragraph in terms of the actualized enlightenment.

This section elucidates the fact that all consciousnesses are unproduced. It seeks to explain that, originally, all the consciousnesses are produced in accordance with ignorance. Now, via the actualized enlightenment, [these consciousnesses] return to the fountainhead of the mind, and once they return to the fountainhead of the mind none of the consciousnesses is then produced. Because the consciousnesses are not produced, the actualized enlightenment is perfectly complete. . . . When the actualized enlightenment is complete, the eight consciousnesses are not produced. This is because, to the extent that enlightenment is devoid of enlightenment, all the consciousnesses will not exist, and because, to the extent that that enlightenment is ultimate, one returns to the fountainhead of the mind. Hence the statement was made that "all the consciousnesses then access [enlightenment]." *KSGR* 2, p. 979a25–b6.

inspiration that is innate in all sentient beings. And why is this? Because these are present originally in the bodies of all sentient beings."[39]

The Buddha replied, "So it is. And why is this so? Although all sentient beings are originally free from outflows and all wholesome benefits are originally innate in them, they are being pricked by the thorn of desire, which they have yet to overcome [and thus do not realize that they are originally enlightened]."[40]

Muju Bodhisattva asked, "If there is a sentient being who has yet to draw on the original inspiration and who [continues to have the desire to] gather and accumulate [mundane experiences], then how will he overcome that which is difficult to overcome?"

The Buddha replied, "Whether discrimination and, therewith, the taints occur en masse or solitarily, if his spirit reverts (*hoesin*) to abide in the cave of voidness, he will overcome that which is difficult to overcome.[41] Liberated from the bonds of Māra [demonic forces personified], he will sit supernally on the open ground where the consciousnesses and the skandhas [will be in a state of] *parinirvāṇa*."[42]

---

[39] Wǒnhyo explains that the one enlightenment is actually both the actualized and original enlightenments, which are nondual since "the perfection of the actualized enlightenment is in fact identical to the original enlightenment." Wǒnhyo then goes ahead to draw a tautology between the one enlightenment, the dharmakāya of the buddhas, and the original enlightenment that is inherent in all sentient beings. That immanent original enlightenment is the "enlightened inspiration that is innate in all sentient beings . . . , which influences the minds of sentient beings to perform the two kinds of action [benefitting oneself and others]." *KSGR* 2, p. 979c17–25.

[40] "In original enlightenment, the immeasurable meritorious qualities inherent in the [enlightened] nature are not tainted or affected by the three outflows; hence, the statement was made that [sentient beings] 'are originally free from outflows.' With these [qualities] as the basis, one produces all wholesome actions and benefits; hence, the statement 'all wholesome benefits are originally innate.' However, while one may be endowed with the original enlightenment, one is [still] overwhelmed by adventitious defilements and 'the thorn of desire.' Therefore, one has not yet gained one's own original enlightenment." *KSGR* 2, pp. 979c28–980a2.

[41] This sentence is adapted from a citation to *Udānavarga* (*Fa-chi yao-sung ching* 4, *T* 213.4.799a26–27) appearing in *Mahāyānasaṃgraha*; see *She ta-sheng lun* 2, *T* 1593.31.119a18–19. Noted by Liebenthal, p. 364, though his citation to *T* 212 is wrong.

[42] The phrase "sit supernally on the open ground" is cited also in *Li-tai fa-pao chi* (*T* 2075.51.193a8), the Pao-t'ang doxography compiled in the late eighth century, and appears to derive from a passage in the *Lotus Sūtra* (*Miao-fa lien-hua ching*, *T* 262.9.12c14–15). The entire sentence appears also in the biography of the Korean Sǒn monk, Sunji (fl. 858); see *Chodang chip* 20, p. 356c24–25. This exchange explains, according to Wǒnhyo, the practices by which the hindrances are overcome (in technical terms, the "counteracting path," or *pratipakṣamārga*) and realization catalyzed. There are two benefits accruing from eradicating the hindrances. First is the fruition of bodhi, which transcends the five skandhas; in such an achievement, "one sits at the *bodhimaṇḍa* and gains supreme enlightenment; hence the statement 'one will sit supernally on the open ground.' Second, one realizes nirvāṇa via this supreme enlightenment. One's en-

Muju Bodhisattva remarked, "The mind that gains nirvāṇa is isolated and autonomous. Lingering perpetually in nirvāṇa, [the mind] perforce is liberated."

The Buddha responded, "Lingering perpetually in nirvāṇa is the bondage of nirvāṇa. Why is this? Nirvāṇa is the inspiration of original enlightenment, and that inspiration is originally nirvāṇa. The enlightened aspects (bodhyaṅga) of nirvāṇa are in fact the aspects of original enlightenment. As the enlightened nature is undifferentiated, nirvāṇa is undifferentiated. As enlightenment is originally unproduced, nirvāṇa is unproduced. As enlightenment is originally free from extinction, nirvāṇa is free from extinction. Because nirvāṇa is innate, there is no attainment of nirvāṇa. And if nirvāṇa cannot be attained, then how can one linger therein?

"Oh son of good family! One who is enlightened need not linger in nirvāṇa. Why is this? Enlightenment originally is unproduced; it is far removed from the maculations (mala) of sentient beings. Enlightenment is originally free of calmness; it is far removed from the agitation of nirvāṇa [i.e., the presumption that there is a process by which nirvāṇa is achieved]. The mind of one who lingers at such a stage lingers nowhere. Free from both egress and access, it accesses the amala-consciousness."

Muju Bodhisattva asked, "If the amala-consciousness has some place where it can be accessed,   [369a]   [does this mean it is] something that is attained—that is, an attained dharma?"

The Buddha replied, "No, it does not. Why is this? It is like a deluded son who carries gold coins in his hands, but does not know that he has them. Roaming throughout all the ten directions, he passes fifty years in poverty and destitution, hardship and suffering. Though he devotes all his efforts to eeking out a living, he is unable to support himself. Seeing his son in such dire straits, his father tells him, 'You're carrying around gold coins! Why don't you use them? Then you'll be free to satisfy your needs in every possible way.' His son awakens and discovers the gold coins. His mind greatly joyous, he shouts, 'I found the gold coins!' His father replies, 'My deluded son! You should not be elated [at your good fortune]. The gold coins you've found have always been in your possession; they are not something you've "found." So how can you be happy?'[43]

---

lightened understanding will then be free from [any semblance of] enlightenment and all the consciousnesses will access [nirvāṇa]; hence the statement 'the consciousnesses and skandhas [will be in a state of] parinirvāṇa.' " KSGR 2, p. 980a7–25.

[43] As Liebenthal (p. 363 n. 3) notes, attempts to trace this simile to the allegory of the compassionate father and his ignorant sons in the Lotus Sūtra are dubious. Liebenthal instead proposes to trace it to a simile in the Nirvāṇa Sūtra (Ta-pan-nieh-p'an ching 24, T 374.12.510b1)

"Oh son of good family! It is just the same with the *amala*-consciousness. It originally is not something from which you have departed. It is not something that has now been accessed. Even though in the past you were unaware of it, it was not nonexistent. Even though now you have awakened to it, it is not accessed."

Muju Bodhisattva asked, "If that father knew his son was deluded, why did he wait until [his son] had spent fifty years roaming throughout the ten directions in poverty and destitution, hardship and suffering, before he told him [about the gold coins he was carrying]?"

The Buddha replied, "The passage of fifty years is but the agitation of a single moment of thought. Roaming throughout the ten directions is but the fantasy of distant travel."[44]

Muju Bodhisattva asked, "What is 'the agitation of a single moment of thought'?"

The Buddha replied, "The five skandhas all arise in the action of a single moment of thought.[45] In the arising of the five skandhas all fifty evils are contained."[46]

---

about a destitute person who finds a diamond (= adamant), though I am not entirely convinced by this suggestion. Wŏnhyo treats this passage as a simile for the delusion of any sentient being ("a deluded son"), whose grasping at defilements obscures the original purity of his mind ("carries gold coins in his hands, but does not know that he has them"). The buddhas are able to arose resolute faith (*adhimukti*) in such a being through the Mahāyāna teachings ("You're carrying around gold coins!"), and finally that being is able to access the first *bhūmi* ("[he] discovers the gold coins"). But he then grasps at the achievement of that state ("I found the gold coins!"), which the buddhas must counter by admonishing him, "The gold coins you've found have always been in your possession; they are not something you've 'found.' So how can you be happy?" *KSGR* 2, pp. 980c23–981a23. See also Chu-chen's explanation in *T'ung-tsung chi* 6, p. 260a.

[44] The translation is tentative. Rhi's rendering (*Kŭmgang sammaegyŏng-ron*, p. 153), "One imagines this while assuming that there is nothing that is far off," seems hardly plausible. Neither Wŏnhyo, Yüan-ch'eng, nor Chu-chen provides any gloss on the phrase that might guide the translation. Might this phrase have something to do with the (mistaken) belief that practice has to continue through a complex series of steps? Or perhaps it is intended simply to imply a spatial interpenetration to complement the temporal interpenetration expressed in the preceding line.

[45] "The purpose here is to explain that the four marks [*saṃskṛtalakṣaṇa*; of production, subsistence, decay, and extinction] that are contained in a single moment of thought include all of birth and death." *KSGR* 2, p. 981b24–25.

[46] These fifty evils comprise a rather complex list, based on different dharmas associated with the five skandhas. Wŏnhyo explains that the consciousness skandha has eight evils: the eight consciousnesses. Both feeling and perception skandhas have eight apiece: the mental states (*caitta*) associated with mind (*cittasaṃprayukta*). The formations skandha has nine: eight that are *cittasaṃprayukta* and one that is dissociated from mind (*cittaviprayukta*). The form skandha has seventeen: four great elements, thirteen derivative elements (five sense-bases, five sense-objects,

Muju Bodhisattva asked, "The fantasy of distant travel and roaming throughout the ten directions—both these arise in a single moment of thought and include all the fifty evils. How can one prompt those sentient beings not to give rise to a single thought [so that the fifty evils will not arise]?"

The Buddha replied, "One should prompt those sentient beings to sit with their minds and spirits calm, abiding in the adamantine stage. Once thoughts are tranquillized so that nothing is produced, the mind will be constantly calm and serene. This is what is meant by the absence of even a single thought."[47]

Muju Bodhisattva said, "This is inconceivable. When one is enlightened to the fact that thoughts are unproduced, one's mind becomes calm and serene. That is the inspiration of original enlightenment. That inspiration is motionless; it exists in perpetuity and is not nonexistent. But this does not mean that it is not nonexistent, or that there is nothing to which it is not enlightened. Awakening to the knowledge that there is no enlightenment is the original inspiration and original enlightenment. Enlightenment is pure and immaculate, perdurable and unchanging, because its nature is fixed. It is inconceivable!"

The Buddha replied, "So it is."

After Muju Bodhisattva heard these words, he gained what he had never had before and recited gāthās:

The Lord is the Lord of Great Enlightenment,
He explains the dharma that produces no-thought,

---

and three kinds of *rūpa* included in the *dharmadhātu*). These make a total of fifty, which are called evil "because they all flow counter to nirvāṇa, and because they are in opposition to the genuine goodness of nirvāṇa." *KSGR* 2, pp. 981b25–981c4.

   [47] Chu-chen (*T'ung-tsung chi* 6, p. 260c) construes this paragraph as presenting the major meditation technique of *VS*. He also relates it to various passages in Ch'an writings attributed to Bodhidharma, Seng-ts'an, and Hui-neng to illustrate its affinities with Ch'an praxis.

Wŏnhyo here finishes his outline of the process of actualized enlightenment with a treatment of the experiences forthcoming through consummating one's practice. "Those sentient beings" are those ordinary persons who have not yet attained the ten faiths, the preliminary stage of the path. "Sit with their minds and spirits calm" refers to the completion of the ten abidings, the actual inception of the mārga. "Abiding in the adamantine stage" is the first *bhūmi* on up, where one realizes the dharmakāya. "Once thoughts are tranquillized so that nothing is produced" is the inception of the stage of sublime enlightenment. "The mind will be constantly calm and serene" is the access to the sublime-enlightenment stage, where one gains a vision of the fountainhead of the mind, which is free from production and extinction. *KSGR* 2, p. 981c7–16.

The mind that is free of thoughts and is unproduced,
That mind endures in perpetuity and is never extinguished.
The inspirations of one enlightenment and original enlightenment,
Inspire all those who are endowed with original enlightenment.
It is like he who [recovered] gold coins,
But what he recovered was in fact not recovered at all.

At that time, the congregation heard these words and all gained prajñā-pāramitā, which is the inspiration of original enlightenment.

# Chapter Five

# Approaching the Edge of Reality

[369b1]  At that point, the Tathāgata made this statement:[48] "All bodhisatt-vas, and the rest [of the congregation], who have been deeply affected by the original inspiration, are sentient beings who are worthy of salvation. If later,[49] during an inappropriate time,[50] one were to preach the dharma ac-cordingly, it would be neither timely nor beneficial. Speech that is neither accordant nor discordant,[51] neither identical nor different,[52] would be speech that accords with thusness. [Such speech] guides all affective knowledge so that it flows into the sea of *sarvajña* [all-knowledge]. It prevents the assembly that is capable [of salvation] from being swept away[53] by the empty breeze

---

[48] According to Wŏnhyo, this chapter explains the absolute, true-thusness aspect of the one mind, complementing the phenomenal aspect, which was covered in the preceding chapter. I ask the reader's patience during the portions of this chapter that bracket the discussion of the two accesses and guarding the one. The extant recensions seem corrupt here and their readings are often difficult to render intelligibly. I have relied heavily on Wŏnhyo's exegesis in attempt-ing to bring some sense to these sections, but not always with the greatest success. It appears to me that much of this chapter is intended to provide a medium in which to embed these two Ch'an teachings, and little more.

[49] That is, after the Buddha's *parinirvāṇa*; after the end of the orthodox-dharma age; or during the last, and most degenerate, of the five five-hundred-year periods leading up to the demise of Buddhism. *KSGR* 2, p. 982b29–c1.

[50] When beings are neither innocent nor mature; when enlightenment does not come easily; and when heterodox views are rampant. *KSGR* 2, p. 982c2–3.

[51] "Accordant" means speech that accords with the principle. "Discordant" means speech that obstructs the production of faith. To avoid any potential clinging to the principle or any obstruction of right faith, one should use "speech that is neither accordant nor discordant." *KSGR* 2, p. 982c6–11.

[52] "Identical" means to speak in accordance with the view that existence is real, creating a "difference" with the view that voidness is real. Since such identities and differences only ex-acerbate doctrinal controversies, one should speak in a way that is "neither identical nor differ-ent." *KSGR* 2, p. 982c11–15.

[53] A free rendering for the logograph *ŭp* ("to pour", "to extract"). Wŏnhyo glosses it by

[of the sense realms] and prompts them to aspire for[54] the spiritual cavern,[55] which has but a single taste [because it is calm and equanimous].

"The world is not the world; an abiding place [nirvāṇa] is not a refuge. In withdrawing from or accessing the five voidnesses [*infra*], [one who has realized voidness] neither clings to nor rejects anything. Why is this? All dharmas are marked by voidness. The dharma nature is not nonexistent, but that which lacks nonexistence [i.e., the principle of the dharma nature] is not nonexistent [in that it is not rejected by the practitioner] and that which is not nonexistent is not existent [for it is not clung to by the practitioner]. As it has no fixed nature, it does not linger in either existence or nonexistence. Neither ordinary nor sanctified knowledge is distressed by existence or nonexistence.[56]

"Once all you bodhisattvas, and everyone else, are aware of this inspiration, you will attain bodhi."[57]

At that time there was a bodhisattva in the assembly named Taeryŏk [Great Power; Mahābala]. Arising from his seat, he came before the Buddha and addressed him, saying: "Lord! As you have said, 'In withdrawing from or accessing the five voidnesses, one neither clings to nor rejects anything.' How is it that there is no clinging or rejection with regard to these five voidnesses?"

The Buddha replied, "Bodhisattva! The five voidnesses are: [1] the three realms of existence are void; [2] the shadows [i.e., the karmic effects] of the six destinies [hell-denizens, animals, hungry ghosts, humans, aśuras, and gods] are void; [3] the characteristics of dharmas [the four *saṃskṛtalakṣaṇas* of production, subsistence, decay, and extinction] are void; [4] names and characteristics are void; [5] the objects of the mind and consciousnesses are

---

*ch'im* ("measuring", "conjecture"), and says that it has the meaning of grasping. *KSGR* 2, p. 982c24–25.

[54] Following Wŏnhyo's interpretation of the logograph *sŏ* ("multitude," "nearly"), which he glosses as *hŭimang* ("hope," "aspiration"). *KSGR* 2, p. 982c28.

[55] Following the Wŏnhyo and K'ai-pao recensions, Koryŏ II/Taishō replaces *kong* ("cavern") with the near-homographic *yu* ("milk"), which might be better considering its characterization as having a single taste. See *VS*, p. 369b5 n. 5. Wŏnhyo explains: " 'Spiritual cavern' refers to the cave of spiritually perfected beings, which is far away from the cities, an uneventful place of tranquillity and longevity. It is a simile for great nirvāṇa, the immortal refuge." *KSGR* 2, pp. 982c28–983a1.

[56] Following the K'ai-pao and Three Editions reading. *VS*, p. 369 n. 7.

[57] "If a bodhisattva who has yet to achieve the *bhūmis* knows that the dharma nature is neither existent nor nonexistent, he will then attain full enlightenment at the moment of the generation of the thought [of enlightenment; *bodhicittotpāda*]." *KSGR* 2, p. 983a25–26.

void.[58] Bodhisattva! These kinds of voidness may be void but they do not linger in voidness, for voidness is not marked by voidness. And how can dharmas that are signless involve either clinging or rejection? Accessing that place which is free from clinging is identical to accessing the three void-nesses."

Taeryŏk Bodhisattva asked, "What are the three voidnesses?"

The Buddha replied, "The three voidnesses are: [1] the characteristic of voidness is also void; [2] the voidness of voidness is also void; [3] that which is voided is also void.[59] These kinds of voidness do not subsist in the three characteristics,[60] and they are not devoid of true reality [because they lead to the revelation of what is real]. Eradicating the pathways of words and speech is inconceivable."

Taeryŏk Bodhisattva said, "If they 'are not devoid of true reality,' then it must be assumed that they do in fact exist."

The Buddha retorted, "Nonexistence does not linger in nonexistence. Existence does not linger in existence.[61] Neither is nonexistent or existent. A nonexistent dharma does not in fact linger in nonexistence. A characteristic that is not nonexistent does not in fact linger in existence. One may not refer successfully to the principle in terms of either existence or nonexistence.

"Bodhisattva! That characteristic which has neither name or meaning is inconceivable. Why is this? The name that is nameless is not without name; the meaning that is meaningless is not without meaning."

Taeryŏk Bodhisattva said, "Such names and meanings are true and are characterized by thusness; they are the tathāgatas' characteristic of thusness. Thusness does not linger in thusness: thusness has no characteristic of thus-

---

[58] According to Wŏnhyo, the first two of the five types of voidness are intended to counter the deception that phenomenal objects, which are the objects of clinging, are real; the latter three are designed to counter the deceptions produced by the consciousnesses that are the cata-lysts for that clinging. *KSGR* 2, p. 983b26–29.

[59] According to Wŏnhyo, the first of these three types of voidness shows that rejecting the reality of mundane objects ("characteristic of voidness") is in turn to be rejected as well, thereby reconciling absolute truth with conventional truth. The second type suggests that descriptions of existence or nonexistence made according to conventional truth are also to be rejected; this reconciles conventional truth with absolute truth. The last demonstrates that both of the two preceding accounts of the significance of voidness are also void; this fuses both conventional and absolute truths into a single truth and reveals the one *dharmadhātu* (*il pŏpkye*), which is the one mind. *KSGR* 2, p. 983c8–26.

[60] Wŏnhyo glosses the three characteristics as conventional, absolute, and neither; *KSGR* 2, p. 983c27–28.

[61] This line is omitted in the Wŏnhyo and K'ai-pao recensions; *VS*, p. 396b19 n. 9.

ness, because its characteristic is to be free from thusness. [But] it is not that it has not 'come thusly' [ = tathāgata]. As far as the mental characteristics of sentient beings are concerned, those characteristics are identical to the tathā-gata. Hence, the minds of sentient beings should also be free from any dis-crete sense realms."

The Buddha said, "So it is. The minds of sentient beings are actually free from any discrete sense realms. Why is that? It is because the mind is origi-nally pure, and the principle unsullied. It is due to being soiled by the dust [of sensory objects] that [this world] comes to be called the three realms of existence. The mind that is involved in these three realms of existence comes to be called the discrete sense realms. These sense realms are empty and false, and are projections of the mind. If the mind is free from deception, there then will be no discrete sense realms."[62]

Taeryŏk Bodhisattva remarked, "If the mind    [369c]    remains pure, no sense objects will arise. When this mind is pure, the three realms of existence will perforce no longer exist."[63]

The Buddha responded, "So it is, Bodhisattva! If the mind does not pro-duce sense objects, those sense objects will not produce mind. Why is this? All visible objects are nothing but the mind that sees them. If the mind does not illusorily project them, there will be no visual objects.

"Bodhisattva! If sentient beings have no existence internally and the three natures [internal, external, and medial] are void and calm, there then will be no personal aggregation [viz., things involving oneself] or impersonal ag-gregation [viz., things separate from oneself]. Even the two accesses will also not produce mind. For one who has been so inspired, there will then be no three realms of existence."[64]

---

[62] "The mind is originally pure, and the principle unsullied" represents original enlighten-ment. "Soiled by the dust [of sensory objects, this world] comes to be called the three realms of existence" represents the common state of unenlightenment. "If the mind is free from decep-tion, there then will be no discrete sense realms": this represents the stage of the actualized enlightenment, which takes one from unenlightenment back to original enlightenment. *KSGR* 2, p. 984c6–15.

[63] " 'When this mind is pure, the three realms of existence will perforce no longer exist': [Bodhisattvas] from the first *bhūmi* onward have a realization of original purity; therefore, in accordance with their attainment, the three realms of existence vanish. The phenomenal char-acteristics of the three realms vanish on the first *bhūmi* or, alternatively, the eighth *bhūmi*. The own-nature of the three realms vanishes at the stage of equal enlightenment. The habit-energies (*vāsanā*) of the three realms vanish only on attaining the stage of sublime enlightenment." *KSGR* 2, p. 984c22–26.

[64] " 'If sentient beings have no existence internally': this is because on the level of the ten abidings, one realizes the voidness of the internal sense of self (*pudgala*). 'The three natures are

Taeryŏk Bodhisattva asked, "What is meant by your statement, 'the two accesses will also not produce mind'? The mind is originally unproduced; so how can there be an access to it?"

The Buddha replied, "There are two accesses: the first is called the access of principle (*iip*); the second is called the access of practice (*haengnip*). Access of principle means one has deep faith that sentient beings are not different from the true nature, and thus are neither identical nor counterpoised.[65] [This true nature] is obscured and obstructed merely by adventitious sense objects. Without either going or coming, one abides frozen in attentive contemplation (*ŭngju kakkwan*).[66] One contemplates according to truth (*ch'egwan*) that the buddha-nature is neither existent nor nonexistent. It is neither self nor others and is no different in either ordinary person or sage. One abides firmly without wavering in the state of the adamantine mind,

---

void and calm': this is because on the level of the ten practices, one realizes the voidness of the internal dharmas. 'There then will be no personal aggregation or impersonal aggregation': this is because at the level of the ten transferences, one gains the equanimous voidness which rejects totally all such personal and impersonal aggregations, or persons and dharmas." *KSGR* 2, p. 985a4–7.

[65] "Counterpoised" (*kong*) may be a mistake for "different" (*i*), the top portion of the latter logograph somehow having been deleted. This emendation is not corroborated in any of the recensions, however.

[66] "Attentive contemplation" (*kakkwan*) replaces Bodhidharma's renowned, but problematic, term, "wall contemplation" (*pi-kuan*). The precise denotation of this term as used in *VS* is somewhat unclear, since *kakkwan* (Ch. *chüeh-kuan*) as the *dvandva* "attention and contemplation" is the equivalent in older Chinese translations of "thought and imagination" (*vitarka-vicāra*)—the scourge of any meditation deeper than the first dhyāna. Wŏnhyo's interpretation seeks to give the term a rather more salutary connotation, taking it as "attention and examination" or "attentive examination" (*kakch'al*; Ch. *chüeh-ch'a*), adopting the rendering of *vitarka-vicāra* used in the translation of the *Laṅkāvatāra*; see discussion in Mizuno, p. 53, and for the *Laṅkāvatāra*'s translation of *vitarkavicāra* as *chüeh-kuan*, see Suzuki, *Studies*, p. 442 ad loc. All in all, *VS*'s gloss seems to suggest that "wall contemplation" is a form of detached, but nevertheless vigilant awareness, in which the adept remains constantly focussed on the utter ineffability of the buddha-nature. This is extremely close, as we shall see, to *VS*'s interpretation of "guarding the one."

There is also an interesting allusion in Hui-ssu's (515–576) *Sui-tzu-i san-mei* to a type of samādhi that combines the vajrasamādhi and wall contemplation. This is the "adamantine-wall samādhi" (*chin-kang-pi ting san-mei*). Hui-ssu's explication of this samādhi draws on the same *Āgama* story of Śāriputra's attack by a demon that we mentioned in treating the vajrasamādhi in part 1, chapter 3. The power of the vajrasamādhi (what Hui-ssu terms instead "adamantine-wall samādhi") was such that Śāriputra was completely unaware he had been struck a deadly blow over the head by a demon, illustrating that samādhi's ability to leave one totally senseless to the external world. Somewhat the same connotation is brought out in the reference to "abiding frozen" in either "wall contemplation" or "attentive contemplation" in the two corresponding passages of *VS* and *Erh-ju ssu-hsing lun*. See *Sui-tzu-i san-mei* 1, *ZZ* 1, 98, 350d–51a; discussed in Jorgensen, "*Long Scroll*," p. 194, and McRae, p. 306 n. 21.

calm, quiet, inactive, and free from discrimination. This is called the access of principle.

"The access of practice means that the mind has no bias or inclination; its shadows [the sense objects] are free from flux. Wherever [the mind] finds itself, its tranquil thoughts seek nothing. It is not buffeted by the winds [of the sense realms], and [remains still] like the great earth. It rejects [any notions of] mind and self and rescues sentient beings. It is not subject to production, has no characteristics, and is free from both clinging and rejection.

"Bodhisattva! The mind [that has realized the principle] is free from either egress or access. As the mind that is free from either egress or access accesses without accessing anything, I therefore referred to 'access.'

"Bodhisattva! The characteristic of that dharma which in this wise accesses the dharma is not void; and the dharma that is not void—that dharma is not frivolously discarded. Why is this? Those dharmas which are not nonexistent are replete with all meritorious qualities. They are neither mind nor its shadows; they are naturally (*niyati*) pure."

Taeryŏk Bodhisattva asked, "What is meant by this statement 'they are neither mind nor its shadows; they are naturally pure'?"

The Buddha replied, "The dharma that is void and thus is neither one of the dharmas of mind and consciousness [i.e., the eight consciousnesses], nor one of the dharmas that drive the mind [i.e., the six classes of mental concomitants (*caitta*)]. That dharma is not marked by voidness. That dharma is not marked by materiality. That dharma is not one of the dharmas dissociated from mind (*cittaviprayuktasaṃskāra*). It is not a dharma that accords with the unconditioned quality of the mind. It is neither a shadow that is cast [viz., a sense-object projected by the mind] nor [the mind] that projects [sense objects]. It has no nature of its own and is not discrete. It is neither name, characteristic, nor object (*artha*). Why is this? Because [that dharma] is thus.

"Those dharmas that are not thus also do not lack thusness and [dharmas] that do not exist do not lack thusness. But it is wrong [to claim that] there exists [any dharma] that lacks thusness.[67] Why is this? The dharma of the fundamental principle is neither principle nor fundamental. It is far removed from all controversy and manifests no characteristics.

"Bodhisattva! The production of this sort of pure dharma is not produced by production [for its essence is unproduced]; its extinction is not extinguished by nonextinction [for its essence is unextinguished]."

---

[67] The translation of these two sentences is tentative. Wŏnhyo's interpretation seeks to force exactly the opposite sense from the passage. *KSGR* 2, p. 968a7–9.

Taeryŏk Bodhisattva remarked, "This is inconceivable! Such characteristics of dharmas are produced neither in combination [i.e., they are not mind or mental characteristics, which are always produced in association with each other] nor independently [for they have no own-nature and are not differentiated]. They are neither bridled [for they are neither name nor object] nor bound [for they are not associated with the senses]. They are neither amassed [viz., materiality] nor scattered [viz., voidness]. They are neither produced nor extinguished. They are free from any characteristic of either coming or going. This is inconceivable!"

The Buddha said, "So it is. It is inconceivable. The inconceivable mind—that mind is also thus. Why is this? Thusness is not    [370a]    different from the mind, for the mind is originally thus.

"Sentient beings and the buddha-nature are neither one nor different. The natures of sentient beings are originally free from both production and extinction. This nature of production and extinction—that nature is originally nirvāṇa. The nature [of sentient beings] and the characteristics [of production and extinction] are originally thus, for thusness is motionless.

"No characteristics of dharmas are generated by conditions, for the nature of this characteristic of generation (utpādalakṣaṇa) is to be thus and motionless. The characteristics of conditionality—those characteristics are originally void and nonexistent. As each and every condition is void, there is no conditioned generation (pratītyasamutpāda). All conditioned dharmas are the illusory visions of the deluded mind. Their appearance is originally unproduced, since the conditions [that produce them] are originally nonexistent. The thusness of the mind, that principle of dharma—its self-essence is void and nonexistent. It is like 'King Space,'⁶⁸ which originally has no abode; the minds of ordinary people wrongly perceive [all-encompassing space] as differentiated [into this space and that space].

"That characteristic of thusness originally neither exists nor does not exist. The characteristics of existence and nonexistence are perceived only by the mind and consciousness. Bodhisattva! So too is it with the nature of the mind: it is not devoid of self-essence, but that self-essence is [also] not existent, for nonexistence is actually not nonexistent. Bodhisattva! Those characteristics of both nonexistence and not nonexistence are not part of the stage of speech and language. Why is this? The dharma of true thusness is

---

⁶⁸ " 'King Space' is the so-called dharma of space, which is the support of all materiality, in the same way that a king is the support of all his subjects. Hence, space is said to be King Space." *KSGR* 2, p. 986c9–11.

empty, vacant, and signless. It is not something that may be reached by dualities[69] [such as thought and imagination (*vitarkavicāra*)].

"The realm of emptiness cannot be fathomed by either those inside or outside [the Buddhist religion]. Only a master of the six practices may come to know of them."

Taeryŏk Bodhisattva asked, "What are these six practices? I beg of you to explain them."

The Buddha replied, "First is the practice of the ten faiths. Second is the practice of the ten abidings. Third is the practice of the ten practices. Fourth is the practice of the ten transferences. Fifth is the practice of the ten *bhūmi*s. Sixth is the practice of equal enlightenment. One who practices these sorts of practices may then come to know [the realm of emptiness]."[70]

Taeryŏk Bodhisattva asked, "The enlightened inspiration of the edge of reality has neither egress nor access. Through what sort of dharma or thought does one approach the edge of reality?"

The Buddha replied, "The dharma of the edge of reality—that dharma has no limit. The mind that is limitless thence approaches the edge of reality."

Taeryŏk Bodhisattva asked, "The knowledge of this limitless mind—that knowledge is boundless. The boundless mind—that mind gains autonomy. Autonomous knowledge gains access to the edge of reality. This is also the case for ordinary persons, feeble-minded sentient beings—that is, those whose minds are subject to severe panting (*ch'ŏn*).[71] Through what dharma may they control that [panting], steady their minds, and gain access to the edge of reality?"

---

[69] Following the Wŏnhyo and K'ai-pao recensions. Koryŏ II/Taishō has "it is not reached by two-vehicle [adherents]," which is also plausible; *VS*, p. 370a11 n. 2.

[70] This is the expanded outline of the *mārga* as found in such Chinese apocryphal compositions as *P'u-sa ying-lo pen-yeh ching*, *Fan-wang ching*, and *Jen-wang ching*; Wŏnhyo himself notes that the outline of this *mārga* comes from *P'u-sa ying-lo pen-yeh ching* and its full explication appears in *Avataṃsaka-sūtra*. He then correlates the first four stages of this *mārga* (the ten faiths through the ten transferences) with the access of principle and the latter two (the ten *bhūmi*s and equal enlightenment) with the access of practice. *KSGR* 2, p. 987a16–18.

[71] Wŏnhyo: " 'The panting (*ch'ŏn/ch'uan*) of the mind': the mind that is startled is not at rest, and one's inhalations and exhalations become extremely rapid: this is 'panting.' It is used as a simile for the agitation of the six [sensory] consciousnesses, which are never at rest." *KSGR* 2, p. 987b16–17. See also Yüan-ch'eng's comments (*Chu-chieh* 3, p. 208a), who seeks to trace the idea of "panting" to the *Laṅkāvatāra-sūtra*. "Panting" appears commonly in early Chinese translations of dhyāna texts. One of An Shih-kao's translations associates panting with the rapid breath that accompanies the onset of the dying process; see *Ma-i ching*, *T* 732.17.533b14. Panting is also equated with distracted thought in Chu Fa-hu's translations; see *Fa-kuan ching*, *T* 611.15.241a24.

The Buddha replied, "Bodhisattva! This panting of the mind is driven both internally [by the sense of self that is a product of the *kliṣṭamanovijñāna*] and externally [by the sense realms]. [The defilements (kleśa)] flow along following those impulsions, until their drips [their manifestations (*samudā-cāra*)] become a sea. The heavenly[72] winds [of the passions] buffet [the sea of the proclivities (*anuśaya*) creating] the waves [of the seven consciousnesses], thereby startling the great dragon [of ignorance]. Because the mind is startled and alarmed, one begins to pant severely.[73]

"Bodhisattva! One should urge those sentient beings to preserve the three and guard the one, in order to access the tathāgatadhyāna.[74] Due to this concentrated absorption, their minds will come to be free of panting."

Taeryŏk Bodhisattva asked, "What do you mean by 'preserve the three and guard the one, in order to access the tathāgatadhyāna'?"

The Buddha replied, " 'Preserve the three' means to preserve the three liberations. 'Guard the one' means to guard the thusness of the one mind. 'Access the tathāgatadhyāna' means the noumenal contemplation (*igwan*) on the thusness of the mind. Accessing such a state is in fact what is meant by approaching the edge of reality."

Taeryŏk Bodhisattva asked, "What exactly are these three liberations? Through what dharma may one enter this noumenal-contemplation samādhi?"

The Buddha replied, "The three liberations are void liberation, adamantine liberation, and prajñā liberation. The mind that engages in noumenal contemplation means that once the mind    [370b]    is pure in accordance with the principle, there is then nothing that cannot be the mind."

Taeryŏk Bodhisattva asked, "How do you perform this act of preservation? How does one contemplate it?"

The Buddha answered, "Preservation is put into operation when mind and objects are nondual. Whether withdrawing from or accessing internal or external practices, [these remain] nondual.[75] One does not dwell on any

---

[72] Following Wŏnhyo's reading (*KSGR* 2, p. 987b13). All other editions read the near-homograph *tae* ("great") for *ch'ŏn* ("heavenly"); see *VS*, p. 370a22.

[73] The glosses for this simile are drawn from Wŏnhyo; *KSGR* 2, p. 987b.

[74] The last, and most profound, of the four types of dhyāna mentioned in the *Laṅkāvatāra-sūtra*, in which the person is able to go out into the world to aid sentient beings while still maintaining the full depth of his concentration; see *Leng-ch'ieh ching* 2, *T* 670.16.492a22–24; *Ta-sheng ju Leng-ch'ieh ching* 3, *T* 672.16.602a12; Suzuki, trans., pp. 85–86; it is discussed in Suzuki, *Studies*, pp. 367–68.

[75] " 'Internal practice' is the practice of calm radiance, which is generated through accessing contemplation. 'External practice' is the practice of transforming objects, which occurs through withdrawing from contemplation. Whether withdrawing or accessing, one does not

particular characteristic and the mind is free from gain or loss. The mind, purified, flows freely into the one-and-many *bhūmi*.[76] [All of] this is what is meant by 'contemplate it.'

"Bodhisattva! Such a person does not linger over any dualistic character-istics. Although he does not go forth into homelessness (*pravrajita*) he is no longer part of the household. For this reason, while he does not wear the dharma-robes and neither observes all the Prātimokṣa precepts [monk's dis-ciplinary rules] nor participates in the Poṣada [fortnightly religious observ-ance], he does not engage in personal licentiousness in his own mind and obtains the fruition of sainthood. He does not linger over either of the two vehicles but accesses the bodhisattva path. Subsequently he will complete all the *bhūmi*s and attain the bodhi of the buddhas."

Taeryŏk Bodhisattva remarked, "This is inconceivable! Even though such a person has not gone forth into homelessness, he cannot but have gone forth. Why is this? He has entered the domicile of nirvāṇa, where he dons the robe of the tathāgatas and sits on the bodhi-seat (*bodhimaṇḍa*). Such a person should be worshipped respectfully even by śramaṇas [religious men-dicants]."

The Buddha said, "So it is. Why is this? Accessing the domicile of nir-vāṇa, the mind transcends[77] the three realms of existence.[78] Donning the robe of the tathāgatas, he accesses the site of the voidness of dharmas. Seated on the bodhi-seat, he ascends to the unique[79] *bhūmi* of right enlightenment. The mind of such a person transcends the two types of [belief in] selfhood

---

lose the middle way: hence, the statement '[these remain] nondual.' This is as has been explained in the 'Ten Transferences' section of the *Pen-yeh ching*." KSGR 2, p. 988b4–6. For the passage from the *P'u-sa ying-lo pen-yeh ching*, see *T* 1485.24.1014a7–14.

[76] " 'The-one-and-many [lit., 'one-and-not-one'] *bhūmi*': this is an alternate name for the first *bhūmi*. This is because the first *bhūmi* is in fact the ten *bhūmi*s, for in one moment one may suddenly access the ten types of *dharmadhātu*. The ten *bhūmi*s are in fact the first *bhūmi*, for they may all be directly accessed through this initial gate [of the first *bhūmi*]. Owing to the fact that the ten *bhūmi*s are in fact the first *bhūmi*, [the first *bhūmi*] is called the 'one.' But because the first *bhūmi* is in fact the ten *bhūmi*s, it is 'many.' Consequently, [the first *bhūmi*] is called the 'one-and-many *bhūmi*.' " KSGR 2, p. 988b19–23.

[77] Following the Koryŏ II/Taishō reading; no alternate readings are given by the Taishō editors. Wŏnhyo's recension reads *ki* ("to activate") for *wŏl* ("to transcend"). KSGR 2, p. 988c14.

[78] Liebenthal (p. 366 and n. 2) traces this phrase to allusions in Paramārtha's translation of *Shih-pa-k'ung lun* (*T* 1616), though I believe the page and line numbers are miscited; apparently, he means to refer to *T* 1616.31.861c28, 862a1.

[79] Lit., "single" (*il*). This work is missing in the Koryŏ II/Taishō recension and is added following the Wŏnhyo, K'ai-pao, and Three Editions; *VS*, p. 370b13 n. 11.

[i.e., believing in the selfhood of the individual person and of dharmas]. So why wouldn't the śramaṇas worship him respectfully?"

Taeryŏk Bodhisattva remarked, "Adherents of the two vehicles do not see such a unique *bhūmi* or the sea of voidness."

The Buddha responded, "So it is. Two-vehicle adherents savor samādhi, and gain the samādhi-body [i.e., they are attached to the trance of extinction (*nirodhasamāpatti*)]. With regard to that unique *bhūmi* and the sea of voidness, they become like alcoholics who stay drunk and never sober up. Continuing through numerous kalpas [eons], they remain unable to gain enlightenment. But once the liquor has worn off and they finally awaken, they will then be able to cultivate these practices and eventually gain the body of a buddha.[80] From the moment that such a person abandons the [status of] *icchantika* [a person who is blocked from attaining enlightenment], he may access the six practices. On those stages of practice, his mind is purified in a single moment of thought and he gains absolute clarity and brightness. The power of his adamantine knowledge renders him *avaivartaka* [not subject to spiritual retrogression]. He ferries sentient beings across to liberation and has inexhaustible friendliness and compassion."[81]

Taeryŏk Bodhisattva said, "But such a person would not need to maintain the codes of morality and thus should be reproached by the śramaṇas."

The Buddha replied, "I explain moral codes to you because of your unwholesome actions and haughtiness, and because of the waves and swells [the first seven consciousnesses, which disturb the calm surface] of the sea [the innate purity of the mind]. Once the mind-ground [has realized the voidness of dharmas], its sea of the eighth consciousness is limpid and the flow of its ninth consciousness is pure. The winds [of the sense realms] cannot buffet them, so waves and swells do not arise.[82]

"The nature of the moral codes is equanimous and void; [the śrāvakas]

---

[80]  This simile is adapted from *Laṅkāvatāra-sūtra*: "It is like a drunkard,/ Whose liquor wearing off, later awakens,/ He gains the supreme essence of buddhahood,/ Which is my true dharma-body." (*Ju Leng-ch'ieh ching* 4, *T* 671.16.540b7–8). The Sanskrit is somewhat different (as rendered by Suzuki, trans., p. 116, v. 210): "Like unto the drunkard who, being awakened from his intoxication, regains his intelligence, [the Śrāvakas] will have the realisation of the Buddha's truth, which is his own body."

[81]  *VS*'s correlation of the *icchantika* with two-vehicle adherents who are hopelessly attached to samādhi is without parallel in other scriptures, so far as I am aware. Mahāyāna texts have, however, frequently equated *icchantikas* with Hīnayānists, as for example *Laṅkāvatāra-sūtra*; Suzuki, trans., p. 59. The Mahāyāna conception of *icchantika* is discussed by Suzuki in his companion volume, *Studies*, pp. 217–21; and see the citations to other Mahāyāna texts in Takasaki Jikidō, *A Study on the Ratnagotravibhāga*, introduction, p. 40, and translation, p. 205.

[82]  Cf. the simile of waves and water in *Ta-sheng ch'i-hsin lun, T* 1666.32.476c.

who hold fast to them are deluded and confused. For a person [who knows the true nature of the precepts], the seventh and sixth [consciousnesses] will not be produced, and all origination [of mind and mental concomitants] ceases [for he achieves] the meditative absorption [engendered by accessing the principle]. Remaining close to the three buddhas [*infra*], he arouses [the thought of] bodhi. His mind, which conforms [with the dharma of the one mind], mysteriously accesses the three [types of] signlessness [for he has perfected the access of practice and has eradicated ignorance]. He deeply reveres the triratna, and does not neglect his dignified demeanor (*īryāpatha*). All of those śramaṇas will have to venerate him!

"Bodhisattva! That humanhearted person will not linger over any worldly dharmas, whether active [leading to rebirth in the heavens of the desire realm] or motionless [leading to rebirth in the form and formless realms]. Rather, he will access the three types of voidness and extinguish the mind that is involved with the three realms of existence."

Taeryŏk Bodhisattva asked, "That virtuous one arouses the thought of bodhi at the sites of the [three] buddhas: that is, [1] the buddha endowed with all meritorious qualities, who has brought to fruition [the process of the actualization of enlightenment]; [2] the tathāgatagarbha-buddha[83] [the original enlightenment innate in all sentient beings]; and [3] the corporeal buddha.  [370c]  He accesses the three codes of morality [see chapter 6 *infra*] but does not linger over their characteristics. He extinguishes all thoughts of the three realms of existence, but does not reside in that calm place. Not forsaking the assembly that is capable [of salvation], he reenters the untamed stage [of ordinary sentient beings]. It is inconceivable!"

At that time, Śāriputra rose from his seat, came forward, and recited these gāthās:

> He perfects the sea of prajñā,
> And does not dwell in the city of nirvāṇa,
> Just as the exotic lotus blossom,
> Does not grow in the high plains.[84]
> All the buddhas over immeasurable kalpas,

[83] The term tathāgatagarbha-buddha appears only in *VS* and another suspected Korean apocryphal composition, *Sŏk Mahayŏn-ron* (cf. *k.* 10, *T* 1668.32.667c21–22, which reads the "tathāgatagarbha-buddha of original enlightenment").

[84] Taken from the *Wei-mo-chieh so-shuo ching* (*Vimalakīrtinirdeśa*) 2, *T* 475.14.549b6; cf. Robert Thurman, trans., *The Holy Teaching of Vimalakīrti*, p. 66. The locus classicus for this metaphor is *Dhammapada* (Pupphavagga), vv. 58, 59.

Did not forsake all the defilements.
Only after saving the world did they gain [nirvāṇa],
Like the lotus rising from the mud.
Just as those six levels of practice,
Are what are cultivated by the bodhisattvas,
So too are those three types of voidness,
The true path to bodhi.
Whether I now linger [in the tranquillity of nirvāṇa] or not,
It will be just as the Buddha has explained:
I will return again to this place whence I came,
And discard [this body] only after I have completed [all the bodhisattva
    practices].
Furthermore, I will urge all sentient beings,
To join with me [in pursuing the same vow] and not remain apart,
May those who came before or will come afterward,
All be encouraged to climb to right enlightenment.

At that time, the Buddha proclaimed to Śāriputra: "This is inconceivable! You are certain to complete later on the path to bodhi. Innumerable sentient beings will transcend the sea of birth and death."

At that time, the great assembly [of Mahāyānists] all awakened to bodhi, and all the lesser assembly [of Hīnayānists] together accessed the sea of the five voidnesses.

Chapter Six

# The Voidness of the True Nature

[370c17]   At that time, Śāriputra addressed the Buddha, saying: "Lord! The cultivation of the bodhisattva path is free from either names or characteristics. The three [codes of] morality do not demand a dignified demeanor.[85] How should we receive and keep these [codes] so that we may then preach them to sentient beings? I beg that the Buddha may proclaim this for us, out of his compassion."

The Buddha replied, "Oh son of good family! May you now listen well and I will proclaim this for you.

"Oh son of good family! Both wholesome and unwholesome dharmas are projections of the mind. All the sense realms[86] are but the discriminations of ratiocination and verbalization. Control this [discrimination through] one-pointedness of mind and all conditioning will be brought to an end. Why is this? Oh son of good family! The one [original enlightenment, which is the basis of the three moral codes,] originally is not generated [because it is fundamentally calm and tranquil]. The functioning of the three [moral codes] is inoperative. Abiding in that thus-like principle, the gates leading to the six destinies are closed and the four conditions that accord with thusness become imbued with the three moral codes."

Śāriputra asked, "How is it that 'the four conditions that accord with thusness become imbued with the three moral codes'?"

The Buddha replied, "The four conditions are: (1) The condition that keeps [the precepts] through the power of the cessation engendered by analytical consideration (pratisaṃkhyānirodha; t'aengmyŏl); it is the moral code

---

[85] This sentence provides the tie in with the statement toward the end of the previous chapter, "He accesses the three codes of morality but does not linger over their characteristics"; VS, chap. 5, after n. 83. See discussion at KSGR 3, p. 990c8–9.

[86] Wŏnhyo glosses these instead as the six destinies: hell-denizens, hungry ghosts, animals, humans, aśuras, gods. KSGR 3, p. 990c20.

that maintains both the discipline and the deportments. (2) The condition that is originated and generated through the power of the pure basis of original inspiration; it is the moral code that accumulates wholesome dharmas. (3) The condition that is the power of the great compassion of original wisdom; it is the moral code that aids all sentient beings.[87] (4) The condition that is the power of the penetrative knowledge of the one enlightenment; it accords with abiding in thusness. These are called the four conditions.[88]

"Oh son of good family! In this wise, the power of the four great conditions does not linger over phenomenal characteristics and does not lack efficacious functioning. As it remains separate from any one    [371a]    locus, it cannot be sought.

"Oh son of good family! In this wise, the one phenomenon [one enlightenment] completely contains the six practices. It is the buddhas' sea of bodhi and *sarvajña*."

Śāriputra remarked, "[You said that] it 'does not linger over phenomenal

[87] These three moral codes are common in Yogācāra and Yogācāra-influenced literature and have been adopted frequently in sinitic Buddhist apocrypha. See discussion in part 1, chapter 4, "Reductionist Tendencies" section.

[88] This list of four conditions is peculiar to *VS*. Wŏnhyo explains:

"The four conditions": this means that within the one mind's inspiration of original enlightenment is contained four powerful functions, which act as the conditions for the three moral codes. These are: (1) the condition that is based on extinction; (2) the condition based on production; (3) the condition based on absorption; (4) the condition based on separation. [1] "Based on extinction" means that the meritorious qualities inherent in original enlightenment, [which are engendered by] the tranquillity of the nature, are diametrically opposed in their own-natures to all the defilements. It is by means of this condition that one is able to perfect the moral conduct that maintains both the discipline and deportments. [2] "Based on production" means that the meritorious qualities inherent in original enlightenment, [which are engendered by] the wholesomeness of the nature, completely harmonize in their own natures with the wholesome faculties (*kuśalamūla*). It is by means of this condition that one is able to perfect the moral conduct that accumulates wholesome dharmas. [3] "Based on absorption" means that great compassion produced in the nature, which is inherent in original enlightenment, does not of its own accord abandon any sentient being. It is by means of this condition that one completes the moral conduct that embraces sentient beings. [4] "Based on separation" means that the prajñā produced in the nature, which is inherent in original enlightenment, stays far removed of its own accord from all phenomenal characteristics. It is by means of this condition that one causes the three moral codes to stay separate from phenomenal characteristics and abide in accordance with thusness. The prior three conditions have a specific application; the last one is a condition that is of universal application.

When a bodhisattva arouses the thought [of enlightenment] and receives the three moral codes, he receives and keeps these while remaining in harmony with the benefit of original enlightenment; hence these four conditions are replete in the three [groups of] precepts. Such is the general import [of this passage].

*KSGR* 3, p. 991a.

characteristics and does not lack efficacious functioning.' Such a dharma would be true voidness, which is permanent, blissful, selfhood, and pure. As it transcends [the attachment to] the two types of selfhood [viz., the self-hood of person and dharmas], it is great *parinirvāṇa*. That mind has no bonds: this is a contemplation that has considerable force. All the thirty-seven aspects of enlightenment (*bodhipakṣikadharma*) are necessarily contained in this contemplation and in this [original] enlightenment [where subject and object are balanced]."

The Buddha said, "So indeed does it contain the thirty-seven aspects of enlightenment. What are these? They are the four applications of mindfulness (*smṛtyupasthāna*); the four right efforts (*samyakprahāṇa*); the four bases of psychic power (*ṛddhipāda*); the five faculties (*indriya*); the five powers (*bala*); the seven limbs of enlightenment (*bodhyaṅga*); the eightfold path (*mār-gāṅga*), and so forth. These many classifications have but one meaning [i.e., they all conduce to enlightenment], for they are neither unitary nor separate. But because their designations are manifold, they are merely names and merely letters;[89] those dharmas are unascertainable (*anupalabdhi*). An unas-certainable dharma has but a single meaning and is free from locution. That characteristic of being free from locution is the nature of true and real void-ness. The meaning of that void nature accords with reality (*yathābhūta*) and is thus. That principle which is thus contains all dharmas. Oh son of good family! A person who abides in that principle which is thus thereby crosses over the sea of the three sufferings."

Śāriputra asked, "Each and every one of the myriads of dharmas is but verbalization and locution. That which is characterized by verbalization and locution has no meaning and a meaning that accords with reality cannot be explained verbally. So why now does the Tathāgata preach the dharma?"

The Buddha replied, "I preach the dharma because you sentient beings persist in needing explanations. I preach what cannot be spoken of. This is why I preach [the dharma]. My speech consists of meaningful words, not mere locution; sentient beings' speech consists of mere locution and is not meaningful. Meaningless words are all vain and worthless. Vain and worth-less words say nothing about meaning, and anything that does not convey meaning is false speech.

"As far as speaking in accordance with meaning is concerned, the real is void and yet not void; voidness is real and yet unreal. [Speaking in accor-

[89] See *Mo-ho po-jo po-lo-mi ching* 1 (*T* 223.8.221c19) where the Buddha also addresses Śāri-putra, telling him that all concepts "are explained merely with names and letters."

dance with meaning] remains separate from dualistic characteristics, but also is not centered in between. The dharma that is not so centered remains far removed from these three characteristics [voidness, reality, and their interstice]; its location cannot be found.

"[Those words which remain separate from these three characteristics] are spoken according to thusness. Thusness is nonexistent and makes existence nonexistent, for there is no existence in nonexistence. Thusness is nonexistent and makes nonexistence existent, for there is nonexistence in existence. Neither existence nor nonexistence applies. Because such statements are inapplicable, [the concept] 'thusness' [too] is inapplicable. Thusness is not said to be either thusness that is existent or thusness that is nonexistent."[90]

Śāriputra said, "All sentient beings begin as *icchantikas*.[91] On what levels should the *icchantika*'s thoughts abide in order to reach the [level of] the tathāgatas and the tathāgatas' real characteristic?"

The Buddha said, "From the [level of] the *icchantika*'s mind up until one reaches the tathāgatas and the real characteristic of the tathāgatas, one passes through five levels.[92]

"First is the level of faith [comprising the ten faiths]. [The practitioner] has faith that in this body there is a seed of true thusness,[93] which is obscured by the deceptions [of incredulity and nescience]. By relinquishing the deceptive thoughts and leaving them far behind, the pure mind will become clear and transparent and one will know that all the sense realms are just the discriminations of ratiocination and verbalization [i.e., they are mere-representation].

"Second is the level of consideration [comprising the ten abidings, ten practices, and ten transferences]. 'Consideration' means that one contemplates the fact that all the sense realms are nothing more than ratiocination

[90] This paragraph is one of the worst sections of *VS* to construe. Wŏnhyo has to bring all of his exegetical talents to bear to make any sense of the passage; see his convoluted explanations at *KSGR* 3, p. 992c12–29.

[91] *Icchantika* here is used to refer to anyone who has yet to generate the aspiration for full enlightenment (*bodhicittotpāda*), or who does not have faith in the Mahāyāna. See *KSGR* 3, p. 993a9–16.

[92] The following section outlines the five major divisions of the bodhisattva path found in many sinitic apocryphal scriptures, such as *P'u-sa ying-lo pen-yeh ching* (*T* 1485.24.1017a3, 1010b27, 1022b13). The correlations Wŏnhyo draws between the *VS* schema and the more standard list found in other scriptures are bracketed in the translation.

[93] See the discussion of the significance of this passage in the development of the buddha-nature concept in Tokiwa Daijō, *Busshō no kenkyū*, p. 406.

and verbalization. [As those sense realms are] the discriminations of ratiocination and verbalization, they manifest according to one's mind (*manas*).
Those sense realms which are perceived are not my original consciousness,[94]
for I know that the original consciousness is neither a dharma, nor its meaning, nor [those external sense objects] to which one clings, nor [that men-
tality] which clings.

"Third is the level of cultivation [the ten *bhūmis*]. Cultivation involves
constant training in that which catalyzes spiritual development [the simultaneous cultivation of calmness (*śamatha*) and insight (*vipaśyanā*)]. Training
and cultivation are to be simultaneous and initially guided by [preparatory]
knowledge [*kahaeng-chi*; *sambhārajñāna*]. Overcoming all hindrances and difficulties, one removes all   [371b]   restraints and shackles and stays far removed from them.

"Fourth is the level of practice [equal enlightenment]. Practice means to
leave behind all the stages of practice [the ten *bhūmis*]. The mind that is free
from both clinging and rejection [manifests] the extremely pure, fundamental inspiration [viz., original enlightenment]. The thusness of the mind will
be motionless [because the adept accesses the vajrasamādhi], and the real
nature will become fixed. This is great *parinirvāṇa*. Its nature alone is void
and vast.

"Fifth is the level of relinquishment [sublime enlightenment, the stage of
buddhahood]. Not lingering in the voidness of the nature, right knowledge
flows freely. Great compassion is characterized by thusness but that characteristic does not linger in thusness. *Samyaksaṃbodhi* empties the mind so that
there is nothing to realize. As the mind is boundless and limitless, it does
not focus on a single, limited spot. This [is what is meant by] reaching the
tathāgatas.

"Oh son of good family! These five levels are but one enlightenment;
they are accessed through the inspiration of original [enlightenment]. The
proselytization of sentient beings must occur from that original locus."

Śāriputra asked, "What do you mean by 'must occur from that original
locus'?"

The Buddha replied, "Originally there is no original locus. On the brink

---

[94] " 'Original consciousness' is so called, because the sixth consciousness is the origin of the
three realms of existence. As a gāthā recited by [Ārya]Deva Bodhisattva says, 'The mind-consciousness is the basis of the three [realms of] existence. . . .' " *KSGR* 3, p. 993b20–21. I have
been unable to locate the precise verse cited here by Wŏnhyo. However, a similar verse appears
in *Kuang Po-lun pen* [*Śataśāstra*], *T* 1570.30.185c10–11, and see exegesis at *Ta-sheng Kuang Po-
lun shih-lun* 9, *T* 1571.30.236a.

of voidness, which has no locus, one accesses reality and, arousing bodhi, completes the sanctified path. Why is this? Oh son of good family! Like a hand grabbing air, [enlightenment] is neither obtained nor not obtained."

Śāriputra remarked, "As the Lord has explained, at the inception of one's vocation, one should cleave therewith to the inspiration of original [enlightenment]. Such a state of mind is calm and extinguished, and that calm extinction is thus. [Thusness] encodes all the meritorious qualities [of original and actualized enlightenments] and contains the myriad of dharmas: this is consummate interfusion, which is nondual. It is inconceivable! We should know that this dharma is in fact mahāprajñāpāramitā [great perfection of wisdom]. It is the great spiritual spell, the spell of great clarity, the unsurpassed spell, the unequalled spell."[95]

The Buddha said, "So it is, so it is! True thusness has voidness as its nature. As its nature is void, its knowledge is empyreal, incinerating all the fetters. In an equipoised and balanced manner, the three stages of equal enlightenment (tŭnggak) and the three bodies of sublime enlightenment (myogak) shine brilliantly in the ninth consciousness so that there are no shadows.[96]

"Oh son of good family! This dharma is not subject either to causes or conditions, because it is just wisdom functioning on its own. It is neither moving nor still, because the nature of that functioning is void. Its meaning neither exists nor does not exist, because the characteristic of voidness is void.

---

[95] This passage is taken from the final line of Hsüan-tsang's rendering of the Prajñāpāramitāhṛdaya-sūtra [Heart Sūtra], (T 251.8.848c14–15), which was made on July 8, 649 (Lancaster and Park, The Korean Buddhist Canon, p. 11). This date provides the terminus a quo for the composition of VS.

[96] "The three stages of equal enlightenment" are distinct levels in which the lifespan of the bodhisattva lasts for respectively a hundred kalpas, a thousand kalpas, and ten thousand kalpas. On the first level, the bodhisattva practices all the samādhis and finally enters the vajrasamādhi. On the second level, he practices all the deportments of a buddha, until he finally sits at the bodhimaṇḍa and overcomes Māra's hordes. On the final level, he leads the life of a fully enlightened buddha. These derive from P'u-sa ying-lo pen-yeh ching 1, T 1485.24.1012c27–1013a9. The three bodies of sublime enlightenment are the three buddha-bodies: the dharmakāya, saṃbhogakāya, and nirmāṇakāya. Explaining "[these] shine brilliantly in the ninth consciousness so that there are no shadows," Wŏnhyo says: "The previous stage of equal enlightenment is still involved with birth and death and has not yet depleted the fountainhead of the mind; for this reason, it is located within the eight consciousnesses. Arriving at sublime enlightenment, one now leaves birth and death behind forever and returns completely to the fountainhead of the one mind of original enlightenment. Hence, he accesses the clear purity of the ninth consciousness. . . . Now, returning to the fountainhead of the mind, that original substance becomes one's essence, and due to this, all shadows—all characteristics—become extinct." KSGR 3, p. 994c25–29.

"Oh son of good family! If one proselytes sentient beings, one should make those sentient beings access this meaning through contemplation. One who accesses this meaning will see the tathāgatas."

Śāriputra remarked, "Contemplation of the tathāgatas' meaning does not linger in any of the currents [of existence]. One should leave behind the four dhyānas and transcend the summit of existence (*bhavāgra*)."[97]

The Buddha said, "So it is. And why is this? All dharmas are but names and classifications. This is also the case with the four dhyānas. If one sees the tathāgatas, [one's own] tathāgata-mind will become autonomous (*aiśvarya*) and remain eternally in a state of extinction, neither withdrawing from [that state] nor accessing it. This is because both internal [the mind] and external [the sense objects] will be in equilibrium.

"Oh son of good family! In the same way, all [eight types of] dhyānic contemplations are absorptions that involve past conceptions.[98]

"But this thusness, furthermore, is not the same as those [types of dhyāna]. Why so? One who contemplates thusness through thusness perceives no sign that he is 'contemplating thusness.' All signs are already calm and extinct. Calm extinction is in fact the meaning of thusness.

"In the same way, a dhyānic absorption that involves such conceptions is active [because it clings to the characteristics of mundane dhyāna] and is not [true] dhyāna.[99] Why is this? The nature of dhyāna is separate from all movement. It neither taints nor is tainted; it is neither a dharma nor its shadow. It is far removed from all discrimination, because it is the meaning of the original inspiration.[100] Oh son of good family! This sort of contemplative absorption alone deserves to be called dhyāna."

Śāriputra asked, "It is inconceivable! The tathāgata constantly proselytes sentient beings by means of that which accords with reality (*yathābhūta*). In this wise,   [371c]   the real meaning has many locutions and vast import.

---

[97] The summit of existence refers to the last of the four formless dhyānas, the absorption of neither perception nor nonperception (*naivasaṃjñāsaṃjñāyatana*).

[98] Following Wŏnhyo's recension (*KSGR* 3, p. 995b9); no variants are noted by the Taishō editors; *VS*, p. 371b24. Wŏnhyo glosses "absorptions that involve past conceptions" as follows: "This is because they do not leave behind past grasping at the beginningless deceptive thoughts that cling to all the [mundane] characteristics." *KSGR* 3, p. 995b17.

[99] A parallel phrase ("activity is not dhyāna") appears in the apocryphal *Dharmapada*, *p'in* 11, *Fa-chü ching*, *T* 2901.85.1435a22. That *p'in* is frequently cited in Ch'an writings; see discussion in Mizuno, "Gisaku no *Hokkukyō*," pp. 17–20.

[100] Following the Koryŏ II/Taishō recension. The Wŏnhyo, K'ai-pao, and Three Editions read instead "the meaning of its original meaning," a probable dittography of the first "meaning." *VS*, p. 371b27 n. 7.

Sentient beings of sharp faculties alone are able to cultivate it; sentient beings of dull faculties find it difficult to recall. Through what expedient device may we prompt those of dull faculties to gain access to this truth?"

The Buddha replied, "One should encourage those of dull faculties to receive and keep one four-line gāthā; this will then allow them access to the real truth. All of the buddhadharma is contained within a single four-line[101] gāthā."

Śāriputra asked, "What is this four-line gāthā? I beg you to recite it."

Thereupon, the Lord recited the gāthā:

Objects[102] that are produced by causes and conditions,
Those objects are extinguished, not produced.
Extinguish all objects subject to production and extinction,
And those objects will be produced, not extinguished.[103]

At that time, the great congregation heard this gāthā and all were utterly rapturous. Everyone came to understand both extinction and production. The prajñā [that comprehends] extinction and production is a sea that knows the nature is void.

---

[101] The Wŏnhyo and K'ai-pao recensions omit "four-line." *KSGR* 3, p. 995c19; *VS*, p. 371c4 n. 8.

[102] "Objects" here renders the logograph *ŭi* (Skt. *artha*), which can refer to either meaning or object; both senses are probably implicit in the gāthā. "Dharma" is used for "object" in the text from which this gāthā derives (see next note).

[103] The first line of this gāthā is taken, with minor modifications, from Kumārajīva's translation of the *Madhyamakakārikā* (*Chung-lun*, *T* 1654.30.33b11–12, *Mūlamadhyamakakārikā* xxiv.19); see also *Chung-kuan lun shu* (*T* 1824.42.152b1), *Ju ta-sheng lun*, *T* 1634.32.41b; *Fo-tsu t'ung-chi* 37, *T* 2035.49.352a4–5; *Mo-ho chih-kuan* 1a, *T* 1911.46.1b29–c1. These and other sources are cited at Liebenthal (pp. 375–76, 375 n. 3, and 382). For the import of this gāthā, see Ko Ikchin, pp. 246–47. In his exegesis, Wŏnhyo clarifies that the first half of the gāthā refers to all dharmas as explained from the standpoint of conventional truth; it reconciles the mundane with the absolute. The second half refers to the dharma of calm extinction (i.e., nirvāṇa) as explained from the standpoint of absolute truth; it reconciles the absolute with the mundane. *KSGR* 3, pp. 996c27–997a19.

Chapter Seven

# The Tathāgatagarbha

[371c10]  At that time, the Elder Pŏmhaeng arose from the original limit
(*ponje*)[104] and addressed the Buddha: "Lord! "The object that is produced is
not extinguished; the object that is extinguished is not produced. In this
wise, the object that is thus is in fact the bodhi of the buddhas. The nature
of bodhi is in fact free from discrimination. The nondiscriminative knowledge cannot be fathomed by discrimination. This characteristic of being unfathomable is just the extinction of discrimination.[105] In this wise, both objects and characteristics are inconceivable, and in this inconceivability there
is accordingly no discrimination.

"Lord! All the classifications of dharmas are immeasurable and limitless,
but that limitless characteristic of dharmas has but one real meaning.[106] [The
many doctrinal teachings] have but a single nature. How can that be?"

The Buddha replied, "Elder! It is inconceivable! I preach all the dharmas
because of my concern for those who are deluded, and because it is an expedient way. All the characteristics of dharmas are but the knowledge of this
one real meaning. Why it this? It is just like four gates that open upon a
single city: one may return to that single city through any of those four
gates. And just as the populace [of that city] may freely enter [through any
gate], just so is it the same with the tastes of the myriad types of dharmas
[all of which merge in the single taste]."[107]

---

   [104] "Listening to the Buddha's words is in fact accessing the original limit." *KSGR* 3, p.
996b15–16.

   [105] This is the earliest quoted portion of *VS*; see Fa-tsang's *Hua-yen ching i-hai po-men*, *T*
1875.45.628c21–22, and discussion in part 1, chapter 4.

   [106] A problematic passage. I follow Wŏnhyo in ignoring the logograph "nature" (*sŏng*) in
my rendering. *KSGR* 3, 996b27–c2.

   [107] This simile is used also in Wŏnhyo's *Pŏmmang-kyŏng posal kyebon sagi* (Personal notes to
the "Bodhisattva Vinaya" text of the *Fan-wang ching*) 1, *HTC* 95.108b7–15.

The Elder Pŏmhaeng remarked, "If this is indeed how dharmas are, I should be able to imbibe each and every taste while lingering in that single taste."

The Buddha replied, "So it is, so it is! Why is this? The true meaning of the single taste—its taste[108] can be compared to that of the one ocean: there is none of the myriad of streams that does not flow into it. Elder! The tastes of all the dharmas are just like those streams: while their names and classifications may differ, that water is indistinguishable.[109] And once [those streams] have flowed into the ocean, [that seawater] then[110] absorbs all those streams.[111] [In the same way,] if one lingers in the single taste, then all tastes are imbibed."

The Elder Pŏmhaeng asked, "If all dharmas are of a single taste, then how is it that there are [separate] paths for the three vehicles? Does their knowledge have distinctions?"

The Buddha replied, "Elder! It is like the [Ch'ang]-chiang [Yangtze River], the [Hwang-]ho [Yellow River], the Huai [River], and the ocean: because there are variations in their size, disparities in their depth, and differences in their names, when water is in the [Ch'ang-]chiang it is called Chiang water, when it is in the Huai it is called Huai water, and when it is in the Ho it is called Ho water. But once all these types [of water] enter the ocean, they are just called seawater.[112] The dharmas [i.e., the three vehicles] are also the same: once they all abide in true thusness they are just called    [372a]    the path to buddhahood.

"Elder! One who dwells in the one path to buddhahood[113] then comprehends three practices."

The Elder Pŏmhaeng asked, "What are those three practices?"

---

[108] "Taste" is missing in the Koryŏ II/Taishō edition (*VS*, p. 371c22) and is added from Wŏnhyo's recension; *KSGR* 3, p. 996c22.

[109] See part 1, chapter 3, for discussion of this common metaphor, which is often used to explain the soteriological purport of the teachings of Buddhism.

[110] Following the Koryŏ II/Taishō recension, which reads *chŭk* ("then") for Wŏnhyo's *chŭk* ("is in fact"); *KSGR* 3, p. 996c24, *VS*, p. 371c24; and passim throughout chapters 7 and 8.

[111] An allusion to this passage appears in *Platform Sūtra*: "It is like the great sea which gathers all the flowing streams, and merges together the small waters and large waters into one." *Liu-tsu t'an ching*, *T* 2007.48.340b18–19; Yampolsky, trans., p. 150.

[112] Compare *Udāna* 5.4: "Whatsoever great rivers there are—namely, Gaṅgā, Yamunā, Aciravatī, Sarabhū, Mahī—these, when they reach the mighty ocean, abandon their former names and lineage, and go henceforth by the name of just 'mighty ocean.' " Translation from F. L. Woodward, *The Minor Anthologies of the Pali Canon*, p. 64. The use of native geographical names in this passage is a strong piece of textual evidence suggesting the non-Indian origin of this scripture; see Mizuno, pp. 42–43; Liebenthal, p. 361.

[113] The first *bhūmi* on up. *KSGR* 3, p. 997a20.

The Buddha replied, "First is that practice that cleaves to phenomena. Second is the practice that cleaves to consciousness. Third is the practice that cleaves to thusness.[114] Elder! In this wise, the three practices subsume completely all approaches; there are no approaches to dharma that are not accessed thereby. One who accesses these practices does not produce the characteristic of voidness. And one who accesses [these practices] in this manner can be said to have accessed the tathāgata.[115] One who accesses the tathāgata accesses that access via nonaccess."

The Elder Pŏmhaeng asked, "This is inconceivable! Accessing the tathāgatagarbha has no access point; it is like a sprout that matures into a fruit. Through the power of the fundamental inspiration, that inspiration will bring about the recovery of the original [edge of reality].[116] In attaining that original edge of reality, how many kinds of knowledge would one have?"

The Buddha replied, "His knowledge would be unfathomable. But were we to explain it in brief, he would have four types of knowledge. What are the four? First is fixed knowledge: that is, [knowledge] that accords with thusness. Second is adaptable knowledge: that is, [knowledge] that expediently extirpates and destroys [the defilements]. Third is nirvāṇa knowledge: that is, [knowledge] that removes lightning[-like] sensory awareness.[117] Fourth is ultimate knowledge: that is, [knowledge] that accesses reality and perfects the path.[118]

---

[114] I reproduce the passage again with Wŏnhyo's glosses added: "The practice that cleaves to phenomena: (while relying on the four noble truths and the twelvefold chain of conditioned generation,) one cleaves to (the *bodhipakṣika-dharma*s) in accordance with phenomena (that are governed by cause and effect). The practice that cleaves to consciousness: all sentient beings are merely products of the one mind. They cleave to the practice (of the four means of conversion [*saṃgrahavastu*]: giving [*dāna*], kind words [*priyavadya*], helpfulness [*arthacaryā*], and cooperation [*samanārthatā*]) in accordance with (the principle that there is just) consciousness. The practice that cleaves to thusness: all dharmas are equal. One cleaves to the practice (of the six pāramitās) in accordance with the thusness (that is equal). To 'cleave' here means to absorb these practices in the mind; it does not mean to cling to the subject-object distinction." See *KSGR* 3, p. 997a22–26.

[115] Following Wŏnhyo's recension (*KSGR* 3, p. 997b1). Wŏnhyo glosses tathāgata here as the "sea of the tathāgatagarbha"; *KSGR* 3, p. 997b9.

[116] " 'Sprout' is a simile for the inspiration of original [enlightenment]. 'Fruit' is a simile for attaining that original [inspiration]." *KSGR* 3, p. 997b18.

[117] "Lightning" refers to the production and extinction of the five sensory consciousnesses, the speed of which is compared to the flash of lightning; *KSGR* 3, p. 997c7.

[118] Wŏnhyo correlates the first type of knowledge, fixed knowledge, with the equanimous wisdom (*samatājñāna*), the second of the four types of wisdoms recognized in the Yogācāra school. The second type, adaptable knowledge, is the wisdom of sublime observation (*pratyāvekṣaṇājñāna*). The third type, nirvāṇa knowledge, is the wisdom gained through the accom-

"Elder! In this wise, the operation of these four great matters has been explained by all the buddhas of antiquity as being a great bridge and a great ford. If you are to proselyte sentient beings, you should make use of these knowledges.

"Elder! The operation of these great functions involves, furthermore, three great matters. First, the internal [consciousnesses] and the external [sense realms] do not mutually infringe[119] on one another in the three samādhis [see *infra*]. Second, in the great matrix of meaning [see *infra*], the analytical suppression (*pratisaṃkhyānirodha*) occurs in accordance with the path.[120] Third, the wisdom and concentration that are thus are both inspired by compassion. In this wise, these three matters perfect bodhi. One who does not practice these matters will then be unable to flow into the sea of the four knowledges and will be subject to the whims of all the great *māras*.

"Elder! Until all of you in the congregation attain buddhahood, you ought constantly to cultivate and train, without even a temporary respite."

The Elder Pŏmhaeng asked, "What are the three samādhis?"

The Buddha replied, "The three samādhis are the samādhi of voidness (*śūnyasamādhi*), the samādhi of signlessness (*ānimittasamādhi*), and the samādhi of wishlessness (*apraṇihitasamādhi*).[121] These are the samādhis."

The Elder Pŏmhaeng asked, "What is the great matrix of meaning?"

The Buddha replied, " 'Great' means the four great elements. 'Meaning' means the aggregates (skandha), elements (*dhātu*), and sense-fields (*āyatana*), and other [lists, such as the twelvefold chain of conditioned origination]. 'Matrix' means the original consciousness. This is called the great matrix of meaning."

The Elder Pŏmhaeng said, "It is inconceivable! In this wise, the [three]

---

plishment of what was to be done (*kṛtyānusthānajñāna*). The fourth type, ultimate knowledge, is equated with great perfect mirror wisdom (*ādarśanajñāna*). *KSGR* 3, p. 997b2–c10.

[119] Lit., snatch away. Cf. the celebrated usage of this term by Lin-chi I-hsüan (d. 866) in his four approaches to practice (snatch away the man, but don't snatch away the objects; etc.); see *Lin-chi lu*, *T* 1985.47.497a.

[120] "One analyzes the four great elements and the three main dharma classifications [skandha, *dhātu*, and *āyatana*] according to the principle; this eradicates all signs and brings to an end the fundamental consciousness's seeds of conceptual proliferation (*prapañca*). The preceding [*sic*] three samādhis overcome the bonds that have manifested at present; this analytical wisdom destroys their seeds. Because of this, at the time that one perfects accordingly the four wisdoms, one can uproot the seeds and bring about the evolution of the eight consciousnesses [into the pure ninth consciousness]." *KSGR* 3, p. 998a4–8.

[121] These last two types of samādhis are transposed in the Wŏnhyo and K'ai-pao recensions; *VS*, p. 372a20 nn. 6, 7. For this common list, see *Mo-ho po-jo po-lo-mi ching* 24, *T* 223.8.394c26–27.

matters [that bring about the perfection of the four] knowledges inspire both oneself and others, transcend the lands of the three realms, do not linger in nirvāṇa, and access the bodhisattva path.

"These sorts of characteristics of dharmas are things that are subject to production and extinction, because they involve discrimination. If one stays far removed from discrimination, these dharmas ought not be subject to extinction."

Wishing to proclaim this idea, the Tathāgata then recited this gāthā:

Dharmas are produced by discrimination,
And in turn are extinguished due to discrimination,
Extinguish all dharmas that are subject to discrimination,
And those dharmas will be neither produced nor extinguished.

At that time, the Elder Pŏmhaeng heard the recitation of this gāthā and his mind was jubilant and elated. Wishing to proclaim its meaning, [372b] he recited gāthās:

All dharmas are originally calm and extinguished,
But this calm extinction is also unproduced.
All those dharmas that are subject to production and extinction,
Those dharmas are not unproduced.
Those [dharmas that are calm, extinct, and unproduced] are thence not
    associated with these [dharmas subject to production and extinction],
Because each is subject to either annihilationism or eternalism,[122]
This [dharma spoken by the Buddha] thence leaves behind all such dualities,
But also does not persist in lingering in oneness.
If it is said that dharmas are one,
This characteristic will be like a hairnet.[123]
It is like mistaking heat-waves for water,
This is because all [such conceptions] are false and deceptive.[124]
If you perceive the nonexistence of dharmas,
Those dharmas will be identical to voidness,

---

[122] Dharmas subject to production and extinction would be subject to annihilationism; calm-and-extinct dharmas would be subject to eternalism. *KSGR* 3, p. 998c24–27.

[123] For "hairnet" (*moryun*) as a metaphor for something "gossamery," viz., illusory, see *Ju Leng-ch'ieh ching* (*Laṅkāvatāra-sūtra*) 9, *T* 671.16.565c16; *Jen-wang ching* 1, *T* 246.8.839a23.

[124] The last two lines of this verse derive from *Laṅkāvatāra-sūtra*; see *Ju Leng-ch'ieh ching* 3, *T* 671.16.532b28; and cf. *Ta-sheng ju Leng-ch'ieh ching* 3, *T* 672.16.601c11; both noted (though the first citation is misprinted) at Liebenthal, pp. 367–68. Cf. also Suzuki's rendering of the Sanskrit in *Laṅkāvatāra Sūtra*, p. 83, v. 150.

Just like a blind man who mistakenly believes that the sun is nonexistent,
Your preaching of the dharma would be as [deceptive as] the [nonexistent]
    hair of a tortoise.
I have now heard the Buddha say,
Knowledge of the dharma is not [achieved through] dualistic views,
It also does not depend on remaining in between,
It therefore is grasped by not abiding anywhere.
The dharma spoken by the tathāgatas,
Derives completely from this nonabiding,
It is from that nonabiding place,
That I worship the tathāgatas.
Respectfully worshipping the characteristic of the tathāgatas—
That motionless wisdom which is equal to empty space,
At that place which is free from grasping [at the two extremes] and which
    does not exist [in between],
I respectfully worship their nonabiding bodies.
I, in all places,
Constantly see all the tathāgatas,
I wish only that all the tathāgatas,
Will explain the perpetual dharma to me.

At that time the Tathāgata made this statement: "All you good men! Listen well and I will explain for all of you the perpetual dharma.

"Oh son of good family! The perpetual dharma is not a perpetual dharma; it is neither the spoken nor written word; it is neither truth nor liberation. It is neither nonexistence nor the sense realms and remains completely apart from the extremes of deceptive [grasping] and annihilationism. But this dharma is also not impermanent, for it remains far apart from either eternalism or annihilationism. [At the moment of] cognition, the consciousnesses are permanent. The consciousnesses are perpetually calm and extinct; but that calm extinction is also calm and extinct.

"Oh son of good family! Since he [i.e., the adept from the first *bhūmi* onward] who knows that dharmas are calm and extinct need not make his mind calm and extinct, his mind remains constantly calm and extinct. The mind of one who attains calm extinction constantly contemplates [according to] truth. He knows that all mentality and materiality are nothing but the ignorant mind. The discriminations of the ignorant mind differentiate all the dharmas; [all the dharmas] are nothing apart from name and materiality. If in this wise one knows dharmas and does not pursue written and spoken language, the mind will think only of meaning and will not distinguish the self [as the thinker of that thought]. Knowing that the self is a hypothetical name is in fact the attainment of calm extinction. If one attains calm extinction, one then attains *anuttarasamyaksaṃbodhi*."

Once the Elder Pŏmhaeng had heard this speech, he recited gāthās:

> Names and characteristics, which are phenomena [created by]
>     discrimination,
> Together with dharmas—these are called the three.    [372c]
> True thusness and orthodox, sublime knowledge:
> Together with the [above] make five.[125]
> I now know that these dharmas,
> Are fettered by annihilationism and eternalism.
> Accessing the path of production and extinction,
> Is annihilationism, not eternalism.
> The dharma of voidness spoken by the Tathāgata,
> Remains far removed from annihilationism and eternalism,
> As there are no causes or conditions, [that dharma] is unproduced,
> And because it is unproduced, it is not extinguished.[126]
> Grasping at the existence of causes and conditions,
> Is like reaching for a flower in the sky,
> Or expecting a barren woman's child—
> Ultimately it is unascertainable.[127]
> Leaving behind all clinging to causes and conditions,
> One also does not follow anything else to extinction,
> Or assume the selfhood of the [threefold matrix of] meaning and the [four]
>     great [elements].
> Because of relying on thusness one attains reality.
> Therefore the dharma of true thusness,
> Is constantly autonomous and thus;
> All the myriads of dharmas,
> Are transformations of those [affective] consciousnesses which are not thus.
> That dharma which remains separate from consciousness is void,
> Hence it is explained from the standpoint of voidness.

[125] This verse also is adapted from *Laṅkāvatāra-sūtra*. See *Ju Leng-ch'ieh ching* 3, *T* 671.16.527c16–17; cf. *Ta-sheng ju Leng-ch'ieh ching* 2, *T* 672.16.598a6; all noted by Liebenthal, pp. 366–67. See also Suzuki, trans., p. 60, v. 134.

[126] Adapted from *Laṅkāvatāra-sūtra*; *Ju Leng-ch'ieh ching* 3, *T* 671.16.529b5–6, 530c8–9; noted by Liebenthal, p. 367. See Suzuki, trans., p. 68, v. 137, and p. 75, v. 140, though the Sanskrit differs radically.

[127] Adapted from *Laṅkāvatāra-sūtra*; see *Ju Leng-ch'ieh ching* 530c14–15; see Liebenthal, p. 367; Suzuki, trans., p. 75, v. 143.

One who extinguishes all those dharmas which are subject to production
    and extinction,
And thence dwells in nirvāṇa,
He will be snatched away by the great compassion [of the buddhas],
So that he will not linger in the extinction of nirvāṇa.
Transmuting (*parivṛtti*) both the subject and object of clinging [mind and
    sensory objects],
He accesses the tathāgatagarbha.

At that time the great assembly heard this meaning and all attained right
vocation (*samyagājīva*) and accessed the tathāgata's [wisdom] and the sea of
the tathāgatagarbha.

# Chapter Eight

# Dhāraṇī (Codes)

[372c18]   At that time, Chijang (Earth-store; Kṣitigarbha) Bodhisattva arose from amidst the congregation and came before the Buddha.[128] Joining his palms together and genuflecting in foreign fashion, he addressed the Buddha: "Lord! I observe that the congregation entertains doubts that have yet to be resolved. The Tathāgata is now about to remove those doubts. I will now ask questions on behalf of this congregation concerning the doubts that remain; I beg that the Tathāgata, out of his friendliness and compassion, will take pity on us and grant this request."

The Buddha replied, "Bodhisattva-*mahāsattva*! That you are interested in rescuing sentient beings shows that your great compassion and empathy is inconceivable. You should question me extensively, and I will answer you."

Chijang Bodhisattva asked, "How is it that all dharmas are not conditionally produced?"

Wishing to proclaim this meaning, the Tathāgata then recited a gāthā:

If dharmas are produced by conditions,
Then no dharmas could exist apart from conditions.
How is it that conditions can produce dharmas,
When the dharma-nature is nonexistent?[129]

---

[128] "In [this chapter] are resolved all the doubts remaining from the previous chapters. It encodes (*dhārayati*) the important meanings, without forgetting them; this is why it gets the name 'Dhāraṇī.' Moreover, because Chijang Bodhisattva had already attained the dhāraṇī of the meaning of language (*munŭi t'arani*), he thoroughly retained the meaning of all the passages in the [preceding] chapters and remembered the points on which the congregation had doubts. Next, he asks questions in order to resolve well all those doubts. Hence, because he was able to ask these questions, this chapter is entitled 'Dhāraṇī.' " *KSGR* 3, p. 1001a20–21.

[129] "This exchange is intended to resolve doubts remaining from the 'Tathāgatagarbha' chapter. It was said there [*VS*, chap. 7, at n. 126], 'As there are no causes and conditions, [that dharma] is unproduced,/ And because it is unproduced, it is not extinguished.' In this passage

At that time, Chijang Bodhisattva asked, "If dharmas are unproduced, then how is it that in your dharma-talks you say that dharmas are produced by the mind?"

Thereupon, the Lord recited a gāthā:    [373a]

Dharmas that are produced by the mind,
Those dharmas cling to subject and object,
They are like sky-flowers in a drunkard's eyes,
Those dharmas are just-so and not otherwise.

At that time, Chijang Bodhisattva remarked, "If this is what dharmas are like, then those dharmas would have no analogues[130] [and they would be like thusness]. Dharmas that have no analogues—those dharmas ought to be generated spontaneously [without causes]."

Thereupon the Lord recited a gāthā:

Dharmas are originally free from both existence and nonexistence,
So too is this the case for self and others,
As [those dharmas] have neither beginning nor end,
Both accomplishment and failure are in fact meaningless [lit.,
    nonabiding].[131]

At that point Chijang Bodhisattva said, "The characteristics of each and every dharma are originally nirvāṇa. This is also the case with nirvāṇa and the characteristic of voidness. The dharma that remains once these types of dharmas are nonexistent ought to be thus."

The Buddha replied, "Once there are no such dharmas, that [remaining] dharma will be thus."

---

there is clinging to the existence of causes and conditions as being that which catalyzes production, but a doubt remains as to why the fruition [of that causal process] would not [also] be conditionally produced. Hence, [Chijang] uses this doubt in order to ask about conditioned generation." *KSGR* 3, p. 1001b16–19.

[130] "Analogue" (*tae*) here might also be rendered as "counterpart," or "complementarity." The sense is that the production of those dharmas would not be dependent on the existence of any other dharma—i.e., they would not be conditionally generated.

[131] These last two exchanges were intended to resolve doubts remaining from the "Voidness of the True Nature" chapter. It was said there (*VS*, chap. 6, after n. 89), "I preach the dharma because you sentient beings persist in needing explanations. I preach what cannot be spoken of. This is why I preach [the dharma]." The issue in this passage is that if the dharma spoken by the Buddha arises from his mind, as the "Voidness of the True Nature" chapter implied, then it would be impossible for that dharma to be unproduced, as Chijang remarks in his initial question. *KSGR* 3, p. 1001b25–28.

Chijang Bodhisattva said, "This is inconceivable. The characteristic of thusness is in this wise neither associated nor dissociated. Clinging to mentality and clinging to action are in fact both void and calm. The void and calm mind-dharma may not cling to both [saṃsāra and nirvāṇa] or neither, for it too is perforce calm and extinct."[132]

Thereupon, the Lord recited a gāthā:

All void and calm dharmas,
Those dharmas are calm but not void,
When the mind is not void,
That will bring about the nonexistence of the mind.[133]

At that point, Chijang Bodhisattva said, "This dharma [of the one mind] does not involve the three truths, for [the three truths of] materiality, voidness, and mind are also extinguished. When these [three] dharmas are originally extinguished, that dharma [of the one mind] ought also to be extinguished."

Thereupon the Lord recited a gāthā:

Dharmas are originally devoid of own-nature,
They arise from that [mind of original enlightenment],
While not found in this sort of [discriminative] loci,
They are involved in this wise with that [one enlightenment which is signless].[134]

[132] "Associated" means that the distinction between two types of thusness—the thusness of the original nirvāṇa, and the thusness that is an amalgamation of nirvāṇa and the characteristic of voidness—would not be true thusness. "Dissociated" refers to the fact that these two types are not void, for they are instead a single thusness. "Clinging to mentality" refers to nirvāṇa, for the calm and extinct mind may become an object of clinging. "Clinging to action" refers to saṃsāra, because it is the object to which all defiled action clings. *KSGR* 3, p. 1002a7–16. The first line of this passage is easier to construe if *kong* (associated) is read as instead a misprint for *i* (different), which has occurred previously in the text. This first line would then read: "The sign of thusness is in this wise neither different nor identical."

[133] The preceding exchanges were intended to resolve doubts remaining from the "Approaching the Edge of Reality" chapter. It was said there (*VS*, chap. 5, before n. 62), "Taeryŏk Bodhisattva said, . . . 'As far as the mental characteristics of sentient beings are concerned, those characteristics are identical to the tathāgata. Hence, the minds of sentient beings should also be free from any discrete sense realms.' The Buddha said, 'So it is. The minds of sentient beings are actually free from any discrete sense realms. Why is that? It is because the mind is originally pure, and the principle unsullied.' " The issue in this passage is that the person might confuse this original purity of the mind, which corresponds to thusness, with that heterodox nonexistence, which does not correspond to thusness. *KSGR* 3, p. 1001c21–27.

[134] This exchange has countered doubts raised in the "Inspiration of Original Enlightenment" chapter. As a passage there stated (*VS*, chap. 4, after n. 34), "Muju Bodhisattva said, 'If

At that time, Chijang Bodhisattva asked, "All dharmas are neither produced nor extinguished. So how is it that they are not all one?"
Thereupon, the Lord recited a gāthā:

An abiding place for dharmas does not exist,
Both characteristics and [dharma] classifications are void and therefore
    nonexistent.
These two—name and locution—together with dharmas,
These in fact involve grasping at subject and object.[135]

At that point, Chijang Bodhisattva remarked, "No characteristics of
dharmas linger on either of the two shores [of saṃsāra or nirvāṇa]; they also
do not linger in the current between them [i.e., they are not unitary]. Mind
and consciousness are similarly [free from both production and extinction];
so how is it that all the sense realms are produced by consciousness? If consciousness is the cause of that production, then consciousness too must be
produced by [something else]. So how then can consciousness be unproduced? If there is production then there must be a product."
Thereupon, the Lord recited a gāthā:

These two things—product and production,
These two are causality and the caused.
Both are originally [mere] names and are themselves nonexistent,
Clinging to their existence is an illusion, like a sky-flower.    [373b]
When consciousness has not yet been produced,
Objects then are not produced either.
When objects have not yet been produced,
Consciousness is then also extinguished.
These are both originally nonexistent,

---

all sense realms are void, all bodies are void, and all consciousnesses are void, then enlightenment too must be void.' The Buddha replied, 'Each and every enlightenment has a given nature
that is neither destroyed nor annihilated. They are neither void nor nonvoid, for they are free
from voidness or nonvoidness.' " The issue here is that if the one mind is also nonexistent and
therefore calm and extinct, why did it say in that previous passage that the enlightened mind is
neither destroyed nor annihilated, and thus continues to exist? *KSGR* 3, p. 1002b3–9.

[135] This exchange has been intended to counter doubts raised in the "Practice of Nonproduction" chapter. It was said there (*VS*, chap. 3, after n. 24), "These conditions are generated,
but there is no production; these conditions decay, but there is no extinction. . . . There is no
place where they abide, nor is there seen anything that abides, because their natures are fixed.
This fixed nature is neither unitary nor different." The issue here is if both form and mental
dharmas are unproduced and unextinguished, then they would just be identical, a conclusion
that would controvert the traditional distinction between *nāma* and *rūpa* and would illogically
imply that production and extinction were identical. *KSGR* 3, p. 1002b25–1002c3.

They neither exist nor do not exist.
Consciousness that is unproduced is also nonexistent,
So how is it that objects exist on account of it?[136]

At that time, Chijang Bodhisattva remarked, "In this wise, the character-istics of dharmas are void both internally [viz., the sense-consciousnesses] and externally [viz., sense objects]. These two groups—objects and sensory awareness—are originally calm and extinct. As the Tathāgata has explained, a dharma that in this wise is the real characteristic and true voidness would not be subject to origination."

The Buddha responded, "So it is. Dharmas that accord with reality are formless and nonabiding. They are neither originated nor do they prompt origination. They are neither meaning [i.e., the skandhas, *dhātus*, and *āya-tanas*] nor the great [elements]. They are the aggregation of the profound, meritorious qualities [inherent in] the dharma of the matrix of the one orig-inal [enlightenment]."[137]

Chijang Bodhisattva said, "It is inconceivable! It is inconceivable! The seventh [consciousness] and the five [sensory consciousnesses] are unpro-duced. The eighth and sixth [consciousnesses] are calm and extinct. The characteristic of the ninth [consciousness] is to be void and nonexistent. Ex-istence is void and nonexistent. Nonexistence is void and nonexistent. As the Lord has explained, dharmas and phenomena are both void. Accessing the voidness [gate to liberation], there are no longer any practices [that need to be cultivated], but one also does not neglect any actions [such as the six pāramitās]. [In the signless gate to liberation,] there are neither self nor ob-jects-of-self, neither subject nor object views. All the internal and external defilements are calm and still. Accordingly, [in the wishless gate to libera-tion,] wishes are also assuaged. In this wise, noumenal contemplation is the

---

[136] This exchange has been intended to counter doubts raised in the following passage in the "Signless Dharma" chapter (*VS*, chap. 2, before n. 16): " 'What is meant by "that characteristic of discriminative awareness, subject to production and extinction"?' The Buddha replied, 'The principle is free from either acceptance or rejection. If there were acceptance or rejection, then all kinds of thoughts would be produced. The thousands of conceptions and myriads of men-tations are marked by production and extinction.' The issue there is that if consciousness is the source of such things as acceptance and rejection, and thus produces the various types of thoughts, then it should be subject itself to production and extinction. So how then could it be said that it does not abide on either of the two shores of saṃsāra and nirvāṇa? But if the con-sciousnesses are neither produced nor extinguished, then how could it be said that they produce the sense realms?" *KSGR* 3, p. 1002c19–25.

[137] Wŏnhyo interprets the term "dharma of the matrix of the one original" as the " 'one original enlightenment,' because with that as the basis, it can catalyze the production of all formations (saṃskāra) and all meritorious qualities (guṇa)." *KSGR* 3, p. 1003a29–1003b2.

true thusness in which wisdom and concentration [are perfectly balanced]. The Lord constantly explains that, in this wise,[138] the dharma of voidness is an excellent medicine."

The Buddha replied, "So it is. Why is this? Because [voidness] is void. As this void-nature is unproduced, the mind [that accesses voidness] is perpetually unproduced. As this void-nature is not extinguished, the mind is perpetually unextinguished. As the void-nature is nonabiding, the mind is also nonabiding. As the void-nature is inactive (*muwi*), the mind is also inactive. Voidness is free from both egress and access, and leaves behind both gain and loss. The skandhas, elements, and sense realms, and so forth, are also all nonexistent. So too is this the case with the mind that accords [with voidness in not clinging to egress and access] and does not grasp [at the skandhas, etc.]. Bodhisattva! I have discussed the various aspects of voidness in order to destroy [the grasping at] all [types of] existence."

Chijang Bodhisattva said, "Lord! Would that meditator be considered wise who knows that existence is unreal, like heat-waves that are [not] water, and that reality is not nonexistent, like the sovereignty of fire that is inherent [in wood]?"[139]

The Buddha replied, "So it is. Why is this? This person's true contemplation contemplates the calm extinction of the one [mind]. Signs and signlessness are grasped in voidness as being equal, and since voidness is cultivated [and one therefore accords with the buddha-mind], one does not lose one's vision of the buddhas. Because one sees the buddhas, one does not flow along with the three currents.

"In the Mahāyāna, the path of the three liberations [here, voidness, signlessness, wishlessness] has but a single essence and is devoid of nature. Because it is devoid of nature, it is void; because it is void, it is signless; because

---

[138] Following Wŏnhyo's gloss; *KSGR* 3, p. 1003c10.

[139] For this simile, see *Kuang Po-lun pen*, *T* 1570.31.185b21–26. The translation follows Wŏnhyo's interpretation. Wŏnhyo comments,

"Like the sovereignty of fire that is inherent [in wood]": this is to say, it is just like in wood is innate the nature of the great element of fire, but if one splits [that wood] in order to find that [fire] one will never discover its characteristic of heat. And yet, that nature of fire is really not nonexistent in wood, because if one searches for it using friction [lit., drilling] that fire will perforce appear. The one mind is also the same. One cannot find the nature of the mind by analyzing [lit., splitting] all its characteristics. And yet in reality it cannot be nonexistent in all dharmas, because if the mind cultivates the path in order to find it, the one mind will appear. In this wise, as far as the nature of fire is concerned, its characteristic [of heat] is hidden but its power is great, just like the sovereign of a kingdom; hence, it is called "sovereign."

*KSGR* 3, p. 1004a17–22.

it is signless, it is wishless; because it is wishless, it seeks nothing; because it seeks nothing, it is free from anticipation. Due to this action, the mind is purified. Because the mind is purified, one sees the buddhas. Because one sees the buddhas, one then will be reborn in the Pure Land.

"Bodhisattva! Diligently cultivate the three transformations[140] with regard to this profound dharma. Wisdom and concentration will then be completely perfected, and one will immediately transcend the three realms of existence."

Chijang Bodhisattva asked, "As the Tathāgata has said, nonproduction and nonextinction are impermanent, so extinguish this production and extinction. Once production and extinction have been extinguished, [373c] this calm extinction will be permanent. Because it is permanent, it cannot be excised. That dharma which cannot be excised remains far removed from all the active and motionless dharmas of the three realms of existence. [One should avoid] the conditioned dharmas as if avoiding a fiery pit.

"Through relying on what dharma may one admonish oneself and access that one approach [to dharma]?"[141]

The Buddha replied, "Admonish your mind concerning the three great matters; access this practice via the three great truths."

Chijang Bodhisattva asked, "How may one admonish one's mind in regard to these three matters? How may one access the one practice via the three truths?"

The Buddha replied, "As for the three great matters: the first is cause; the second is fruition; the third is consciousness. These three matters are, in this wise, void and nonexistent from their inception; they are not self [for their natures are void] but instead are true self [for they have no limiting identity]. So how is it that the taint of craving (*tṛṣṇā*) arises concerning them? Contem-

---

[140] "The three transformations" (*saṃhwa*) are glossed by Wŏnhyo as the three voidnesses: i.e., the voidness of the characteristic of voidness; the voidness of voidness itself; and the voidness of that which is void. *KSGR* 3, p. 1004b22–25. There is also a proselytic listing: (1) past transformation: previous preachings of the Mahāyāna; (2) adaptable transformation: the bodhisattva entering into saṃsāra in order to rescue beings from their plight; (3) ultimate transformation: prompting those beings to attain complete buddhahood. See *Fa-hua hsüan lun* 7, *T* 1720.34.417a; *Fa-hua i-shu* 7, *T* 1721.34.546a.

[141] This question opens another exchange, which is intended to resolve a second doubt remaining from the "Tathāgatagarbha" chapter. As a passage in that chapter said (*VS*, chap. 7, after n. 124), "[At the moment of] cognition, the consciousnesses are permanent. The consciousnesses are perpetually calm and extinct; but that calm extinction is also calm and extinct." This state would seem so rarified to the average person, however, that he might think that there were no means available for him to cultivate his mind and realize calm extinction. *KSGR* 3, p. 1004c3–7.

plate these three matters as being bound[142] by the bonds [*grantha*; of covet-ousness, ill-will, attachment to rules and rituals, and dogmatic fanaticism] and being aimlessly adrift in the sea of suffering. It is because of such matters that one constantly admonishes oneself.

"As for the three truths: the first truth is that the path to bodhi is equal [in its accessibility, for the bodhi-nature is inherent in all sentient beings], not unequal. The second truth is that great enlightenment is gained through the orthodox knowledge [of the Buddhists], not through the perverse knowledge [of the non-Buddhists]. The third truth is that truth is accessed by not differentiating the practices of wisdom and concentration; truth is not accessed by practicing them randomly. The person who cultivates the path to buddhahood by means of these three truths cannot but attain right en-lightenment concerning these dharmas [of the three truths]. Gaining the knowledge of right enlightenment, one spreads immense friendliness, in-spires both oneself and others, and achieves the bodhi of the buddhas."

Chijang Bodhisattva asked, "Lord! Such a dharma would in fact be free from causes and conditions. If a dharma is unconditioned, there then would be no causes that are generated. So how can such a motionless dharma prompt access to the tathāgata[garbha]?[143]

Wishing to proclaim this meaning, the Tathāgata then recited these gāthās:

The characteristics of all dharmas,
Their natures are void, nonexistent, and motionless.
These dharmas are not produced in the present,
But they are not produced in another time [past and future] either.[144]
Dharmas are neither moving nor motionless,
As their natures are void, they are calm and extinct,

[142] Following the Koryŏ II/Taishō reading of *pak* ("to bind"). The Wŏnhyo and K'ai-pao recensions wrongly dittograph the following character *p'yo* ("to whirl"; "to be adrift"); *VS*, p. 373c8 n. 14.

[143] This question initiates an additional exchange concerning a doubt remaining from the "Tathāgatagarbha" chapter. The concluding verse in that chapter said (*VS*, chap. 7, after n. 127), "Transmuting both the subject and object of clinging,/ He accesses the tathāgatagar-bha." It was commonly assumed, however, that realization of the tathāgatagarbha—represent-ing the "equal truth" just discussed, in which the bodhi-nature is inherent in all sentient beings—was not brought about through specific causes and conditions, such as spiritual prac-tice. Hence, how then could this passage imply that there was some explicit soteriological means by which the "subject and object of clinging" were transmutted so that access to the tathāgatagarbha could occur? *KSGR* 3, p. 1005b9–13.

[144] Adapted from *Mūlamadhyamakakārikā* (vii.28); see *Chung-lun* 2, *T* 1564.30.11c11–12. Noted in Liebenthal, p. 366.

Only at the time when their natures are void, calm, and extinct,
Will those dharmas then appear.
As they leave behind all characteristics, they abide calmly,
And as they abide calmly, they are unconditioned.
All these conditionally produced dharmas,
Those dharmas are not produced by conditions.
Because there is no production or extinction due to causes and conditions,
The natures of production and extinction are void and calm.
The nature of conditions involves both the subject and object conditions,[145]
These conditions arise from the original condition.
Hence the production of dharmas is not due to conditions,
This is also the case with the nonproduction of conditions.
Dharmas that are produced according to causes and conditions,
Those dharmas [in turn function as] causes and conditions.
[Those dharmas which] are characterized by being produced and
     extinguished according to causes and conditions,
Those are in fact free from production and extinction.
Those characteristics which are thus, true, and real,
Originally make no appearance,    [374a]
All dharmas in the present moment,
Produce their appearances themselves.
Accordingly that consummately pure origin,
Is originally not caused by the multitude of forces,
Precisely when this is subsequently obtained,[146]
One [re]attains the original attainment.[147]

At that time, Chijang heard what the Buddha said and his mind-ground
became enraptured. There was then no one in the congregation who enter-
tained any further doubts. Once [Chijang] had known all their minds, he
recited gāthās:

I knew the doubts in all their minds,
And accordingly questioned cordially and sincerely,
Through his virtue of great friendliness, the Tathāgata
Has analyzed [these doubts] and left none remaining.
Everyone in these two congregations,

---

[145] Wŏnhyo glosses these as the *adhipatipratyaya* (predominant condition) and *ālambanaprat-yaya* (cooperative condition), respectively; *KSGR* 3, p. 1005c.

[146] Glossed by Wŏnhyo as "after [the completion of] the mārga, or what was earlier briefly referred to as 'the time when these are calmed and extinguished.' " *KSGR* 3, p. 1006a16–17.

[147] Wŏnhyo interprets this as meaning that the actualization of enlightenment leads to the re-"attainment" of the original enlightenment. *KSGR* 3, p. 1006a18–20.

Has clearly understood everything.
Through my understanding, I now
Proselyte universally all sentient beings.
Just as the great friendliness of the Buddha,
Does not allow him to abandon his great vow,
Hence at that only-child stage,
[The bodhisattva continues to] linger in defilement.[148]

At that time, the Tathāgata addressed the congregation: "This bodhi-sattva is inconceivable! He constantly relieves sentient beings from their suf-fering through his great friendliness. If there is a sentient being who keeps the dharma [taught in] this sūtra or keeps this bodhisattva's name, he then will not fall into the evil destinies, and all obstructions and difficulties will completely vanish. If there are sentient beings who have no extraneous thoughts remaining, but reflect exclusively on the dharma of this sūtra and cultivate and train in it, then this bodhisattva will constantly manifest a transformation body and speak the dharma to them. He will guard and pro-tect those persons, never abandon them even for a moment, and prompt them quickly to attain *anuttarasamyaksaṃbodhi*.

"All of you bodhisattvas! When you proselyte sentient beings, you should encourage all of them to cultivate and train in this decisive, definitive meaning (*nitārtha*) of the Mahāyāna."

## Epilogue

At that time, Ānanda arose from his seat and, coming forward, addressed the Buddha: "As the Tathāgata has said, the Mahāyāna's aggregate of merits is certain to eradicate the fetters. The inspiration of the enlightenment that is unproduced is inconceivable. What sūtra title should such a teaching be given? How much merit will be forthcoming from receiving and keeping such a sūtra? I beg the Buddha to explain this for us, out of his friendliness and compassion."

[148] "Only-child stage" (*ilcha chi*) is a term that derives from the *Nirvāṇa Sūtra*; see the de-scription at *Ta-pan-nieh-p'an ching* 16, *T* 374.12.458c–459a, upon which Wŏnhyo seems to draw in his explanation: " 'Only-child stage' (*ilcha chi*) is the first *bhūmi* and above. [There,] one has already realized that all sentient beings are equal, and one regards all sentient beings as if they were one's own only child. . . . 'Linger in defilement': Although a bodhisattva gains the equal-ity of all dharmas, by means of his power of expedients, he does not abandon defilements (*kleśa*). This is because, if one were to abandon all defilements and proclivities (*anuśaya*) and thence access nirvāṇa, this would controvert one's original vow." *KSGR* 3, p. 1006a29–1006b4.

The Buddha replied, "Oh son of good family! The name of this sūtra is inconceivable. It has been protected by all the buddhas of antiquity; it is able to catalyze access into the sea of the tathāgatas' all-embracing knowledge. If there is a sentient being who keeps this sūtra, then he will have nothing more to seek in any other sūtras. The dharma [teaching] of this scripture encodes all dharmas and includes the essentials of all sūtras. It is the unifying thread (*kyejong*) of the dharmas of all these sūtras. As far as the title of this sūtra is concerned, it is named *Sŏp taesŭng kyŏng* (*Mahāyānasaṃgraha-sūtra*; Compendium of Mahāyāna scripture); *Kŭmgang sammae* (*Vajrasamādhi*), and *Muryang-ŭi chong* (Source of immeasurable doctrine). If there is a person who receives and keeps this scripture,    [374b]    he will be called one who welcomes and supports [lit., receives and keeps] hundreds of thousands of buddhas. Such meritorious qualities may be compared to the limitlessness of space, which is inconceivable. It is this sūtra alone with which I now charge you."

Ānanda asked, "What sort of person, with what sort of mental attitude, would receive and keep this scripture?"

The Buddha replied, "Oh son of good family! The mind of the person who receives and keeps this scripture is free from gain or loss and constantly cultivates the religious life (*brahmacaryā*). If he constantly gladdens his mind and calms its conceptual proliferation (*prapañca*), then even amidst the crowded masses, his mind will remain ever concentrated; even if he dwells in the household life, he will not grasp at the three realms of existence.

"There are five types of merits accruing from this person's appearance in the world. First, he is honored by the congregation. Second, he will not die an untimely death. Third, he will eruditely rebut perverse opinions. Fourth, he will joyfully ferry across sentient beings. Fifth, he will be able to access the sanctified path. It is this sort of person who will receive and keep this scripture."

Ānanda asked, "Will one who ferries across all sentient beings be as worthy of receiving offerings as that person, or not?"

The Buddha replied, "Such a person is able to become a great field of merit for sentient beings. He constantly practices great knowledge, and displays both expedients and truth. He receives all manner of offerings from the four saṃghas upon which one may depend,[149] including even their

---

[149] A listing that derives from *Nirvāṇa Sūtra*. (1) The educated *pṛthagjana* (ordinary person) who keeps precepts and preaches dharma, but still retains the defiled nature; he has not yet reached the first *bhūmi*. (2) The *srotaāpanna* (streamwinner) and *sakṛdāgāmin* (once-returner); these are bodhisattvas who have reached the first *bhūmi* and received prediction of their future buddhahood, but have not yet reached the second or third *bhūmi*. (3) The *anāgāmin* (nonre-

heads, eyes, marrow, and gray matter. So how could he not but receive clothes and provisions? Oh son of good family! Such a person is your spiritual mentor, your bridge; how could an ordinary person not but worship him?"

Ānanda asked, "If, at that person's place, one receives and keeps this sūtra and worships that person, how much merit will one accrue?"

The Buddha answered, "If, furthermore, there is a person who gives a city-full of gold and silver, it would not measure up to the inconceivable amount [of merit] forthcoming from receiving and keeping one four-line gāthā of this scripture at that person's place, or from worshipping that person. It is inconceivable![150]

"Oh son of good family! The mind of a person who encourages all sentient beings to keep this sūtra will be constantly concentrated; he will never forget his original mind. If one forgets his original mind he then must repent. This practice (dharma) of repentance produces coolness (śītībhūta)."

Ānanda asked, "If one repents, don't previous evil deeds recede into the past?"

The Buddha replied, "So it is. It is like bringing a bright lamp into a dark room: that darkness instantly vanishes. Oh son of good family! This is not to speak only of repenting from previous [evil deeds]: indeed all evil deeds can be said to recede into the past."

Ānanda asked, "What is meant by 'repentance'?"

The Buddha replied, "By relying on the teachings of this sūtra, one accesses the true and real contemplation; as soon as one accesses that contemplation, all evil deeds will completely vanish. Leaving behind all evil destinies, one will be reborn in the Pure Land, where one will quickly achieve *anuttarasamyaksaṃbodhi*."

When the Buddha had finished preaching this sūtra, Ānanda, the bodhisattvas, and the great fourfold congregation were all enraptured and elated, and their minds achieved the certitude [that they would attain enlightenment]. Worshipping the Buddha's feet with their foreheads, they were enraptured and elated, and practiced [his teaching] respectfully.

---

turner), who has received this prediction and is destined soon to attain *anuttarasamyaksaṃbodhi*. (4) The arhat, who has achieved the tenth *bhūmi*. See *Ta-pan-nieh-p'an ching* 6, *T* 375.12.637a–c; *Ta-pan-ni-huan ching* 4, *T* 376.12.875c–876b.

[150] Added following the Koryŏ II/Taishō recension; *VS*, p. 374b17. This line is missing in Wŏnhyo; *KSGR* 3, p. 1007b12.

# GLOSSARY OF CHINESE LOGOGRAPHS

Ado *hwasang* 阿道和尙
*ammara* 菴摩羅
Amnyang-kun 押梁國
*a-mo-lo* 阿摩羅
*an-chu* 安住
*an-hsin* 安心
*an-mo-lo* 菴摩羅
An Shih-kao 安世高
Ansim-sa 安心寺
Chajang 慈藏
Chakchegŏn 作帝建
*ch'an* 禪
Ch'ang-an 長安
Changsan 章山
Chan-jan 湛然
*Ch'an-men ching* 禪門經
*chaŭn purhyŏn* 自隱不現
*ch'e* 體
Ch'egwan 諦觀
*ch'eng-fa hsing* 稱法行
Ch'eng-kuan 澄觀
*chen-ju* 眞如
*chen-shih fa* 眞實法
*chi* 知
Chiang-nan 江南
Chidŏk 智德
*chien-chiao* 漸教
*chigwan* 止觀
Chih-chou 智周
Chih-i 智顗
*chih-kuan* 止觀
Chih-sheng 智昇

Chih-yen    智儼

*ch'im*    斟

*chi-mieh jen*    寂滅忍

Ching-chüeh    淨覺

Ching-chung    淨衆

Ching-t'u    淨土

Ching-ying Hui-yüan    淨影慧遠

Ch'ing-yüan Hsing-ssu    青原行思

Chinhŭng (king)    眞興

*chin-kang-pi ting san-mei*    金剛壁定三昧

*Chin-kang san-mei ching*    金剛三昧經

*Chin-kang shang-wei ching*    金剛上昧經

Chinul    知訥

*chinyŏ*    眞如

Chisŏn Tohŏn    智詵道憲

Chi-tsang    吉藏

Ch'oe Ch'iwŏn    崔致遠

Ch'ogae    初開

*chŏlp'il*    絕筆

*ch'ŏn/ch'uan*    喘

*ch'ongji*    總持

Chŏngt'o    淨土

*chonsim*    存心

*chonsin*    存神

*chon/tsun*    存

*chu* (abiding)    住

*chüan*    卷

*ch'uan*    喘

Ch'uan-ao *ta-shih*    傳澳大師

*Ch'uan fa-pao chi*    傳法寶記

*Chuang-tzu*    莊子

*chüan-shih*    轉識

Chu-chen    誅震

*chüeh-ch'a*    覺察

Chüeh-fan Hui-hung    覺範慧洪

*chüeh-kuan*    覺觀

*Chüeh-kuan lun*    絕觀論

*ch'üeh-pen*    闕本

Chuhaeng-sa    住行寺

*chŭk* (is in fact) 即
*chŭk* (then) 則
Chunbŏm 遵範
*Ch'un-ch'iu* 春秋
*chung* 中
*chung-shu* 忠恕
Enchō 圓超
Ennin 圓仁
*Erh-ju ssu-hsing lun* 二入四行論
Fa-ching 法經
Fa-ch'ung 法沖
Fa-hsiang 法相
Fa-ju 法如
Fa-jung 法融
*fan* 返
*fan-chao* 返照
*fan-ching ta-teh* 翻經大德
Fan-hsing p'in 梵行品
*fan-yüan k'an* 返源看
Fa-shang 法上
Fa-tsang 法藏
*Fa-wang ching* 法王經
Fa-yen 法眼
*fa-yün ti* 法雲地
Fei Ch'ang-fang 費長房
*fo chi-shih hsin* 佛即是心
*Fo-hsing lun* 佛性論
Fu Chien 符堅
Fu Hsi 傅翕
Fu *ta-shih* 傅大師
*Haedong ko Sinhaeng sŏnsa chi pi* 海東故信行禪師之碑
*Haengjang* 行狀
Haengmyŏng-sa 行名寺
*haengnip/hsing-ju* 行入
Haet'al 解脫
*hoegwang panjo/hui-kuang fan-chao* 迴光返照
*hoesin/hui-shen* 廻神
Hogŏ 踋踞
*hoguk pulgyo* 護國佛教

*hogwe*  胡(蹴)跪

*ho-ho*  和合

Hsiang-fa  像法

*hsien-ch'ien ti*  現前地

*hsin*  信

*hsin-an*  心安

*hsing*  行

*hsing-ju*  行入

*hsin-hsiang*  心相

*hsin pu-ch'i*  心不起

*Hsin-wang ching*  心王經

*Hsin-wang p'u-sa shuo t'ou-t'o ching*  心王菩薩說投陀經

*Hsiu-hsin yao-lun*  修心要論

Hsüan-tsang  玄奘

Hsüan-tse  玄賾

Hsüan-tsung (emperor)  玄宗

*hsün*  旬

Hua-yen  華嚴

*Hua-yen chin-kuan ch'ao*  華嚴錦冠鈔

Hui-chiao  慧皎

Hui-k'o  慧可

Hui-kuan  慧觀

*hǔimang*  希望

Hui-neng  慧能

Hui-ssu  慧思

Hŭiyang-san  曦陽山

Hu-kuo p'in  護國品

Hung-chou  洪州

Hung-jen  弘忍

*hwadu/hua-t'ou*  話頭

*hwangnyong*  黃龍

Hwangnyong-sa  黃龍寺

Hwaŏm  華嚴

*Hwaŏm chongyo*  華嚴宗要

*Hwaŏmgyŏng chongyo*  華嚴經宗要

*Hwaŏmgyŏng-so*  華嚴經疏

*hwarang*  花郎

*Hyangjŏn*  鄉傳

Hyeŭn  惠隱

Hyet'ong   惠通
Hyoso   孝昭(王)
*i* (different)   異
Ich'adon   異次頓
*i-chieh*   義解
*i-ching* (anomalous sūtras)   異經
*i-ch'u*   異出
*iip/erh-ju*   二入
*iip/li-ju*   理入
*il*   一
*ilcha chi*   一子地
*ilch'e*   一切
*i/li* (inspiration)   利
*Ilmi chinsil musang musaeng kyŏlchŏng silche pon'gangnihaeng*
    一味真實無相無生決定實際本覺利行
*ilmi kwanhaeng/i-wei kuan-hsing*   一味觀行
*il-pŏpkye*   一法界
Imok   璃目
*in* (acceptance)   忍
*Inwang-kyŏng*   仁王經
*ip/ju*   入
Iryŏn   一然
*Jen-wang ching*   仁王經
*ju cheng-ting wei*   入正定位
*ju-kuan*   入觀
Ju-lai kuang-ming-chüeh p'in   如來光明覺品
*ju nieh-p'an*   入涅槃
*ju-tao*   入道
*Ju-tao an-hsin yao-fang-pien fa-men*   入道安心要方便法門
*ju-ting*   入定
*Ju-tsang lu*   入藏錄
*kae*   開
Kaesŏng   開城
*kagyong/chüeh-yung*   覺用
*kahaeng-chi*   加行智
*kail*   可一
Kaji-san   迦智山
*kakch'al*   覺察
*kakkwan*   覺觀

Kaksŭng (Enlightenment Vehicle)  覺乘
Kaksŭng (Horn Rider)  角乘
*k'an*  看
*k'an-hsin*  看心
*kanhwa/k'an-hua*  看話
Kanhye-chi  乾慧地
*Kegon engi emaki*  華嚴緣起繪卷
*ki* (to activate)  起
Kim Hŏnjŏng  金獻貞
Kim *hwasang*  金和尙
Kim Pusik  金富軾
Kim Wŏn  金遠
*kŭmgang sammae/chin-kang san-mei*  金剛三昧
*Kŭmgang sammaegyŏng-chu*  金剛三昧經注
*Kŭmgang sammaegyŏng-ron*  金剛三昧經論
*Kŭmgang sammae-kyŏng*  金剛三昧經
Koguryŏ  高句麗
*kong* (associated)  共
*kong* (cavern)  孔
*kongan/kung-an*  公案
*Kongōzammaikyōgi*  金剛三昧經記
*Kongōzammaikyō ronso*  金剛三昧經論疏
*Kongōzammaikyō shiji*  金剛三昧經指事
*Kongōzammaikyō shiki*  金剛三昧經私記
Koryŏ  高麗
*Kosŏn-sa Sŏdang hwasang t'appi*  高仙寺誓幢和上塔碑
*kuan-hsin*  觀心
*Kuan-hsin lun*  觀心論
K'uei-chi  窺基
*ku-i-ching*  古異經
Kusan Sŏnmun  九山禪門
*kwanhaeng/kuan-hsing*  觀行
*kwŏn*  卷
*kyejong*  繫宗
*kyŏlchŏng sŏng*  決定性
Kyŏngju  慶州
*kyŏnsŏng/chien-hsing*  見性
Kyunyŏ  均如
*Leng-ch'ieh jen-fa chi*  楞伽人法記

Liang-chou   涼州
*Liang-t'u i-ching lu*   涼土異經錄
Liao-tung   遼東
*li-ju*   理入
*li-kou san-mei*   離垢三昧
Lin-chi   臨濟
Lin-chi I-hsüan   臨濟義玄
*liu-ju fa-men*   六入法門
*liu-li*   琉璃
*lüeh-shu*   略疏
*lun*   論
*malna [sik]*   末那識
*miao-chüeh*   妙覺
*miao-hsüeh ti*   妙學地
Mich'u (king)   味鄒
*mo-chao hsieh Ch'an*   默照邪禪
*moryun*   毛輪
Muae   無礙
*mubunbyŏl-chi/wu-fen-pieh chih*   無分別智
Muju   無住
Mukhoja   墨胡子
Munmu (king)   文武
*munŭi t'arani*   文義陀羅尼
*munyŏm/wu-nien*   無念
*Muryangŭi chong*   無量義宗
*Muryangŭijong-kyŏng*   無量義宗經
*Muryangsu chongyo*   無量壽宗要
Musang   無相
*musoŭi/wu-so-wei*   無所為
Muyŏm   無染
*myogak/miao-chüeh*   妙覺
Myŏngnang   明朗
Naksan-sa   洛山寺
Nam-ak   南岳
Nangji   朗智
*ning-jan*   凝然
Niu-t'ou   牛頭
*non*   論
Nulchi (king)   訥祇

*ŏnŏdodan*　言語道斷

Paekche　百濟

*pak* (to bind)　縛

*p'alsang pangp'yŏn*　八相方便

*p'an-chiao*　判教

*pan'gyo*　判教

*panjo/fan-chao*　返照

*P'an piryang-ron*　判比量論

*panwŏn kan*　返源看

*pao-i*　抱一

Pao-t'ang　保唐

*pao-yüan hsing*　報冤行

Pei-Liang　北涼

Pei tsung　北宗

*pen-chüeh*　本覺

*pi-kuan*　壁觀

*p'in*　品

*Po-jo-hsin ching chu-chieh*　般若心經注解

Pŏmhaeng　梵行

Pŏmil　梵日

Pŏmnang　法朗

*pon'gak/pen-chüeh*　本覺

Pongnim-san　鳳林山

*pon silche/pen shih-chi*　本實際

Pŏphŭng (king)　法興

*porri*　本利

Poyang　寶壤

P'u-chi　普寂

*pudong/pu-tung*　不動

Puk-san　北山

Pulchi　佛地

*punbyŏl/fen-pieh*　分別

*pun'gu ŏ paeksong*　分軀於百松

Punhwang-sa　芬皇寺

Pusŏk-sa　浮石寺

*pu-ssu-i san-mei*　不思義三昧

P'u-t'i ta-mo　菩提達摩

*pu-tung ti*　不動地

*p'yo* (to whirl; to be adrift)　飄

*saengmyŏl*　生滅
Sagul-san　闍崛山
Saja-san　獅子山
*samhwa*　三化
*san-ching*　散經
San-i　三一
*san-mei ching*　三昧經
*san-mei-ching lei*　三昧經類
*san-tsang*　三藏
Seng-chao　僧肇
Seng-ts'an　僧璨
Seng-yu　僧祐
*shan-hui ti*　善慧地
Shan-tung　山東
Shan-wu-wei　善無畏
She-lun　攝論
*sheng-mieh*　生滅
Shen-hsiu　神秀
Shen-hui　神會
*shen-i*　神異
*shih*　世
*shih-hsing*　十行
*Shih hui-hsiang p'in*　十廻向品
*shih-i p'ien-ju*　拾遺編入
*shih-shih wu-ai*　事事無礙
*shou-chen pao-i*　守真抱一
*shou-chih*　守直
*shou-chung*　守中
*shou-hsin*　守心
*shou-i*　守一
*shou-i ning-jan*　守一凝然
*shou-i pu-i*　守一不移
*shou-i teh-tu*　守一得度
*shou pen chen-hsin*　守本真心
*shou tzu pen-hsin*　守自本心
*shu*　蜀
Sidan　始旦
*sigak/shih-chüeh*　始覺
Silla　新羅

*Silla-kuk Muju Kaji-san Porim-sa si Pojo sŏnsa yŏngt'ap pimyŏng*
新羅國武州迦智山寶林寺謚普照禪師靈塔碑銘

*sim* 心

*Simmun hwajaeng-ron* 十門和諍論

Simwang/Hsin-wang 心王

Sinhaeng 信行/神行/愼行

*sini* 神異

Sinmun (king) 神文

*Sinp'yŏn chejong kyojang ch'ongnok* 新編諸宗教藏總錄

*siphaeng/shih-hsing* 十行

Sŏl Ch'ong 薛聰

Sŏndŏk 善德

*sŏng* 性

Sŏngdŏk 聖德

*sŏ* 庶

*so* 疏

Sŏngju-san 聖住山

*Sŏp taesŭng-kyŏng* 攝大乘經

*suil/shou-i* 守一

*sui-yüan hsing* 隨緣行

Suje 樹提

Sumi-san 須彌山

*sun* 旬

Sŭngdun 僧遁

Sŭngnang 僧郎

Sunji 順之

Suro 首羅

*susim/shou-hsin* 守心

Su-tsung 肅宗

*suyŏn/sui-yüan* 隨緣

Ta-chao Chih-k'ung 大照志空

*tae* (analogue) 待

*tae* (great) 大

Taean 大安

Taebŏmhaeng 大梵行

T'ai-i 太一

T'ai-shang Lao-chün 太上老君

T'ai-tsung 太宗

T'ang 唐

*T'ang Hsin-lo-kuo Huang-lung-ssu Yüan-hsiao chuan*
唐新羅國黃龍寺元曉傳

T'an-lin  曇林

*tan-pen shih-i*  單本失譯

Tao-an  道安

Tao-hsin  道信

Tao-hsüan  道宣

Tao-hsüan  道璿

Tao-sheng  道生

Tao-shih  道世

Tao-shun  道舜

*teng-chüeh*  等覺

*t'i*  體

T'ien-t'ai  天台

*t'ien-tsun*  天尊

Ti-lun  地論

*T'i-wei Po-li ching*  提謂波利經

*tŭnggak/teng-chüeh*  等覺

Toŭi  道義

T'ongdo-sa  通度寺

Tongni-san  桐裡山

*t'ong pulgyo*  通佛教

Toryun  道倫

Tsan-ning  贊寧

Ts'ao-tung  曹洞

*tso-ch'an*  坐禪

*Tsui-miao sheng-ting ching*  最妙勝定經

*tsun*  尊

*tsung*  宗

Tsung-mi  宗密

*tsun-san*  存三

Tu Cheng-lun  杜正倫

*tui-chih*  對治

Tullyun  遁倫

*tun-chiao*  頓教

Tung-shan fa-men  東山法門

Tung-shan *wu-sheng* fa-men  東山無生法門

*tun-wu*  頓悟

Tzu-hsüan  子璿

*tzu-yin pu-hsien*　自隱不現

*ŭi* (idea)　意

*ŭi* (object)　義

Ŭich'ŏn　義天

*ŭihae*　義解

Ŭisang　義湘

*ŭisik*　意識

*ŭngju kakkwan*　凝住覺觀

*ŭn i purhyŏn*　隱而不顯

Unjŏng　運精

*ŭp* (to pour)　挹

Wai-yü　外域

Wang Kŏn (king)　王建

Wang Pi　王弼

*wei-ching*　偽經

Wei-shih　唯識

*wŏl* (to transcend)　越

Wŏlch'ung　月忠

Wŏnch'ŭk　圓測

Wŏnhyo　元曉

*Wŏnhyo pulgi*　元曉不羈

*wŏnsŏng/yüan-sheng*　圓聲

*wŏnyung/yüan-jung*　圓融

Wu Chao　武曌

Wu-chu　無住

*wu-fa*　無法

*Wu fang-pien*　五方便

*wu-hsing*　無性

*wu-kou ti*　無垢地

*wu-nien*　無念

*wu-sheng fa*　無生法

*wu-shih*　無時

*wu-so-chiu hsing*　無所求行

Wu Yüeh　吳越

*yak chon kwansim/jo ts'un kwan-hsin*　若存觀心

*yakso*　略疏

Yang-chou Kao-li-seng Chih-teh　楊州高麗僧智德

Yen Fo-t'iao　嚴佛調

Yen-shou　延壽

Yen-ts'ung  彥琮
*yin-fu*  隱覆
*yin-yang*  陰陽
*yong*  用
Yongŏi  龍魚異
*yüan*  緣
Yüan-ch'eng  圓澄
*yüan-hsing ti*  遠行地
*yukhaeng/liu-hsing*  六行
*yu* (milk)  乳
*yung*  用
Yung-hui  永徽
*yuri*  琉璃
Yusik  唯識
*Yusim allak-to*  遊心安樂道
*Yu Tang Silla-kuk ko Hŭiyang-san Pongam-sa kyo si Chijŏng taesa Chŏkcho
    chi t'ap pimyŏng*  有唐新羅國故曦陽山鳳岩寺教謚智證大師寂照之塔碑銘

**(G.10)**

# WORKS CITED

Citations to the *Hsü-tsang-ching* (*HTC*) are to the Hong Kong reprint edition of the *Dai-Nihon zokuzōkyō* (Hsiang-kang ying-yin Hsü-tsang-ching wei-yüan-hui, eds.). All citations from Pali texts are to the Pali Text Society editions.

## WORKS IN BUDDHIST CANONICAL COLLECTIONS

*A-pi-ta-mo ta-pi-p'o-sha lun* 阿毘達磨大毘婆沙論. *T* 1545.27.1a–1004a.

*Chan-ch'a shan-o yeh-pao ching* 占察善惡業報經. *T* 839.17.901c–910c.

*Ch'an-yüan chu-chüan-chi tou-hsü* 禪源諸詮集都序. *T* 2015.48.397b–413a.

*Ch'eng wei-shih lun* 成唯識論. *T* 1585.31.1a–59a.

*Chieh-shen-mi ching* 解深密經. *T* 676.16.688b–711b.

*Chieh-shen-mi ching shu* 解深密經疏. *ZZ* 1, 34, 291a–476c, *ZZ* 1, 35, 1a–55d.

*Chih-kuan fu-hsing ch'uan-hung chüeh* 止觀輔行傳弘決. *T* 1912.46.141a–446c.

*Ching-lu i-hsiang* 經律異相. *T* 2121.53.1a–268c.

*Ching-teh ch'uan-teng lu* 景德傳燈錄. *T* 2076.51.196a–467a.

*Ching-t'u sheng wu-sheng lun* 淨土生無生論. *T* 1975.47.381a–384a.

*Chin-kang po-jo po-lo-mi ching* 金剛般若波羅密經. *T* 235.8.748c–752c.

*Chin-kang san-mei ching*. See *Kŭmgang sammae-kyŏng*.

*Chin-kang san-mei ching chu-chieh* 金剛三昧經注解. *ZZ* 1, 55, 2–3, 186a–222a.

*Chin-kang san-mei ching t'ung-tsung chi* 金剛三昧經通宗記. *ZZ* 1, 55, 3, 223a–299a.

*Chin-kang san-mei pen-hsing ch'ing-ching pu-huai pu-mieh ching* 金剛三昧本性清淨不壞不滅經. *T* 644.15.697a–699b.

*Chin-kang-ting ching ta yu-ch'ieh pi-mi hsin-ti fa-men i-chüeh* 金剛頂經大瑜伽秘密心地法門義訣. *T* 1798.39.808a–821a.

*Chin-kuang-ming ching* 金光明經. *T* 663.16.335a–359b; *T* 664.16.359b–402a; *T* 665.16.403a–456c.

*Chin-kuang-ming ching hsüan-i* 金光明經玄義. *T* 1783.39.1a–12a.

*Chinyŏk Hwaŏmgyŏng-so* 晉譯華嚴經疏. *T* 2757.85.234c–236a.

*Chiu-ching i-sheng pao-hsing lun* 究竟一乘寶性論. *T* 1611.31.831a–848a.

*Ch'oesangsŭng-ron* 最上乘論. *T* 2011.48.377a–379b.

*Chuan-shih lun* 轉識論. *T* 1587.31.61c–63c.

*Chüeh-ting-tsang lun* 決定藏論. *T* 1584.30.1018b–1035b.

*Chung-ching mu-lu* 衆經目錄. *T* 2147.55.150a–180b.

*Chung-kuan lun shu* 中觀論疏. *T* 1824.42.1a–169b.

*Chung lun* 中論. *T* 1564.30.1a–39b.

*Ch'u san-tsang chi-chi* 出三藏記集. *T* 2145.55.1a–114a.

*Chu Wei-mo-chieh ching* 註維摩詰經. *T* 1775.38.327a–419c.

*Fa-chi yao-sung ching* 法集要頌經. *T* 213.4777a–799c.

*Fa-chü ching* 法句經. *T* 2901.85.1432b–1435c.

*Fa-hua hsüan-lun* 法華玄論. *T* 1720.34.361a–450c.

*Fa-hua i-shu* 法華義疏. *T* 1721.34.451a–633b.

*Fa-kuan ching* 法觀經. *T* 611.15.240b–242a.

*Fang-kuang po-jo ching* 放光般若經. *T* 221.8.1a–146c.

*Fan-i ming-i chi* 翻譯名義集. *T* 2131.54.1055a–1185b.

*Fan-wang ching* 梵網經. *T* 1484.24.997a–1010a.

*Fo-hsing lun* 佛性論. *T* 1610.31.787a–813a.

*Fo-i-chiao ching* 佛遺教經. *T* 389.12.1110c–1112b.

*Fo-shou p'u-sa nei-hsi liu po-lo-mi ching* 佛說菩薩內習六波羅密經. *T* 778.17.
    714b–715a.

*Fo-tsu t'ung-chi* 佛祖統紀. *T* 2035.49.129a–475c.

*Fo wei Hsin-wang p'u-sa shuo t'ou-t'o ching* 佛為心王菩薩說投陀經. *T* 2886.85.
    1401c–1403b.

*Gyōrinshō* 行林抄. *T* 2409.76.1a–501c.

*Haedong kosŭng-chŏn* 海東高僧傳. *T* 2065.50.1015a–1023a.

*Hsin-hsin ming* 信心銘. *T* 2010.48.376b–377a.

*Hsiu-hsin yao lun* 修心要論. See *Ch'oesangsŭng-ron.*

*Hsü Kao-seng chuan* 續高僧傳. *T* 2060.50.425a–707a.

*Hua-yen ching*. See *Ta-fang-kuang fo hua-yen ching.*

*Hua-yen ching i-hai po-men* 華嚴經義海百門. *T* 1875.45.627a–636c.

*Hua-yen ching nei-chang men teng-tsa k'ung-mu chang* 華嚴經內章門等雜孔目章.
    *T* 1870.45.536c–589b.

*Hua-yen ching shu*. See *Ta-fang kuang fo hua-yen ching shu.*

*Hua-yen wu-shih yao wen-ta* 華嚴五十要問答. *T* 1869.45.519a–536b.

*Hui-yin san-mei ching* 慧印三昧經. *T* 632.15.460c–468a.

*Hwaŏm ilsŭng pŏpkye-to* 華嚴一乘法界圖. *T* 1887A.45.711a–716a.

*Jen-wang hu-kuo po-jo ching shu* 仁王護國般若經疏. *T* 1705.33.253a–286a.

*Jen-wang po-jo ching shu* 仁王般若經疏. *T* 1707.33.314b–359a.

*Jen-wang po-jo po-lo-mi ching* 仁王般若波羅蜜經. *T* 246.8.834c–845a.

*Ju Leng-ch'ieh ching* 入楞伽經. *T* 671.16.514c–586b.

*Ju Ta-sheng lun* 入大乘論. *T* 1634.32.36a–49c.

*K'ai-yüan shih-chiao lu* 開元釋教錄. *T* 2154.55.477a–723a.

*Kegonshū shōsho byō immyōroku* 華嚴宗章疏并因明錄. *T* 2177.55.1132c–1135b.

*Kuang Po-lun pen* 廣百論本. *T* 1570.29.182a–187a.

*Kuang-po yen-ching pu-t'ui-chuan-lun ching* 廣博嚴淨不退轉輪經. *T* 268.9.254b–
    285c.

*Kuang-tsan ching* 光讚經. *T* 222.8.147a–216b.

*Kŭmgang sammaegyŏng-ron* 金剛三昧經論. *T* 1730.34.961a–1008a.

*Kŭmgang sammae-kyŏng* 金剛三昧經. *T* 273.9.365c–374b.

*Leng-ch'ieh-a-po-to-lo pao ching* 楞伽阿跋多羅寶經. *T* 670.16.479a–514b.

*Leng-ch'ieh ching*. See *Leng-ch'ieh-a-po-to-lo pao ching*.

*Leng-ch'ieh shih-tzu chi* 楞伽師資記. *T* 2837.85.1283a–1290c.

*Lien-hua-mien ching* 蓮華面經. *T* 386.12.1070b–1077c.

*Lin-chi lu* 臨濟錄. *T* 1985.47.495a–506c.

*Li-tai fa-pao chi* 歷代法寶記. *T* 2075.51.179a–196b.

*Li-tai san-pao chi* 歷代三寶紀. *T* 2034.49.22c–127c.

*Liu-tsu t'an ching* 六祖壇經. *T* 2007.48.237a–345b.

*Ma-i ching* 罵意經. *T* 732.17.530a–534c.

*Miao-fa lien-hua ching* 妙法蓮華經. *T* 262.9.1a–62b.

*Mo-ho chih-kuan* 摩訶止觀. *T* 1911.46.1a–140c.

*Mo-ho po-jo po-lo-mi ching* 摩訶般若波羅蜜經. *T* 223.8.217a–424a.

*Mo-ho po-jo po-lo-mi-to hsin ching* 摩訶般若波羅蜜多心經. *T* 251.8.848c.

*Pao-tsang lun* 寶藏論. *T* 1857.45.143b–150a.

*Pei-hua ching* 悲華經. *T* 157.3.167a–233c.

*Pŏmmang-kyŏng posal kyebon sagi* 梵網經菩薩戒本私記. *HTC* 95.108a–121b.

*Pŏpkye toji ch'ongsu-rok* 法界圖記叢髓錄. *T* 1887B.45.716a–767c.

*P'u-sa ts'ung Tou-shu-t'ien chiang shen-mu-t'ai shuo kuang-p'u ching* 菩薩從兜術天
降神母胎說廣普經. *T* 384.12.1015a–1058b.

*P'u-sa ying-lo pen-yeh ching* 菩薩瓔珞本業經. *T* 1485.24.1010b–1023a.

*Pu-t'ui-chuan fa-lun ching* 不退轉法輪經. *T* 267.9.226a–254b.

*Samguk yusa* 三國遺事. *T* 2039.49.953c–1019a.

*San-lun hsüan-i* 三論玄義. *T* 1852.45.1a–15a.

*Shan-hai-hui p'u-sa ching* 山海慧菩薩經. *T* 2891.85.1405c–1409c.

*Sheng-man ching* 勝鬘經. *T* 353.12.217a–323b.

*She Ta-sheng lun* 攝大乘論. *T* 1593.31.112b–132c.

*Shih ch'an po-lo-mi tz'u-ti fa-men* 釋禪波羅蜜次弟法門. *T* 1916.46.475c–548c.

*Shih-hsiang po-jo-po-lo-mi ching* 實相般若波羅蜜經. *T* 240.8.776a–778b.

*Shih-men Hung Chüeh-fan lin-chien lu* 石門洪覺範林間錄. *ZZ* 2b, 21, 4.

*Shih-men kui-ching i* 釋門歸敬儀. *T* 1896.45.854c–868c.

*Shih Mo-ho-yen lun*. See *Sŏk Mahayŏn-ron*.

*Shih pa-k'ung lun* 十八空論. *T* 1616.31.861a–867a.

*Shih-ti ching* 十地經. *T* 286.10.497c–535a; *T* 287.10.535a–574c.

*Shih-ti ching lun* 十地經論. *T* 1522.26.123a–203b.

*Shih-ti i-chi* 十地義記. *T* 2758.85.236a–239c.

*Shokyō yōshō* 諸經要抄. *T* 2819.85.1192c–1197c.

*Shou-leng-yen ching* 首楞嚴經. *T* 945.19.105b–155b.

*Shou-leng-yen i-shu chu-ching* 首楞嚴義疏注經. *T* 1799.39.823a–976c.

*Sinp'yŏn chejong kyojang ch'ongnok* 新編諸宗教藏總錄. *T* 2184.55.1165b–1178c.

*Sŏk Mahayŏn-ron* 釋摩訶衍論. *T* 1668.32.591c–668c.

*Sui-tzu-i san-mei* 隨自意三昧. *HTC* 98.344a–354a.

*Sung Kao-seng chuan* 宋高僧傳. *T* 2061.50.709a–900a.

*Ta-ai-tao pi-ch'iu-ni ching* 大愛道比丘尼經. *T* 1478.24.945b–955a.

*Ta-chih-tu lun* 大智度論. *T* 1509.25.57a–756c.

*Ta-Chou lu* 大周錄. *T* 2153.55.373b–476a.

*Taesŭng kisillon-so* 大乘起信論疏. *T* 1844.44.202a–226a.

*Taesŭng kisillon pyŏlgi* 大乘起信論別記. *T* 1845.44.226a–240c.

*Ta-fang-kuang fo hua-yen ching* 大方廣佛華嚴經. *T* 278.9.395a–788b; *T* 279.10.
1a–444c.

*Ta-fang-kuang fo hua-yen ching shu* 大方廣佛華嚴經疏. *T* 1735.35.503a–963a.

*Ta-fang-teng ju-lai-tsang ching* 大方等如來藏經. *T* 666.16.475a–460b.

*Ta-fang-teng ta-chi ching* 大方等大集經. *T* 397.13.1a–407a.

*T'ang Ta-chien-fu-ssu ku-ssu-chu fan-ching ta-teh Fa-tsang ho-shang chuan* 唐大薦
福寺故寺主翻經大德法藏和尚傳. *T* 2054.50.280a–289c.

*Ta-pan-nieh-p'an ching* 大般涅槃經. *T* 374.12.365a–603c.

*Ta-pan-nieh-p'an ching chi-chieh* 大般涅槃經集解. *T* 1763.37.377a–611a.

*Ta-pan-ni-huan ching* 大般泥洹經. *T* 376.12.853a–899c.

*Ta-pao-chi ching* 大寶積經. *T* 310.11.1a–658a.

*Ta-p'i-lou-che-na ch'eng-fo ching shu* 大毘盧遮那成佛經疏. *T* 1796.39.579a–689c.

*Ta-sheng a-p'i-ta-mo tsa-chi lun* 大乘阿毘達磨雜集論. *T* 1606.31.694b–774a.

*Ta-sheng ch'i-hsin lun* 大乘起信論. *T* 1666.32.352a–583b.

*Ta-sheng ch'i-hsin lun i-shu* 大乘起信論義疏. *T* 1843.44.175a–201c.

*Ta-sheng chuang-yen ching lun* 大乘莊嚴經論. *T* 1604.31.589b–661c.

*Ta-sheng i chang* 大乘義章. *T* 1851.44.465a–875c.

*Ta-sheng ju Leng-ch'ieh ching* 大乘入楞伽經. *T* 672.16.1a–640c.

*Ta-sheng ju-tao tz'u-ti* 大乘入道次弟. *T* 1864.45.449b–467c.

*Ta-sheng kuang po-lun shih-lun* 大乘廣百論釋論. *T* 1571.30.187a–250b.

*Ta-sheng pei fen-t'o-li ching* 大乘悲分陀利經. *T* 158.3.233c–289a.

*Ta-T'ang nei-tien lu* 大唐內典錄. *T* 2149.55.219a–342a.

*T'ien-t'ai ssu-chiao i* 天台四教儀. *T* 1931.46.774c–780c.

*Tōiki dentō mokuroku* 東域傳燈目錄. *T* 2183.55.1145c–1165b.

*Tseng-i a-han ching* 增一阿含經. *T* 125.2.549a–830b.

*Tsui-shang-sheng lun*. See *Ch'oesangsŭng-ron*.

*Tsung-ching lu* 宗鏡錄. *T* 2016.48.417b–957b.

*Tzu-men ching-hsün* 緇門警訓. *T* 2023.48.1040c–1097c.

*Wan-shan t'ung-kuei chi* 萬善同歸集. *T* 2017.48.957b–993c.

*Wei-mo-chieh so-shuo ching* 維摩詰所說經. *T* 475.14.537a–557b.

*Wei-mo ching shu* 維摩經疏. *T* 2772.85.375c–423c.

*Wei-mo-ching lüeh-shu* 維摩經略疏. *T* 1778.38.562c–710a.

*Wu-liang-i ching* 無量義經. *T* 276.9.383b–389b.

*Wu-men kuan* 無門関. *T* 2005.48.292a–299c.

*Wu-shang-i ching* 無上依經. *T* 669.16.468a–477c.
*Yŏlban-kyŏng chongyo* 涅槃宗要. *T* 1769.38.239a–255c.
*Yüan-chüeh ching* 圓覺經. *T* 842.17.913a–922a.
*Yuan-chüeh ching lüeh-shu chu* 圓覺經略疏注. *T* 1795.39.523b–578a.
*Yu-ch'ieh-shih ti lun* 瑜伽師地論. *T* 1579.30.279a–882a.
*Yugaron-ki* 瑜伽論記. *T* 1828.42.311a–868b.
*Yu-p'o-sai chieh ching* 優婆塞戒經. *T* 1488.24.1034a–1075c.


## OTHER WORKS IN ASIAN LANGUAGES

An Kyehyŏn 安啓賢. *Silla Chŏngt'ogyo sasangsa yŏn'gu* 新羅淨土教思想史研究
(The history of Silla Pure Land thought). 1976. Reprint, Seoul: Hyŏnŭmsa,
1987.
Ch'ae Inhwan 蔡印幻. *Shiragi bukkyō kairitsu shisō kenkyū* 新羅仏教戒律思想
研究 (Silla Buddhist Vinaya thought). Tokyo: Kokusho Kankōkai, 1975.
Chang Wŏn'gyu 張元圭. "Hwaŏm kyohak wansŏnggi ŭi sasang yŏn'gu" 華嚴
教學完成期의思想研究 (Hwaŏm scholastic thought during its mature
period). *PGHP* 11 (1974): 11–43.
*Chodang chip* 祖堂集 (Collection from the bascilica of the patriarchs). In
*Hyosong Cho Myŏnggi paksa hwagap kinyŏm pulgyo sahak nonch'ong* 曉城趙明
基博師華甲記念:佛教史學論叢 (Essays on Korean buddhist history, in honor
of Prof. Cho Myŏnggi's sixtieth birthday), appendix, pp. 1–29. Seoul, 1965.
Cho Myŏnggi 趙明基. *Koryŏ Taegak kuksa wa Ch'ŏnt'ae sasang* 高麗大覺國師와
天台思想 (National Master Ŭich'ŏn of Koryŏ and Ch'ŏnt'ae thought).
Seoul: Tongguk Munhwasa, 1964.
————. *Silla Pulgyo ŭi inyŏm kwa yŏksa* 新羅佛教의理念과歷史 (The ideology
and history of Silla Buddhism). Seoul: Sin t'aeyangsa, 1962.
————, ed. *Wŏnhyo taesa chŏnjip* 元曉大師全集 (The complete works of
Wŏnhyo). Seoul: Poryŏn'gak, 1978.
Ch'oe Pyŏnghŏn 崔柄憲. "Silla hadae Sŏnjong Kusanp'a ŭi sŏngnip: Ch'oe
Ch'iwŏn ŭi sasan pimyŏng ŭl chungsim ŭro" 新羅下代禪宗九山派의成立:
崔致遠의四山碑銘을中心으로(The establishment of the Nine Mountains
Sŏn lineage during the latter Silla, focusing on Ch'oe Ch'iwŏn's stelae
inscriptions from four mountains). In *Han'guk sa nonmun sŏnjip* (*Kodae
p'yŏn*) 韓國史論文選集(古代篇) (Essay-collection on Korean history: ancient
period), vol. 2, edited by Yŏksa hakkoe 歷史學會, pp. 265–321. Seoul:
Ilchogak, 1976.
Chōsen sōtokufu 朝鮮總督府, ed. *Chōsen kinseki sōran* 朝鮮金石總覽 (Collection of Korean metal and lithic inscriptions). Keijō (Seoul): Chōsen Sōtokufu, 1919.
Ch'üan An 船菴. "Wu-tsu Hung-jen ch'an-shih" 五祖弘忍禪師 (The Fifth

Patriarch, Ch'an master Hung-jen). *Hsien-tai fo-hsüeh* 現代佛學 (Contemporary Buddhist Studies) 82 (June 1957): 26–29.

*Dai-Nihon zokuzōkyō* 大日本續藏經 (The Japanese supplement to the Buddhist canon). Kyoto: Zōkyō Shoin, 1905–1912.

Etani Ryūkai 惠谷隆戒. "Shiragi Gangyō no Jōdokyō shisō" 新羅元曉の淨土教思想 (The Pure Land thought of Wǒnhyo of Silla). In *Jōdokyō no shin kenkyū* 淨土教の新研究 (New research on Pure Land Buddhism), pp. 71–92. Tokyo: Sankibō Busshorin, 1976.

———. "Shiragi Gangyō no *Yūshin anrakudō* wa gisaku ka" 新羅元曉の「遊心安樂道」は偽作か (Is Wǒnhyo's *Yusim allak-to* apocryphal?) *IBK* 23 (1974): 16–23.

Fukaura Seibun 深浦正文. *Yuishikigaku kenkyū* 唯識学研究 (Studies in Yogācāra teachings). 2 vols. 1954. 2d ed. Kyoto, 1977.

Han Kidu 韓基斗. *Silla sidae ǔi Sǒn sasang*, Han'guk Sǒn sasang yǒn'gu, 新羅時代의禪思想; 韓國禪思想研究 (Sǒn thought during the Silla, Studies in Korean Sǒn thought), no. 1. Iri: Wǒn'gwang Taehakkyo Ch'ulp'anbu, 1974.

Hattori Masaaki 服部正明. "Zen to Indo bukkyō" 禪とインド仏教 (Zen and Indian Buddhism). In *Zen no honshitsu to ningen no shinri* 禪の本質と人間の真理 (The essence of Zen and human truth), edited by Hisamatsu Shin'ichi 久松真一 and Nishitani Keiji 西谷啓治, pp. 509–24. Tokyo: Sōbunsha, 1969.

Hayashi Taium 林岱雲. "Bodaidarumaden no kenkyū" 菩提達摩傳の研究 (The biography of Bodhidharma). *Shūkyō kenkyū* 宗教研究 (Religious studies) 9 (1932): 62–72.

Hayashiya Tomojirō 林屋友次郎. *Kyōroku kenkyū* 經錄研究 (Studies on Buddhist scriptural catalogues). Tokyo: Iwanami Shoten, 1941.

Hirakawa Akira 平川彰, et al., eds. *Index to the Abhidharmakośabhāṣya* (*Kusharon sakuin* 倶舍論索引). Tokyo: Daizō Shuppan Kabushikikaisha, 1977.

Hǒ Hǔngsik 許興植. "Sǒnjong Kusan-mun kwa *Sǒnmun yech'am-mun* ǔi munjejǒm" 禪宗九山門과禪門禮懺文의問題點 (The Nine Mountains schools of Sǒn and the problem of the *Sǒnmun yech'am-mun*). In *Han'guk Pulgyo Sǒnmun ǔi hyǒngsǒng sa-chǒk yǒn'gu: Kusan Sǒnmun-ǔl chungsim-ǔro*, edited by Pulgyo hakhoe, pp. 139–59.

Hongmun'gwan 弘文舘, ed. (*Chǔngbo*) *Munhǒn pigo* 增補文獻備考 (Comprehensive references to documentary materials, revised and expanded edition). P'yǒngyang: Sahoe Kwahagwǒn Ch'ulp'ansa, 1967.

Hong Yunsik 洪潤植. "Koryǒ Pulgyo ǔi sinang ǔirye" 高麗佛教의信仰儀禮 (Koryǒ Buddhism and religious observances). In *Pak Kilchin Festschrift*, pp. 655–98.

———. "*Samguk yusa* wa Pulgyo ǔirye" 三國遺事와佛教儀禮 (*Samguk yusa* and Buddhist ceremonies). *PGHP* 16 (1979): 221–46.

Hsiang-kang ying-yin Hsü-tsang-ching wei-yüan-hui 香港影印續藏經委員會,

eds. *Hsü-tsang ching* 續藏經. Hong Kong: Hong Kong Buddhist Association, 1967.

Hwang Suyǒng 黃壽永. "Silla *Sǒdang hwasang pi* ǔi sinp'yǒn" 新羅「誓幢和上碑」의 新片 (New fragments of the *Memorial inscription to Sǒdang Upādhyāya of Silla*). *Kogo misul* 考古美術 (Archaeology and art) 108 (1970): 1–6.

Inoue Hideo 井上秀雄. "Chōsen ni okeru bukkyō juyō to shinkan'nen" 朝鮮における佛教受容と神観念 (The reception of Buddhism in Korea and the concept of spirits). *Nihon bunka kenkyūsho kenkyū hōkoku* 日本文化研究所研究報告 (Research reports of the Japanese Cultural Research Center) 13 (1977): 45–69.

Jan Yün-hua 冉雲華. "Tung-hai ta-shih Wu-hsiang chuan yen-chiu" 東海大師無相傳研究 (The biography of the Korean monk Musang). *Tun-huang hsüeh* 敦煌學 (Tun-huang studies) 4 (1979): 47–60.

Kamata Shigeo 鎌田茂雄. *Chōsen bukkyō no tera to rekishi* 朝鮮佛教の寺と歷史 (The history and temples of Korean Buddhism). Tokyo: Daihōrinkaku, 1980.

———. *Chūgoku bukkyō shisōshi kenkyū* 中國仏教思想史研究 (Studies in Chinese Buddhist thought). Tokyo: Shunjūsha, 1969.

———. *Chūgoku Kegon shisōshi no kenkyū* 中國華嚴思想史の研究 (Studies in the history of Chinese Hua-yen thought). Tokyo: Tokyo University Press, 1965.

Kamata Shigeo and Ueyama Shunpei 鎌田茂雄, 上山春平. *Bukkyō no shisō VII (Chūgoku Zen)* 仏教の思想7(中國禪) (Buddhist thought: Chinese Ch'an). Tokyo, 1969.

Kameda Tsutomu 亀田孜, ed. *Kegon engi*, Nihon emakimono zenshū 華嚴緣起, 日本繪卷物全集 (The story of Kegon, anthology of Japanese scroll-paintings), vol. 8. Tokyo: Kadokawa Shoten, 1976.

Kashiwagi Hiroo 柏木弘雄. *Daijō kishinron no kenkyū: Daijō kishinron no seiritsu ni kansuru shiryōron teki kenkyū* 大乘起信論の研究:大乘起信論の成立に関する資料論的研究 (Studies on *Ta-sheng ch'i-hsin lun*: Text-critical research concerning the composition of *Awakening of Faith in Mahāyāna*). Tokyo: Shunjūsha, 1981.

Kim Chigyǒn 金知見. "Silla Hwaǒmhak ǔi churyu ko" 新羅華嚴學의主流考 (Investigation of the mainstream of Silla Hwaǒm studies). In *Pak Kilchin Festschrift*, pp. 257–75.

———. "Silla Hwaǒmhak ǔi kyebo wa sasang" 新羅華嚴學의系譜와思想 (The thought and lineage of Silla Hwaǒm). *Haksurwǒn nonmunjip* 學術院論文集 (Essay-collection of the Academy of Arts and Sciences) 12 (1973): 31–65.

———, ed. *Wǒnhyo yǒn'gu nonch'ong: kǔ ch'ǒrhak kwa in'gan ǔi modǔn kǒt* 元曉研究論叢—그哲學과人間의모든것 (Wǒnhyo studies: Aspects of his philosophy and humanism). Seoul: Wǒnhyo Sasang Yǒn'guwǒn, 1987.

Kim Chigyŏn and Ch'ae Inhwan 蔡印幻, eds. *Shiragi bukkyō kenkyū* 新羅佛教研究 (Studies in Silla Buddhism). Tokyo: Sankibo Busshorin, 1973.

Kim Hyŏnghŭi 金炯熙. "Hyŏnjon ch'anso–rŭl t'onghae pon Wŏnhyo ŭi *Hwaŏm-kyŏng* kwan" 現存撰疏를通해본元曉의華嚴經觀 (Wŏnhyo's view of the *Avataṃsaka-sūtra* according to his extant commentaries). M.A. Thesis, Tongguk University, 1980.

Kim Ingsŏk 金芿石. *Hwaŏm-hak kaeron* 華嚴學概論 (A primer of Hwaŏm studies). Seoul: Pŏmnyunsa, 1974.

Kim Kangmo 金彊模. "Shiragi Gangyō no bungakukan" 新羅元曉の文学観 (The literary perspectives of the Silla monk Wŏnhyo). In *Shiragi bukkyō kenkyū*, edited by Kim Chigyŏn and Ch'ae Inhwan, pp. 111–36.

Kim Pusik 金富軾. *Samguk sagi* 三國史 (Historical records of the Three Kingdoms). Edited by Sin Sŏkho 申奭鎬, translated by Kim Chonggwŏn 金鍾權. Seoul: Sŏnjin Munhwasa, 1960.

Kim Sanggi 金庠基. "Song-tae e issŏsŏ ŭi Koryŏ-pon ŭi yut'ong e taehayŏ" 宋代에있어서의高麗本의流通에對하여 (The transmission of Koryŏ books during the Sung period). *Asea yŏn'gu* 亞細亞研究 8, 2 (1965): 273–79.

Kim Talchin 金達鎮, trans., with Ko Ikchin 高翊晋. *Kŭmgang sammaegyŏng-ron* 金剛三昧經論 (Exposition of the *Vajrasamādhi-Sūtra*) Wŏnhyo chŏnjip 元曉全集 (The collected works of Wŏnhyo) vol. 1. Seoul: Yŏrŭmsa, 1986.

Kim Unhak 金雲學. "Wŏnhyo ŭi hwajaeng sasang" 元曉의和諍思想 (Wŏnhyo's thought on reconciling doctrinal controversies). *PGHP* 15 (1978): 173–82.

Kim Yŏngt'ae 金英泰. "Chŏn'gi wa sŏrhwa rŭl t'onghan Wŏnhyo yŏn'gu" 傳記와說話를通한元曉研究 (A study of Wŏnhyo from the standpoint of biographies and legends). *PGHP* 17 (1980): 33–76.

———. "Hŭiyang-san Sŏnp'ae ŭi sŏngnip kwa kŭ pŏpkye e taehayŏ" 曦陽山禪派의成立과그法系에대하여(The foundation of the Huiyang-san Sŏn school and its dharma-lineage). *Han'guk Pulgyo-hak* 韓國佛教學 (Korean Buddhist studies) 4 (1979): 11–38.

———. "Ogyo Kusan e taehayŏ" 五教九山에對하예 (On the Five Scholastic Sects and the Nine Mountains of Sŏn). *PGHP* 16 (1979): 59–77.

———. "Silla Pulgyo e issŏsŏ ŭi yongsin sasang: *Samguk yusa* rŭl chungsim ŭro" 新羅佛教에있었서의龍神思想:三國遺事를中心므로 (The ideology of dragon-spirits in Silla Buddhism, focusing on the *Samguk yusa*) *PGHP* 11 (1974): 123–54.

———. "Silla Pulgyo sasang" 新羅佛教思想 (Silla Buddhist thought). In *Pak Kilchin Festschrift*, pp. 89–132.

———. "Silla Pulgyo taejunghwa ŭi yŏksa wa kŭ sasang yŏn'gu" 新羅佛教大衆化의歷史와그思想研究 (A study of the history of, and ideology behind, Buddhism's popularization in Silla). *PGHP* 6 (1969): 145–91.

Kimura Senshō 木村宣彰. "*Kongōzammaikyō* no shingi mondai" 金剛三昧經の

真偽問題 (The issue of the authenticity of the *Vajrasamādhi-sūtra*). *Bukkyō shigaku kenkyū* 佛教史学研究 (Buddhist historical studies) 18 (1976): 106–17.

Ko Ikchin 高翊晋. "Han'guk kodae ŭi Pulgyo sasang" 韓國古代의佛教思想 (Buddhist thought in ancient Korea). In *Ch'ogi Han'guk Pulgyo kyodansa ŭi yŏn'gu* 初期韓國佛教教団史의研究 (History of Buddhist sectarianism in early Korea), Pulgyohak nonjip 佛教學論集 (Essays in Buddhist studies), no. 1, ed. Pulgyo hakhoe, pp. 11–106. Seoul: Minjŏksa, 1986.

———. "Wŏnhyo ŭi sasang ŭi silch'ŏn wŏlli" 元曉의思想의實踐原理 (Praxis in Wŏnhyo's thought). In *Pak Kilchin Festschrift*, pp. 225–55.

Kondō Haruo 近藤春雄. *Tōdai shōsetsu no kenkyū* 唐代小説の研究 (Studies in T'ang-period tales). Tokyo: Kasama Shoin, 1978.

*Koryŏ taejanggyŏng* 高麗大藏經 (*Tripiṭaka Koreana*) [*sic*]. Photolithographic edition. Seoul: Tongguk University Press, 1976.

Kwŏn Sangno 權相老. "Han'guk kodae sinang ŭi illan" 古代信仰의一臠 (A cross-section of ancient Korean beliefs). *PGHP* 1 (1963): 81–108.

———. "Han'guk Sŏnjong yaksa" 韓國禪宗略史 (A brief history of the Korean Sŏn school). In *Pulgyo-hak nonmunjip*, Paek Sŏnguk paksa songsu kinyŏm 佛教學論文集―白性郁博士頌壽記念 (Essays on Buddhist studies: Festschrift in honor of Dr. Paek Sŏnguk's sixtieth birthday), edited by Paek Sŏnguk paksa songsu kinyŏm saŏp wiwŏnhoe 白性郁博士頌壽記念事業委員會, pp. 265–98.

Makita Tairyō 牧田諦亮. *Gikyō kenkyū* 疑經研究 (Studies on apocryphal scriptures). Kyoto: Jimbun Kagaku Kenkyūsho, 1976.

———. "Tendai daishi no gikyō kan" 天台大師の疑經観 (Chih-i's view of apocryphal scriptures). In *Shikan no kenkyū* 止観の研究 (Studies in calmness and insight), edited by Sekiguchi Shindai 関口真大, pp. 201–15. Tokyo: Iwanami Shoten, 1975.

Masunaga Reihō 増永靈鳳. "Shoki Zenshi to Dōgen zenshi no buppō" 初期禪史と道元禪師の佛法 (Early Ch'an history and the teachings of Zen master Dōgen). *Komazawa daigaku kenkyū kiyō* 駒沢大学研究紀要 (Research reports of Komazawa University) 13 (1955): 58–75.

Matsubayashi Kōshi 松林弘之. "Shiragi Jōdokyō no ichikōsatsu: Gangyō no Jōdokyō shisō o megutte" 新羅淨土教の一考察:元曉の淨土教思想をめぐって (An examination of Silla Pure Land teachings, with reference to Wŏnhyo's Pure Land thought). *IBK* 15, 1 (1966): 196–98.

Matsumae Takeshi 松前健. "Kodai Kanzoku no ryūda sūhai to ōken" 古代韓族の龍蛇崇拜と王權 (Royal authority and the ancient Korean people's worship of dragons and snakes). *Chōsen gakuhō* 朝鮮学報 (Korean studies) 57 (1970): 53–68.

Min Yŏnggyu 閔泳珪. "Iryŏn ŭi Sŏn Pulgyo: Silla wa Koryŏ ŭi Kusan Sŏn-mun ŭn Namjong i anigo Pukchong ida" 一然의禪佛教―新羅와高麗의九山禪門은南宗이아니고北宗이다(Iryŏn's Sŏn Buddhism: The Silla and

Koryŏ Nine Mountains school of Sŏn was not the Southern school but the Northern school). In *Han'guk kojŏn simp'ojium* 韓國古典심포지움 (Symposium on Korean classical texts), vol. 1, ed. Chindan hakhoe, pp. 2–9. Seoul: Ilchogak, 1980.

Minamoto Hiroyuki 源弘之. "Shiragi Jōdokyō no tokushoku" 新羅淨土教の特色 (The special characteristics of Silla Pure Land thought). In *Shiragi bukkyō kenkyū*, edited by Kim Chigyŏn and Ch'ae Inhwan, pp. 285–317.

Mishina Akihide 三品彰英 (a.k.a. Shōei). *Nissen shinwa densetsu no kenkyū* 日・鮮神話傳説の研究 (Studies in Japanese and Korean myths and legends). 1943. Reprint edition, Mishina Akihide ronbunshū 三品彰英論文集 (Mishina Akihide essay collection), vol. 4. Tokyo: Heibonsha, 1972.

———. "Shiragi no Jōdokyō" 新羅の淨土教 (Silla Pure Land teachings). In *Bukkyō shigaku ronshū*, Tsukamoto hakushi shōju kinen 佛教史学論集, 塚本博士頌寿紀念 (Essays on the history of Buddhism, presented to Professor Tsukamoto Zenryū on his retirement from the Research Institute for Humanistic Studies), pp. 727–45. Kyoto: Kyoto University, 1961.

Mitomo Kenyō 三友健容. "*Muryōgikyō* Indo senjutsu setsu" 無量義経インド撰述説 (The Indian provenance of the *Wu-liang-i ching*). *Nichiren kyōdan no shomondai* 日蓮教団の諸問題 (Issues in the Nichiren Sect) (1983): 1119–45.

Mizuno Kōgen 水野弘元. "Bodaidaruma no *Ninyūshigyō* setsu to *Kongōzam-maikyō*" 菩提達摩の二入四教説と金剛三昧經 (Bodhidharma's *Explanation of the two accesses and four practices* and the *Vajrasamādhi-sūtra*). *Komazawa daigaku kenkyū kiyō* 駒澤大学研究紀要 (Research report of Komazawa University) 13 (1955): 33–57.

———. "Gisaku no *Hokkukyō* ni tsuite" 偽作の法句經について (On the apocryphal *Dharmapada*). *Komazawa daigaku bukkyōgakubu kenkyū kiyō* 駒沢大学佛教学部研究紀要 (Research report of the Komazawa University Buddhist Studies department) 19 (1961): 11–33.

Mochizuki Shinkō 望月信亨. *Bukkyō kyōten seiritsu shiron* 佛教経典成立史論 (Studies on the history of the composition of Buddhist scriptures). Kyoto: Hōzōkan, 1946.

Motoi Nobuo 本井信雄. "Shiragi Gangyō no denki ni tsuite" 新羅元曉の傳記について (On the biography of Wŏnhyo). *Ōtani gakuhō* 大谷学報 (Ōtani University reports) 41 (1961): 33–52.

Naitō Ryūo 内藤龍雄. "*Shutsu sanzō kishū* no senshū nenji ni tsuite" 出三藏記集の撰集年次について (The completion date of *Chu san-tsang chi-chi*). *IBK* 7 (1958): 162–63.

———. "Sōyū no chosaku katsudō" 僧祐の著作活動 (Seng-yu's literary activities). *IBK* 20 (1971): 284–87.

Ninomiya Keinin 二宮啓任. "Chōsen ni okeru Ninnōkai no kaisetsu" 朝鮮における仁王会の開設 (The establishment of *Jen-wang ching* assemblies in Korea). *Chōsen gakuhō* 14 (1959): 155–63.

Nishitani Keiji 西谷啓治 and Yanagida Seizan 柳田聖山, eds. *Zenke goroku II* 禪家語録 (Zen recorded-sayings). Tokyo: Chikuma Shobō, 1974.

Nukariya Kaiten 忽滑谷快天. *Zengaku shisōshi* 禪學思想史 (History of Zen thought), vol. 1. Tokyo: Genkōsha, 1923.

Obata Hironobu 上畠宏允. "Chibetto no Zenshū to *Rekidai hōbōki*" チベット の禪宗と歴代法寶記 (The Tibetan Ch'an school and *Li-tai fa-pao chi*). *Zen bunka kenkyūsho kiyō* 禪文化研究所紀要 (Research reports of the Zen Cultural Institute) 6 (1974): 139–76.

Ogawa Kan'ichi 小川貫弌. *Bukkyō bunkashi kenkyū* 佛教文化史研究 (Studies in the history of Buddhist culture). Kyoto: Nagata Bunshōdō, 1973.

Okabe Kazuo 岡部和雄. "Sōyū no giggikyō-kan to shōkyō-kan" 僧祐疑偽経 観と抄経観 (Seng-yu's views on apocryphal sūtras and abbreviated scriptures). *Komazawa daigaku bukkyōgakubu ronshū* 駒沢大学佛教学部論集 (Essay-collection of the Komazawa University Buddhist Studies department) 2 (1971), pp. 63–74.

———. "Zensō no chūsho to gigi kyōten" 禮僧の注抄と疑偽経典 (Scriptural citations by Ch'an monks and apocryphal scriptures). In *Tonkō butten to Zen* 敦煌仏典と禪 (Tun-huang Buddhist texts and Ch'an), Kōza Tonkō 講座敦煌, vol. 8, edited by Shinohara Hisao 篠原壽雄 and Tanaka Ryōshō 田中良昭, pp. 335–76.

Okimoto Katsumi 沖本克己. "Chibetto yaku *Ninyūshigyōron* ni tsuite." チベット 訳「二入四行論」について (On the Tibetan translation of the *Two accesses and four practices treatise*). *IBK* 24 (1976): 999–92 [*sic*].

———. "Zenshūshi ni okeru gikyō: *Hōōkyō* ni tsuite" 禪宗史に於ける偽経: 「法王経」について (Apocryphal scriptures in the history of the Ch'an school: The *Fa-wang ching*). *Zen bunka kenkyūsho kiyō* 禪文化研究所紀要 (Annals of the Buddhist Cultural Institute) 10 (1978), pp. 27–61.

Ōminami Ryūshō 大南竜昇. "Sanmai kyōten no yakushutsu to juyō" 三昧経 典の訳出と受容 (The translation and reception of *samādhisūtras*). *Bukkyō bunka kenkyū* 仏教文化研究 (Studies on Buddhist culture) 21 (1976).

Paek Sŏnguk paksa songsu kinyŏm saŏp wiwŏnhoe 白性郁博士頌壽記念事業 委員會, ed. *Pulgyo-hak nonmunjip*, Paek Sŏnguk paksa songsu kinyŏm 白性 郁博士頌壽記念:佛教學論文集 (Essays on Buddhist studies: Festschrift in honor of Dr. Paek Sŏnguk's sixtieth birthday). Seoul: Tongguk University, 1957.

Pak Chonghong 林鍾鴻. *Han'guk sasang sa: Pulgyo sasang p'yŏn* 韓國思想史: 佛教思想篇 (History of Korean thought: Buddhist thought), Sŏmun mun'go 瑞文文庫, no. 11. Seoul: Sŏmun Mun'go, 1972.

*Pak Kilchin Festschrift*. See Sungsan Pak Kilchin paksa hwagap kinyŏm saŏphoe, ed. *Han'guk Pulgyo sasangsa*, Sungsan Pak Kilchin paksa hwagap kinyŏm.

*Po-na-pen erh-shih-ssu shih* 百衲本二十四史 (Po-na edition of the twenty-four histories). *Ssu-pu ts'ung-kan* 四部叢刊 edition. Shanghai: Commercial Press, 1920–1922.

Pulgyo hakhoe, ed. *Han'guk Pulgyo Sŏnmun ŭi hyŏngsŏng sa-chŏk yŏn'gu: Kusan Sŏnmun-ŭl chungsim-ŭro* 韓國佛教禪門의形成史的研究—禪門九山中心 (Historical studies on the formation of the Sŏn school of Korean Buddhism, focusing on the Nine Mountains school of Sŏn). Pulgyohak nonjip 佛教學論集 (Essays in Buddhist studies), no. 2, pp. 11–106. Seoul: Minjŏksa, 1986.

Rhi Ki-yong [Yi Kiyŏng] 李箕永, trans. *Han'guk ŭi Pulgyo sasang* 韓國의佛教思想 (Korean Buddhist thought), Segye sasang chŏnjip 世界思想全集, vol. 11. Seoul: Samsŏng Ch'ulp'ansa. 1977.

———. "*Inwang panya-kyŏng* kwa hoguk Pulgyo" 仁王般若經과護國佛教 (The *Jen-wang ching* and National-protection Buddhism). In *Han'guk Pulgyo yŏn'gu*, Puryŏn Yi Kiyŏng paksa hwagap kinyŏm 韓國佛教研究—不然李箕永博士華甲紀念 (Studies on Korean Buddhism, in commemoration of the sixtieth birthday of (Puryŏn) Dr. Rhi Ki-yong), pp. 163–93. Seoul: Han'guk Pulgyo Yŏn'guwŏn, 1982.

———, trans. *Kŭmgang sammaegyŏng-ron*, Han'guk myŏngjŏ taejŏnjip 金剛三昧經, 韓國名著大全集 (*Commentary to the Vajrasamādhi-sūtra*, the great works of Korea). Seoul: Taeyang Sŏjŏk, 1973.

———. "Kyŏngjŏn in'yong e nat'anan Wŏnhyo ŭi tokch'angsŏng" 經典引用에 나타난元曉의獨創性 (The uniqueness of Wŏnhyo as manifested in his citations of scriptures). In *Pak Kilchin Festschrift*, pp. 177–224.

———. *Wŏnhyo sasang: segye kwan* 元曉思想：世界觀 (Wŏnhyo's thought: His world view). Seoul: Hongbŏp Wŏn, 1967,

*Samguk sagi.* See Kim Pusik.

Satō Ken 佐藤健. "*Anrakushū* to gikyō" 安樂集と偽經 (The *An-lo chi* and apocryphal scriptures). *Bukkyō daigaku kenkyū kiyō* 佛教大学研究紀要 (Research reports of Bukkyō University) 60 (1976): 79–134.

Sekiguchi Shindai 関口真大. *Bukkyō no jissen genri* 仏教の実践原理 (The principles of Buddhist practice). Tokyo: Sankibō Busshorin, 1977.

———. *Tendai shikan no kenkyū* 天台止観の研究 (Studies in the calmness and insight meditations of the T'ien-t'ai school). Tokyo: Iwanami Shoten, 1969.

*Shih-san ching chu-shu* 十三經注疏 (Annotations and commentaries to the Thirteen Classics). Taipei: Ch'eng-wen Ch'u-p'an-she, 1966.

*Sinjŭng Tongguk yŏji sŭngnam* 新增東國輿地勝覽 (Revised survey of Korean geography). Edited by No Sasin 盧思慎. Photolithographic reprint of 1530 revised and enlarged edition. Seoul: Tongguk Munhwasa, 1959.

Shimizu Yōkō 清水要晃. "*Nyūryōgakyō* no shiki no sansōsetsu ni tsuite: nyoraizō to arayashiki no dōshi o megutte" 入楞伽經の識の三相說について—如來藏とアーラャ識の同視をめぐって (The theory of the three characteristics of consciousness in the *Laṅkāvatāra-sūtra*: With special reference to the identification of tathāgatagarbha and ālayavijñāna). *IBK* 25 (1976): 162–63.

Shinohara Hisao 篠原壽雄 and Tanaka Ryōshō 田中良昭, eds. *Tonkō butten to Zen* 敦煌仏典と禪 (Tun-huang Buddhist scriptures and Ch'an), Kōza Tonkō 講座敦煌, vol. 8. Tokyo: Daitō Shuppansha, 1980.

Shiratori Kiyoshi 白鳥清. "Rei to tatsu tono kankei o ronjite 'Lingism' no setsu o teishōsu" 靈と龍との關係を論じて 'Lingism'の說を提唱す (Proposing the theory of "Ling-ism" [Numinosity] with special reference to the relation between *ling* [numinosity] and *lung* [dragons]). In *Tōyōshi shūsetsu, Katō hakushi kanreki kinen* 東洋史集說, 加藤博士還暦記念 (Essays on oriental history, presented in commemoration of Dr. Katō's sixtieth birthday), pp. 363–97. Tokyo, 1941.

Shizutani Masao 靜谷正雄 "Indo bukkyōshi to Nāga (tatsu)" ンド仏教史とナーガ (Indian Buddhist history and Nāgas [dragons]). *Ryūkoku shidan* 龍谷史壇 (Historical circle of Ryūkoku University) 73, 4 (1978): 131–46.

Sŏng Nakhun 成樂熏, trans. *Wŏnhyo, Wŏnch'ŭk, Ŭisang, Hyech'o, Ch'egwan, Ŭich'ŏn*, Han'guk ŭi sasang taejŏnjip 元曉圓測義湘慧超諦觀義天, 韓國의思想大全集 (Great books of Korean thought), vol. 1. Seoul: Tonghwa Ch'ulp'an Kongsa, 1972.

Sungsan Pak Kilchin paksa hwagap kinyŏm saŏphoe 崇山朴吉真博士華甲紀念, eds. *Han'guk Pulgyo sasangsa*, Sungsan Pak Kilchin paksa hwagap kinyŏm 韓國佛教思想史, 崇山朴吉真博士華甲紀念(History of Korean Buddhist thought, presented in commemoration of the sixtieth birthday of [Sungsan] Dr. Pak Kilchin). Iri (Chŏlla bukto): Wŏn pulgyo sasang yŏn'guwŏn, 1975.

Suzuki Daisetsu 鈴木大拙. "Daruma no Zenbō to shisō oyobi sono ta" 達摩の禪法と思想及びその他 (Bodhidharma's Zen teachings, thought, etc). In *Kōkan Shōshitsu issho oyobi kaisetsu* 校刊少室逸書及解說 (Fragments from Bodhidharma's chambers, with explication). Osaka: Ataka Bukkyō Bunko, 1936.

———. *Zen shisōshi kenkyū* 禪思想史研究 (Studies in the history of Zen thought), Suzuki Daisetsu zenshū 鈴木大拙全集 (The complete works of D. T. Suzuki), vol. 2. Tokyo, 1968.

*Taishō shinshū daizōkyō* 大正新修大藏經 (Revised tripiṭaka compiled during the Taishō reign-period). Edited by Takakusu Junjirō 高楠順次郎 and Watanabe Kaikyoku 渡辺海旭. Tokyo: Daizōkyōkai, 1924–1935.

Takamine Ryōshū 高峯了州. *Kegon shisōshi* 華嚴思想史 (History of Hua-yen thought). Revised ed. Kyoto: Hyakkaen, 1963.

———. *Kegon to Zen to no tsūro* 華嚴と禪との通路 (The convergence of Hua-yen and Ch'an). Nara: Nanto Bukkyō Kenkyūkai, 1956.

Takasaki Jikidō 高崎直道. *Nyoraizō shisō no keisei* 如来蔵思想の形成 (The formation of Tathāgatagarbha thought). Tokyo: Shunjūsha, 1974.

Tamura Enchō 田村圓澄. *Kodai Chōsen bukkyō to Nihon bukkyō* 古代朝鮮仏教と
日本仏教 (Ancient Korean Buddhism and Japanese Buddhism). Tokyo:
Yoshikawa Kōbunkan, 1980.

Tanaka Ryōshō 田中艮昭. "Gisaku no *Hokkukyō* to sono ihon ni tsuite" 偽作
の「法句經」と疏の異本について (The apocryphal *Dharmapada*: Its commentaries and editions). *IBK* 23, 1 (1974): 122–29.

Tatsuzawa Toshiaki 瀧澤俊亮. "Chūgoku minzoku to ryūda no denshō" 中國
民族と龍蛇の伝承 (The Chinese people and legends of dragons and snakes).
*Tōyō bungaku kenkyū* 東洋文学研究 (Studies on Oriental literature) 9 (1961):
81–106.

Tokiwa Daijō 常盤大定. *Busshō no kenkyū* 佛性の研究 (Studies on the buddha-
nature). Tokyo: Kokusho Kankōkai, 1973.

Tongbang sasang nonch'ong kanhaeng wiwŏnhoe 東方思想論叢刊行委員會,
ed. *Tongbang sasang nonch'ong*, Yi Chongik paksa hagwi kinyŏm nonmunjip 東方思想論叢, 李鍾益博士學位紀念論文集 (Essays in Oriental thought,
presented in commemoration of Dr. Yi Chongik's doctoral degree). Seoul:
Poryŏn'gak, 1975.

Tongguk taehakkyo Pulgyo munhwa yŏn'guso 東國大學校佛教文化研究所,
ed. *Han'guk Pulgyo ch'ansul munhŏn ch'ongnok* 韓國佛教撰述文獻總錄 (A
comprehensive catalogue of Korean Buddhist materials and literature).
Seoul: Tongguk Taehakkyo Ch'ulp'anbu, 1976.

Ui Hakuju 宇井伯壽. *Zenshūshi kenkyū* 禪宗史研究 (Studies in the history of
Zen sect). 3 vols. Tokyo: Iwanami Shoten, 1939/1941/1943.

Wang Chung-min 王重民. *Tun-huang i-shu tsung-mu so-yin* 敦煌遺書總目索引
(General index to the catalogues of the manuscript remains from Tun-
huang). Peking, 1962.

Yabuki Keiki 矢吹慶輝. *Meisha yoin* 鳴沙餘韻 (Echoes of the desert). Tokyo:
Iwanami Shoten, 1930.

―――. *Meisha yoin kaisetsu* 鳴沙餘韻解說 (Annotation to Echoes of the
desert). Tokyo: Iwanami Shoten, 1933.

―――. "Tonkō shutsudo gigi kobutten ni tsuite" 敦煌出土疑偽古佛典に就
いて (Ancient apocryphal Buddhist scriptures from Tun-huang). *Shūkyō
kenkyū* 宗教研究 (Religious studies) 3, 10 (1919): 41–121.

Yamaguchi Zuihō 山口瑞鳳. "Chibetto bukkyō to Shiragi Kin oshō" チベッ
ト仏教と新羅金和尚 (Tibetan Buddhism and Reverend Kim). In *Shiragi
bukkyō kenkyū* (Studies on Silla Buddhism), ed. Kim Chigyŏn and Ch'ae
Inhwan, pp. 1–36.

Yanagida Seizan 柳田聖山. *Shoki Zenshū shisho no kenkyū* 初期禪宗史書の研究
(Research on early Ch'an historiographical works). Kyoto: Hōzōkan, 1967.

―――. *Daruma no goroku* 達摩の語錄 (The records of Bodhidharma), Zen no
goroku 禪の語錄 (Recorded-sayings of Ch'an), vol. 1. Tokyo: Chikuma
Shobō, 1969.

————. *Shoki no Zenshi 1: Ryōga shijiki, Denhōbōki* 初期の禪史：楞伽師資記, 伝法寶紀 (Early Ch'an histories: The *Leng-ch'ieh shih-tzu chi* and *Ch'uan fa-pao chi*), Zen no goroku, vol. 2. Tokyo: Chikuma Shobō, 1971.

————. *Shoki no Zenshi 2: Rekidai hōbōki* 初期の禪史2：歷代法寶記 (Early Ch'an histories: The *Li-tai fa-pao chi*), Zen no goroku, vol. 3. Tokyo: Chikuma Shobō, 1976.

Yi Chongik 李鍾益. "Han'guk Pulgyo chejongp'a sŏngnip ŭi yŏksa chŏk koch'al" 韓國佛教諸宗派成立의歷史的考察 (A historical investigation of the foundation of Korean Buddhist sects). *PGHP* 16 (1979): 29–58.

————. "Silla Pulgyo wa Wŏnhyo sasang" 新羅佛教와元曉思想 [Silla Buddhism and Wŏnhyo's thought]. In *Tongbang sasang nonch'ong*, Yi Chongik paksa hagwi kinyŏm nonmunjip 東方思想論叢—李鍾益博士學位紀念論文集 (Essays on Oriental thought: Festschrift in honor of Professor Yi Chongik's doctoral degree), pp. 183–97. Seoul: Poryŏn'gak, 1975.

————. *"Wŏnhyo ŭi kŭnbon sasang: Simmun hwajaeng-ron yŏn'gu* 元曉의根本思想：十門和諍論研究 (Wŏnhyo's fundamental thought: Research on *Ten approaches to the reconciliation of doctrinal controversy*). Seoul: Tongbang Sasang Yŏn'guwŏn, 1977.

————. "Wŏnhyo ŭi saengae wa sasang" 元曉의生涯와思想 (The life and thought of Wŏnhyo). In *Tongbang sasang nonch'ong*, pp. 198–239.

Yi Hŭisu 李喜秀. *T'och'ak-hwa kwajŏng esŏ pon Han'guk pulgyo* 土着化過程에서 본韓國佛教 (The adaptation of Korean Buddhism to indigenous culture). Seoul: Pulsŏ Pogŭpsa, 1971.

Yi Kiyŏng. See Rhi Ki-yong.

Yi Nŭnghwa 李能和. *Chosŏn Pulgyo t'ongsa* 朝鮮佛教通史 (A comprehensive history of Korean Buddhism). 3 vols. 1918. Reprint, Seoul: Poryŏn'gak, 1979.

Yi Pyŏngdo 李丙燾, trans. *Samguk sagi* 三國史記 (Historical records of the Three Kingdoms). 2 vol. Seoul: Ŭryu Munhwasa, 1977.

————, trans. *Samguk yusa* 三國遺事 (Memorabilia and mirabilia of the Three Kingdoms). Seoul: Tongguk Munhwasa, 1962.

Yi Pyŏngdo and Kim Chaewŏn 金載元. *Han'guksa: kodae p'yŏn* 韓國史：古代篇 (A history of Korea: Ancient period). Seoul: Ŭryu Munhwasa, 1959.

Yi Usŏng 李佑成. "*Samguk yusa* sojae Ch'ŏyong sŏrhwa ŭi ilbunsŏk" 「三國遺事」所在處容說話의一分析 (An analysis of the Ch'ŏyong story contained in *Samguk yusa*). In *Kim Chaewŏn paksa hoegap kinyŏm nonch'ong* 金載元博士回甲紀念論叢 (Festschrift in honor of Dr. Kim Chaewŏn's sixtieth birthday), pp. 89–127. Seoul, 1969.

Yoritomi Motohiro 賴富本宏. "Gokoku kyōten to iwareru mono: *Ninnōkyō* o megutte" 護國経典と言われるもの—「仁王経」をめぐって (The national-protection class of scriptures: On the *Jen-wang ching*). *Tōyō gakujutsu kenkyū* 東洋学術研究 (Oriental scholarship) 14 (1975): 45–62.

Yoshimura Shūki 芳村修基. "The Denkar-Ma, An Oldest Catalogue of the Tibetan Buddhist Canons." In *Indo daijō bukkyō shisō kenkyū: Kamarashīra no shisō* インド大乗仏教思想研究―カマラシーラの思想 (Studies on Indian Buddhist Mahāyāna thought: The thought of Kamalaśīla), pp. 99–199. Kyoto: Hyakkaen, 1974.

Yoshioka Yoshitoyo 吉岡義豊. "Bukkyō no zenpō to Dōkyō no shuitsu" 仏教の禪法と道教の守一 (Buddhist meditation techniques and "guarding the one" in Taoism). *Chizan gakuhō* 智山学報 27–28 (November 1964): 109–25. Reprinted in *Dōkyo to bukkyō* 道教と佛教 (Taoism and Buddhism), vol. 3, pp. 287–314. Tokyo: Kokusho Kankōkai, 1976.

―――. "Shoki Dōkyō no shuitsu shisō to Bukkyō: tokuni *Taiheikyō* o chūshin toshite" 初期道教の守一思想と仏教―とくに太平経を中心として (The conception of "guarding the one" in early Taoism, and Buddhism: with special reference to the *Book of Great Peace*). *Taishō daigaku kiyō* 大正大学紀要 (Taishō University reports) 53 (1968): 61–82. Reprinted as "*Taiheikyō* no shuitsu shisō to bukkyō" 太平経の守一思想と仏教 (Buddhism and the conception of "guarding the one" in the *T'ai-p'ing ching*). In *Dōkyō to bukkyō*, vol. 3, pp. 315–51. Tokyo: Kokusho Kankōkai, 1976.

Yoshizu Yoshihide 吉津宜英. "Hōzō-den no kenkyū" 法蔵伝の研究 (The biography of Fa-tsang). *Komazawa daigaku bukkyō gakubu kenkyū kiyō* 駒澤大学仏教学部研究紀要 37 (1979), pp. 168–93.

Yūki kyōju shōju kinen rombunshū knakōkai 結城教授頌寿紀念論文集刊行会 ed. *Bukkyō shisōshi ronshū*, Yūki kyōju shōju kinen 結城教授頌寿記念: 佛教思想史論集 (The history of Buddhist thought: Festschrift in commemoration of Prof. Yūki Reimon's sixtieth birthday). Tokyo: Daizō Shuppansha, 1964.

Yūki Reimon 結城令聞. "Shina Yuishiki gakushijō ni okeru Ryōgashi no chii" 支那唯識学史上に於ける楞伽師の地位 (The place of the Laṅka teachers in Chinese Vijñānavāda history). *Shina bukkyō shigaku* 支那佛教史学 (Studies in Chinese Buddhist history) 1 (1937): 21–44.

Zengaku Daijiten Hensansho 禪学大辞典編纂所, ed. *Zengaku daijiten* 禪学大辞典 (Great dictionary of Zen studies). 3 vols. Tokyo: Komazawa University, 1977.

An, Kye-Hyŏn. "Silla Buddhism and the Spirit of the Protection of the Fatherland." *Korea Journal* 17, 4 (April 1977): 27–29.

Anderson, Poul. *The Method of Holding the Three Ones: A Taoist Manual of Meditation of the Fourth Century A.D.* Studies on Asian Topics, no. 1, Scandinavian Institute of Asian Studies. London: Curzon Press, 1980.

Austerlitz, Robert, et al. "Report of the Workshop Conference on Korean Romanization." *Korean Studies* 4 (1980): 111–25.

Bascom, William R. "Four Functions of Folklore." In *Study of Folklore*, edited by Alan Dundes, pp. 279–98.

Beal, Samuel. *A Catena of Buddhist Scriptures from the Chinese.* London: Trübner, 1871.

Best, Jonathan. "Buddhism, Art and the Transforming Power of Faith in Early Korea." Paper read at the Forces of Tradition in Modern Korea Symposium, May 12, 1988, University of California, Los Angeles.

Bielefeldt, Carl. "Ch'ang-lu Tsung-tse's *Tso-ch'an I* and the 'Secret' of Zen Meditation." In *Traditions of Meditation in Chinese Buddhism*, edited by Peter Gregory, pp. 129–61.

Bielefeldt, Carl, and Lewis Lancaster. "T'an Ching (Platform Scripture)." *Philosophy East and West* 25 (1975): 197–212.

Bokenkamp, Stephen R. "Stages of Transcendence in Taoism: The Influence of the Buddhist *Bhūmi* Scheme." In *Chinese Buddhist Apocrypha*, edited by Robert Buswell.

Brock, Karen. "Tales of Gishō and Gangyō: Editor, Artist, and Audience in Japanese Picture Scrolls." Ph.D. diss., Princeton University, 1984.

Brough, John. "Thus Have I Heard. . . ." *Bulletin of the School of Oriental and African Studies* 13 (1950): 416–26.

Broughton, Jeffrey. "Early Ch'an Schools in Tibet." In *Studies in Ch'an and Hua-yen*, Studies in East Asian Buddhism, no. 1, edited by Robert M. Gimello and Peter N. Gregory, pp. 1–68. Honolulu: University of Hawaii Press, 1983.

Buswell, Robert E., Jr. "The Biographies of the Korean Monk Wŏnhyo (617–686): A Study in Buddhist Hagiography." In *Biography as a Genre in Korean Literature*, edited by Peter H. Lee. Berkeley: Center for Korean Studies, 1989.

———. "Buddhism in Korea." In *The Encyclopedia of Religion*, edited by Mircea Eliade, vol. 2, pp. 421–26. New York: Macmillan, 1987.

———. "Ch'an Hermeneutics: A Korean View." In *Buddhist Hermeneutics*, Studies in East Asian Buddhism no. 6, edited by Donald S. Lopez, Jr., pp. 231–56. Honolulu: University of Hawaii Press, 1988.

———, ed. *Chinese Buddhist Apocrypha*. Honolulu: University of Hawaii Press, forthcoming, 1989.

———. "Chinul's Systematization of Chinese Meditative Techniques in Korean

Sŏn Buddhism." In *Traditions of Meditation in Chinese Buddhism*, edited by Peter N. Gregory, pp. 199–242.

———. "The Chronology of Wŏnhyo's Life and Works: Some Preliminary Considerations." In *Wŏnhyo yŏn'gu nonch'ong: kŭ ch'ŏrhak kwa in'gan ŭi modŭn kŏt* (Wŏnhyo Studies: Aspects of his philosophy and humanism), edited by Kim Chigyŏn, pp. 931–64.

———. "Did Wŏnhyo Write Two Versions of his *Kŭmgang sammaegyŏng-ron* [Exposition of the *Book of Adamantine Absorption*]?: An Issue in Korean Buddhist Textual History." *Proceedings of the Fifth International Conference on Korean Studies*. Sŏngnam, Korea: Academy of Korean Studies, in press.

———. *The Korean Approach to Zen: The Collected Works of Chinul*. Honolulu: University of Hawaii Press, 1983.

———. "The Korean Origin of the *Vajrasamādhi-Sūtra*: A Case Study in Determining the Dating, Provenance, and Authorship of a Buddhist Apocryphal Scripture." Ph.D. diss., University of California, Berkeley, 1985.

———, trans. "The Reception of Buddhism in Korea and Its Impact on Indigenous Culture." Translation of Inoue Hideo, "Chōsen ni okeru bukkyō juyō to shinkan'nen." In *Introduction of Buddhism to Korea: New Cultural Patterns*, Studies in Korean Religion and Culture, vol. 3, edited by Lewis Lancaster and Chai-sin Yu. Berkeley: Asian Humanities Press, forthcoming.

———. "The 'Short-Cut' Approach of *K'an-hua* Meditation: The Evolution of a Practical Subitism in Chinese Ch'an Buddhism." In *Sudden and Gradual: Approaches to Enlightenment in Chinese Thought*, edited by Peter N. Gregory, pp. 321–77.

Campbell, Joseph. *The Hero with a Thousand Faces*. Princeton: Princeton University Press, 1949.

———. *The Masks of the Gods II: Oriental Mythology*. New York: Viking Press, 1962.

Chan Hing-ho. "Ta Sung Kao-seng chuan." In *A Sung Bibliography (Bibliographie des Sung)*, edited by Etienne Balazs and Yves Hervouet, pp. 349–50. Hong Kong: The Chinese University Press, 1978.

Chappell, David W. "Early Forebodings of the Death of Buddhism." *Numen* 27, 1 (1980): 122–54.

———. "The Teachings of the Fourth Ch'an Patriarch Tao-hsin (580–651)." In *Early Ch'an in China and Tibet*, edited by Whalen Lai and Lewis Lancaster, pp. 89–129.

Chappell, David W., ed., and Masao Ichishima, comp. *T'ien-t'ai Buddhism: An Outline of the Fourfold Teachings*. Tokyo: Daiichi Shobō, 1983.

Charles, R. H. *The Apocrypha and Pseudepigrapha of the Old Testament in English*. 2 vols. Oxford: Clarendon Press, 1913.

Ch'en, Kenneth K. S. *Buddhism in China: A Historical Survey*. Princeton: Princeton University Press, 1964.

Chou Yi-liang. "Tantrism in China." *Harvard Journal of Asiatic Studies* 8 (1945): 241–332.

Chun Shin-yong [Ch'ŏn Sinyŏng], ed. *Korean Folk Tales*. Korean Culture Series no. 7. Seoul: Si-sa-yong-o-sa Publishers, 1982.

Cleary, J. C., trans. *Zen Dawn: Early Zen Texts from Tun Huang*. Boston: Shambhala, 1986.

Cohen, Alvin P., ed. *Selected Works of Peter A. Boodberg*. Berkeley: University of California Press, 1979.

Collcutt, Martin. "The Early Ch'an Monastic Rule: *Ch'ing kuei* and the Shaping of Ch'an Community Life." In *Early Ch'an in China and Tibet*, edited by Whalen Lai and Lewis Lancaster, pp. 165–84.

Collins, Steven. *Selfless Persons: Imagery and Thought in Theravāda Buddhism*. Cambridge: Cambridge University Press, 1982.

Combaz, Gisbert. "Masques et dragons en Asie." *Mélanges chinois et bouddhiques* 7 (1945): 1–328.

Conze, Edward. *Buddhism: Its Essence and Development*. New York: Harper and Row, Harper Torchbooks, 1959.

———. *Buddhist Thought in India: Three Phases of Buddhist Philosophy*. 1962. Reprint, Ann Arbor: University of Michigan Press, 1967.

———. trans. *The Perfection of Wisdom in Eight Thousand Lines and Its Verse Summary*. Bolinas, Calif.: Four Seasons Foundation, 1975.

Conze, Edward, et al., eds. *Buddhist Texts Through the Ages*. New York: Harper and Row, 1964.

Dalia, Albert A. "The 'Political Career' of the Buddhist Historian Tsan-ning." In *Buddhist and Taoist Practice in Medieval Chinese Society: Buddhist and Taoist Studies II*, Asian Studies at Hawaii, no. 34, edited by David W. Chappell, pp. 146–80. Honolulu: University of Hawaii Press, 1987.

Demiéville, Paul. *Le concile de Lhasa: une controverse sur le quiétisme entre bouddhistes de l'Inde et de la Chine au VIIIᵉ siècle de l'ère chrétienne*. Bibliothèque de l'Institut des hautes études chinoise, vol. 7. Paris: Impr. nationale de France, 1952.

Demiéville, Paul, Hubert Durt, and Anna Siedel, eds. *Répertoire du canon bouddhique Sino-Japonais*. Revised ed. Tokyo and Paris: L'Académie des Inscriptions et Belles-lettres, Institut de France, 1978.

Donner, Neal. "Sudden and Gradual Intimately Conjoined: Chih-i's T'ien-t'ai View." In *Sudden and Gradual: Approaches to Enlightenment in Chinese Thought*, edited by Peter N. Gregory, pp. 201–26.

Dumoulin, Heinrich. *A History of Zen Buddhism*. Boston: Beacon Press, 1963.

Dundes, Alan, ed. *The Study of Folklore*. Englewood Cliffs, N.J.: Prentice-Hall, 1965.

Durt, Hubert. "La Biographie du Moine Coréen Ŭi-Sang d'après le Song Kao Seng Tchouan." In *Kim Chaewŏn paksa hoegap kinyŏm nonch'ong* (Essays presented in commemoration of Dr. Kim Chaewŏn's sixtieth birthday), pp. 411–22. Seoul, 1969.

Eberhard, Wolfram, ed. *Folktales of China*. Chicago: University of Chicago Press, 1965.

Edgerton, Franklin. *Buddhist Hybrid Sanskrit Dictionary*. New Haven: Yale University Press, 1953.

Elwin, Verrier. *Myths of Middle India*. Specimens of the Oral Literature of Middle India. Oxford: Oxford University Press, 1949.

Emeneau, Murray B. *Kota Texts: Part Three*. University of California Publications in Linguistics, vol. 3. Berkeley: University of California Press, 1946.

Epstein, Ronald. "The *Śūraṅgama-sūtra* with Tripiṭaka Master Hsüan-hua's Commentary *An Elementary Explanation of Its General Meaning*: A Preliminary Study and Partial Translation." Ph.D. diss., University of California, Berkeley, 1975.

Faure, Bernard. "Bodhidharma as Textual and Religious Paradigm." *History of Religions* 25 (1986): 187–98.

———. "The Concept of One-Practice Samādhi in Early Ch'an." In *Traditions of Meditation in Chinese Buddhism*, edited by Peter Gregory, pp. 99–128.

———, trans. *Le Traité de Bodhidharma*. Paris: Le Mail, 1986.

———. "La Volonté d'Orthodoxie: Généalogie et doctrine du bouddhisme Ch'an de l'école du Nord—d'après l'une de ses chroniques, le *Leng-chia shih-tzu chi* (début du 8è siècle)." Ph.D. diss., University of Paris, 1984.

Forte, Antonino. *Political Propaganda and Ideology in China at the End of the Seventh Century: Inquiry into the Nature, Authors and Function of the Tunhuang Document S. 6502 Followed by an Annotated Translation*. 2 vols. Napoli: Istituto Universitario Orientale, 1976.

Foulk, Theodore Griffith. "The 'Ch'an School' and Its Place in the Buddhist Monastic Tradition." Ph.D. diss., University of Michigan, Ann Arbor, 1987.

Frauwallner, Eric. "Amalavijñānam und Alayavijñānam." *Beitrage zur Indischen Pilologie und Altertumskunde: Festschrift W. Schubring*, pp. 148–59. Hamburg: Cram, 1951.

Fujieda, Akira. "The Tun-huang Manuscripts." In *Essays on the Sources for Chinese History*, edited by Donald D. Leslie, Colin Mackerras, and Wang Gungwu, pp. 120–28. 1973. Reprint, Columbia: University of South Carolina Press, 1975.

Giles, Lionel, ed. *A Descriptive Catalogue of the Chinese Manuscripts from Tunhuang in the British Museum*. London: British Museum, 1957.

Gimello, Robert M. "Apophatic and Kataphatic Discourse in Mahāyāna: A Chinese View." *Philosophy East and West* 26 (1976): 117–36.

———. "Chih-yen (602–668) and the Foundation of Hua-yen Buddhism." Ph.D. diss., Columbia University, 1976.

————. "Random Reflections on the 'Sinicization' of Buddhism." *Bulletin of the Society for the Study of Chinese Religions* 5 (1978), pp. 52–89.

Gómez, Luis O. "Indian Materials on the Doctrine of Sudden Englightenment." In *Early Ch'an in China and Tibet*, edited by Whalen Lai and Lewis Lancaster, pp. 393–434.

————. "Proto-Mādhyamika in the Pāli Canon." *Philosophy East and West* 26 (1976): 137–65.

————. "Purifying Gold: The Metaphor of Effort and Intuition in Buddhist Thought." In *Sudden and Gradual: Approaches to Enlightenment in Chinese Thought*, edited by Peter N. Gregory, pp. 67–165.

————. "The Structure and Meaning of a Pali *Sutta*." Paper delivered at the Eighth Annual Conference of the International Association of Buddhist Studies. Berkeley, California, August 10, 1987.

Grayson, James Huntly. *Early Buddhism and Christianity in Korea: A Study in The Emplantation of Religion*. Studies in the History of Religions, no. 47. Leiden: E. J. Brill, 1985.

Gregory, Peter N. "The Problem of Theodicy in the *Awakening of Faith*." *Religion* 22 (1986): 63–78.

————, ed. *Sudden and Gradual: Approaches to Enlightenment in Chinese Thought*. Studies in East Asian Buddhism, no. 5. Honolulu: University of Hawaii Press, 1987.

————. "Sudden Enlightenment Followed by Gradual Cultivation: Tsung-mi's Analysis of Mind." In *Sudden and Gradual: Approaches to Enlightenment in Chinese Thought*, edited by Peter Gregory, pp. 279–320.

————, ed. *Traditions of Meditation in Chinese Buddhism*. Studies in East Asian Buddhism, no. 4. Honolulu: University of Hawaii Press, 1986.

————. "Tsung-mi's Synthetic Vision." Photocopied manuscript, n.d.

Grosnick, William. "*Cittaprakṛti* and *Ayoniśomanaskāra* in the *Ratnagotravibhāga*: A Precedent for the *Hsin-Nien* Distinction of *The Awakening of Faith*." *Journal of the International Association of Buddhist Studies* 6, 2 (1983): 35–47.

————. "Nonorigination and *Nirvāṇa* in the Early *Tathāgatagarbha* Literature." *Journal of the International Association of Buddhist Studies* 4, 2 (1981): 33–43.

Guenther, Herbert B. *Philosophy and Psychology in the Abhidharma*. Delhi: Motilal Banarsidass, 1957.

Ha, Tae-hung, and Grafton K. Mintz, trans. *Samguk Yusa: Legends and History of the Three Kingdoms of Ancient Korea*. Seoul: Yonsei University Press, 1972.

Hadas, Moses, and Morton Smith. *Heroes and Gods: Spiritual Biographies in Antiquity*. 1965. Reprint, Freeport, N.Y.: Books for Libraries Press, 1970.

Hakeda, Yoshito S., trans. *The Awakening of Faith, Attributed to Aśvaghosha*. New York: Columbia University Press, 1967.

Hong Jung-Shik [Hong Chŏngsik]. "The Thought and Life of Wŏnhyo." In *Buddhist Culture in Korea*. Korean Culture Series, vol. 3, edited by Chun Shin-yong, pp. 15–30 (Korean version, pp. 163–81). Seoul: International Cultural Foundation, 1974.

Hurvitz, Leon. "Chih-I (538-597): An Introduction to the Life and Ideas of a Chinese Buddhist Monk." *Mélanges chinois et bouddhiques* 12 (1962): 1–372.

———, trans. *Scripture of the Lotus Blossom of the Fine Dharma*. New York: Columbia University Press, 1976.

In Kwŏn-hwan. "Buddhist Preachings and Their Korean Acculturation." *Korea Journal* 12, 10 (October 1972): 18–27.

Inaba, Shōju. "On Chos-grub's Translation of the *Chieh-shên-mi-ching-shu*." In *Buddhist Thought and Asian Civilization: Essays in Honor of Herbert V. Guenther on his Sixtieth Birthday*, edited by Leslie S. Kawamura and Keith Scott, pp. 105–13. Emeryville, Calif: Dharma Publishing, 1977.

Jackson, Roger. "Terms of Sanskrit and Pāli Origin Acceptable as English Words." *Journal of the International Association of Buddhist Studies* 5 (1982): 141–42.

Jan, Yün-hua. "Buddhist Historiography in Sung China." *Zeitschrift der deutschen morgenländischen Gesellschaft* 114 (1964): 360–81.

———. "Hui Chiao and His Works, a Reassessment." In *Indo-Asian Culture*, pp. 177–90. New Delhi, 1964.

———. "Tsung-mi: His Analysis of Ch'an Buddhism." *T'oung Pao* 58 (1972): 1–54.

Jansen, Wm. Hugh. "The Esoteric-Exoteric Factor in Folklore." In *Study of Folklore*, edited by Alan Dundes, pp. 43–278.

Jorgensen, John A. "The Earliest Text of Ch'an Buddhism: The *Long Scroll*." M.A. thesis, Australian National University, 1979.

Keel, S. [Hee-Sung]. "Buddhism and Political Power in Korean History." *Journal of the International Association of Buddhist Studies* 1 (1978): 9–24.

Kluckhohn, Clyde. "Recurrent Themes in Myths and Mythmaking." In *Study of Folklore*, edited by Alan Dundes, pp. 158–68.

Koh, Ik-Jin [Ko Ikchin]. "Wŏnhyo's Hua-yen Thought." *Korea Journal* 23, 8 (August 1983): 30–33.

Koseki, Aaron L. "Prajñāpāramitā and the Buddhahood of the Non-Sentient World: The San-lun Assimilation of Buddha-Nature and Middle Path Doctrine." *Journal of the International Association of Buddhist Studies* 3, 1 (1980): 16–33.

Lai, Whalen. "The Pure and the Impure: The Mencian Problematik in Chinese Buddhism." In *Early Ch'an in China and Tibet*, edited by Whalen Lai and Lewis Lancaster, pp. 299–326.

———. "T'an-ch'ien and the Early Ch'an Tradition: Translation and Analysis of the Essay 'Wang-shih-fei lun.' " In *Early Ch'an in China and Tibet*, edited by Whalen Lai and Lewis Lancaster, pp. 65–87.

———. "Tao-sheng's Theory of Sudden Enlightenment Re-examined." In *Sud-*

*den and Gradual: Approaches to Enlightenment in Chinese Thought*, edited by Peter N. Gregory, pp. 169–200.

Lai, Whalen W., and Lewis R. Lancaster, eds. *Early Ch'an in China and Tibet.* Berkeley Buddhist Studies Series, vol. 5. Berkeley, 1983.

Lancaster, Lewis R. "Buddhist Apocryphal Words." Paper delivered at panel on Chinese Buddhist Apocrypha, American Academy of Religion, Annual Meeting, November 24, 1986.

————. Review of *Répertorie du Canon Bouddhique Sino-Japonais*, edited by Paul Demiéville, Hubert Durt, and Anna Seidel. *Journal of the International Association of Buddhist Studies* 5 (1982): 128–31.

Lancaster, Lewis R., and Sung Bae Park. *The Korean Buddhist Canon: A Descriptive Catalogue.* Berkeley: University of California Press, 1979.

Ledyard, Gari. "Yin and Yang in the China-Manchuria-Korea Triangle." In *China Among Equals*, edited by Morris Rossabi, pp. 313–53.

Lee, Ki-Baik. *A New History of Korea.* Translated by Edward W. Wagner, with Edward J. Shultz. Cambridge: Harvard University Press, 1984.

Lee, Leo. *Le maître Wôn-hyo de Sil-la du VIIè siècle: Sa vie, ses écrits, son apostolat.* Seoul: Librairie Catholique, 1986.

Lee, Peter H. *Anthology of Korean Literature.* Honolulu: University Press of Hawaii, 1981.

————. "Fa-tsang and Ŭisang." *Journal of the American Oriental Society* 82 (1962): 56–62.

————, trans. *Lives of Eminent Korean Monks: The Haedong Kosŭng chŏn*, Harvard-Yenching Institute Studies, no. 25. Cambridge: Harvard University Press, 1969.

————, trans. *Songs of Flying Dragons: A Critical Reading.* Cambridge: Harvard University Press, 1975.

Leverrier, R. P. Roger. "Buddhism and Ancestral Religious Beliefs in Korea." *Korea Journal* 12, 5 (1972): 37–42.

————. "Étude sur les rites bouddhiques a l'époque du royaume de Koryŏ: le rôle du bouddhisme et de la prière pour la protection du royaume." *Revue de Corée* 4, 3 (1972): 61–72.

Liebenthal, Walter. "A Biography of Tao-sheng." *Monumenta Nipponica* 11 (1955).

————. "New Light on the Mahāyāna Śraddhotpāda Śāstra." *T'oung Pao* 44 (1958): 155–216.

————. "Notes on the 'Vajrasamādhi.' " *T'oung Pao* (1956): 347–86.

Liu, Ming-wood. "The *P'an-chiao* System of the Hua-yen School in Chinese Buddhism." *T'oung Pao* 67 (1981): 10–47.

Maspero, Henri. *Taoism and Chinese Religion*, trans. Frank A. Kierman, Jr. Amherst: University of Massachusetts Press, 1981.

McClung, David H. "The Founding of the Royal Dragon Monastery: Translated, with Annotations, from Iryŏn's *Samguk Yusa.*" *Transactions of the Royal Asiatic Society, Korea Branch* 53 (1978): 69–80.

McRae, John R. *The Northern School and the Formation of Early Ch'an Buddhism,* Studies in East Asian Buddhism, no. 3. Honolulu: University of Hawaii Press, 1986.

———. "The Ox-Head School of Chinese Ch'an Buddhism: From Early Ch'an to the Golden Age." In *Studies in Ch'an and Hua-yen,* Studies in East Asian Buddhism, no. 1, edited by Robert M. Gimello and Peter N. Gregory, pp. 169–252. Honolulu: University of Hawaii Press, 1983.

Minn Young-gyu (Min Yŏnggyu). "Le bouddhisme Zen de Silla et de Koryŭ: d'après la relation du moine Il-yŏn." *Revue de Corée* 6, 2 (1974): 47–59.

Miyakawa Hisayuki. "Local Cults around Mount Lu at the Time of Sun En's Rebellion." In *Facets of Taoism: Essays in Chinese Religion,* edited by Holmes Welch and Anna Seidel, pp. 83–101. New Haven: Yale University Press, 1979.

Mizuno, Kōgen. "On the *Pseudo-Fa-kiu-king.*" *Indogaku bukkyōgaku kenkyū* 9, 1 (1961): 402–395 [*sic*].

Mundkur, Balaji. *The Cult of the Serpent: An Interdisciplinary Survey of Its Manifestations and Origins.* Albany: State University of New York Press, 1983.

Ñāṇamoli, Bhikkhu. *The Life of the Buddha: As it Appears in the Pali Canon the Oldest Authentic Record.* Kandy: Buddhist Publication Society, 1972.

Ñāṇananda, Bhikkhu. *Concept and Reality in Early Buddhist Thought: An Essay on "Papañca" and "Papañca-Saññā-Saṅkhā."* Kandy, Sri Lanka: Buddhist Publication Society, 1971.

———. *The Magic of the Mind: An Exposition of the Kalākārāma Sutta.* Kandy, Sri Lanka: Buddhist Publication Society, 1974.

Ōchō, Enichi. "The Beginnings of Tenet Classification in China." *The Eastern Buddhist,* New Series 14, 2 (1981), pp. 71–94.

Olrik, Axel. "Epic Laws of Folk Narrative." In *Study of Folklore,* edited by Alan Dundes, pp. 129–41.

Paul, Diana Y. *Philosophy of Mind in Sixth-Century China: Paramārtha's "Evolution of Consciousness."* Stanford: Stanford University Press, 1984.

Park, Sung Bae (Pak Sŏngbae). "A Comparative Study of Wŏnhyo and Fa-tsang on the Ta-Ch'eng Ch'i-Hsin Lun." In *Che-il hoe Han'gukhak Kukche haksurhoe ŭi nonmunjip (Papers of the First International Conference on Korean Studies),* pp. 579–97. Sŏngnam, Korea: Academy of Korean Studies, 1979.

———. "Wŏnhyo's Commentaries on the *Awakening of Faith in Mahāyāna.*" Ph.D. diss., University of California, Berkeley, 1979.

———. "On Wŏnhyo's Enlightenment." *Indogaku bukkyōgaku kenkyū* 29, 1 (1980): 470–67 [*sic*].

Pradhan, Prahlad, ed. *Abhidharmakośabhāṣyam of Vasubandhu.* Patna: K. P. Jayaswal Research Institute, 1975.

Raglan, Lord. *The Hero: A Study in Tradition, Myth, and Drama*. Westport, Conn.: Greenwood Press, 1956.

Reischauer, Edwin O. *Ennin's Travels in T'ang China*. New York: The Ronald Press, 1955.

Reynolds, Frank E., and Donald Capps, eds. *The Biographical Process: Studies in the History and Psychology of Religion*. Religion and Reason 11. The Hague: Mouton, 1976.

Rhi Ki-yong [Yi Kiyŏng]. "Wŏnhyo and His Thought." *Korea Journal* 11, 1 (January 1971): 4–9.

Robinet, Isabelle. *Méditation taoïste*. Paris: Dervy Livres, 1979.

Rogers, Michael C. "*P'yŏnnyŏn T'ongnok*: The Foundation Legend of the Koryŏ State." *Korean Studies* (University of Washington) 4 (1982–1983): 3–72.

Rossabi, Morris, ed. *China Among Equals: The Middle Kingdom and its Neighbors, 10th–14th Centuries*. Berkeley: University of California Press, 1983.

Ruegg, David Seyfort. "On the Knowability and Expressibility of Absolute Reality in Buddhism." *Indogaku bukkyōgaku kenkyū* 20 (1971): 495–89 [*sic*].

———. *La Théorie du Tathāgatagarbha et du Gotra: Études sur la Sotériologie et la Gnoséologie du Bouddhisme*. Publications de l'École Française d'Extrême-Orient, vol. 70. Paris, 1969.

Rump, Ariane, and Wing-tsit Chan, trans. *Commentary on the Lao Tzu by Wang Pi*, Monograph of the Society for Asian and Comparative Philosophy, no. 6. Honolulu: University Press of Hawaii, 1979.

Rutt, Richard. "The Flower Boys of Silla (Hwarang): Notes on the Sources." *Transactions of the Korea Branch of the Royal Asiatic Society* 38 (1961): 1–66.

Schafer, Edward. "Combined Supplements to *Mathews*." Mimeographed. University of California, Berkeley: Department of Oriental Languages, n.d.

Schopen, Gregory. "Filial Piety and the Monk in the Practice of Indian Buddhism: A Question of 'Sinicization' Viewed from the Other Side." *T'oung Pao* 70 (1984): 110–26.

Shih, Robert. *Biographies des moines éminents (Kao seng tchouan) de Houei-kiao* (The Biographies of eminent monks by Hui-chiao). Bibliothèque de Muséon, vol. 54. Louvain: Institut Orientaliste, 1968.

Sorensen, Henrik H. "Ennin's Account of a Korean Buddhist Monastery, 839–840 A.D." *Acta Orientalia* 47 (1986): 141–55.

———. "The History and Doctrines of Early Korean Sŏn Buddhism." Ph.D. diss., University of Copenhagen, 1987.

Strickmann, Michel. "On the Alchemy of T'ao Hung-ching." In *Facets of Taoism: Essays in Chinese Religion*, edited by Holmes Welch and Anna Seidel, pp. 123–92. New Haven: Yale University Press, 1979.

Suzuki, Daisetz Teitaro. *Essays in Zen Buddhism*. Series 1. London: Routledge and Kegan Paul, 1970.

Suzuki, Daisetz Teitaro, trans. *The Laṅkāvatāra Sūtra.* 1932. Reprint, Boulder: Prajñā Press, 1978.

———. *Studies in the Laṅkāvatāra Sūtra.* 1932. Reprint, Boulder: Prajñā Press, 1978.

Takasaki, Jikidō. *A Study on the Ratnagotravibhāga (Uttaratantra): Being a Treatise on the Tathāgatagarbha Theory of Mahāyāna Buddhism.* Serie Orientale Roma 33. Rome: Istituto Italiano per il Media ed Estremo Oriente, 1966.

Tambiah, Stanley Jeyaraja. *The Buddhist Saints of the Forest and the Cult of Amulets: A Study in Charisma, Hagiography, Sectarianism, and Millennial Buddhism.* Cambridge: Cambridge University Press, 1984.

Tamura, Enchō. "Japan and the Eastward Permeation of Buddhism." *Acta Asiatica* 47 (1985): 1–30.

Thich, Thien-an. *Buddhism and Zen in Vietnam: In Relation to the Development of Buddhism in Asia.* Edited by Carol Smith. Rutland, Vt., and Tokyo: Charles E. Tuttle, 1975.

Thompson, Stith, and Jonas Balys. *Oral Tales Of India.* Bloomington: Indiana University Press, 1958.

Thurman, Robert A. F., trans. *The Holy Teaching of Vimalakīrti: A Mahāyāna Scripture.* University Park: Pennsylvania State University Press, 1976.

Tokiwa, Gishin, trans. *A Dialogue on the Contemplation-Extinguished: A Translation Based on Professor Seizan Yanagida's Modern Japanese Translation and Consultations with Professor Yoshitaka Iriya.* Kyoto: Institute for Zen Studies, 1973.

Tokuno, Kyoko. "The Evaluation of Indigenous Scriptures in Chinese Buddhist Bibliographical Catalogues." In *Chinese Buddhist Apocrypha*, edited by R. Buswell.

Twitchett, Denis. "Problems of Chinese Biography." In *Confucian Personalities*, edited by Arthur F. Wright and Denis Twitchett, pp. 24–39.

Ueda, Yoshifumi. "Two Main Streams of Thought in Yogācāra Philosophy." *Philosophy East and West* 17 (1967): 155–65.

Ueyama, Daishun. "The Study of Tibetan Ch'an Manuscripts Recovered from Tun-huang: A Review of the Field and Its Prospects." Translated by Kenneth W. Eastman and Kyoko Tokuno. In *Early Ch'an in China and Tibet*, edited by Whalen W. Lai and Lewis R. Lancaster, pp. 327–49.

Visser, M. W. de. *The Dragon in China and Japan.* Amsterdam: Johannes Müller, 1913.

Watson, Burton, trans. *The Complete Works of Chuang-tzu.* New York: Columbia University Press, 1968.

Wayman, Alex. "Notes on the Three Myrobalans." *Phi Theta Annual* 5 (1954–1955): 63–77.

Wayman, Alex, and Hideko Wayman. *The Lion's Roar of Queen Śrīmālā.* New York: Columbia University Press, 1974.

Wei, Tat, trans. *Ch'eng Wei-Shih Lun: The Doctrine of Mere-Consciousness*. Hong Kong: Ch'eng Wei-shih Lun Publication Committee, 1973.

Weinstein, Stanley. "A Biographical Study of Tz'u-en." *Monumenta Nipponica* 15 (1959): 119–49.

———. "Chinese Buddhism." In *The Encyclopedia of Religion*, edited by Mircea Eliade, vol. 2, pp. 482–87. New York: Macmillan, 1987.

———. "The Concept of *Ālaya-vijñāna* in Pre-T'ang Chinese Buddhism." In *Bukkyō shisōshi ronshū* (Essays on the history of Buddhist thought), edited by Yuki Kyōju Kenkōkai, pp. 33–50.

———. "Imperial Patronage in the Formation of T'ang Buddhism." In *Perspectives on the T'ang*, edited by Arthur F. Wright and Denis Twitchett, pp. 265–306. New Haven: Yale University Press, 1973.

Werner, E. T. C. *Myths and Legends of China*. New York: Farrar and Rinehart, 1936.

Woodward, F. L., trans. *The Minor Anthologies of the Pali Canon*. London: Oxford University Press, 1948.

Worthy, Edmund H., Jr. "Diplomacy for Survival: Domestic and Foreign Relations of Wu Yüeh, 907–978." In *China Among Equals*, edited by Morris Rossabi, pp. 17–44.

Wright, Arthur F. "Biography and Hagiography: Hui-chiao's *Lives of Eminent Monks*." In *Silver Jubilee Volume of the Zinbun-kagaku-kenkyusyo, Kyoto University*, pp. 383–432. Kyoto, 1954.

———. "Values, Roles, and Personalities." In *Confucian Personalities*, edited by Arthur F. Wright and Denis Twitchett, pp. 3–23.

Wright, Arthur F. and Denis Twitchett., eds. *Confucian Personalities*. Stanford: Stanford University Press, 1962.

Yampolsky, Phillip. "New Japanese Studies in Early Ch'an History." In *Early Ch'an in China and Tibet*, edited by Whalen Lai and Lewis Lancaster, pp. 1–11.

———, trans. *The Platform Sūtra of the Sixth Patriarch*. New York: Columbia University Press, 1967.

Yanagida Seizan. "The *Li-Tai Fa-Pao Chi* and the Ch'an Doctrine of Sudden Awakening." Translated by Carl Bielefeldt. In *Early Ch'an in China and Tibet*, edited by Whalen Lai and Lewis Lancaster, pp. 13–49.

Zimmer, Heinrich. *Myths and Symbols in Indian Art and Civilization*, edited by Joseph Campbell. Princeton: Princeton University Press, 1946.

Zŏng, In-sŏb [Chŏng Insŏp]. *Folk Tales from Korea*. 3d ed. Elizabeth, N.J.: Hollym International, 1982.

Zürcher, Erik. *The Buddhist Conquest of China: The Spread and Adaptation of Buddhism in Early Medieval China*. 2 vols. Leiden: E. J. Brill, 1959.

# INDEX